D0034285

TimeOut
Dublin

timeout.com/dublin

Published by Time Out Guides Ltd, a wholly owned subsidiary of Time Out Group Ltd.
Time Out and the Time Out logo are trademarks of Time Out Group Ltd.

© Time Out Group Ltd 2007
Previous editions 1998, 1999, 2002, 2004.

10 9 8 7 6 5 4 3 2 1

This edition first published in Great Britain in 2007 by Ebury Publishing
Ebury Publishing is a division of The Random House Group Ltd,
20 Vauxhall Bridge Road, London SW1V 2SA

Random House Australia Pty Limited 20 Alfred Street, Milsons Point, Sydney, New South Wales 2061, Australia
Random House New Zealand Limited 18 Poland Road, Glenfield, Auckland 10, New Zealand
Random House South Africa (Pty) Limited Isle of Houghton, Corner Boundary
Road & Carse O'Gowrie, Houghton 2198, South Africa

Random House UK Limited Reg. No. 954009

Distributed in USA by Publishers Group West
1700 Fourth Street, Berkeley, California 94710

Distributed in Canada by Publishers Group Canada
250A Carlton Street, Toronto, Ontario M5A 2L1

For further distribution details, see www.timeout.com

ISBN 10: 1-904978-65-7
ISBN 13: 9781904978 8657

A CIP catalogue record for this book is available from the British Library

Colour reprographics by Wyndeham Icon, 3 & 4 Maverton Road, London E3 2JE

Printed and bound in Germany by Appl

Papers used by Ebury Publishing are natural, recyclable products made from wood grown in sustainable forests

St Stephen's Green. *See p71.*

Time Out Guides Limited
Universal House
251 Tottenham Court Road
London W1T 7AB
Tel + 44 (0)20 7813 3000
Fax + 44 (0)20 7813 6001
Email guides@timeout.com
www.timeout.com

Editorial

Editor Sam Le Quesne
Deputy Editor Simon Cropper
Listings Editor Juliet Martin
Proofreader Sylvia Tombesi-Walton
Indexer Johnny Cox

Editorial/Managing Director Peter Fiennes
Series Editor Ruth Jarvis
Deputy Series Editor Lesley McCave
Business Manager Gareth Garner
Guides Co-ordinator Holly Pick
Accountant Kemi Olufuwa

Design

Art Director Scott Moore
Art Editor Pinelope Kourmouzoglou
Senior Designer Josephine Spencer
Graphic Designer Henry Elphick
Digital Imaging Dan Conway
Ad Make-up Jenni Prichard

Picture Desk

Picture Editor Jael Marschner
Deputy Picture Editor Tracey Kerrigan
Picture Researcher Helen McFarland

Advertising

Sales Director Mark Phillips
International Sales Manager Ross Canadé
International Sales Executive Simon Davies
Advertising Sales (Dublin) LDP Media Ltd
Advertising Assistant Kate Staddon

Marketing

Group Marketing Director John Luck
Marketing Manager Yvonne Poon
Marketing & Publicity Manager, US Rosella Albanese

Production

Group Production Director Mark Lamond
Production Manager Brendan McKeown
Production Coordinator Caroline Bradford

Time Out Group

Chairman Tony Elliott
Managing Director Mike Hardwick
Financial Director Richard Waterlow
TO Magazine Ltd MD David Pepper
Group General Manager/Director Nichola Coulthard
TO Communications Ltd MD David Pepper
Group Art Director John Oakey
Group IT Director Simon Chappell

Contributors

Introduction Sam Le Quesne, Christi Daugherty. **History** Sam Le Quesne, Jack Jewers (*Boiling point* Yousef Eldin; *Neutral ground* Christi Daugherty). **Dublin Today** Emily Hourican (*The property boom* Yousef Eldin). **Architecture** Emma Cullinan. **New Novel Army** Sam Le Quesne, Sam Bungey. **Where to Stay** Christi Daugherty. **Sightseeing** Bridget Hourican, Emily Hourican, Sam Le Quesne (*Key notes: The Guinness family* Eoin Higgins). **Restaurants** Domini Kemp (*Vine dining* Sam Le Quesne). **Cafés & Coffee Shops** Eoin Higgins. **Pubs & Bars** Eoin Higgins. **Shops & Services** Emily O'Sullivan. **Festivals & Events** Sam Le Quesne (*A breath of air* Eoin Butler). **Children** Emily Hourican. **Film** Bridget Hourican. **Galleries** Bridget Hourican. **Gay & Lesbian** Stephen O'Farrell. **Music** Yousef Eldin, Sam Bungey (*Doyle on troubled waters* Mark O'Connell). **Nightlife** Yousef Eldin, Jonathan Rothwell. **Sport & Fitness** Sam Le Quesne (*Field of greens* Christi Daugherty). **Theatre & Dance** Bridget Hourican. **Trips Out of Town** Christi Daugherty (*Walk: Sutton Head* Emily Hourican). **Directory** Lisa Plumridge.

Maps john@jsgraphics.co.uk, except DART & Rail and Luas maps.

All photography by Britta Jaschinski, except: pages 12, 60 Getty Images; pages 14, 18 Mary Evans Picture Library; page 17 AP/Empics; page 155 (top right) Emmanual Jal; page 160 Leon Farrell; page 165 An Lar Films; page 182 Karl Blackwell.

The following images were supplied by the featured establishments/artists: pages 32, 33, 34, 48, 155 (top left), 156, 163, 179, 188.

The Editor would like to thank *Mongrel* magazine and all contributors to previous editions of *Time Out Dublin*, whose work forms the basis for parts of this book.

Contents

Dublin Castle. *See p67.*

Introduction

So far-reaching is the Irish diaspora, and so strong is the Irish compulsion to talk, that scarcely a corner of the globe has been left untouched by tales of Dublin's fair city, and its bitter-sweet heritage of grim hardship and rare oul' times. The shtick, in short, is well polished: but is it the truth? Roddy Doyle thinks not: 'It's a big con job. We have sold the myth of Dublin as a sexy place incredibly well; because it's a dreary little dump most of the time.' But tourism statistics tell a different story. Visitors are flocking to the city in their millions, and not just lads and ladettes on pre-wedding piss-ups or Americans following the filigree thread of their ancestry from the other side of the Atlantic. Real people come here too – and it's easy to see why.

The city's mercurial rise from provincial town to one of the brightest stars in the European firmament has been well documented. In 2006, the Irish Business and Employers Confederation estimated that the national economy was growing at three times the average European rate, making it the fastest-growing developed economy in the world. And the impact of this affluence is evident everywhere you look: Grafton Street is bulging with high-end clothing stores; every neighbourhood boasts its own destination restaurants and style bars; business is clearly booming in the city's new office developments; big-name architects are jetting into town to construct a glittering new landscape of iconic bridges and bold new public buildings.

But the biggest change has been in the psyche of Dubliners. For years, while the rest of the world was charmed by Dublin, the locals simply didn't share that opinion. The contempt that many of them felt for their city can be traced back centuries. In 1727, the author Jonathan Swift dismissed his hometown as 'the most disagreeable place in Europe'. But recently, Dublin took a step back and looked at itself, and liked what it saw. The dirty old town had become a healthy mix of the old and the new – historic buildings standing side-by-side with gorgeous new construction. The grimy 18th-century walls had been scrubbed clean and it all had the faint gleam of polish about it. Dublin was standing on its own.

Today, Dublin is all that it was before, and much more; it has embraced the modernity it long rejected. This means it's not the stodgy, sweet, dare-we-say backward place that you might have loved years ago. Now its bars are sleek, its nightclubs are packed and its restaurants are pricey. But don't be put off by that, because the fact is, its heart is still Irish. Scratch that new chrome and you'll find there's still solid old oak underneath. So you haven't lost much, and Dubliners have gained the one thing they've always wanted: at last they're proud of their city. And rightly so.

ABOUT TIME OUT CITY GUIDES

This is the fifth edition of *Time Out Dublin*, one of an expanding series of Time Out guides produced by the people behind the successful listings magazines in London, New York and Chicago. Our guides are all written by resident experts who have striven to provide you with all the most up-to-date information you'll need to explore the city or read up on its background, whether you're a local or a first-time visitor.

THE LIE OF THE LAND

To make the book (and the city itself) easier to navigate, we have divided Dublin into small areas, each of which is easily walkable. These are: Temple Bar & Around, Around Trinity College, St Stephen's Green & Around, O'Connell Street & Around, the North Quays & Around, Liberties & Kilmainham, Dublin Bay & the Coast. These are our own breakdowns, and are not official areas that you'll see signposted around town, but we hope they'll give you a quick handle on the city's layout. The borders of these sightseeing areas are clearly marked on p248.

ESSENTIAL INFORMATION

For all the practical information you might need for visiting the area – including visa and customs information, details of local transport, a listing of emergency numbers, information on local weather and a selection of useful websites – turn to the Directory at the back of this guide. It begins on p219.

THE LOWDOWN ON THE LISTINGS

We have tried to make this book as easy to use as possible. Addresses, phone numbers, bus information, opening times and admission prices are all included in the listings. However, businesses can change their arrangements at any time. Before you go out of your way, we'd

Bull Island. *See p93.*

strongly advise you to phone ahead to check opening times and other particulars. While every effort and care has been made to ensure the accuracy of the information contained in this guide, the publishers cannot accept responsibility for any errors it may contain.

PRICES AND PAYMENT

We have noted where venues such as shops, hotels, restaurants and theatres accept the following credit cards: American Express (AmEx), Diners Club (DC), Discover (Disc), MasterCard (MC) and Visa (V). Many will also accept travellers' cheques, and/or other cards such as Carte Blanche.

The prices we've listed in this guide should be treated as guidelines, not gospel. If prices vary wildly from those we've quoted, ask whether there's a good reason. If not, go elsewhere. Then please let us know. We aim to give the best and most up-to-date advice, so we want to know if you've been badly treated or overcharged.

Advertisers

We would like to stress that no establishment has been included in this guide because it has advertised in any of our publications and no payment of any kind has influenced any review. The opinions given in this book are those of Time Out writers and entirely independent.

TELEPHONE NUMBERS

The country code for Ireland is 353. The code for Dublin is 01 (drop the 0 if dialling from outside Ireland). Mobile phones do not require the 01 prefix. All telephone numbers in this guide take these codes unless otherwise stated. For more on telephones and codes, *see p234.*

MAPS

The map section at the back of this guide includes useful orientation and overview maps of the country and city. The maps start on p245. Street maps to the centre of Dublin are on pp250-252; all map references in this book indicate the page number and the grid square on those maps. There's also a street index on p253, as well as useful maps of the DART and Suburban Rail (p255) and Luas transport systems (p256) to help you find your way around the city and further afield.

LET US KNOW WHAT YOU THINK

We hope you enjoy *Time Out Dublin*, and we'd like to know what you think of it. We welcome tips for places that you consider we should include in future editions and take note of your criticism of our choices. You can email us at guides@timeout.com.

There is an online version of this book, along with guides to over 100 international cities, at **www.timeout.com**.

In Context

Feature boxes

Trinity College. *See p59*.

Bloody Sunday reprisals. See p21.

History

The hand the Celts were dealt.

There is no conveniently straightforward answer to the question of how old Dublin is. Historians are forever deliberating over where to draw the line between seasonal, nomadic settlement and thriving village – from whence to trace Ireland's first and largest city. In 1988 the powers that be made the questionable decision to mark the city's thousandth anniversary, counting from the first imposition of taxes in Dublin, but the area around the city is known to have been inhabited in one form or another since around 8,000 BC. The Gaels, who arrived sometime around the first century AD, are believed to have come up with the name 'Dubhlinn' (meaning 'the black pool', probably referring to a tidal pool in the estuary of the now-subterranean River Poddle). The city's modern Irish name, Baile çtha Cliath, is derived from 'Ath Cliath' ('the ford of the hurdles'), believed to have been the name of an occasional Celtic settlement some 400 years earlier.

FIRST FOOTINGS

After the arrival in the early fifth century of the Welsh missionary Maewyn Succat (see p18 **Key notes**), Dublin became the centre of one of the earliest Christian orthodoxies in Europe. Something of a golden age of Christianity followed, producing some of the finest religious art in the world, including the Ardagh Chalice, the *Book of Durrow* and, perhaps most famously, the *Book of Kells* (see p61).

By 841, Norwegian Vikings had established a permanent urban settlement in the area and were using Dublin as a base from which to plunder surrounding regions. Enriched Dublin became a powerful stronghold, and the first permanent dwellings were constructed near what is now Temple Bar.

Viking Dublin came under regular attack from the Irish after 936, particularly by Brian Borœ and Mael Sechnaill, the last great High Kings of Ireland. It would be Borœ who at last defeated them on Good Friday 1014.

THE ENGLISH ARRIVE

The English stepped firmly into the Irish fray in 1166, after the King of Leinster (which included Dublin) was deposed by a neighbouring king. He turned to Henry II, King of England, for help. In return he offered to make Leinster subject to Henry's overlordship. As an added incentive, he promised his eldest daughter to whoever led the invasion.

And so it was that an expeditionary force, led by the Earl of Pembroke, Richard de Clare (better known as Strongbow), set sail in August 1170 to seize Dublin. The deposed king was restored, and Strongbow remained in Dublin as governor. The following year, Henry II proclaimed Dublin to be under his control, thus cementing a political sphere of influence that was to remain for almost 1,000 years.

TUDOR RULE

In many respects, Dublin was a medieval town like any other. It certainly suffered from the same insidious problems, mostly related to chronic overcrowding. With a population of 5,000 crammed inside the city walls, both disease and fire were hazards. Other threats included open sewers, filthy drinking water and, worst of all, starvation. In 1295 food shortages were so severe that it was said that the poor were driven to eat the criminals on the gallows. During the famine of 1317 gruesome rumours spread that mothers had resorted to eating their own babies. While that's almost certainly apocryphal, the horrors of the Black Death certainly were not. By 1348 the city's population had mushroomed to nearly 35,000, but the epidemic would claim a third of them.

As Dublin grew and stumbled, the rest of Ireland was living under tribal kingdoms, largely beyond English control. The area under direct English rule extended only 48 kilometres (30 miles) from Dundalk to the Wicklow Hills, an area known even now as 'the Pale'. This boundary gave rise to the expression 'beyond the pale', meaning something that is uncontrollable or unacceptable.

It was not until the Tudor period (1485-1603) that English power was consolidated across Ireland. When Henry VIII split England from the Roman Catholic Church in 1531, he took the opportunity to seize Church land in Ireland, redistributing it among his supporters, both English and Irish. It took him no great leap of imagination from proclaiming himself head of an Anglicised Irish Church to fully fledged King of Ireland.

When Henry's youngest daughter, Elizabeth, became queen (after a brief period of Catholic restoration under his eldest, Mary), she launched a campaign to civilise Ireland, 'for the reformation', as she put it, 'of this barbarous people'.

During this time, Catholic Dubliners were constantly persecuted. Acts of Parliament in 1536 and 1539 dissolved the city's monasteries, forever altering the urban landscape. In 1558, the Bacall Iosa (a wooden staff said to have been bequeathed to the city by St Patrick) was ritually burned, and the following year all relics and icons were removed from the city's churches. In 1560 the English proclaimed Ireland an Anglican country, and Protestants took over the Catholic churches, leaving the dispossessed Catholics to worship in cellars. The closure of the monasteries would have disastrous effects on the city's economy and social order. The knock-on effects of unemployment and the curtailing of Catholic charitable funds all but cancelled out initiatives to clean the city and improve the living conditions of its poorest inhabitants. In 1575 another outbreak of Black Death claimed a further third of the population.

CROMWELL

By the mid 1600s Dublin was pronounced to be overwhelmingly Protestant, widening the gulf between the Anglicised capital and the rest of Ireland. Outside the city, discontent grew among the oppressed Catholic majority. Civil unrest was rife.

By 1649, though, the English civil war was over. Oliver Cromwell, now head of the fledgling new republic, was obsessed by the idea that, if it were not brought to heel, Ireland could be used to mount an invasion of England. And so it was that on 15 August of that year Cromwell landed an army of 12,000 in Dublin and (after a short pause in which he commandeered St Patrick's Cathedral as a stable) proceeded to Drogheda. What followed was to be remembered as one of the most shameful acts of English – indeed, of any nation's – military history, an act of such irrepressible wickedness that the shadow it cast over Anglo-Irish relations has never fully healed. Over 3,000 Irish soldiers were murdered on a single night in Drogheda – most had already surrendered and some were burned alive while taking refuge in a church. Another bloody day in Wexford saw the deaths of 2,000 people, including hundreds of civilians. Slowly but inexorably, the country was, in fact, 'brought to heel'. Land amounting to nearly 60,000 square kilometres was seized from Catholic landowners and redistributed among Cromwell's Protestant supporters. That act alone would help keep the country tied to England for centuries.

Oliver Cromwell. *See p13.*

RENAISSANCE

After the restoration removed the Cromwells from the picture, the Duke of Ormond was appointed Lord Deputy of Ireland and, at the end of the 17th century, the city again began to change rapidly. Narrow medieval streets were rebuilt in the wide, neo-classical style that had become popular in Paris and Amsterdam, and squares and parks were created. This is when Temple Bar was developed; Marsh's Library was built in 1702, and Trinity College library was started in 1712.

The Earl of Drogheda, Henry Moore, purchased land north of the river on which he built Henry Street and its environs. Banker Luke Gardiner set out Henrietta Street, a prime aristocratic quarter north of the river, and later Gardiner Street, which was overseen by architect James Gandon. Indeed, Dublin without the iconic influence of Gandon would be, in many ways, an unrecognisable place; he also designed Beresford Place, Custom House, the Kings Inns and the Four Courts. The new Parliament House was opened in 1731, and, 20 years later, building began on the new façade of Trinity College, the largest piece of collegiate architecture in Europe.

'A storm was gathering over the country, and the results would be devastating.'

As the aesthetic influence of the Enlightenment merged with the city's growing wealth, Dublin entered something of a cultural golden age in the 1770s. For the upper classes at least, it was a belle époque, and many took great advantage of their new-found status. During this time Dublin was second only to London in terms of music, theatre and publishing. George Frideric Handel lived on Abbey Street in 1741-2; indeed, the debut performance of his *Messiah* was held just around the corner in Fishamble Street. At the same time, playwrights Richard Sheridan, Oliver Goldsmith and William Congreve all lived and worked in Dublin, as did philosopher and politician Edmund Burke, satirist Jonathan Swift and the founder of the *Spectator* magazine, Richard Steele.

However, the glamorous façade hid an underbelly of growing dissent. The crushing defeat of King James II at the Battle of the Boyne in 1690 forever ended the hopes of Catholic England. The newly installed Protestant monarch, William of Orange, passed laws that didn't exactly outlaw Roman Catholicism, but that made life very difficult for those who practised it. Catholics

were forbidden to hold any office of state, stand for Parliament, join the armed forces or practise law. Most crucially, they could neither vote nor buy any land. It is no big surprise, given all of that, that by the latter half of the 18th century, barely five per cent of the land in Ireland was in Catholic hands. Disenfranchised Catholics migrated from the countryside, and Dublin found itself with a Catholic majority. Into the city's thriving intellectual scene came rich new seams of dissent. All the ingredients were there to make Dublin a hotbed for radical political thinking. And for radical political activities as well.

In an all-too-familiar pattern, sectarian animosity turned into violence. Gangs like the Liberty Boys (mostly Protestant tailors' apprentices) slugged it out daily on the streets with the Ormond Boys (mostly Catholic butchers' assistants). On one particularly violent occasion, a gang of victorious Liberty Boys left their rivals hanging by their jaws from their own meat hooks.

REBELS WITH A CAUSE

In 1782, after months of negotiation, the reformist politician Henry Grattan won legislative independence from the English Privy Council, which had been required to approve all laws passed in Ireland since the time of Henry VII. An excited crowd gathered outside the parliament building on 16 April to hear Grattan proclaim, 'Spirit of Swift, spirit of Molyneux, your genius has prevailed! Ireland is now a nation!' Some, though not all, of the anti-Catholic legislation was repealed, most notably the restriction on Catholics being allowed to practise law (although the ban on holding public office remained). Grattan became something of a hero, but he was certainly no revolutionary. He did not believe in full independence from England. Indeed, one of the first acts of his new parliament was to approve the sending of 20,000 Irish sailors to assist the English navy.

When, in 1798, a fleet of French troops arrived to assist a Catholic uprising in County Kilkenny, the English government got jittery. Two years later, when Dubliner Wolfe Tone orchestrated his own, pan-sectarian rebellion of 'United Irishmen' (*see p18* **Key notes**), London became convinced that it had cut Ireland too much slack. When another French fleet attempted to land at Lough Swilly, the reprisals were brutal. As many as 10,000 rebels were executed or deported. With all of this rebellion in the air, Grattan's parliament lacked the teeth to save itself from being abolished by the Act of Union in 1801, which reimposed direct rule from London.

The effect on Dublin was crushing. Much of the former ruling class left, and they took their wealth with them. The city was left without effective representation. A storm was gathering over the country, and the results would be devastating.

In 1803, after an abortive rebellion led by 25-year-old Dubliner Robert Emmet, the British once more became concerned about French support for the Irish nationalist cause. Emmet's botched rebellion was a sad saga – in strategic terms at least, a complete failure – but the romantic mythology to which he contributed was a more powerful gift to the nationalist cause than anything he achieved in his short and tragic revolutionary career. The most influential nationalist movement of the 19th century appreciated the value of mythology only too well, and it was that, rather than any strategic success, that would make the Fenians vital players in the struggle for an independent Ireland.

The devastating potato famine of 1846-51, and England's slow and disinterested response to it, galvanised support for the independence movement, and the next 15 years saw the growth and spread of the Fenians, first in Dublin, then among the burgeoning Irish-American community in the US (many of whom had fled to America to escape the famine and anti-Catholic oppression). Fenian newspapers were printed on both sides of the Atlantic, and although the group made attempts at armed rebellion, their exploitation of the media was far more successful than their relatively modest paramilitary activities. Much of the Fenian's initial activity amounted to little more than publicity stunts, exercises in what would now be termed 'public relations', albeit audacious ones (nobody can seriously have expected success when, in 1866, they tried to invade Canada with an army of 800 men). No, the Fenians tapped into something much more potent, something immeasurably more significant to the nationalist cause than the symbolic occupation of a public building, or the assassination of British dignitaries. By far the most powerful weapon in their arsenal was Ireland's burgeoning sense of national identity, a celebration of its history, language and culture; the very stuff, in short, of what it meant to be Irish.

THE EASTER UPRISING

By the turn of the 20th century, the end of direct rule from London seemed closer than ever. The Home Rule Bill received its third reading in the British Parliament, and looked all but certain to become law within months.

However, a vociferous loyalist movement had emerged among the Protestant majority in the north. At a meeting in Belfast Town Hall, half a million men and women signed a covenant to resist Home Rule – many signed with their own blood. Senior political figures demanded the exclusion of six counties from any independent Irish state – Derry, Antrim, Tyrone, Down, Armagh and Fermanagh – known collectively as Ulster. The passage of the bill was slowed, and the outbreak of World War I the following year kicked the issue into the long grass.

Nearly 200,000 Irish men volunteered for service with the British army in World War I, some hoping that their loyalty would win concessions after what everybody thought would be a relatively short conflict. With the prospect of Home Rule – at least for the time being – a split occurred in the independence movement. Some, such as John Redmond, the leader of the Irish Parliamentary Party, believed that no further action should be taken while Britain was at war. Others, though, saw the chaos and confusion of war as perfect cover from which to strike a decisive blow for the nationalist cause.

A group of men from the Irish Volunteers and the Irish Republican Brotherhood planned a rebellion to occur in Dublin on Easter Sunday 1916. Plans for the rebellion were beset with problems from the start. A shipment of 20,000 rifles was seized en route from Germany, and Roger Casement, a former British diplomat and prominent member of the Irish Volunteers, was arrested. When the ostensible leader of the Volunteers, Eoin MacNeill, found that he had not been kept fully informed about plans for the rebellion, he petulantly took out a newspaper advertisement announcing that the Sunday 'manoeuvres' had been postponed for 24 hours.

The fact that they must have known how remote was their chance of success serves to highlight the magnitude of what the rebels were about to attempt – men like trade unionist James Connolly, schoolteacher Patrick Pearse, barman Sean MacDermott must have known that martyrdom was the most they could hope for. Others took part out of fervour, swept along by the romantic appeal of such a hopeless gesture of defiance. Still, it would be wrong to assume that, when Patrick Pearse read out the proclamation of independence on the steps of the General Post Office building on that Easter Monday morning, he did so with the full weight of public opinion on his side. Some Dubliners found the actions of the Easter rebels treacherous, especially as many of the city's sons were at that moment fighting in Flanders.

Boiling point

The riot of O'Connell Street on 25 February 2006 was an unexpected event for everyone, including the so-called 'knackers' that many Dubliners cite as the instigators behind it. The events of that Saturday afternoon were not so much a clash between Republicans and Unionists as perhaps the first real rebellion against the Celtic Tiger's growth: for an afternoon, the city's disenfranchised took back the capital, whose recent wealth has seemingly passed them by.

A Unionist march was planned in memory of the victims of Republican violence and was to pass in front of O'Connell Street's General Post Office, a bastion landmark of Irish Republicanism. Sinn Feín leaders, viewing the march as deliberate provocation, had issued a stay-away order to all party members. It seemed, then, that any protest to the march would be unlikely (anarchists are generally not drawn into the North-South division, and the smaller Republican splinter groups, who may have been up for a ruck, arguably do not have the organisation to mobilise it). So when a thousand rioters descended on the city's largest boulevard, with little regard for the usual rules of engagement at a protest, An Garda Síochána were clearly overwhelmed. What the state had not accounted for was the animosity of

the 'bar-stool Republicanism' from some of the harder inner-city neighbourhoods, which viewed the state's allowance for such a march to take place on their turf as one final betrayal too many. It was also an opportunity for many to have a pop at the Establishment who, as they see it, has only taken an interest in poorer neighbourhoods during the country's huge growth of the last decade when opportunities for 'regentrification' have occurred, and prices on formerly state-subsidised houses can be bumped up.

What started off with a couple of hundred insurgents in the first wave of protests on O'Connell Street steadily grew in numbers as more and more friends were called in for the action. As the troubles spread over the river into the more salubrious south-side shopping streets, looters began to chance their luck in some of the city's high-street stores, in the knowledge that police back-up was unlikely to arrive for some time. In fact, police officers were so stretched that containment and general crowd control around the city were proving hopelessly unattainable; at one point, bystanders could view a trail of torched cars alongside Trinity College on Nassau Street, to the left, and the surreal prospect of usual Saturday shoppers lining Grafton Street to the right.

Key notes St Patrick

Separating the man from the myth is never an easy task when the man in question died 1,500 years ago, but perhaps the most surprising fact about the single most potent figure in Irish folklore is that in all probability he was not Irish. The Scots, the English and even the Italians all have reasonable claims to the illustrious man, but the general consensus among historians is that St Patrick was actually a Welshman named Maewyn Succat.

Born sometime between AD 373 and 390, Maewyn was the son of Roman parents, Calpurnius and Conchessa. Kidnapped and taken to Ireland as a slave at 16, he spent years labouring in the forest of Foclut (believed to have been somewhere in County Antrim) before escaping on a ship bound for France. There, Maewyn studied under the Bishop of Auxerre in St Germain, until he was inspired by a series of prophetic dreams to return to Ireland as a missionary. His tactic of preaching at pagan sites and festivals frequently put him at odds with the political and religious establishment (such as it was), but by the time of his death in 461, Maewyn's popularity was such that half a dozen feudal landowners fought viciously over the right to bury him on their land. A group of friends resolved matters by stealing his body and interring it in an unmarked grave, probably somewhere in County Down.

Maewyn was responsible for founding a number of churches during his lifetime, although it is not known whether the site of St Patrick's Cathedral was, in fact, one of them. One of the most notable stories associated with Maewyn is his use of the shamrock to demonstrate the Holy Trinity to spectators – hence the flower's current status as the national emblem. The popular myth about his banishing of the snakes from Ireland is believed to be a metaphor for his conversion of the pagans.

In any case, five strategic sites were seized that morning and occupied by the rebels – the Four Courts, St Stephen's Green, Liberty Hall, Jacob's Biscuit Factory and Boland's Flour Mill. Disorder ensued, and 5,000 soldiers were sent from London to assist the police. After almost a week of fighting, the rebels were beaten into submission, and the city centre lay in ruins. Horrified by the bloodshed, Pearse surrendered the following Sunday evening, and was later executed in Kilmainham Gaol. In all, 77 death sentences were issued. Last to be killed was James Connolly, who, unable to stand because of a broken ankle, was shot sitting down.

THE CONFLICT INTENSIFIES

Anti-British feeling, subdued by the onset of war, was inflamed by the list of those executed or imprisoned after the rebellion. Meanwhile, a power vacuum was left at the heart of the nationalist cause, and it was to be filled by two men whose names have become synonymous with the fight for independence. Eamon De Valera was an Irish-American maths teacher who led the garrison at Boland's Mill, while Michael Collins was a West Cork man and former English émigré, who returned home to help the Irish Republican Brotherhood. In 1918 De Valera's new party, Sinn Féin, won 75 per cent of Irish seats in the British general election, but the new MPs convened not in London, but in Dublin, at the Dáil Éireann (the Irish Parliament), where they once again declared Ireland a republic. While De Valera went to rally support in America, Collins concentrated on his work as head of the military wing of the Irish Volunteers (later to become the Irish Republican Army, or IRA). The long, bloody war for Irish independence was now well under way.

The conflict reached its nadir when, on 21 November 1920, Michael Collins ordered 14 undercover British operatives to be executed in their beds. In retaliation, British troops opened fire on a crowd of football spectators at Croke Park in Dublin, killing 12 people. Later the same day, two senior IRA men and a Sinn Féin supporter (an innocent one, as it happened) were executed at Dublin Castle. Collins came out of hiding to lay a wreath at their funeral. The tit-for-tat cycle continued for another eight months, until a truce was declared on 9 July 1921. A delegation led by Collins travelled to London, where they met with representatives of the British government, including Lloyd George (then prime minister) and Winston Churchill. Negotiations culminated on 6 December with the signing of the Anglo-Irish Treaty, after which Collins is said to have remarked that he had signed his own death warrant.

The treaty conferred dominion status on 26 counties, known collectively as the Irish Free State. The remaining six (all largely Protestant) Ulster counties refused to join, thereby partitioning Ireland along geographical, political and religious lines. Dominion status brought limited independence for the so-called Free State, with important elements of British authority enshrined in the constitution. King George V remained head of state in Ireland, represented by a governor general (as in Canada, Australia and New Zealand). A requirement that members of the Dáil swear allegiance to the British Crown was almost as contentious an issue as the partition.

Supporters of the treaty, led by Michael Collins and Arthur Griffith, argued that it offered the best terms available and should be seen as a start. But the opponents, led by Eamon De Valera, would accept nothing less than full independence. De Valera disassociated himself from the treaty, and Sinn Féin was divided. The treaty was ratified by just seven votes. Even the withdrawal of British troops from the capital for the first time in eight centuries, or the handing over of Dublin Castle to the provisional government, did not quell the rising tide of Republican anger.

The flashpoint came in April 1922, when anti-treaty forces clashed with Free State troops at the Four Courts area of Dublin. Fighting also broke out at the General Post Office on O'Connell Street, and the battle lasted for eight days until De Valera's supporters were forced to surrender. The fledgling government passed emergency legislation that allowed the army to shoot armed Republicans on sight; 77 people were executed and 13,000 imprisoned in seven months, with many more on hunger strikes. In Ulster, the death toll for the first half of 1922 was 264 people. The Civil War rolled on for a year, characterised by a vicious, bloody cycle of aggression and reprisal, until De Valera suspended his anti-treaty efforts in 1923.

Whether Collins was right – that a fully united Irish Republic could be achieved by peaceful means – is something we shall never know. His death at the hands of an IRA hit man in August 1922 ensured that it would be De Valera's more callous brand of political conviction that would define Irish politics until the British finally caved in to the inevitability of an Irish Republic a decade and a half later. But the road was far from smooth, the route a long way from consensus. The deep wounds inflicted by civil war on a people already scarred by oppression, privation and battle are all too evident even today in those six awkward little counties to the north. Perhaps Collins' vision of the road from Free State to republic was altogether too optimistic – romantic, even – and the depth of division meant that civil war was, indeed, simply inevitable.

Years later, though, even De Valera conceded that not accepting the treaty had been a mistake. In any case, the blood price was dear. Eight decades on, the shadow of the gun has still not been removed from Irish politics.

The aftermath of civil war dominated the political scene for the rest of the decade. In 1926 De Valera split from the Republicans to form Fianna Fáil ('Warriors of Ireland'). He became a passionate critic of what he saw as the Free State's betrayal of the Irish people, and in the election of 1927 his party won as many seats as the government. Fianna Fáil members refused en masse to take the oath of allegiance, and were for a time disallowed from taking their seats. The election of 1932 returned a Fianna Fáil victory, thanks in part to the 'help' of the IRA, which indulged in a judicious touch of ballot rigging and voter intimidation in support of De Valera. (He felt little in the way of obligation, however; when the organisation refused to disarm a few years later, he was the one who declared it illegal.)

BUILDING THE REPUBLIC
In the subsequent years, the streets of Dublin became relatively free from violence for the first

time in decades (with a few notable exceptions), and the capital experienced something of a cultural renaissance. The Four Courts and O'Connell Street were rebuilt; the city gained a clutch of new theatres, fashionable shops and coffee houses (most famously, Bewley's on Grafton Street) and Ireland's first radio station started broadcasting from a small office on Little Denmark Street in 1926.

The Fianna Fail government lasted for 17 years, during which time the gap between Britain and Ireland widened as never before. The enforced oath of allegiance was scrapped, Roman Catholicism was officially prioritised as the majority religion and in 1937 the name of the Free State was formally changed to Eire. However, the general perception that De Valera's government was more interested in abstract Republican ideals, rather than immediate issues such as social welfare, would eventually cost them dearly. Fianna Fail was ousted by a coalition of Fine Gael ('Tribe of the Gaels') and Sean MacBride's Clann na Poblachta ('Republican Party') in 1948. A year later, Ireland – still minus the six counties – was at last declared a Republic.

THE DARK BEFORE DAWN

Although Ireland remained neutral throughout World War II, this did not by any means make it immune to the austerity of the times. Rationing of basic items including clothes, fuel and food ended in 1949, but for a variety of reasons Ireland saw little of the economic boom that lifted Europe over the next 50 years. Industrial output fell significantly and wage

Neutral ground

When war was declared in Europe on 3 September 1939, Ireland didn't exactly rush to enlist. In fact, Taoiseach Eamon De Valera declared that Ireland would remain neutral throughout the conflict. His justification – that Ireland was a small nation that could not easily defend itself against major powers, and that it would not fight on the same side as a country (England) that was currently occupying Irish territory (Northern Ireland) – made considerable sense, but nonetheless the country was in the strange position of failing to assist its allies and friends, while openly favouring their side of the struggle.

This ambivalence didn't make the situation easier for anybody – including many Irish – to swallow. Thousands of them found ways to enlist into Allied Forces. Nobody knows precisely how many Irish soldiers fought as part of this shadow army, but in 1944 more than 165,000 'British' soldiers listed next-of-kin addresses in Ireland, while newspapers at the time gave varying estimates for numbers of Irish soldiers fighting: the *Manchester Guardian* said 300,000, the *New Yorker* thought 250,000, and the *Daily Telegraph* suggested 150,000. It is believed that as many as 50,000 Irish died in the war. In his poem 'Neutrality', the poet Louis MacNeice writes bitterly of the 'neutral island facing the Atlantic... while off to the west off your own shores the mackerel/are fat on the flesh of your kin'.

For its part, Ireland had great military significance to both sides in the war – Hitler longed to put bases on Irish soil from which to launch attacks, and the Allies were no different – Churchill begged De Valera to reconsider his decision. Some German agents did parachute into Ireland between 1939 and 1945, but all were invariably captured, astray and hopelessly lost.

Once captured, they were interred in prison camps, and, given Ireland's strange situation, it's no surprise that these were very strange places. The K-Lines camp at Curragh, about 30 miles (48 kilometres) outside Dublin, became famous. The Irish government imprisoned both Allied and Axis soldiers in the camp, as any Allied soldiers who crash-landed in or around Ireland had to be imprisoned too, in order for Ireland to maintain the protection of neutrality. From the outside, K-Lines was not unlike other prison camps in Europe at that time. It was modelled on an internment camp that had been built by the British for IRA members. Inside, though, it was more summer camp than prison camp, with low walls, regular day-release passes for detainees and a famous pub where the Germans drank on one side and the Allies on the other.

Fascinating though this is, recently declassified information has revealed what many suspected: Irish neutrality was at least part myth. De Valera allowed Irish agents to spy on and hamper German movements; and RAF planes were allowed to cross Irish airspace on their way to and from their Northern Ireland bases. And, of course, occasional Allied 'escapes' from K-Lines were encouraged.

controls were introduced, while shortages continued to force up the price of basic goods. All of these factors, combined with extremely high unemployment, contributed to a surge in economic migration, particularly to Britain, with an average of 40,000 people a year leaving Ireland by the early 1950s.

There was no small irony in the fact that the post-war depression that hit so hard was caused by a conflict Ireland had resolutely avoided being part of. But the country had nobody to blame but itself for the self-inflicted cultural oppression that followed, as the government used strict censorship laws to ban works by, among others, Brendan Behan, Austin Clarke, Edna O'Brien, George Bernard Shaw and Samuel Beckett, as well as an occasionally baffling list of international authors, from Marcel Proust, Jean-Paul Sartre and Sigmund Freud to Noel Coward, Dylan Thomas, Ernest Hemingway, John Steinbeck, Tennessee Williams and even Apuleius, the second-century philosopher. Meanwhile, tensions between the Church, the government and the population were intensified when pressure from the Catholic Church forced the government to abandon plans for a progressive programme of pre- and post-natal healthcare legislation that was, by all accounts, desperately needed at the time.

'By the early 1970s the violence became more serious.'

Things began to change in the 1950s, when an ambitious programme of grants and tax breaks attracted a new wave of foreign investment. When Sean Lemass took over as president, he became Ireland's first true economic manager; his expansionist policies led away from an agrarian economy as the country took its first steps to competing in the world market. In 1973 Ireland joined the European Economic Community.

In Dublin, in a kind of celebratory demolition derby, monuments erected by the British during the occupation were destroyed by the IRA – most symbolic among them, Nelson's Pillar on O'Connell Street, a replica of London's Nelson's Column.

By the early 1970s, though, the violence became more serious, with the resumption of sectarian strife in Northern Ireland reopening old political and religious wounds. After the notorious Bloody Sunday killings in January 1972, a crowd of up to 30,000 protestors laid siege to the British Embassy in Dublin for three days before burning it down.

CHURCH AND STATE

In 1983 the so-called pro-life movement launched a vociferous campaign to have the constitution amended to include a ban on abortion (despite the fact that such a ban already existed in Irish law). Enthusiastically backed by the Catholic Church, the referendum passed. Campaigning on both sides rumbled on until 1992, when the issue again hit the headlines with the infamous 'X Case', in which a 14-year-old Dublin girl was raped, became pregnant, but was restrained from travelling to England for an abortion. An impassioned public debate ensued, heightened when the girl herself declared that she would commit suicide unless the decision was overturned. Eventually, the Supreme Court ruled that not only was it legal for her to travel, but that under those circumstances it was not unconstitutional for her to have an abortion performed in Ireland.

For many, the ultimate sign of the changing times came when divorce was finally legalised after a referendum in 1995. Although the result was close enough to keep it mired in the courts for another couple of years (the final count had a margin of victory of just half a per cent), the passage of a law that would have been unthinkable a generation earlier told of the immense change happening in the country.

When a series of well-publicised scandals rocked the Irish religious establishment in the 1990s (a damaging rap sheet of embezzlement and child abuse), it seemed that the days of the all-powerful Church in Ireland were numbered.

THE HERE AND NOW

The 1990s may have been a period of great social upheaval, but they were also a time of unprecedented economic prosperity, and Dublin reaped the rewards. Investment soared and unemployment plummeted. Expats returned in droves. Those were heady days – 'Celtic Tiger' became as familiar a buzzword as 'dot-com', and Ireland's burgeoning high-tech industries were what gave the tiger its sharpest teeth.

Prosperity, however, did not come without a price. In Dublin, crime went up, threatening the city's traditionally easygoing reputation. In 1996 journalist Veronica Guerin was murdered while investigating organised crime in the capital, and her death shocked the nation. Affluent Dublin became an attractive destination for economic migrants, especially Romanians and Nigerians, and fresh tensions began to bubble up.

At the end of the 20th century, the tiger began to falter. The EU, which had lavished money on the country, shifted its attention, and funds, to Eastern Europe, and could yet come calling on Dublin with its palm out, asking for

Hunger strikes

In 1845 a fungus ravaged potato crops in Ireland, destroying much of the staple food of the poor. The famine that followed has gone down in Irish history as the country's biggest struggle. It was not so much the famine itself, as the callousness of the upper class that forever rankles here.

As the blight grew worse, many Irish landlords still shipped grain to England. Their reasoning was purely mathematical – with no crops, the peasants could not pay rent, so the grain was sent for export to offset the loss. The effects were multiplied by the fact that the English Parliament was reluctant to send any food to Ireland. One official declared in 1846, 'It is not the intention at all to import food for the use of the people of Ireland.' In a truly immortal display of hubris, British Prime Minister Robert Peel said the Irish had 'a tendency to exaggerate'.

Enormous cargo loads of imported corn sat in Irish depots for months, until the government felt that releasing the corn for sale would not adversely affect food prices. Huge quantities of cattle, pork, sheep, oats, eggs and flour were exported from Ireland as the people starved. Irish shipping records indicate that nearly 10,000 Irish calves were exported to England during the year that became known as 'Black '47' – this was a 33 per cent increase over the previous year.

While Irish beef and grain were sent to England, the English supplied the starving Irish with cheap Indian cornmeal. Tragically, this meal contained virtually no nutrients, and ultimately contributed to the spread of disease among the weak and starving. In the end, most famine victims died from malnutrition-related diseases such as dropsy, dysentery, typhus, scurvy and cholera, rather than directly from starvation. The cornmeal

was not simply given to those who needed it. The British government feared handouts would encourage laziness and undermine the Irish economy, so it set up pointless projects so that the Irish could earn their gruel. Starving men built roads that began in the middle of a field and went nowhere, and others that ended pointlessly on a sandy beach.

Conveniently for the British, one of the only options open to the poor was emigration, and during the four long years before the brutal famine finally ended, more than a million people took it up. About three quarters of them went to America; the others to Europe or to England. In 1841 Ireland's population had been around eight million; a decade later it was 6.5 million.

Dublin's own famine experience was somewhat different from that of people in rural Ireland. What wealth there was in Ireland was largely kept in the city, and so, in many respects, life continued as normal for the upper classes as the famine raged. Balls were held at the Mansion House, and plans were made to establish a library, museums and public galleries. But the population of Dublin had surged from some 10,000 in 1600 to just under a quarter of a million in 1851, and the city was strained to its limits. The quality of water, air and housing soon degenerated and the mortality began to skyrocket.

In response to the many deaths, the city established a series of initiatives designed to improve its infrastructure; rail and tram networks were built, the Grand and Royal canals were constructed, and hospitals were opened. Most important, permanent social housing for the city's neediest citizens was built, ensuring that such a catastrophe would never happen again.

returns on its investment. It's too early to tell if the Celtic Tiger has turned to Celtic Tabby. Ireland has weathered the global economic downturn better than most European economies, but the pinch has been felt: growth is down, unemployment up, and the adoption of the euro keeps prices artificially high.

Social and political tensions in Dublin society persist (see p17 **Boiling point**), but such problems are no longer confined to the internecine disputes of the Irish people. In May 2006, an estimated 41 Afghan asylum seekers

occupied St Patrick's Cathedral for several days, threatening to starve themselves to death unless they were granted leave to remain in the country. Their claim, that a return to Afghanistan would be tantamount to a death sentence, struck a familiar chord, echoing the rhetoric of similar protests around the world. When police finally cleared St Patrick's, bearing waif-like figures on stretchers and with no satisfactory conclusion reached, Dubliners were left with precious few answers and a feeling of growing unease.

Dublin Today

Making history.

The Celtic Tiger may have lost its teeth, and Ireland may no longer be the envy of the developing world, but it is still a remarkable example of the kind of change that can be telescoped into a generation. From poverty that was almost as much a feature of the middle class as of the working classes, to breathtaking wealth in just 20 years; picking up the pieces of traditional Irish society has been a big job.

Pessimists still wait for the crash, but the rest of the country, particularly Dublin, is busy getting on with life in radically altered circumstances. People buy houses when and where they can, shutting their ears to talk of bust because the alternative might be never getting on the property ladder; they resign themselves to daily traffic problems; submit to being overcharged for a vast range of goods and services; only show occasional signs of temper; and generally adapt easily enough to a shiny new lifestyle.

Of course, not everyone is happy, or reaping the economic miracle. Although analysts predict that economic growth is poised for a six

per cent gain in 2006, the country has many of the hallmarks of a struggling nation: a wretched health service, inadequate public transport and alarming rich–poor divide. As interest rates climb ever higher, those with lower incomes and big mortgages are being squeezed. And, though Ireland is ostensibly a low-taxation country, there's still no such thing as a free lunch. Stealth taxes are everywhere, and contribute to the regular surplus accumulated by the Exchequer. VAT on every overhead charge such as gas and electricity, hefty stamp duty on property purchases, and corporation tax: these all fill the government's coffers. Indirect taxation stands at 41 per cent, compared with an EU average of 33 per cent, and the result is the 'Rip-off Ireland' label that just won't seem to go away.

The most recent census put the population of the country at about 4.2 million, the highest since the Great Famine of the late 1800s. Almost half that number, roughly 2 million, live in the greater Dublin area. But these days, they aren't all Irish.

Taxi!

In the bad old days, taxis were as rare as four-leafed clovers – and more useful. The one certainty of a weekend night out was that it would end with a dismal last stand; the 3am taxi queue. During rush hours, waits were long and no-shows frequent, even after booking hours in advance. All of which meant that one of the most sought-after pieces of information was a reliable driver's mobile number.

Then deregulation happened – despite a legal challenge by the National Taxi Drivers' Union, which was understandably reluctant to break up its lucrative status quo – and a flood of new cars took to the roads. That brought with it a new set of problems. First came tales of criminals flocking to the new opportunity, then there were stories of taxi drivers involved in rapes and other criminal activity, leading to questions in the Dail and serious concern among the Gardai.

Multi-millionaire Ryanair CEO Michael O'Leary also took advantage of deregulation, spending €6,000 on taxi plates for his chauffeur-driven Mercedes so that he could use the taxi lanes and beat the traffic. Perfectly legal, of course – and typically O'Leary.

Another casualty of deregulation has been the standards of cleanliness. Indeed, the whole taxi experience has become very touch-and-go. There are cars out there it is an affront to sit in: stinking, with surly, foul-mouthed drivers and outrageous prices. In fact, the situation has become so bad that one local magazine, the *Dubliner*, runs a campaign for a basic taxi charter that would ensure a minimum standard.

Pricing can be erratic, with a complicated system of charges for numbers of passengers, extra bags, airport trips, and others more obscure. When the Taxi Regulator – who recently moved into one of the finest buildings in Dublin, a Georgian townhouse on Fitzwilliam Square – launched a plan to standardise fares across the country, drivers called a one-day strike.

So, not exactly a drive in the park, but still an improvement on the 3am last stand.

For the first time ever, the city can be said to be truly cosmopolitan. There are 140,000 Poles with registered PPS numbers, and an estimated same again without them: Poles are the biggest non-Irish group. Six Polish newspapers are published regularly, the *Herald* produces a Polish supplement every Friday (most other daily papers do one from time to time), and the newly launched City Channel has a regular Polish magazine show.

Lithuanians are the next largest group, with 50,000-100,000 of them registered for work. Chinese, Spanish and Africans all have their cultural stamping grounds. The Islamic population is around 20,000, although there's no dominant ethnicity; that number is drawn from East Asia, China, Indonesia, sub-Saharan Africa and the Arab world.

Evidence of the new diversity can be seen in the many ethnic shops and restaurants springing up around the city. Moore Street, once famous for brusque Irish women selling fruit, veg and fish from battered babies' prams, has been transformed into a cultural melting pot, where African hairdressers squash up alongside Middle Eastern delis, functional Chinese restaurants and endless cheap internet and phone shops. Parnell Street is fast turning into Chinatown, with rows of restaurants and snack bars, most serving delicious food in fuss-free surroundings. Meanwhile, the area around Camden Street and the South Circular Road has a number of excellent Middle Eastern and Indian shops, all selling good vegetables, spices, orange flower water, almond flour, ground coconut and other weird and wonderful things at reasonable prices.

By and large these new communities live peacefully and happily alongside each other and the established population. Despite much soul-searching and some racist cant at the outset of the steady influx, nasty incidents have been few, and the meshing of cultures successful. The benefits in terms of the look, feel and taste of the city are well recognised, and Dubliners are generally a welcoming lot.

The other big difference in Dublin society is money. Conspicuous wealth is a defining characteristic of the capital today; almost everywhere you look you'll see evidence of consumption: new cars, big houses, designer boutiques, smart restaurants, hotels with heli-pads and luxurious spas. There's no doubt the city is spending money furiously and enjoying every second of it. Every once in a while, respectable newspapers like *The Irish Times* run features on the escalating debt problem, but sounding the alarm bell does nothing to slow the pace of borrowing. As with the possibility of a property crash, Dubliners just don't want to know. And given that there are apparently more millionaires per head of population in Ireland than anywhere else in the world except America, maybe they don't need to.

'There are apparently more millionaires per head of population than anywhere except America.'

Traffic and public transport are still a source of daily irritation to most of the city's inhabitants, particularly that sector of the population – mostly first-time property buyers and families – forced to live in the rapidly expanding 'commuter zone.' This commuter zone now extends in an arc all the way to Kildare and Mullingar in the west, Drogheda in the north and Arklow in the south-east. Houses may be more affordable, but quality of life is compromised by a three-hour daily commute, and the infrastructure of many of the dormitory towns is wholly inadequate to cope with the influx. The Port Tunnel is now years behind schedule, with no end in sight, and is a major embarrassment to the government. Although

the Luas has finally become operational, and is an excellent resource for those living or working along its route, it doesn't go far enough in any direction to really ease the traffic.

Development in the city continues, with some great new public additions, particularly the Dundrum Town Centre – the opening of which precipitated an avalanche of media pieces asking whether shopping is the new religion in modern Ireland – and the Docklands, where work is soon to begin on a national conference centre and Daniel Libeskind-designed theatre. Lansdowne Road rugby stadium is also being redeveloped.

Politically, this is not a country of great variety. The dominant party, Fianna Fáil, has formed the government seven times since independence in 1921, and in 1997 it was the only party to be returned at a general election since 1969. There is no huge ideological difference between the main political parties; rather, the profound allegiances felt to one or the other tend to go back to the creation of the state. However, Fianna Fáil is seen to be a safe pair of hands and more effective that Fine Gael, despite regular waves of dissatisfaction and grumbles.

In a global context, the American connection is as strong as ever; America is still the ideology to which Ireland aspires, far more than anything Europe has to offer. The day of mourning announced by the government after the attacks on the World Trade Center in

Where all the money goes: shoppers on **Grafton Street**.

September 2001 has never been seen before or since – not even for the funeral of Pope John Paul II.

The last few years have seen a gentle radicalisation among Dubliners, mainly spurred by the Iraq War. In spite of the close relationship Ireland still enjoys with the USA, huge anti-war demonstrations have been held, and people who had never marched before took to the streets in significant numbers. Instead of the usual motley selection, the people who marched were largely middle-class, middle-ground families with children. And the matter of American planes refuelling at Shannon airport in the west has become highly controversial. Considerable pressure brought to bear by the Americans means the practice continues, but regular demonstrations are held outside the airport, and cases of planes attacked by anti-war activists are, at the time of going to press, still being heard in the courts. A cleaning woman boarded a supposedly empty American plane to find a prisoner handcuffed and hooded, to the very great embarrassment of the Irish government, which had been given public assurances that prisoners would not be transferred along this route. A Council of Europe report named Ireland as one of the countries used for 'extraordinary rendition', the secret transfer of prisoners – although the Irish government denies it.

And then there was the death of CJ Haughey, the man who, many say, helped create this modern Ireland, though others insist he discredited it. With his Celtic chieftain affectations and good life aspirations, he certainly personified a link between the country and its romantic past. Loved, hated, feared, mocked and revered, Haughey dominated the political scene for over 35 years – though it's impossible to determine exactly how much his policies contributed to the creation of the boom economy; the extent to which he gets credit is usually dependent on his popularity. Although he was investigated almost to the time of his death for corruption, nothing ever stuck. For each person who mourns the death of the Big Fella, there's another who hopes his passing means the end of an Ireland of corruption and cronyism.

Visitors to the city will see little of the latter, of course. On a short acquaintance, Dublin is a fascinating city to explore, with enough traditional entertainment – music, strolling, shopping, food, pub life – to recommend it. The stunning natural setting means fresh air – from sea or mountain – is always accessible, and trips around the country are easily taken. And there are still charming pockets where, on a quiet morning, it seems that very little has changed in more than 50 years. Long may they last.

The property boom

For over a decade, analysts have prophesied a bubble burst for the Irish property market. It hasn't happened yet. The exponential rise in housing prices continues, and 2005 saw the construction of 75,000 new houses in Ireland (a figure that looked set to be surpassed in 2006). And the government has predicted a ten per cent rise in property prices for 2007.

The unflinchingly bullish market has made many of Ireland's existing homeowners filthy rich and has made matters virtually impossible for first-time buyers. Properties bought in the 1980s for tens of thousands of pounds are now valued at seven figures (euros, admittedly, but that's still a big mark-up): a modest two-bedroom house in Crumlin, on the outskirts of Dublin, goes for around €555,000. For most young people, the only option is to rent – an increasingly pricey proposition in itself. A space in a shared flat within half an hour of the city centre is unlikely to go for less than €500/month, and luxury one-bedroom flats in the centre go for up to €1,500.

The thirst for development has left the city scarred: dozens of cranes dot the horizon in any direction on any given day and commercial or letting developments have been big on speed and small on looks. Heritage sites are also put in jeopardy by the rapid expansion: protests failed to stop Temple Bar properties going up over ancient Viking grounds; and, outside Dublin, the clout of Stuart Townsend's celebrity appears unlikely to halt the M3's progress through the prehistoric site of the Hill of Tara. The pressure to develop has seen the council try to apply models derived elsewhere to areas where they're not always appropriate.

The gentrification drive reached a comic peak this year, with Dublin City Council's announcement of plans to restyle a tough area of the city known as the Liberties into a Dublin version of SoHo: in a dubious homage to Manhattan's South of Houston, the acronym now stands for 'South of Heuston Station'.

Architecture

Grand designs.

The word Georgian is very nearly synonymous with Dublin, and the Georgian era was a period of mercurial advancement for the city – at least in architectural terms. Most of the city's memorable buildings were constructed during the reigns of kings George I to IV (from 1714 to 1830), when Ireland was in the fold of the British Empire. Elegant Georgian buildings line the wide streets in the south inner city as well as pockets north of the river Liffey, creating a cityscape that is more than the sum of its parts.

Recent times have been less glorious. An economic slump during much of the 20th century led to a bleak time in Irish architecture, with few notable buildings. Exceptions include: the International-style **Busáras**, designed in 1953 by Michael Scott, with its glazed façade that echoes Le Corbusier's Maison Suisse and Cité de Refuge in Paris; and the beautiful **Guinness Storehouse**, built in 1904 as a homage to the urban elegance of the Chicago

School. During the 1960s and '70s, too many Georgian buildings were knocked down to make way for office blocks. The longest Georgian terrace in Dublin, Fitzwilliam Street, was severed in the 1970s when a chunk was knocked out to make way for offices. However, the demolition caused an outcry, and was a turning point in the preservation of period buildings. When the recent building boom began in the mid 1990s, everything was in place to make the most of it: native architects, who had coped with the slump by working abroad, returned with knowledge gleaned at the drawing boards of the likes of Frank Lloyd Wright, Le Corbusier, Renzo Piano, Richard Rogers and Norman Foster. Ronnie Tallon even designed a bank building in Lower Baggot Street that resembles the façade (not the plan) of Mies van der Rohe's Seagram building in New York.

▶ see also p73 **Walk Georgian Dublin**.

Making an entrance: **Fitzwilliam Square**.

So although an awful lot of mean, dark apartment blocks and semi-detached housing remains, the last decade has seen a rise in the quality of architecture across the country. Architects such as O'Mahoney Pike are leading the way in the design of a new type of light-filled apartment. Good examples of their work can be seen at Hanover Quay, draped in glass 'winter gardens', in Dublin's Docklands, and the wedge-shaped apartments in a circular Victorian gas storage facility (South Lotts Road). Also in the Docklands are the beautiful stepped-back Clarion Quay apartment buildings, in timber, render and glass.

THE OLD AND THE NEW

Dublin's core is small and many interesting buildings huddle near the centre, so it's easy to undertake an architectural tour on foot.

To the west of the city centre is the former medieval area, and if you search around in **Christ Church Cathedral** (*see p69*) and **St Patrick's Cathedral** (*see p70*) you'll discover bits of medieval structure that were retained when the cathedrals were substantially rebuilt in the late 1800s. These include Christ Church's 12th-century Romanesque doorway on the end of its southern transcept, and the early 15th-century tower of St Patrick's. Then again,

from Essex Street in Temple Bar you can gaze down on to the old city wall and the outline of Isolde's Tower.

Substantial neo-classical buildings, dating from the 18th and early 19th centuries, face the River Liffey and areas just to the south of it. The architects behind these projects included Edward Lovett Pearce, Richard Cassels, William Chambers, James Gandon and Thomas Cooley, all of whom played vital roles in the history of Irish architecture. They came from well-connected families, and many had either taken the grand tour to France and Italy themselves, or were under the influence of those who had. Pearse, who was related to Sir John Vanburgh (who designed Blenheim Palace and Castle Howard in England), toured Italy, and his love of Palladian architecture is evident in the design of the granite **Bank of Ireland** building (College Green), dressed in ionic columns made of Portland stone. It was later extended by Gandon.

Sir William Chambers' **Casino** garden building for the Marino Estate, in north Dublin, resembles Andrea Palladio's 1571 Villa Rotunda in Vicenza, Italy. His protégé, James Gandon, took the style with him when he went on to design the **Four Courts** (Inns Quay), a granite building with Portland stone trimmings

overlooking the Liffey, and the monumental yet neatly scaled **Custom House** (Custom House Quay), modelled after Chambers' Somerset House in London. (Look across from the Custom House to see the ill-considered, pyramid-topped recent office building that has been dubbed 'canary dwarf'.) Gandon gained the Four Courts commission on the death of the original architect, Thomas Cooley. Cooley had already designed another neo-classical gem, the Exchange (now **City Hall**) on Cork Hill.

'Trinity has commissioned some of the best architects over the centuries.'

Richard Cassells also took up the reins when his mentor Pearse died. He continued the Palladian theme, albeit using classical adornment in a more subtle way, when he designed a huge town house for the Earl of Kildare, on Kildare Street. Leinster House, as it is known, is now the seat of parliament. It's flanked by the neo-classical **National Library** and **National Museum** (both designed by two Thomas Deanes, a father-and-son team, in the late 19th century), creating a grand classical

courtyard marred somewhat by the car park in its midst. The new glass pavilion through which you enter the courtyard is a finely detailed structure that was designed by Bucholz McEvoy Architects, one of the city's most gifted young practices.

The other side of the parliament building faces Merrion Square, one of Dublin's finest Georgian squares. Others include nearby Fitzwilliam Square and Mountjoy Square on Dublin's northside, which has suffered from deprivation, but whose innate beauty has seen it through to recent restoration.

Merrion Square is a Dublin architectural highlight. On its north side, at No.8, are the offices and bookshop of the Royal Institute of the Architects of Ireland. A large town house on the west side, at No.45, is home to the Irish Architectural Archive; the fittings for its exhibition room came from the Royal Institute of British Architects' Heinz Gallery in London. To the east is the **National Gallery**, which has been given a new wing by Scottish architects Benson and Forsyth. Its cathedral-like entrance is a truly cavernous, suitably monumental prelude to a trip round the gallery itself. A bookshop and café flank the wide staircase that leads you to the art; high above, visitors cross a thin bridge from one gallery to the next.

Ha'penny Bridge. *See p31.*

From the entrance of the new wing you can head down Nassau Street past the walls of **Trinity College**, above which towers the Ussher Library, designed in 1999. A walk around Trinity is an architectural treat, as the university has commissioned some of the best architects over the centuries: people like Cassels (Printing House, 1734), Chambers (exam hall, 1785; chapel, 1798), and Dean and Woodward (museum, 1857).

A recent addition to an engineering building, an angular composition of white elements by Grafton Architects, picked up the latest in a trophy cabinet full of architectural awards won by Trinity college buildings. The Ussher Library, which has a vast void at its centre overlooked by scarily low-walled balconies, sits next to the Le Corbusier-esque Berkeley Library.

Another compact architectural tour can be conducted in Temple Bar. Many of the new structures in the area were knitted into existing buildings (stand-alone, wow-factor buildings are a rarity in Dublin), and are of a pared-down style, but they revolutionised the acceptance of modern architecture in Ireland. Check out **Meeting House Square**, with its Gallery of Photography in reflecting Portland stone, and the red-brick, zinc-punctuated National Photographic Archive, with its low curved-arch

entrance. On the west side is the Gaiety School of Acting, and to the east is the rear of the Ark Children's Cultural Centre. At the heart of the latter is a band of metal strips, framed by green copper, that opens up to create a canopy over a stage, for outdoor performances.

'Ian Ritchie's landmark Spire replaced Nelson's Column, blown up in 1966 by the IRA.'

On nearby Eustace Street is the **Irish Film Centre**, converted from a mix of old buildings. You walk through to the auditorium and the internal, glass-topped courtyard (with café, bookshop and curved box office) down a passageway floored with blue-lit glass paving slabs that resemble strips of celluloid.

Off Eustace Street is Curved Street, flanked by the Art House and the Temple Bar Music Centre. Both are white buildings with vast, metal-framed and mullioned windows in the industrial Modernist style that permeates many of the 'new' Temple Bar buildings. Don't miss the overtly Modernist Temple Bar Gallery and Studios and the Black Church Print Gallery; the design of the latter's window divides were inspired by a compositor's typeface holder.

Those shiny solar panels and wind turbines you can see on the roof of apartments in Crow Street belong to the Green Building. Its witty and experimental design – balconies are made from old bicycle frames and one door has old piping and other metal scraps behind a Perspex screen – makes for a pleasingly human feel. Get a view of the internal atrium (which provides passive-stack ventilation) by going into the urbanely urban furniture shop, Haus, on the ground floor.

You can enter the Temple Bar quarter in a number of ways, and one of the most dramatic is beneath the 1975 **Central Bank** building by Sam Stephenson, which caused a row when it was built: the striped concrete office block, which stands on one central leg, broke through the low-rise skyline in a brutalist fashion like none other in Ireland.

North of the Liffey, you'll see Ian Ritchie's landmark 120m **Spire**, which was put up in O'Connell Street in 2003. It replaced Nelson's Column, blown up in 1966 by the IRA. The needle-shaped Spire was designed to be free of any political or nationalistic symbols, its metal surface intended to let people fix their own significance on it.

THE NEW AND THE NEWEST

On the other side of Temple Bar is the Liffey, with its clutch of new bridges. The Ha'penny Bridge, built in 1816, has long been a Dublin postcard favourite. In 2000, it got a new neighbour in the form of the **Millennium Footbridge**. With its bronzed aluminium handrail, the design of this sleek steel bridge echoes its arched neighbour, but has a much gentler, more buggy-friendly curve. Another recently completed footbridge, this time in the Docklands, has a steel deck held by two upturned 'claws', giving the neatly scaled bridge a nice dynamic. Upriver, to the west, is Santiago Calatrava's sculptural road bridge, which has the beauty of form shared by his bridges and buildings worldwide, though it's way out of scale for the relatively narrow Liffey. Caltrava's Docklands bridge, due for completion in 2009, looks set to be a much better fit. Watch that space.

Looking ahead, Daniel Libeskind will complete a project in the Docklands in 2009, when the finishing touches are scheduled to be added to his angular, tilted theatre, sliced with geometric openings. This will overlook a square, by US landscape designer Martha Schwartz, that will extend out over the water at Hanover Quay.

Guinness Storehouse. *See p27.*

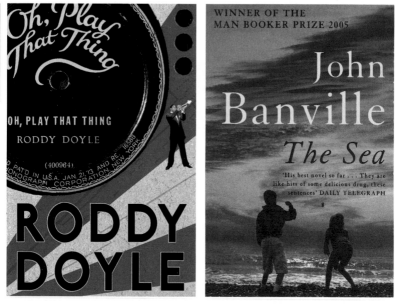

New Novel Army

Contemporary writers living and working in the fair city.

Dublin is a city with an impressive literary pedigree. Several times in recent years, the public has had the chance to steep itself in the achievements of some of Ireland's, if not the world's, most prodigious literary talents: the Beckett centenary of 2006, say; or the Bloomsday centenary in 2004, when 1,300 people descended on the capital to pay homage to Joyce's most famous novel. There is also no shortage of permanent exhibitions enshrining the city's literary past, places like the Dublin Writers' Museum (spanning three centuries of Irish literature; *see p81*), Shaw's Birthplace (*see p77*), the Oscar Wilde House (*see p76*) or the James Joyce Centre (*see p82*). The list goes on. But Dublin's literary present is not so well represented on the tourist trail, despite the fact that many great writers choose to live and work in the city, and often bring home the glory of high-profile prizes.

Today's writers face a different challenge to that of their predecessors. With Irish literature now firmly positioned on the world stage and

recognised as a national treasure at home, the battle is no longer to stake Ireland's claim on the map of world letters. That flag is already flying. Much of contemporary Irish fiction boils down to one common theme: the crisis of a nation struggling to identify itself in the post-colonial age. The Celtic Tiger and the economic and cultural independence bestowed upon the country force its writers to question the validity of a literary culture born out of a colonial past. Ireland's new wave of writing is profoundly international in character, but it can be hard to distance oneself entirely from the influence of the country and its vast history of storytelling. As **Colm Tóibín** explains, Dublin's literary tradition can only be temporarily ignored; it never fails to reassert its presence.

While Tóibín appreciates that tradition, he manages to transcend the limitations of nationality by setting his books across national boundaries, from the hills of Spain to the Irish countryside, and he has achieved international recognition for his efforts: *The Blackwater*

Lightship was shortlisted for the (then) Booker Prize in 1999; *The Master* was shortlisted for the 2004 Man Booker Prize and won the International IMPAC Dublin Literary Award. But his prose is still dominated by themes that resonate in Irish culture – the institution of Catholicism, for example, and the current crisis between belief and non-belief in Irish society.

John Banville is another highly acclaimed modern Irish writer. Two novels exploring the lives of eminent scientists (*Dr Copernicus* and *Kepler*) won him the James Tait Black Memorial Prize and *Guardian* Fiction Prize, respectively. His most recent success has been *The Sea*, his 2005 Man Booker Prize-winning novel about an elderly art historian revisiting his childhood following the death of his wife.

Banville, who was born in Wexford, was very quickly drawn to Dublin. After a brief stint as a clerk for Aer Lingus, and travelling widely, he worked in journalism for 30 years, and was literary editor of *The Irish Times* from 1988 to 1999. Dublin is very much his home and remains a place intrinsically connected to his life as a writer (*see p34* **Banville on Dublin**).

Similarly wide-ranging in his work is **Colum McCann**, who was born in Dublin but moved to America when he was 18. He cycled across the country taking jobs along the way as a mechanic, ranch hand, taxi driver, firefighter and teacher of delinquent teenagers at Miracle Farm in Colorado. His most acclaimed novel, *Dancer*, gives a fictionalised account of Russian dancer Rudolf Nureyev. McCann says the novel was inspired by a story he heard of an Irish boy who, when trying to tune a new television, encountered the fuzzy image of Nureyev and became enraptured by the Russian, establishing a fascinating cross-cultural bond.

Patrick McCabe was likewise moved by the introduction of visual media into Irish life. His novels (twice nominated for the Booker Prize)

Tóibín on Dublin

You travel a lot and you seem to have a special affinity with Spain. What is it that makes you come back to Dublin?
I love the Dublin winter, it's reliable, it's cold and it's dark by half four. Between October and April it's a very good time to finish a book. It's a lovely time because you know exactly how the days go, there's no variation. It's never absolutely freezing like, say, New York.
Is there any particular spot in Dublin where you find comfort or inspiration when you're writing?
I like the three galleries – the National, the Municipal and the Irish Museum of Modern Art – but I mostly stay home.
Is there any way in particular you feel the city has influenced your writing?
I'm from Enniscorthy so Dublin for me remains exotic. We used to come up as kids, and it was an adventure coming up to Dublin, to Clery's, Arnotts, Henry Street and Woolworths and all that. I do love the city. I live in the old Georgian city and I really love the squares, Fitzwilliam Square, Merrion Square, even St Stephen's Green – for country boys it's still exotic.
How do you feel that Dublin compares to other places you've lived in?
I think it is lacking in some ways: it could do with an opera house, it could do with many more traffic restrictions and it could do with many more Luas lines; but then, it is a very leisurely city because of these things, and because the centre is very small.

Do you think it's a good place to be a writer?
Yes, for two reasons. I talked about the winter, the other is that it has a really significant tradition that you can choose to forget about or think about. I love the National Library, where there is an original *Ulysses*... If you walk down out of the National Library, you can see the pub where Barnacle worked, or Clare Street where the Becketts have a business. The city has a lot of literary echoes that other cities don't have.
What changes have you noticed in Dublin over the years?
People travel a lot more, there's a lot more brightness and diversity. It's wonderful walking through the city and seeing all these Chinese, Nigerian and Polish people, who have done wonders for Dublin.
Describe the quintessential Dubliner.
The quintessential Dubliner is someone like me, who came to the city – this old business that you had to be born in Dublin to be a Dubliner is over. I think many people now feel at home in Dublin, whether from China or from Enniscorthy.

describe the difficult transition between poverty and conservatism in Ireland, and the liberation of economic prosperity, providing a dark, highly stylised view of the Irish experience. For McCabe, film eased the transition from a stifling and abusive Ireland (he has cited Hitchcock as an influence) to a more tolerant and diverse society, as he hid away in theatres ignoring the harsh society his parents' generation were struggling to leave behind.

Roddy Doyle sees little in such a transition. While dealing with similar themes of family and adolescence, his accounts of Dublin life are written from his experience growing up in the poverty-stricken North Side. He takes an

unsentimental look at Irish childhood and, much like Frank McCourt, has been criticised for presenting a dismal view of urban life. 'There's always a subtle pressure to present a good image,' he maintains, 'and it's always someone else's image of what's good.' In his honest representations of the tough, macho elements of Irish culture, Doyle nevertheless manages to communicate a romantic view of community.

A bright new member of Dublin's literary elite is **Sean O'Reilly**. His latest novel, *Watermark*, takes place in an unnamed Irish city and tells the story of a woman on the margins of urban society, examining classic and universal themes of love, sex and death.

Banville on Dublin

It would be easy for a visitor to come away from Dublin with the view that it's an inherently literary city, an environment in which a writer can thrive. In your experience, is this true?
Certainly Dubliners, and the Irish in general, are the People of the Word. We love to talk, and love to hear ourselves talking, and will say anything, no matter how cruel, for the sake of a witticism. When a politician or a churchman is caught committing some enormity, what fascinates us is not so much the sin, but the account the sinner gives of himself. In this city, if you tell a good enough story, you can get away with anything.
Has the atmosphere of the city changed a great deal since you moved here?
I came to live in Dublin more than 40 years ago. Of course, the city then was a sleepy, not to say comatose, backwater. Dubliners are hopelessly nostalgic for the 'rare oul' times', but really there was little that was lovely back then, as we busied ourselves in tearing down much of what was left of the great Georgian city that the English had left us. Now we are rich, from exporting computer parts and Viagra – hardware and software, you might say – and all is glitz and speed and greed, yet one cannot regret the better lives the young lead now, compared to our pinched past.
What part of Dublin do you live in? What drew you to that particular area?

I have an apartment in the centre of town, where I work. It's on the river. There is an elegant riverside boardwalk built a few years ago, which gives the sense of pacing the deck of a great luxury liner, where the tourists stroll, the office workers eat their sandwich lunches, the seagulls furiously swoop, and the druggies sun themselves of a morning before cooking up another round of crack.
More generally, are there parts of the city that have certain associations for you?
When I first came to Dublin I had an enormous, shabby and freezing flat in a magnificent Georgian house on Upper Mount Street, one of the world's most impressive sweeps of cityscape, looking down along Merrion Square to the parliament buildings, former home of the Dukes of Ormond, and, in the other direction, giving on to the canal, where the air under the bridges is apple-green and the sky floats in the water. I can think of few moments more poignantly beautiful than a deserted late-summer Sunday afternoon in Mount Street, with copper-coloured sunlight falling along the brick façades.
Which qualities do you associate with the quintessential Dubliner?
Irreverence, humour and resentment; and an unfailing astonishment at the fact of rain.
Do you have any favourite buildings?
St Stephen's Church in Mount Street Crescent, known as The Pepper Canister.
Are there cafés you sit in when you're working?
No real writer will be seen working in public, which puts Sartre and The Beaver in their places. But Dunne & Crescenzi wine bar (*see p118*) is the perfect place to hide out with a book when the Muse is in one of her sulks.

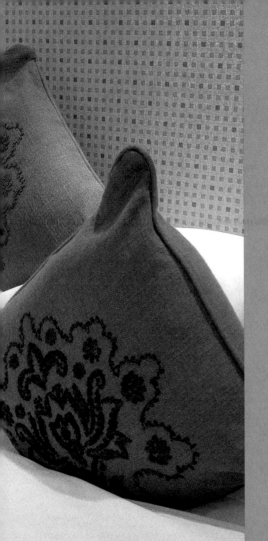

Where to Stay

Feature boxes

Brooks Hotel. *See p39*.

Where to Stay

Top of the morning – and the night before.

There are a few things Dublin does particularly well: bars, churches, city squares, public art – and, happily, hotels. Whether you're looking for a cheap, funky hostel, or planning to put a few five-star nights on your black MasterCard, this town will have something for you.

But beware: Dublin also does bad hotels well. There are plenty of dank, dark, hideous establishments, last decorated in 1981 with plaid curtains, floral carpets and the dirt of decades in the corners, and they all seem to charge €100 a night or more. Choose carefully.

In the following pages, we've carefully weeded out the worst and provided a list of the best each area has to offer. But you may have to be flexible. If you want a sea view but you haven't got much cash, consider staying in a guesthouse – some of them are wonderful and, for the money, better than anything you could expect from a large hotel. Similarly, if you want to stay in Temple Bar or around Dame Street, but you're a light sleeper, bring earplugs – those are noisy areas. It's also worth mentioning that only the most expensive hotels have air conditioning: bear this in mind if you plan to visit in the summer and you hate stuffy bedrooms.

Wherever you stay you're likely to get sick of the standard Dublin breakfast of eggs, bacon and sausage – sometimes with white and black pudding – fairly quickly. The bigger the hotel, generally speaking, the more likely you are to face the hellish prospect of the breakfast buffet. Guesthouses inevitably provide the most innovative morning options.

WHERE ARE WE?

Unlike many other busy tourist towns, Dublin hotels are not concentrated in any particular area of the city; you can stay in virtually any neighbourhood. Budget hotels tend to cluster just north of the river, but there are a few good ones south as well, and luxury just spreads out wherever it damn well pleases: the U2-owned **Clarence** (*see below*) stares down the celeb fave **Morrison** (*see p49*) from opposite sides of the Liffey, while the sleek **Clarion Hotel Dublin IFSC** (*see p50*) stands a bit further down the river, and the gorgeous **Harrington Hall** (*see p47*) and small-but-fabulous **Number 31** (*see p49*) hide away near St Stephen's Green. Meanwhile, out in the suburbs, the big touristy **Fitzpatrick**

Castle Dublin and **Clontarf Castle Hotel** (for both, *see p52*) overlook Dublin Bay.

A WORD ABOUT THE LISTINGS

Rates listed here are given as general guidelines only, and you should always check with the hotel to see if prices have changed before you book a room; hotels can, and do, change their rates frequently. Rates can also vary depending on the day of the week, the month of the year or if any special events are on in the city.

It's wise to check hotel websites for special offers, and always ask if any are available before you book. Many hotels will give lower rates for children if you book in advance.

The hotels listed here all have en-suite rooms with telephones, unless indicated otherwise. Prices do not include breakfast, unless otherwise noted. The abbreviation 'pp' stands for 'per person'. VAT is included, but be aware that at the upper end of the market, hotels may also add a 12 to 15 per cent service charge.

Around Temple Bar

Deluxe

The Clarence

6-8 Wellington Quay, Dublin 2 (407 0800/fax 407 0820/www.theclarence.ie). All cross-city buses/Luas Jervis. **Rooms** 49. **Rates** €340-€370 single/double; €700-€2,500 suite. **Credit** AmEx, DC, MC, V. **Map** p251 E3 ❶

It's the age-old story: struggling musicians hang out in bar of dive hotel while playing grotty pubs; struggling musicians' band, U2, goes stellar; Bono and the Edge buy old dive hotel and turn it into this. The Clarence's large, soundproofed rooms are elegantly decorated in subtle earth tones, and fabrics tend towards the luxurious: crisp sheets with four-digit thread-counts are topped by soft duvets. Tiled bathrooms are filled with covetable bath products. If you can tear yourself away from the views of the Liffey from the big windows in your room, the Tea Rooms restaurant (*see p104*) and the Octagon Bar (*see p129*) downstairs are well worth your time and money; there's also an elegant new spa. Staff are ever-present without being obsequious. There are plans to expand the hotel considerably in the future, though nothing has been decided yet.

Bar. Concierge. Disabled: adapted room. Gym. Internet (high speed, wireless). No-smoking rooms. Parking (€25/night). Restaurant. Room service (24hrs). TV: DVD.

Brooks Hotel. *See p39.*

Expensive

Brooks Hotel

59-62 Drury Street, Dublin 2 (670 4000/fax 670 4455/www.brookshoteldublin.com). All cross-city buses/Luas St Stephen's Green. **Rooms** 98. **Rates** €190-€240 single; €200-€280 double. **Credit** AmEx, MC, V. **Map** p251 E4 **②**

This sophisticated hotel has taken strides towards cool with its recent makeover. The rather cramped guestrooms have been worked over by designers in recent years – at least, some of them come with a dark purple and muted gold colour scheme that will look lovely to some, tacky to others. The hotel lobby has a bright, airy restaurant and bar with generous sofas and elegant furnishings – and if the frenzy of busy Dublin pubs starts to wear you down, soothe your nerves in the exclusive ambience of the Butterlane Bar. This is a favourite of business travellers: expect a preponderance of suits. **Photo** *p37.* *Bar. Business centre. Concierge. Disabled: adapted room. Gym. Internet (high speed, wireless). No-smoking floors. Parking (€6.35/night). Restaurant. Room service (24hrs). TV: DVD.*

The Morgan

10 Fleet Street, Dublin 2 (679 3939/fax 643 7060/ www.themorgan.com). All cross-city buses. **Rooms** 121. **Rates** €140-€2,500. **Credit** AmEx, MC, V. **Map** p251 F3 **③**

This trendy designer hotel packs in the young trustafarian crowd, who seem to feel at home on the red velvet chairs. The cream-coloured walls of the popular Morgan Bar have been expanded in recent years and, as the hotel's press material ominously puts it, 'no space has been overlooked by the design concept'. Indeed, the place has been designed to within an inch of its life. Still, it's not an unattractive place – merely one so trendy that one's lack of £500 shoes seems, somehow, to matter. Bedrooms are spacious, with more design elements, done in calming pale tones and brightened by original Irish art. Be warned: rooms looking out on to Fleet Street can be noisy in the small hours; ask for a room at the back of the hotel or on one of the upper floors. *Bar. Business centre. Concierge. Disabled: adapted rooms (4). Internet (high speed, wireless). No-smoking rooms. Restaurant. Room service (7am-midnight). TV: DVD.*

The Paramount

Parliament Street & Essex Street, Dublin 2 (417 9900/fax 417 9904/www.paramounthotel.ie). All cross-city buses. **Rooms** 70. **Rates** (incl breakfast) €100-€260. **Credit** AmEx, MC, V. **Map** p251 E3 **④**

You'd never guess it from sitting in the Turk's Head bar (*see p130*) on a Saturday night, but this hotel is something of a hidden gem. It's not a peaceful place – the aforementioned bar and nightclub packs in partiers most nights – but it looks quite good. The bedrooms are reminiscent of 1930s chic, done up in subtle tobacco tones, with leather headboards, dark wood furnishings and soft lighting. The spacious

Top Ten Hotels

Buswells Hotel

Political gossip in the bar, big, comfy rooms... What's not to like? *See p43.*

The Clarence

This is the coolest place in town. *See p36.*

The Clarion Hotel Dublin IFSC

Proves that chains sometimes know what they're doing. The view is great and the pool simply gorgeous. *See p50.*

The Gresham Hotel

A chunk of Irish history, with a big, buzzing lobby bar, and sleek renovated rooms. *See p50.*

Harrington Hall

A guesthouse with real class and reasonable prices. *See p47.*

Isaac's Hostel

An in-house restaurant and a spanking new sauna. Hostels didn't used to be like this... *See p51.*

The Morrison

A little something for the modernists. *See p49.*

Number 31

Small but perfectly formed, this lovely, family-run guesthouse has heart – and great breakfasts. *See p49.*

Trinity Lodge

Georgian beauty with an arty touch, for a modest price. *See p44.*

The Westin

Big quiet rooms, subtle luxury: a hotel for grown-ups. *See p40.*

rooms are equally popular with raucous pleasure-seekers and low-key weekenders, but ask for rooms on the upper floors if you're not keen on earplugs. *Bar. Concierge. Disabled: adapted rooms (4). No-smoking floors. Internet. Room service (24hrs). TV: pay movies.*

Temple Bar Hotel

15-17 Fleet Street, Dublin 2 (677 3333/fax 677 3088/www.towerhotelgroup.ie). All cross-city buses/ Luas Abbey Street. **Rooms** 129. **Rates** (pp) €99-€180. **Credit** AmEx, DC, MC, V. **Map** p251 F3 **⑤**

For people over the age of 19, there's something terrifying about Temple Bar. The bright lights, the unrelenting stream of drunken parties on the move, the sick-splashed pavements. Right in the thick of the action is the Temple Bar Hotel, with its hugely popular, raucous nightclub Buskers. Surprisingly, the hotel maintains an air of civility, with a grown-up reception area and comfortable (if plain) rooms. Still, if you're looking for an oasis of serenity, or even a bit of quiet, this place probably isn't for you – but it's a decent spot slap-bang in the centre of the city. *Bar. No-smoking floors. Parking (€8/night). Restaurant. Internet (wireless). Room service (noon-10pm). TV.*

Moderate

Central Hotel
1-5 Exchequer Street, Dublin 2 (679 7302/fax 679 7303/www.centralhotel.ie). Bus 16, 16A. **Rooms** 70. **Rates** (pp, incl breakfast) €90 single; €140 double. **Credit** AmEx, MC, V. **Map** p251 E3 ⑥
This comfortable, 187-year-old hotel is unique in that it's a prime piece of real estate (right off Dame Street near Temple Bar) that the designers haven't yet got their hands on. This, you can't help but think, is how all hotels here used to look: floral fabrics and busy carpet patterns everywhere, and the furniture likely to have battered edges – and a real sense of quirky independence, even though it's part of the Best Western chain. The spacious rooms are a bit tired (and somebody renovate those bathrooms, please), but they have wonderful architectural touches and big, old sash windows. The cosy Library Bar is a haven of civility with its leather armchairs, blazing fires, wood panelling and books: it's the thinking Dubliner's trendy hangout. The restaurant is attractive and particularly pleasant early in the morning, when light streams through its huge windows. *Bars (2). Concierge. Internet (high speed, wireless). No-smoking rooms. Restaurant. Room service (24hrs). TV.*

Eliza Lodge
23-4 Wellington Quay, Dublin 2 (671 8044/fax 671 8362/www.dublinlodge.com). All cross-city buses/Luas Jervis. **Rooms** 18. **Rates** (incl breakfast) €76 single; €130-€150 double; €150-€180 penthouse; €190-€256 suite. **Credit** AmEx, MC, V. **Map** p251 E3 ⑦
The pokey little reception area at this riverside hotel doesn't bode well, but it's a deceptive introduction to what is otherwise a good hotel. Some people may be put off by the incessant clatter and rumble of trucks down on the quays, but double glazing minimises the disturbance, and the sweeping views of the River Liffey more than make up for the pesky traffic. While the rooms won't feature on any television interior design programme, they're big and bright, and the price is very good for what you get. *No-smoking hotel. Restaurant. TV.*

Budget

Ashfield House
19-20 d'Olier Street, Dublin 2 (679 7734/fax 679 0852/www.ashfieldhouse.ie). All cross-city buses.

Rooms 30. **Rates** (pp, incl breakfast) €50 single; €15-€33 dorms; €40-€45 twins; €32-€36 triples. **Credit** AmEx, MC, V. **Map** p251 F2 ⑧
This brightly decorated, cheery guesthouse has basic but clean en-suite rooms (two, four and six beds), and larger dorms. Facilities include a bureau de change and free luggage storage, as well as cosy dining areas, with pool table, television and internet access. Its security is highly rated. *Internet (wireless). No-smoking rooms.*

Kinlay House
2-12 Lord Edward Street, Dublin 2 (679 6644/fax 679 7437/www.kinlaydublin.ie). All cross-city buses. **Rooms** 30. **Rates** (pp, incl breakast) *Jan, Feb, Nov, Dec* €17-€34. *Mar-Oct* €18-€36. **Credit** AmEx, MC, V. **Map** p250 D3 ⑨
Run by the Irish student group USIT and open all year round, Kinlay House is a beautiful red brick building in one of Dublin's oldest neighbourhoods, steps from Christ Church Cathedral and on the edge of trendy Temple Bar. There's a large self-catering kitchen and dining room, a TV room and colourful meeting room. Dorms are small but clean, and the front desk is open round the clock. Toast and coffee are served each morning until 9.30am. *Internet (wireless). No smoking rooms. TV room.*

Deluxe

Westbury Hotel
Grafton Street, Dublin 2 (679 1122/fax 679 7078/ www.jurysdoyle.com). All cross-city buses/Luas St Stephen's Green. **Rooms** 205. **Rates** €220-€402 single/double; €420-€820 suite. **Credit** AmEx, DC, MC, V. **Map** p251 F4 ⑩
This upmarket hotel straddles the line between traditional and modern, and it's not an unpleasant place to stay at, just off the bustling shopping hub of Grafton Street. Rooms are understated but have lavish touches, like minibars stocked with Waterford Crystal; the lobby is spacious and bright, with a restaurant, café terrace and bar – a favourite of Dublin's *beau monde*. But the place has its weaknesses (there's a cheapness to its design and furniture choices), and it's definitely not the most lavish hotel in the city for the price. **Photo** *opposite.* *Bar. Business centre. Concierge. Disabled: adapted rooms (4). Gym. Internet (high speed). No-smoking rooms. Parking (free). Restaurants (2). Room service (24hrs). TV: pay movies.*

The Westin
College Green, Dublin 2 (645 1000/fax 645 1234/ www.westin.com/dublin). All cross-city buses. **Rooms** 163. **Rates** €319-€595 single/double; €795 suite. **Credit** AmEx, DC, MC, V. **Map** p251 F3 ⑪
The Westin has always made good use of its imposing 19th-century façade (the building was once a bank) – a promise of traditional grandeur, exclusivity and modern luxury. The elegant reception area

The spacious surroundings of the **Westbury Hotel**.

4.00am. And our chef is already preparing your dinner.

Attention to quality and knowledge of origin are two key ingredients in the success of Alex. Our reputation depends on every dish that leaves our kitchen. So when the fishing boats come back to the harbour, amongst the fresh halibut, fresh turbot and fresh seabream you'll find our chef - a man full of fresh ideas.

ALEX
RESTAURANT · COCKTAIL BAR

Conrad Dublin, Earlsfort Terrace, Dublin 2. T: 01 6028900 E: dublininfo@conradhotels.com

Gorgeous Georgian architecture? It has to be **Trinity Lodge**. *See p44.*

is all marble columns and exquisite plasterwork; a hall of mirrors lines the Westmoreland Street entrance. Rooms are decorated in mahogany and neutral shades, with comfortable beds, soft linen and modern dataports; many have sweeping views of the city. The hotel's bar, the Mint, is in the old vaults, and the Exchange restaurant is bright and modern. Well worth a splurge.
Bar. Business centre. Concierge. Disabled: adapted rooms (5). Gym. Internet (wireless). No-smoking floors. Parking (€14 per night). Restaurant. Room service (24hrs). TV: pay movies.

Expensive

Buswells Hotel

23-27 Molesworth Street, Dublin 2 (614 6500/ 676 2090/www.quinnhotels.com). Bus 10, 11, 13, 46A/Luas St Stephen's Green/DART Pearse. **Rooms** 69. **Rates** (incl breakfast) €175 single; €240 double; €260 triple. **Credit** AmEx, DC, MC, V. **Map** p251 G4 ⑫
This traditional hotel is saved from feeling stuffy or dated by a strong sense of class. The rooms are distributed across three Georgian buildings and exude charm, from their hefty Georgian windows to the views of the broad streets below. The fact that the hotel is divided into separate buildings gives it a slightly eccentric effect; finding your room could be a tough proposition after a night on the whiskey. But

it's undeniably elegant, the rooms are big and superbly decorated, and the place as a whole has a marvellous quirky spirit – in part because its location near the government buildings make its bar and restaurant hubs of political intrigue.
Bar. Business centre. Concierge. Disabled: adapted room. Gym. Internet (wireless). No-smoking floors. Parking (€2.80/hr; free nights). Restaurant. Room service (24hrs). TV.

Trinity Capital Hotel

Pearse Street, Dublin 2 (648 1000/fax 648 1010/ www.capital-hotels.com). All cross-city buses/DART Pearse. **Rooms** 82. **Rates** (incl breakfast) €95-€165 single; €115-€213 double; €165-€263 mini-suite. **Credit** AmEx, DC, MC, V. **Map** p251 G3 ⑬
Tucked in beside Dublin's fire station, the Capital attracts business and leisure travellers in equal numbers. The brightly painted rooms are enhanced by subtle art deco touches, but they're a bit on the small side; the decor makes some of them look like classy dorm rooms, and some of the bathrooms are tiny. Still, service is friendly, there's a handy restaurant and lobby lounge, and the hotel nightclub and bar is a hectic party spot. The Trinity has a sister hotel on Grafton Street (the Grafton Capital Hotel), where the rooms are a bit bigger and the mood a bit more grown up.
Bar. Disabled: adapted rooms (4). Internet (wireless). No-smoking floor. Parking (€10/24hr). Restaurant. Room service (24hrs). TV: pay movies.

Where to Stay

Moderate

Trinity Lodge

12 South Frederick Street, Dublin 2 (617 0900/fax 617 0999/www.trinitylodge.com). All cross-city buses/Luas St Stephen's Green. **Rooms** 16. **Rates** €120 single; €160-€205 double; €205 deluxe twin. **Credit** AmEx, DC, MC, V. **Map** p251 F3

Trinity's main building dates to 1785. It offers Georgian architecture with chic, laid-back style, and its ten large rooms are nicely done in Georgian style, some with paintings by Irish artist Graham Knuttel. Downstairs there's a pleasant breakfast room where thoughtful touches include freshly baked breads and freshly squeezed orange juice. In a second building across the road, six more rooms have a more contemporary edge but are equally well done. Staff are friendly, and the place is well located for the restaurants and bars of central Dublin. Because the building is listed, there's no lift. **Photo** *p43.*
Bar. Disabled: adapted room. Internet (pay terminal). No-smoking rooms. Parking(€5). Room service (7.30-10am). TV.

Budget

Trinity College

College Green, Dublin 2 (608 1177/fax 671 1267/ www.tcd.ie). All cross-city buses/DART Pearse. **Rooms** 800. **Rates** (pp) €55.30-€66.30. **Credit** MC, V. **Map** p251 F3

From mid June until the beginning of September, Trinity College provides its 800 rooms as budget accommodation. The 16th-century university could

hardly be more central, and there are the added bonuses of stone buildings, cobbled squares and lots of trees. There's a choice of single or twin rooms and double, twin and quad apartments; not all the rooms are en-suite, so make sure you specify what you're after when you book. A continental breakfast is included in the price of a room; facilities include a bar, cafés, laundry, parking and a restaurant. *No smoking rooms.*

Around St Stephen's Green

Deluxe

Conrad Hotel

Earlsfort Terrace, Dublin 2 (602 8900/fax 676 5424/www.conradhotels.com). Bus 10, 11, 13, 14, 15, 44, 46A, 47, 48, 86/Luas St Stephen's Green. **Rooms** 192. **Rates** €200-€420 single/double. **Credit** AmEx, DC, MC, V. **Map** p251 F5

The long-established Conrad, on a prominent site on the corner of St Stephen's Green, is a firm favourite among the suited, laptop-wielding types who've made Dublin the business hub that it is: here are fast internet connections, big desks and fax machines. Bedrooms are nicely done in neutral colours, with big windows, individual temperature controls for the air con and fabulous bathrooms. The gym is excellent, and reduced rates are available for the use of the nearby K Club golf course. The hotel pub might lack character, but local office workers still pack the place every night; and the Alex restaurant is a particularly sleek hotel diner for those with expense accounts.

Bars (2). Business centre. Concierge. Disabled: adapted room. Gym. Internet (high speed, wireless). No-smoking floors. Parking (€7.50). Restaurants (2). Room service (24hrs). TV: pay movies.

Hilton Dublin

Charlemont Place, Grand Canal, Dublin 2 (402 9988/ fax 402 9966/www.dublin.hilton.co.uk). Bus 14, 15, 44, 48A/Luas Charlemont. **Rooms** 192. **Rates** €140-€320 single/double. **Credit** AmEx, DC, MC, V. **Map** p251 F6 ⑰

The main selling point of this modern chain hotel is its tranquil setting overlooking the leafy banks of the Grand Canal, offering a view so bucolic you could forget you're right in the middle of the city. The bedrooms are decorated, as you might expect, in contemporary style (though you might not expect the fabrics to be quite so reliant on strange, checkerboard patterns), and they get lots of light. The hotel's lobby is also decorated rather loudly, although it has recently been toned down a bit. Unsurprisingly, the Hilton has the full complement of business facilities: internet access, fax machines, impressive-looking phones, a boring bar. The restaurant overlooks the canal, which makes up a bit for its somewhat depressing chain-hotel look. To sum up: we've seen better Hiltons.

Bar. Business centre. Concierge. Disabled: adapted rooms (5). Internet (high speed). No-smoking floors. Parking (€5). Restaurant. Room service (24hrs). TV: DVD/pay movies.

Merrion Hotel

Upper Merrion Street, Dublin 2 (603 0600/fax 603 0700/www.merrionhotel.com). Bus 10, 13, 13A/ DART Pearse. **Rooms** 143. **Rates** €275-€450 per room; €765-€1,350 suites. **Credit** AmEx, DC, MC, V. **Map** p251 G4 ⑱

Your mum would love this hotel. Housed inside four restored, listed Georgian houses, the Merrion doesn't shy away from a little frill here, a delicate striped couch there. No, this place is definitely in touch with its feminine side. Downstairs the public spaces are dominated by quiet, girly drawing rooms where fires glow in hearths and you long for tea and scones, and – hey presto! – they're yours at the drop of a few euros. The impressive contemporary art on the walls is part of one of the country's largest private collections. Service is discreetly omnipresent, and the spacious rooms overlook either the government buildings or the hotel's 18th-century-inspired gardens of acacia and lilac. Pamper yourself in the Tethra Spa (*see p48* **Reach for the spas**), stretch your credit card at the Michelin-starred Patrick Guilbaud restaurant (*see p107*) or dine at the somewhat cheaper and more atmospheric Cellar restaurant.

Bars. Business services. Concierge. Disabled: adapted rooms (4). Gym. Internet (high speed). No-smoking (hotel). Parking (€20/night). Restaurants (2). Spa. Swimming pool (indoor). Room service (24hrs). TV: DVD/pay movies.

O'Callaghan Alexander Hotel

Fenian Street, Merrion Square, Dublin 2 (607 3700/ fax 607 3600/www.ocallaghanhotels.com). Bus 10, 13. **Rooms** 102. **Rates** €129-€315 single/double; €295-€395 suite. **Credit** AmEx, DC, MC, V. **Map** p251 H3 ⑲

It's tucked so unobtrusively around the corner from Merrion Square that you might miss it. The place may look historic on the outside, but it's all minimalist and modern on the inside. Bedrooms are relentlessly contemporary – the very bright colour scheme could be a bit dazzling for anyone who forgets the sunglasses. Public areas are similarly modish, and it's all well run by helpful staff. Residents can use the gym, business centre and all facilities at the Davenport Hotel just across the road (*see below*).

Bar. Concierge. Disabled: adapted rooms (6). Gym. Internet (high speed, wireless). No-smoking floors. Parking (free; valet €10). Restaurant. Room service (24hrs). TV: pay movies.

O'Callaghan Davenport Hotel

Merrion Square, Dublin 2 (607 3500/fax 661 5663/ www.ocallaghanhotels.com). DART Pearse/all cross-city buses. **Rooms** 116. **Rates** €119-€315 single/ double; €280-€450 suite. **Credit** AmEx, DC, MC, V. **Map** p251 H4 ⑳

The Davenport's impressive façade, with its columns and dramatic lighting, was built in 1863 as part of Merrion Hall, but that's virtually all that remains of that grand old structure: most of the Davenport was built in the 1990s and, in a rather old-fashioned way, is utterly modern. The lobby is nice enough, but the rooms seem to have been designed by somebody else entirely. Beds are covered in startling fabrics, and the look is a bit odd – as if someone's shortsighted aunt were let loose in a fabric store. Still, it's nicely located, has all you need,

Airline flights are one of the biggest producers of the global warming gas CO_2. But with **The CarbonNeutral Company** you can make your travel a little greener.

Go to **www.carbonneutral.com** to calculate your flight emissions then 'neutralise' them through international projects which save exactly the same amount of carbon dioxide.

Contact us at **shop@carbonneutral.com** or call into the office on **0870 199 99 88** for more details.

CarbonNeutral®flights

staff are helpful enough, and breakfasts are quite good; but it's not the best hotel in town for this price. *Bar. Business centre. Concierge. Disabled: adapted rooms (2). Gym. Internet (high speed, wireless). No-smoking floors. Parking (free; €10 valet). Restaurant. Room service (24hrs). TV: pay movies.*

Shelbourne Hotel
27 St Stephen's Green, Dublin 2 (663 4500/fax 661 6006/www.marriott.co.uk). Bus, 11, 14, 15. **Rooms** call for details. **Rates** €200-€250 single/double; €300-€400 suite. **Credit** AmEx, DC, MC, V. **Map** p251 G4 ㉑

A major landmark in Dublin since 1824, the Shelbourne has long been the doyenne of Dublin hotels, and it remains at the centre of Dublin life. It has always been an idiosyncratic place, badly in need of a renovation, and in 2006 it finally got one. After being bought by Marriott, it was closed for more than a year for a top-to-toe makeover. As this guide went to press, the hotel was still shut, but the finished product is promised to have more consistent elegance. Whatever they do with it, some rooms will still overlook St Stephen's Green, some won't; for regulars and locals, the bars and drawing rooms will still be the main attraction; and Marriott promises that the esteemed Shelbourne and Horseshoe bars will retain their quirky political souls. Tea in the Lord Mayor's Lounge is a Dublin tradition, and long may it reign. **Photo** *opposite.*
Bar. Business centre. Concierge. Gym. Internet (wireless). No-smoking floor. Parking (free). Spa. Swimming pool (indoor). Restaurant. Room service (24hrs). TV: pay movies.

Expensive

Harrington Hall
69-70 Harcourt Street, Dublin 2 (475 3497/fax 475 4544/www.harringtonhall.com). Buses 10, 11, 15A, 15B, 16, 16A, 20B, 62/Luas Harcourt Street. **Rooms** 28. **Rates** (incl breakfast) €140-€187.50 single/double; €290 suite. **Credit** AmEx, DC, MC, V. **Map** p251 F5 ㉒

This beautiful place occupies two adjoining houses close to St Stephen's Green. The property was once the home of Timothy Charles Harrington, former Lord Mayor of Dublin, who clearly had excellent architectural taste. The exquisite stuccoed ceilings have been retained, and there's much to praise here: the warmth, attentiveness and personal touch of the service, the beautifully appointed lobby and the spotless, simple but elegant bedrooms. Rooms at the rear look out across the ethereal Iveagh Gardens. This is one of Dublin's outstanding small hotels. *Disabled: adapted room. Internet (wireless). No-smoking hotel. Parking (free). Room service (24hrs). TV.*

Molesworth Court Suites
Schoolhouse Lane, Dublin 2 (676 4799/fax 676 4982/ www.molesworthcourt.ie). All cross city buses/Luas St Stephen's Green. **Rooms** 11. **Rates** €180 1-room suite; €235-€285 2-room suite; €375 3-room suite. **Credit** AmEx, MC, V. **Map** p251 F4 ㉓

The landmark **Shelbourne Hotel**.

On a quiet side street in the heart of the city, these excellent three- and four-star self-catering apartments make a good option for families or groups of friends. Each of the spacious apartments is fully self-contained, cosy and comfortable, with all bed linen provided. Some are attractively designed, although it's fair to say the complex is due for a refurbishment. Still, the price is right and the location handy, with plenty of shops, restaurants and pubs within a stone's throw.
Internet (high speed, wireless). Parking (free). TV: DVD.

Moderate

Kilronan House
70 Adelaide Road, Dublin 2 (475 5266/fax 478 2841/www.kilronanhouse.com). Bus 11,13, 16, 16A/Luas Harcourt Street. **Rooms** 28. **Rates** (pp, incl breakfast) €45-€85. **Credit** AmEx, MC, V. **Map** p251 F6 ㉔

This friendly, attractive pad has been extended in recent years, and now has 28 spacious bedrooms –

Reach for the spas

Ireland's gone spa crazy lately. The trend took off about three years ago in County Kerry (of all places), but since then has spread as far north as Donegal and as far south as Wicklow. Sometimes it seems every hotel in the hinterlands is having a sauna with 'cooling Irish mist spray shower' installed. The only place that hadn't embraced spa-mania, weirdly enough, was cosmopolitan Dublin. But that may all be changing.

One of the very few to plunge into the spa race years ago was the Merrion (see p45), whose Tethra spa is a soothing, almost dramatic place, with a pale blue 'infinity' pool that seems to stretch for miles (it's an illusion, and a good one). Only guests (and a few choice spa members) are allowed in, so you have a good chance of a little privacy for your paddling. In the attractive treatment rooms you can be gently pummelled with hot stones or sample the usual holistic treatments at surprisingly reasonable prices, given the luxury around you.

If you're staying at the Clarence (see p36), its little spa, Therapy, is yours to plunder. It has all the style and matter-of-fact sophistication you'd expect from this hotel, but a surprisingly limited number of treatments on offer – although the management says that's likely to change.

As this book was being put together, the Morrison Hotel (see p49) was lavishing attention on its plans for a new spa, Headspace, scheduled to open in 2007. The hotel promised it would be 'stylishly designed' with 'a unique Turkish bath', as well as treatment rooms. If we know the Morrison, it will need to be seen to be believed.

Given the limited spa options in the city hotels, you might want to leave them behind and try the city's free-standing establishments for your massages and facials. Therapie (8-9 Molesworth Street, 472 1222) has a calming feel, with soothingly designed treatment rooms, while Nue Blue Eriu (South William Street, 672 5776) is a simply beautiful space, with all the latest treatments from names like Eve Lom and Dr Hauschka.

---

ten of which are en-suite. Unfortunately, prices have gone up as well (nearly doubling in the last few years), so it no longer offers as much in the way of value. Still, it's a surprisingly elegant place, renovated with real class and run with panache. Some of the rooms in the handsome Victorian building still have original period features and high ceilings; newer bedrooms do not, but those give you a bit more space. Big, varied breakfasts are served in a sunny front room.

Internet (wireless). No-smoking hotel. Parking (free). Room service (7am-11pm). TV.

Latchfords of Baggot Street

99-100 Lower Baggot Street, Dublin 2 (676 0784/ fax 662 2764/www.latchfords.ie). Bus 10. **Rooms** 23. **Rates** €155 studio; €180 1-bedroom suite; €200 2-

bedroom suite; €200 superior studio. **Credit** AmEx, MC, V. **Map** p251 H5 ㉕

Latchfords offers all the usual mod cons in a fully self-catering environment. If you prefer to fry your own eggs, this may be your place – and if you choose not to fry your own eggs, there's a restaurant and café on the ground floor that will happily oblige. The building is Georgian and elegant, and each apartment is comfortable, pleasant and quiet.

Internet (wireless). Parking (free, limited). TV: DVD.

MontClare Hotel

Merrion Square, Dublin 2 (607 3800/fax 607 3807/www.ocallaghanhotels.com). Bus 10, 13/ Dart Pearse. **Rooms** 74. **Rates** €125-€225 single/double; €175-€275 suite. **Credit** AmEx, DC, MC, V. **Map** p251 G4 ㉖

Sitting comfortably on the north-west corner of Merrion Square, the MontClare is another cog in the O'Callaghan hotel machine (which also includes the Davenport and the Alexander). As with those other hotels, the decor is nicely done but somewhat on the old-fashioned side, the furniture is a bit elegant and a bit cheap. But overall the emphasis here is determinedly on old-school comfort, both in the public areas and the bedrooms, which are spacious and quiet. The hotel bar is decked out in polished wood and presents a more contemporary face.
Bar. Concierge. Internet (wireless). No-smoking floors. Parking (free). Restaurant. Room service (24hrs). TV: pay movies.

Number 31

31 Leeson Close, Dublin 2 (676 5011/fax 676 2929/ www.number31.ie). Bus 10, 46A/Luas Charlemont.
Rooms 21. **Rates** (incl breakfast) €150-€190.
Credit AmEx, DC, MC, V. **Map** p251 G5 ㉗
Set in one of the city's most fashionable locales, this unique guesthouse is a real find, combining modern design with an almost rural tranquillity. Most of the soothingly decorated bedrooms occupy a Georgian townhouse, although a few are in the beautifully designed modern mews building where delicious home-made breakfasts (the cranberry bread is the stuff of legends) are served in the morning. Warm yourself in front of the peat fire in the sunken lounge or wander through the lush gardens for some gentle therapy. Friendly, convenient and elegant – Number 31 has it all. **Photo** *p44.*
Internet (wireless). No-smoking hotel. Parking (free). TV.

Staunton's on the Green

83 St Stephen's Green, Dublin 2 (478 2300/fax 478 2263). Bus 10, 11, 46A/Luas St Stephen's Green.
Rooms 58. **Rates** (pp, incl breakfast) €88-€96 single; €70-€76 double. **Credit** AmEx, MC, V.
Map p251 F5 ㉘
Staunton's Georgian building has seen better days, but an expansion is underway as this book is going to press, so we hope that while the builders are there, they'll sneak in a little renovation. By Dublin standards this has always been cheapish accommodation, with friendly staff and an old-fashioned idea of breakfast (eggs or cereal from a box), and we suspect that's unlikely to change. The bedrooms are comfortable and spacious – those at the front look across the treetops of the Green, those at the back overlook the peaceful Iveagh Gardens. The public areas are a little on the shabby side, but comfortable enough.
Internet (wireless). No-smoking rooms. Parking (free). TV.

Budget

Avalon House

55 Aungier Street, Dublin 2 (475 0001/fax 475 0303/www.avalon-house.ie). Bus 16, 16A, 19, 22, 155. **Rooms** 78. **Rates** (pp) €15-€38. **Credit** AmEx, MC, V. **Map** p251 E4 ㉙

This pleasantly warm and cheery guesthouse occupies a lovely old red-brick building, and it's well known among those who travel to Dublin on a budget. Its pine floors, high ceilings and open fireplace make it a pleasant place in which to relax, and its café is a popular hangout for international travellers; rooms range from dorms to doubles. This place has all you really need: clean, cheerful rooms in a safe location at a cheap price.
Internet (wireless). No-smoking hostel.

Around O'Connell Street

Deluxe

The Morrison

Ormond Quay, Dublin 1 (887 2400/fax 878 3185/ www.morrisonhotel.ie). Bus 30, 90/Luas Jervis.
Rooms 138. **Rates** €345 single/double; €365-€600 suites; €2,000 penthouse. **Credit** AmEx, DC, MC, V.
Map p251 E2 ㉚
A boutique hotel on a large scale, the Morrison is ideally located across the river from Temple Bar. Savvy guests will immediately recognise the hotel's interior as the work of design maestro John Rocha. His hand is everywhere – from the Waterford Crystal vases to the crushed velvet bed throws in rich colours; such touches transform the place from a good hotel to a great one. The comfortable rooms plead to be enjoyed, with stereos, Egyptian-cotton linens and the sheer decadence of Portuguese limestone in the bathroom; the stylish Café-Bar restaurant and the oh-so-trendy spa urge you never to set foot outside the glossy doors.
Bar. Concierge. Disabled: adapted rooms (4). Internet (high speed, wireless). No-smoking floors. Parking (€14.40). Restaurant. Room service (7am-3am). TV: pay movies.

Expensive

Cassidy's Hotel

Cavendish Row, Upper O'Connell Street, Dublin 1 (878 0555/fax 878 0687/www.cassidyshotel.com). All cross-city buses/Luas Abbey Street. **Rooms** 113. **Rates** (incl breakfast) €85-€125 single; €120-€200 double. **Credit** AmEx, DC, MC, V.
Map p251 F1 ㉛
The family-owned Cassidy's Hotel is across the street from the historic Gate Theatre, and within about 10 minutes' walk of Temple Bar and Dame Street's hustle. The hotel is larger than it looks from the outside (there are over 100 bedrooms in there, somehow), and has a handy restaurant and a cosy bar. Rooms are smallish and simple, but not cramped or uncomfortable. Rooms at the back are quieter, but those at the front have a better view. Charmingly, if you've forgotten to bring a good book, the front desk will lend you one.
Bar. Disabled: adapted rooms (4). Gym. Internet (wireless). No-smoking floors. Parking (free). Restaurant. Room service (5.15am-9.30pm). TV.

The Clarion Hotel Dublin IFSC

*International Financial Services Centre, Dublin 1
(433 8800/fax 433 8811/www.clarionhotelifsc.com).
All cross-city buses/DART Connolly.* **Rooms** 163.
Rates (pp) €145-€200. **Credit** AmEx, DC, MC, V.
Map p251 G2 ⏣

Yes, it's a chain hotel, and big with business travellers; but don't be put off. This is an excellent hotel:
great looking, well run, fabulous location, decent
prices and lots of extras. The guest rooms are spacious with sweeping views of the Liffey; they're done
in soothing neutral colours, all cream and taupe; they
feature Egyptian cotton duvets, large TVs, free
broadband and even video-game consoles. The laid-back atmosphere in the stylish bar and restaurant
is more relaxing than intimidating; those after something more energetic can try out the gym or the truly
gorgeous pool. As chain hotels go, it doesn't get
much better than this. **Photo** *p53.*
*Bars (2). Business centre. Concierge. Disabled:
adapted rooms (7). Gym. Internet (high speed,
wireless). No-smoking rooms. Parking (€10).
Restaurant. Room service (24hrs). Swimming pool
(indoor). TV: pay movies.*

Days Inn

*95-98 Talbot Street, Dublin 1 (874 9202/fax 874
9672/www.daysinntalbot.com). Bus 33, 41/Luas
Abbey Street.* **Rooms** 60. **Rates** (incl breakfast) €89-
€130 single; €99-€150 double. **Credit** AmEx, DC,
MC, V. **Map** p251 F1 ⏣

In its recent renovation, Days Inn clearly looked to
the British homewares chain Habitat (or perhaps it
was America's Pottery Barn) for its decorative inspiration. Now, where the boring chain hotel decor once
was, you'll find lots of brushed wood, chrome and
neutral colours. Bedrooms in the four-storey hotel
are a bit on the small side, but they're nice enough
for resting between bouts of shopping on nearby
O'Connell Street. The fact that the hotel's website
touts a soft drinks machine among the 'amenities' is
an indication of the kinds of extras you can expect
here. There's also an ice machine. Now that's what
we call class.
Disabled: adapted room. Internet (high speed). No-smoking floors. Parking (free, limited). TV.

The Gresham Hotel

*23 Upper O'Connell Street, Dublin 1 (874 6881/fax
878 7175/www.gresham-hotels.ie). Bus 11, 13/Luas
Abbey Street.* **Rooms** 289. **Rates** (incl breakfast)
from €165 single; from €195 double. **Credit** AmEx,
MC, V. **Map** p251 F1 ⏣

A key part of Dublin's political and leisure history,
the Gresham has been taking care of visitors for 200
years. The grand façade, vast lobby and charming
bar are all elegant, but not overwhelmingly so; here
it's all about comfort. A lengthy renovation is giving this grande dame a badly needed upgrade, and
those sections that have been spruced up are well
done. Ask for a renovated room or you may find
yourself in the lap of luxury, 1970s Ireland style.
Renovated rooms have luxurious fabrics in soothing tones, satellite televisions and all the usual four-

star extras; the others have scary headboards and
garish curtains. The gargantuan, buzzy lobby bar
is a popular local meeting point.
*Bars (2). Business centre. Concierge. Disabled:
adapted room. Gym. No-smoking floors. Parking
(€12.50). Internet (high speed). Restaurants (2).
Room service (24hrs). TV: pay movies.*

Hotel Isaac's

*Store Street, Dublin 1 (855 0067/fax 836 5390/
www.isaacs.ie). All cross-city buses/Luas Busaras.*
Rooms 90. **Rates** (incl breakfast) €99-€159 single;
€119-€179 double. **Credit** AmEx, MC, V. **Map**
p251 G2 ⏣

The first thing people tend to notice about Isaac's
(apart from the fact that its neighbourhood is not the
shiniest example of modern Dublin) is the impressive reception area, with its twin-headed elephant
mantelpieces. Bedrooms are a little less OTT, sadly;
but although dull, they have all you need. Isaac's is
distinguished mostly by lovely touches like the verdant courtyard and the snug garden lounge. There's
a small café-bar and an Italian restaurant downstairs for emergencies. But do make sure you take a
cab home at night.
*Bar. Disabled: adapted rooms (3). Internet (high
speed, wireless). No-smoking rooms. Parking (€10).
Restaurant. Room service (7.30-10am). TV.*

Hotel St George

*7 Parnell Square, Dublin 1 (874 5611/fax 874
5582). Bus 10, 11, 11A, 16, 16A, 19, 19A/Luas
Abbey Street.* **Rooms** 46. **Rates** (incl breakfast)
€60-€100 single; €99-€150 double. **Credit** MC, V.
Map p251 F1 ⏣

The public spaces of the Hotel St George are really
quite grand, as the Georgian building has many of
its original architectural touches, including marble
fireplaces, crystal chandeliers and huge antique mirrors. The smallish bedrooms are considerably simpler in design. The decor here is a bit basic (new
curtains wouldn't go amiss, for example). Still, it's a
quiet, pleasant place, and the bar and original 18th-century parlour add to its rather particular charm.
*Bar. Internet (high speed, wireless). No-smoking
floors. Parking (€10). TV.*

Budget

Abbott Lodge

*87-88 Lower Gardiner Street, Dublin 1 (836 5548/
fax 836 5549/www.abbott-lodge.com). All cross-city
buses/Luas Connolly/DART Connolly.* **Rooms** 29.
Rates (pp, incl breakfast) €35-€50. **Credit** MC, V.
Map p251 G1 ⏣

One of the larger accommodation options on
Gardiner Street, Abbott Lodge has 29 en-suite
rooms, many with high ceilings and period details.
All are modestly decorated, but they have nice
touches like large mahogany beds that add to the
sense of space, and all have television and telephone.
The friendly staff will be pleased to point you in the
direction of the area's best pub or restaurant.
No-smoking rooms. TV.

Abraham House

82 Lower Gardiner Street, Dublin 1 (855 0600/fax 855 0598/www.abraham-house.ie). Bus 41/Luas Connolly/DART Connolly. **Rooms** 44. **Rates** €12-€32 dormitory; €32 triple. **Credit** AmEx, MC, V. **Map** p251 G1 ❸

With the results of a major refurbishment still fresh in its memory, now would be a good time to stay at Abraham House. This hostel, situated beside Busáras bus depot and Connolly Street train station, has plenty of space, clean and plentiful cooking facilities and strong security measures – all at affordable rates.
Internet (wireless). No-smoking hostel. Parking (free, limited). TV (triples only).

Dublin International Hostel

61 Mountjoy Street, Dublin 1.(830 4555/fax 830 5808/www.irelandyha.org). All cross city buses. **Rooms** 35. **Rates** (pp, incl breakfast) €18-€21 dormitory; €48-€52 double. **Credit** AmEx, MC, V.

Open all year and run by An Óige, the Irish youth hostel organisation, this hostel is a historic stone building smack in the city centre. The attractively converted public rooms feature polished wood floors, a big self-catering kitchen, internet café, a renovated TV/games room, garden, laundry, and a handsome restaurant where continental breakfast is served for free (full Irish available at extra cost). Dinner is available from June to August. Rooms are small and basic but clean. The hostel is open 24 hours and the front desk is always staffed.

The Four Courts

15-17 Merchants Quay, Dublin 8 (672 5839/fax 672 5862/www.fourcourtshostel.com.) All cross city buses/Luas Four Courts. **Rooms** 35. **Rates** (pp, incl breakfast) €10-€18.50 dormitory; €24-€35 double, triple, quad. **Credit** MC, V. **Map** p250 D3 ❸

Set in several pretty Georgian buildings overlooking the Liffey, this friendly hostel has all the basics, and a few charming details. Its setting at the edge of the river is exceptional, and the guest rooms have big windows, polished wood floors, desks and other nice touches that make the plain, metal bunk beds slightly more bearable. It has 24-hour access, free continental breakfast, good security, laundry facilities, a games room, internet access and a place to park your car: in short, more than most hostels give you for the money.
Internet (high speed). No smoking hostel. Parking (free). Restaurant.

Isaac's Hostel

2-5 Frenchman's Lane, Dublin 1 (855 6215/fax 855 6524/www.isaacs.ie). All cross-city buses/DART Connolly. **Rooms** 53. **Rates** (pp, incl breakfast) €12-€16 dormitory; €32.50-€36.50 single; €28.75-€32.75 twin. **Credit** MC, V. **Map** p251 G2 ❹

Near Busáras bus depot and Connolly Street train station, this is the aristocrat of hostels. Isaac's takes the backpacker concept of humble frugality and turns it on its head. Calling itself 'Dublin's first VIP hostel', it has the usual mix of bunk beds, lockers

and TV rooms, but adds a heady cocktail of extras like polished wood floors, a restaurant and an attractive sauna. There's also internet access, a kitchen for guests to use, pool tables – and a friendly and relaxing atmosphere.
Internet (pay terminal). No-smoking hostel. Restaurant.

Marlborough Hostel

81-82 Marlborough Street, Dublin 1 (874 7629/fax 874 5172/www.marlboroughhostel.com). DART Connolly/Luas Abbey Street. **Rooms** 16. **Rates** (incl breakfast) €19-€25 dorms. **Credit** MC, V. **Map** p251 F1 ❹

This place is unprepossessing from the outside, but inside it's a good, utilitarian hostel with all the extras an impecunious international traveller might wish for. It has eight-bed and four-bed dorms, and a few private rooms. There's a TV lounge, internet access, a games room, clean shower rooms, a kitchen and, for those who care about such things, no curfew.
No smoking hostel.

Mount Eccles Court

42 North Great Georges Street, Dublin 1 (873 0826/ fax 878 3554/www.eccleshostel.com) All cross-city buses/Luas Abbey Street. **Rooms** 20. **Rates** (pp, incl breakfast) €13-€40 dormitory; €31.60-€46 double, twin. **Credit** AmEx, MC, V. **Map** p251 F1 ❹

This lovely little hostel in a Georgian building is a great option for those who find bigger facilities intimidating. Its ten bedrooms and ten dorms are secured with keycard locks and neatly decorated with neutral walls and nice touches, like potted plants. There's 24-hour access, bedding (including sheets), luggage lockers, internet access, bike storage, free hot showers, and TV and music lounges.
Internet (shared terminal). No-smoking hostel. TV (some rooms).

Around North Quays

Expensive

Park Inn

Smithfield Village, Dublin 7 (817 3838/fax 817 3839/www.parkinn.ie). Bus 25, 26, 37, 39, 67, 68, 69, 70/Luas Smithfield. **Rooms** 73. **Rates** (incl breakfast) €110-€140 double; €200-€270 suite. **Credit** AmEx, MC, V.

In charming Smithfield Village, Park Inn is a little piece of easy-living modernity surrounded by a clutch of historic buildings. Irish music is one of the hotel's themes – from the large murals in the spacious café and bar to the CDs on the stereos in most rooms. The bedrooms themselves are modern and bright – perhaps too much so, with splashes of vivid yellow and bright red, and glass-brick walls – but the overall emphasis is on comfort. The café serves modern Irish food and, continuing with the musical theme, often has bands playing trad Irish music.
Bar. Concierge. Disabled: adapted rooms (4). Internet (wireless). No-smoking floors. Parking (€10). Restaurant. Room service (24hrs). TV.

Budget

Phoenix Park House

38-39 Parkgate Street, Dublin 8 (677 2870/fax 679 9769/www.dublinguesthouse.com). Bus 10, 15, 24, 25, 66, 67/Luas Heuston. **Rooms** 28. **Rates** (per person, incl breakfast) €49-€75 single; €34-€55 double. **Credit** AmEx, DC, MC, V.

On the edge of scenic Phoenix Park, this guesthouse has clean and well-appointed en-suite rooms, with an emphasis on good value for money. Though there's no restaurant, there are several good eateries nearby, and staff will cheerfully direct you to the excellent Nancy Hands. All rooms have TVs and telephones. Children are welcome, and there's plenty for them to do nearby.

No-smoking rooms. Room service. TV.

Dublin Bay & the Coast

Deluxe

Clontarf Castle Hotel

Castle Avenue, Clontarf, Dublin 3 (833 2321/fax 833 0418/www.clontarfcastle.ie). Bus 130/DART Clontarf Road. **Rooms** 111. **Rates** (incl breakfast) €91-€400 single/double; €200-€545 suite. **Credit** AmEx, DC, MC, V.

The original castle here was built in 1172 by Hugh de Lacy. Sadly, there's not much left of that structure, but what remains does give the hotel a unique atmosphere; particularly impressive is the vast reception area, with looming castle walls, faded tapestries, stone floors and leather chairs. The historic theme is hammered home in the Templars bistro and Knights bars. But after the regal lobby, the mundane decor in the bedrooms is a disappointment; and the clientele leans more towards busy business traveller than knight errant.

Bar. Business centre. Concierge. Disabled: adapted rooms (2). Gym. Internet (high speed). No-smoking rooms. Parking (free). Restaurant. Room service (24hrs). TV: pay movies.

Portmarnock Hotel & Golf Links

Portmarnock, Co. Dublin (846 0611/fax 846 2442/ www.portmarnockhotel.com). Bus 32, 42. **Rooms** 136. **Rates** (incl breakfast) €120-€310 double; €300-€400 suite. **Credit** AmEx, MC, V.

Justifiably renowned for its excellent golf course overlooking Portmarnock beach, this hotel's emphasis is firmly on conservative luxury. All the sumptuously decorated bedrooms have either a bay view or a view of the links, and you can dine at the excellent Osborne restaurant. The relaxing Jameson bar, with panelled walls and glowing fires, was truly designed for drinking whiskey. The hotel caters equally for business and pleasure, with understated but efficient service; if you're here for the golf, you can be sure your outings will be well organised.

Bars (2). Business centre. Concierge. Gym. Internet (high speed, wireless). No-smoking floors. Parking (free). Restaurant. Room service (24hrs). Spa. TV.

Expensive

Fitzpatrick Castle Dublin

Killiney, Co. Dublin (230 5400/fax 230 5430/www. fitzpatrickhotels.com). DART Dalkey. **Rooms** 113. **Rates** €120-€230 single/double. **Credit** AmEx, DC, MC, V.

Standing nobly at the top of the hill overlooking the village of Dalkey, the Fitzpatrick is a regal-looking place that looks like a castle. It's actually a crenellated manor house, and the owners have a startling way with colour – baby blue, mint green, bright pink – that rather weakens its gravitas. The interior is a similar mix of pros and cons: the views of the sea are extraordinary and the rambling old lounge is a joy, filled with lots of sofas, pianos and working fireplaces. Rooms, however, cry out to be refurbished; the swimming pool is handy, but seems an inappropriate addition; the lifts are rickety and prone to breaking down; and staff can be brusque. However, there's a decent basement restaurant, the Dungeon (naturally), and a more expensive formal restaurant upstairs for fine dining; the Library bar is lively and attractive.

Bars (2). Business centre. Concierge. Gym. Internet (wireless). No-smoking rooms. Parking (free). Restaurants (2). Room service (24hrs). Swimming pool (indoor). TV: pay movies.

Moderate

Deer Park Hotel & Golf Courses

Howth, Co. Dublin (832 2624/fax 839 2405/www. deerpark-hotel.ie). DART Howth/bus 31A, 31B. **Rooms** 77. **Rates** (pp, incl breakfast) €80-€90. **Credit** AmEx, DC, MC, V.

Unquestionably the best thing about this hyper-modern hotel, perched above the sleepy fishing village of Howth, is its sweeping view of the rugged North Dublin coast. The worst thing about the place is that it should have been renovated a few years ago, but it's still got plenty to offer for your money. It's enduringly popular with golfers and rugby weekenders, and its location some distance off the main road makes it tranquil and relaxing. Rooms are spacious, and most enjoy grand sea vistas; there's a large swimming pool with sauna and steam room, and the bar has a large outdoor area. Howth (*see p93*) is a short walk away, and the hotel is close to the DART station.

Bar. Disabled: adapted rooms (3). Gym. Internet (wireless). Parking (free). Restaurant. Room service (24hrs). Spa. Swimming pool (indoor). TV.

Budget

Marina House

7 Dunleary Road, Dún Laoghaire (284 1524/www. marinahouse.com). Bus 7, 46A/DART Monkstown. **Rooms** 9. **Rates** (incl breakfast) €50 double; €15-€21 dorms. **Credit** MC, V.

With a pool like this, it's easy to make a splash: **Clarion Hotel Dublin IFSC**. *See p50.*

This popular hostel has dorms as well as one double and one twin room. Amenities include laundry facilities, a TV room and a kitchen open to guests. This is a cheap way to get a little sea air.
Internet (high speed). No-smoking hostel.

Sanctuary Cove

354 Clontarf Road, Clontarf, Dublin 3 (833 6761). DART Clontarf/bus 130. **Rooms** 4. **Rates** (pp, incl breakfast) €35 double. **No credit cards.**
This handsome yellow house down by the sea in Clontarf, an easy walk from the DART station, offers comfortable rooms at incredibly reasonable prices. The four en-suite bedrooms are neatly fur-

nished, the atmosphere is quiet but friendly, and breakfasts are big and filling.
Parking (free).

Strand House

316 Clontarf Road, Clontarf, Dublin 3 (833 9569). Bus 130/DART Clontarf. **Rooms** 7. **Rates** (incl breakfast) €70 double. **Credit** MC, V.
This attractive Victorian B&B is tucked away near the beach in suburban Clontarf. Ask for a room with a bay window overlooking the sea, and happiness is yours. The five en-suite bedrooms are comfortably, if plainly, furnished.
No-smoking B&B. TV.

The 3-Day Freedom Ticket!

See more of Dublin for less

- 3 DAYS City Tour - Hop on - Hop off
- 3 DAYS Dublin Bus Services
- Airport Transfers (within 3 days)
- Nitelink - Late night bus services

Visit
www.dublinsightseeing.ie
for details

GUINNESS
DRAUGHT

Sightseeing

Dublin Castle. *See p67*.

Introduction

Through streets tall and narrow.

From time to time you have to wonder if they're doing it on pupose: it's so difficult to reach this town – through gridlocked traffic, never-ending construction and poorly marked roads – that it's hard to believe they didn't put all those hurdles there just to stop you from getting in. When you finally arrive, you find Dublin a bit grey and foreboding on the edge of the slow-moving River Liffey, and for just a second you think, 'Am I in the right place? Is this small, modern city the Jerusalem of the Irish diaspora? Is *this* the party capital of the British Isles?'

Well, yes. And no.

Yes, this is Dublin, and no, it is not the place that its reputation has led you to expect, but give it a chance and you'll find that it is just as warm and charming as you hoped it would be.

GETTING STARTED

The best way to experience Dublin is on foot. In fact, if you've got a car, park it right now and try never to think of it again unless you're

heading out of town – the traffic is too heavy and the town too small to make it worthwhile to drive. Get a good map, a bit of sunshine and a sturdy pair of walking shoes, and set out.

You'll find that it's no distance at all from the top of **O'Connell Street** north of the Liffey to the peaceful **Grand Canal** on the south side. Along the way, you can do a little shopping on bustling **Grafton Street** (*see p62*), have a pint in one of its excellent pubs (*see p123*) and take a rest in its dreamy gardens.

The first thing you must do, though, is forget everything you ever heard about Dublin. Leave your preconceptions behind. Then discover the truth about this strange, melancholy, friendly, loveable, complex city.

NEED TO KNOW

For information on using **Dublin Bus, Luas** and the **DART**, *see pp221-223*. For **maps** (including DART and Luas maps), *see pp246-252*. For **tourist information**, *see p235*.

Weekenders

24 hours in Dublin

Start with a wander around the lovely buildings, peaceful gardens and raucous playing fields of **Trinity College** (*see p59*). Pop in to see the **Old Library** (*see p61*), then lunch at **Dunne & Crescenzi** (*see p118*) or the **Cedar Tree** (*see p105*). Afterwards, head down to Dame Street to see the glorious lobby of **City Hall**, then make your way next door to **Dublin Castle** (for both, *see p67*). Don't feel obliged to pay to get inside the building; instead, wander through the Upper Yard to the free **Dubh Linn Gardens** and the **Chester Beatty Library** (*see p66*). Next, take a walk down towards **St Stephen's Green** (*see p71*), stopping in at the **Shelbourne Hotel** (*see p47*) for a cup of tea in the lobby or a cocktail in one of its excellent bars.

48 hours in Dublin

Having done the above on your first day, start the next day in **Temple Bar** (*see p67*) for some local colour, then make for the excellent **National Museum of Archaelogy**

& History (*see p63*) to see its displays of ancient Irish gold and Iron Age metalwork. Lunch on Irish stew at the ever friendly **Porterhouse** microbrewery (*see p130*), before heading down to the impressive **Christ Church Cathdral** (*see p69*) and then on to Swift's **St Patrick's Cathedral** (*see p70*). If the weather's fine, have a cocktail by the mouth of the Grand Canal at the modern **Ocean Bar** (*see p132*); if it's raining, try the gorgeous **Long Hall** instead (*see p129*).

72 Hours in Dublin

If you've followed the advice above, you've now had quite enough of city life, so rent a car and take a daytrip to the glorious **Wicklow Mountains** to see the ancient monastery at **Glendalough** (*see p208*), or up to **Newgrange** (*see p199*) to take in the mysteries of its paleolithic burial mounds. If that sounds too energetic, hop on the DART to **Howth** (*see p93*) or **Dalkey** (*see p96*) for bracing sea walks followed by steaming plates of seafood at **Aqua** (*see p115*) or a pint in one of Dalkey's many lovely pubs.

Sightseeing

One of the Liffey's new bridges.

Trinity College & Around

Visit the intellectual hub of the city.

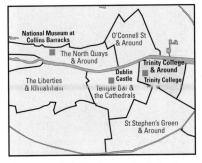

If you can make it, Sunday morning is the time to visit. Before the students are awake and while the bells still toll for morning mass throughout the city, **Trinity College** campus is a perfect oasis of peace and beauty. Although increasingly cluttered with new buildings to cater for a growing student population, the campus is still spacious and gracious, interspersed with elegant walks and gardens, luxuriating in its thesis that a proper education is a matter of more than books and exams. And its mix of old and new buildings, classical with 1970s brutalism and elegant contemporary, is one that works.

Trinity College

Founded in 1592 by Queen Elizabeth I for the scions of the Anglo-Irish Ascendancy in order to protect them from malign popish influences abroad, the university succeeded in stemming the 16th-century brain drain, and drew the sons of notable families back from England and Europe. Past pupils include JM Synge, Bram Stoker, Jonathan Swift, Beckett and Wilde (*see p60* **Old school**); also Edmund Burke – philosopher, statesman and a man who saw nothing contradictory in asserting Ireland's right to independence while insisting it remain part of the British Empire – and Oliver Goldsmith, poet and general wit, whose statue stands guard over the main College Green entrance.

Catholics were uneasily catered for in an academic version of the old famine soup kitchens: those who changed their religion were welcome within its walls. By the time this decree was lifted, in the late 18th century, it was the Catholic hierarchy's turn to snub Trinity. Until 1970 all Catholics were banned by the Church from attending unless granted a special dispensation from the archbishop; one not lightly given.

But this rather troubled history only makes Dubliners more affectionate towards an establishment prized for its aura of doddering academia and ivory-tower impracticality.

Despite the friendly way in which Trinity stands open to the bustle of the city, most of the buildings are still out of bounds to all but students and staff. As you enter Front Square you'll see Sir William Chambers' neo-classical **Chapel** and **Examination Hall**. The Chapel interior – elegant, with a stuccoed ceiling – looks rather like a mini Houses of Parliament, with two rows of pews facing each other rather than the altar. If you're lucky, you'll catch a wedding or choir practice, otherwise there is a sung Eucharist every Sunday at 10.45am and evensong on Thursdays at 5.15pm.

The extremely pretty **Campanile**, designed by Lanyon, rises up directly opposite the main portico, framing beautiful ancient maple trees. During the summer, ambitious students offer 30-minute guided tours of the campus every hour, to which they bring almost more enthusiasm than information.

National Library of Ireland. *See p63.*

Sightseeing

Old school

Some of Ireland's most distinguished writers have honed their crafts at Trinity College – and, thanks to their bequests both literary and financial, a legacy of nurturing talent survives to this day.

No trawl around Trinity's literary past would be complete without mention of one **Oscar Wilde** (1854-1900). Born at 21 Westland Row, Wilde was educated at the university, where he won a gold medal for Greek and became a protégé of the classicist and wit Sir John Pentland Mahaffy. After studying at Magdalen College, Oxford, Wilde embarked on a diverse and brilliant literary career, in which he dabbled as a novelist, poet and, bizarrely enough, editor of *Woman's World* magazine (1887-89). His brilliantly comic plays are still regularly performed: *Lady Windermere's Fan* (1892), *An Ideal Husband* (1895) and *The Importance of Being Earnest* (1895) are probably the best known.

Wilde's devastating wit helped him conquer London, in part because he was regularly quoted in the British press, charming the world with phrases like: 'If you are not too long, I will wait here for you all my life' and 'Men always want to be a woman's first love. Women have a more subtle instinct: what they like is to be a man's last romance'. But Wilde's popularity was to be his undoing, and in 1895 he was prosecuted for homosexuality: *The Ballad of Reading Gaol* (1898) and *De Profundis* (1905) are painful records of his time in prison. Bankrupt and disgraced, he died in Paris in 1900, reminding himself, 'We are all in the gutter, but some of us are looking at the stars.'

Playwright **John Millington Synge** (1871-1909) is another famous Trinity alumnus.

The **Museum Building**, close by the **Old Library** (*see p61*) was inspired by John Ruskin's celebration of Venetian Gothic and designed by Benjamin Woodward and Thomas Deane in 1852. Its immediate success led to a commission for the two architects and the stonemasons (the O'Shea brothers from Cork) to create a similar building for Oxford University. The building can be walked around, and the imposing foyer can be visited – complete with its skeleton of an Irish elk that could be the brother of the one in the Natural History Museum – but the rest is for students and staff only.

Although the elevation from Nassau Street doesn't look like much, it is worth making a detour to check out the new **Ussher Library**, adjacent to the Arts Block, and **Berkely Library**, two fine examples of 1970s brutalism. You won't be allowed into the Ussher – even visiting students need a letter of introduction – but you can press your nose up against the window and catch a glimpse of the large atrium, which creates a lovely column-of-light effect. Outside the Berkely is Pomodoro's *Sphere within a Sphere* (it's that deconstructed golden ball that looks a bit like a Dalek hatching out of an egg, in case you're in any doubt). The

Born to an old clerical family in the suburb of Rathfarnham (and taking his family holidays in County Wicklow, where he got his first taste of the country life he later depicted so vividly in his plays), Synge went on to complete his studies at Trinity. There then followed several years of idling in Paris before visiting the Aran Islands in 1898; the islands and the language of the Irish peasantry were to have a long-lasting effect on him. Upon his return to Dublin, he joined in the tempestuous politics at the Abbey Theatre. His early plays – *Riders to the Sea*, set on the Aran Islands, and *The Well of the Saints* – were performed there, and they were so well received that Synge joined with Yeats and Lady Gregory as a director of the theatre. He wrote to a friend that Yeats looked after the stars while he saw to everything else. However, he would not be famous for looking after things, but for wonderful artistic chaos. When Synge's masterpiece – *The Playboy of the Western World* – was performed at the Abbey Theatre in 1907, the mayhem that ensued became known as the Playboy Riots.

Like the other famed writers before him, Dublin's third Nobel laureate, **Samuel Beckett** (1906-89; pictured), also attended Trinity College (and was the subject of a fascinating on-campus exhibition during the Beckett Centenary of 2006). Also like his predecessors, he spent much of his life after graduating from Trinity outside of Ireland. First, Beckett lived in Paris, and went so far as to write in French in order to disassociate himself from the English literary tradition. While in Paris in the late '20s, he became a friend of Joyce, who dictated some of *Finnegans Wake* to him. Unlike Joyce, though,

Beckett came back from his self-imposed exile and wrote a bitter collection of stories, *More Pricks Than Kicks* (1934), in a garret in Dublin's Clare Street. It seems as though he was still bitter in 1938, when he wrote the story *Murphy*, in which a character assaults the buttocks of the statue of national hero Cúchulainn in the General Post Office. (Careful observers will notice that the statue does not, in fact, possess buttocks.)

Beckett returned to Paris in 1937, and then spent much of World War II on the run from the Gestapo in the South of France. After the war, the man who once said, 'I have my faults, but changing my tune is not one of them', produced the clutch of tartly worded, gloomy but funny masterpieces that would bring him international fame, including his most famous play, *Waiting for Godot* (1955), characterised by its spare dialogue, stark setting and powerful, symbolic portrayal of the human condition. Later works, such as *Endgame* (1958) and *Happy Days* (1961), concentrate even further on language with minimal action.

Dublin never completely disappeared from Beckett's work, however, with Dún Laoghaire pier, Dalkey Island and Foxrock railway station all recognisable in works like *Malone Dies* (1958) and the monologue *Krapp's Last Tape* (1959). Beckett was awarded the Nobel Prize for Literature in 1969, but chose not to accept it in person. With the characteristic modesty of a man who remained obsessively private all his life, Beckett gave away most of the 375,000 kroner that came with the award; he subsidised friends and artists in Paris, and made a substantial donation to his alma mater, Trinity College.

Pavilion (or 'Pav' to anyone who has ever set foot in the place), a drab enough building at the edge of the cricket pitch, comes into its own every summer by virtue of getting sun longer than almost anywhere else in the city. Gangs of students and former alumni mob the place, spilling out of the bar on to the steps and pitch. The **Douglas Hyde Gallery**, in the Arts Block, exhibits intriguing international artists, often to far smaller crowds than it deserves.

The **Dublin Experience**, a multimedia show, runs from May to September in the Arts Block and tells the story of the city. Shows start on the hour from 10am to 5pm.

Old Library & Book of Kells

Trinity College (608 2308/www.tcd.ie/library). All cross-city buses. **Open** *Apr-Sept* 9.30am-5pm Mon-Sat; 9.30am-4.30pm Sun. *Oct-Mar* 9.30am-5pm Mon-Sat; noon-4.30pm Sun. **Admission** €8; €7 concessions; €16 family; free under-12s. **Credit** AmEx, MC, V. **Map** p251 F3.

'Kelly's Book', as it still gets called occasionally, is Trinity's most famous artefact, but it suffers slightly from *Mona Lisa* syndrome: it's so endlessly reproduced that it seems underwhelming in the flesh. The remarkable craftwork and intricate design are highly impressive, but frankly not show-stopping. The book, designed around the ninth century, is an illuminated copy of the Gospels in Latin, lovingly created by early Christian monks; at any one time four pages are on display – two illustrated and two text – inside a bullet-proof glass case. Alongside is the *Book of Durrow*, an even earlier illuminated manuscript of the Gospels, made in about 675. It disappeared in the 16th century for a century, during which time it was used as a lucky charm by a farmer: he used to pour water on it to cure his cattle.

There's also a multimedia exhibition to take you through the process of creating such texts – for die-hard bibliophiles only – but most people just come to gawp at the texts (if that: peering over a fellow tourist's shoulder is about as good as you can hope for). Still, each summer, an average of 3,000 people a day troop through the Old Library, designed by Thomas Burgh and built between 1712 and 1732. And, although the Long Room is just that, and can accommodate more even than are allowed in at any one time, the vaulted, echoing, dimly lit expanse is definitely best seen as empty as possible. This is the city's most beautiful room: a perfect panelled chamber with rows of double-facing shelves holding about 200,000 lovingly bound old volumes. Down the centre of the room are ten large glass cases devoted to texts on Robert Emmet, Trinity's most famous expulsee, kicked out during a purge of United Irishmen in 1798. Emmet's brief, dramatic life and extraordinarily moving and eloquent speech from the dock before his execution have inspired countless newspaper columns, contemporary accounts, biographies, plays and conspiracy theories, many of which are to be found here.

Grafton Street

The bawdiness of the Molly Malone statue, with her low-cut top, heaving bosom and barrow full of cockles and mussels (she's known locally as the Tart with the Cart), is not continued throughout Grafton Street. In fact, because this is Dublin's shopping heartland (the entire street is given over to the pursuit of retail therapy), its most serious problem is that of overcrowding. Come Christmas, the swell of the crowd will propel you irresistibly through the doors of Brown Thomas, whether you want it or not. However, there are a few bright spots even for the retail-shy. **Bewley's** (*see p117*), halfway up on the right, narrowly escaped a dreadful fate recently when two of the city's brightest young entrepreneurs stepped in to prevent the lovely old 19th-century building from being sold. They now run two restaurants from the premises, including **Café Bar Deli**, a branch of the informal pizza-and-pasta joint on South Great George's Street (*see p101*). The grand old interiors have only been improved by the change, and the famous Harry Clarke stained-glass windows look better than ever.

Leading off Grafton Street in every direction are streets filled with pubs, cafés

and restaurants. Worth a visit are the literary pubs: **Davy Byrne's** (*see p124*) on Duke Street for the Joyce aficionados, and **McDaid's** (*see p126*) on Harry Street for the Brendan Behan and Flann O'Brien fans. (And less bookish punters might like to know that opposite McDaid's is a statue of rock icon Phil Lynott, frontman of Thin Lizzy.) At the top of Grafton Street, opposite St Stephen's Green, is a permanent setting for a constantly changing sculpture. Every six months – January and July – the sculpture is replaced by a new piece.

Tucked in behind Bewley's, is **St Teresa's Carmelite Church and Friary**, built towards the end of the 18th century and before Catholic emancipation in a deliberately discreet location. Improbably large and imposing inside, the church still does a good trade in city-centre worshippers. The tiny courtyard outside has a low-key, forgotten appeal. Opposite the courtyard is the back entrance to the **Powerscourt Townhouse Centre** (*see p139*), which still holds its own as a stylish and exclusive shopping centre. The shops and boutiques here have changed little over the years, suggesting that business is brisk in the Wingfield family's former townhouse. On Fridays and Saturdays, a tour takes in original mahogany staircase, tiling and fireplace.

Kildare Street & around

Pleasant side streets lead from the bustle of Grafton Street to Dawson Street and the **Mansion House**. This Queen Anne-style building has been the official residence of the Lord Mayor of Dublin since 1715. **St Anne's Church** next door is where Bram Stoker was married in 1878. The interior dates from 1720, and the loaves of bread left there are hangover from an 18th-century bequest to the city's poor.

From Dawson Street, wander along Molesworth Street towards Kildare Street and **Leinster House** (*see p63*), seat of the Dáil (Irish Parliament) since 1922. Leinster House is flanked by the equally serious grey façades of the **National Library of Ireland** – first stop for researchers into family heritage – and the **National Museum of Archaeology & History** (for both, *see p63*).

The Venetian-inspired red-brick building on the corner of Kildare and Nassau streets, once the Kildare Street Club for the gentlemen of the Ascendancy, now holds the **Heraldic Museum** (*see p63*).

Heraldic Museum

Kildare Street (603 0200/www.nli.ie/h_muse.htm). All cross-city buses/DART Pearse. **Open** 10am-8.30pm Mon-Wed; 10.30am-4.30pm Thur, Fri; 10.30am-12.30pm Sat. **Admission** free. **Map** p251 G4.

In 1886 George Moore said of the Kildare Street Club: 'It represents all that is respectable, that is to say, those who are gifted with that oyster-like capacity for understanding… that they should continue to get fat in the bed in which they were born.' The building is now divided between the Alliance Française and the Heraldic Museum (a dull display of objects showing armorial bearings, scarcely worth a visit since the genealogy and family history section has been moved to the National Library). There is, however, an amusing frieze of monkeys playing billiards carved by the O'Shea brothers, who also did the stonework on Trinity's Museum Building, around the right-hand side of the museum entrance. There is no official account of their significance, so take your pick of two competing stories. According to one, they depict the many strange and wondrous animals to be found throughout the British Empire. The second, more popular, account holds that they represent the gentlemen members of the old Club.

Leinster House

Kildare Street (618 3000/www.oireachtas.ie). All cross-city buses. **Open** *Tours* (when Parliament is not in session) 10.30am, 11.30am, 2.30pm and 3.30pm Mon-Fri. **Admission** free. **Map** p251 G4.
Leinster House is the seat of the Irish Parliament, made up of the Dáil (lower house) and the Seanad (senate or upper house). The first of Dublin's great 18th-century houses to be constructed south of the Liffey, Leinster was built by Richard Castle (between 1745 and 1748) for the Earl of Kildare, who became Duke of Leinster in 1766. The Seanad meets in the sumptuous North Wing Saloon; the Dáil in a rather prosaic room added as a lecture theatre in 1897. The house has two formal fronts – the Kildare Street frontage, designed to look like a townhouse, and a Merrion Square frontage – that are connected by a long central corridor. Leinster House has been claimed as the prototype for the White House in the United States (the White House architect, James Hoban, was born in 1762 in County Kilkenny). The entrance hall and principal rooms were redecorated towards the end of the 18th century with the help of James Wyatt. No cameras or recording equipment are allowed inside.

National Library of Ireland

Kildare Street (603 0200/www.nli.ie). All cross-city buses/DART Pearse. **Open** 10am-9pm Mon-Wed; 10am-5pm Thur, Fri; 10am-1pm Sat. **Admission** free. **Map** p251 G4.
Though the National Library is predominantly a research institution, some parts of it are open to the public. These include the grand domed Reading Room – the place in which Stephen Dedalus expounds his views on Shakespeare in James Joyce's *Ulysses* – and the Exhibition Room, which plays host to changing displays from the Library's extensive collections. There's also a useful walk-in genealogical service for people keen on tracing their family trees. **Photo** *p59*.

National Museum of Archaeology & History

Kildare Street (677 7444/www.museum.ie). All cross-city buses/DART Pearse. **Open** 10am-5pm Tue-Sat; 2-5pm Sun. **Admission** free. **Map** p251 G4.
Established in 1877 by the Science and Art Museums Act, the National Museum is deservedly one of Dublin's most popular attractions. The 19th-century building designed by Thomas Newenham Deane is squeezed into a site to the side of the impassive façade of Leinster House. Its domed entrance hall, or Rotunda, looks like a Victorian reworking of the Pantheon, with windows on the upper gallery that jut inwards so that the space appears to cave in towards the spectator. The most striking exhibition among its many excellent pieces is the Bronze Age Irish gold, displayed in vast glass cases on the ground floor. Further along there are a number of examples of extraordinarily intricate sacred and secular metalwork dating from the Iron Age to the Middle Ages, as well as displays of well-preserved artefacts from prehistoric and Viking Ireland, plus Ancient Egyptian artefacts on the first floor.

Parliament & Bank

Opposite Trinity's main gates, doubtless ready to receive the brightest of its graduates, are Edward Lovett Pearce's **Houses of Parliament**, now the HQ of the Bank of Ireland. This Palladian building was the seat of power from 1728 until, like turkeys calling for an early Christmas (and motivated by huge bribes and handouts), it voted its own dissolution in the 1800 Act of Union, allowing the country to be governed directly from London. Only the hushed and panelled **House of Lords** is still intact, although the former **House of Commons**, where the public now goes about its banking business, is a far more impressive room. Outside stands a statue of Henry Grattan, statesman, orator and the man who first – though prematurely – hailed the new Irish nation in 1782 with the words, 'I am now to address a free people'. Around the corner is the Bank of Ireland Arts Centre, a prestigious if rather corporate venue that hosts regular exhibitions, concerts and poetry readings. Beside it, the **Museum of Banking** (*see below*) has an interactive exhibition on the story of money, though it's a niche interest.

House of Lords

Bank of Ireland, 2 College Green (671 1488). All cross-city buses. **Open** 10am-4pm Mon-Wed, Fri; 10am-5pm Thur. **Guided tours** 10.30am, 11.30am, 1.45pm Tue. **Admission** free. **Map** p251 F3.

Museum of Banking

Bank of Ireland Arts Centre, Foster Place (671 1488). All cross-city buses. **Open** 9.30am-4pm Tue-Fri. **Admission** €1.50; €1 concessions. **Credit** MC, V. **Map** p251 F3.

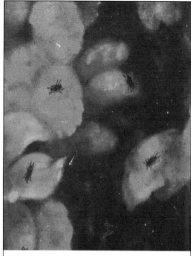

Temple Bar
& the Cathedrals

Steeped in culture, studded with cathedrals and awash with rowdy stags.

Walk this way: **Temple Bar**. *See p67*.

A manic jumble of old, new, tacky and lovely, the area around Temple Bar and up to the cathedrals sometimes seems to belong to different cities. The raucous crowds in Temple Bar on Saturday nights have so little to do with the Sunday morning peace around Christ Church that it seems impossible they should co-exist. But the juxtaposition keeps the Old City dynamic and vibrant; and the rowdy hordes are, in turn, slightly softened by the setting.

Dame Street & around

Dame Street may have the dimensions of a grand old colonial boulevard, but it is a far from pleasant place in which to stroll. Thundering traffic, smoky air and a general aura of frantic scurrying mean it is best used as a means to an end. Luckily, there are plenty of interesting side streets to duck off into. These lead one into

another, allowing you to re-emerge on to the main thoroughfare for points of interest, such as the **Olympia Theatre** (*see p193*), with its pretty coloured-glass canopy and shabby Victorian bordello interior. You might expect to see a row of cancan girls in frilly skirts, but the city's oldest surviving Victorian theatre is now a venue primarily for concerts – Shane McGowan still plays regular gigs here, usually attended by a boozy and partisan crowd.

Further down towards Trinity College is the **Central Bank**. This rather overbearing building was highly controversial when it went up, but is now an accepted part of the cityscape, regarded by most Dubliners with something close to affection. Designed by architect Sam Stephenson, whose legacy is being gradually and favourably reappraised, it looms over Dame Street. In front of it is a plaza where Eamonn O'Doherty's *Crann an Or* (Tree of Gold) sculpture vies with Saturday morning gangs of teenage Goths and skate kids who demonstrate the timeless art of hanging out. Walking up towards Christ Church, opposite the Olympia, is **Dublin Castle** (*see p67*), tucked away down a spindly side street. The castle has a faintly hangdog air, as if unsure of its role: is it a historical monument? A cultural one? Or is it a conference centre? Maybe even a car park? At least one thing's for sure: the Dubh Linn gardens round the back, with their pleasantly elaborate Celtic paving, are usually a reliably peaceful retreat. There too is the magnificent **Chester Beatty Library** (*see p66*); if you only have time for one cultural pit stop while in Dublin, make it this one. Next to the castle entrance and facing down towards Grattan's Bridge is **City Hall** (*see p67*), definitely Dublin's best building. Originally the Royal Exchange, for years this was the HQ of Dublin Corporation, partitioned and subdivided into a rabbit warren for civil servants, its glories totally disguised. After an extensive and expensive renovation programme, it was reopened in 2000 and now is a rarely used but always accessible public resource.

Back down towards Trinity and opposite the Central Bank is **South Great George's Street**, nucleus of one of the city's better

Place of worship for kings and conquerors: **Christ Church Cathedral**. *See p69*.

shopping, eating and bar areas. The **Globe**, **Hogan's** and the **Market Bar** (for all three, *see p129*) have much of the city's nightlife sewn up, although the Market Bar, thanks to its large outdoor area and excellent baby-changing facilities, also has a serious daytime incarnation as a family-friendly spot. Opposite, on Fade Street, is **Le Gueleton** (*see p101*), one of the best cheap restaurants in the city. With a no-reservations policy and constantly changing menu, it manages to be stylish and buzzy as well as cheap. Around the corner from the Globe, on South William Street, **Fallon & Byrne** (*see p151*) is an excellent deli and food market, with a wine bar serving decent plates of oysters, cheeses and charcuterie in the basement, plus there's a very popular restaurant on the first floor (*see p103*).

Located halfway between the Globe and Hogan's is **Café Bar Deli** (*see p101*), good for cheap pizzas and pasta, large groups and kids. Across the road a few doors up is the **Long Hall** (*see p129*), one of a sadly dwindling number of really beautiful old pubs. Opposite is the fine red-brick **George's Street Arcade**, a covered Victorian market full of stalls selling second-hand books, records, clothes, collectable stamps, postcards and, increasingly, deli and organic food. At the far end is the little pedestrianised fashion haven of **Castle Market**. Carry on

up George's Street on the opposite side of the road and, on the corner with Aungier Street, is the **Whitefriar Street Carmelite Church** (*see p67*), built on the site of an ancient 13th-century priory that was confiscated as part of the Dissolution of the Monasteries Act in 1539. The Carmelites returned three centuries later and set up shop in the current building, designed by George Papworth, although the present entrance, with its two-storey Italianate façade, was put up only in 1914.

Further up George's Street, you come to Wexford Street and Camden Street, an area with a lively mix of new cultures known for good Middle Eastern grocery shops and delis. If you're looking for huge vats of almond flour or sticky baklava, this is where to go.

Chester Beatty Library

Clock Tower Building, Dublin Castle, Dame Street (407 0750/www.cbl.ie). All cross-city buses. **Open** *May-Sept* 10am-5pm Mon-Fri; 11am-5pm Sat; 1-5pm Sun. *Oct-Apr* 10am-5pm Tue-Fri; 11am-5pm Sat; 1-5pm Sun. *Guided tours* 1pm Wed; 3pm, 4pm Sun. **Admission** free; donations welcome. **Map** p251 E3.
Many of the finest works from Sir Alfred Chester Beatty's priceless art collection are housed in this purpose-built museum. An Irish-American mining magnate with a passion for the East, Chester Beatty settled here in the 1950s and bequeathed his life's collection to the Irish people in 1969. Manuscripts,

icons, miniature paintings, early prints and objets d'art from Europe and the Far East take you through the differing traditions of belief and learning in the Western, Islamic and East Asian worlds. Beautiful Buddhas, intricate Chinese lanterns, delicate snuff boxes and Japanese woodcuts stand beside illuminated, ninth-century copies of the Koran and some of the earliest Christian scrolls. And if you tire of religious artefacts, a collection of illustrated 20th-century texts includes a storybook by Matisse and charming Parisian fashion plates from the 1920s. Upstairs is a Zen roof garden, while on the ground floor is the Silk Road café, serving good Middle Eastern-style food, and a carefully stocked museum shop offering postcards, wall hangings, cute toys and even some large furniture pieces.

City Hall

Dame Street (222 2204/www.dublincorp.ie/cityhall). All cross-city buses. **Open** 10am-5.15pm Mon-Sat; 2-5pm Sun. **Admission** €4; €1.50-€2 concessions; €10 family. **Credit** MC, V. **Map** p251 E3.

When keeping pace with street life becomes all too much, and you need somewhere to catch your breath and reflect, City Hall has just the right kind of empty grandeur. Entering through the main Dame Street portico, you find yourself in Thomas Cooley's large domed atrium, complete with mosaic floor and sweeping staircases. Around the central space are frescoes by James Ward, showing scenes from the history of Dublin, such as the Battle of Clontarf, and four marble statues, one of which is Daniel O'Connell, taken in out of the rain from its original perch beside what is now the Central Bank. Carvings and stuccowork are equally lovely. In the basement is the Story of the Capital, an exhibition detailing the city's history of government, and a tiny café. **Photo** *p69.*

Dublin Castle

Dame Street (677 7129/www.dublincastle.ie). All cross-city buses. **Open** (by guided tour only) 10am-5pm Mon-Fri; 2-5pm Sat, Sun. **Admission** €4.50; €2.50-€3.50 concessions. **No credit cards**. **Map** p251 E3.

Formerly the seat of British power in Ireland, and efficiently infiltrated by spies during the Michael Collins era, this isn't really a castle – no moat, no drawbridge to lower against invading hordes, no turrets from which to pour boiling oil – more a collection of 18th-century administrative buildings, albeit very fine ones, built on a medieval plan of two courtyards. A figure of Justice stands over the main entrance, dating from the time of British rule, and is something of a sardonic joke – she stands with her back to the city, wears no blindfold and her scales tilt when filled with water. In 1922 this is where the last Lord Lieutenant of Ireland, FitzAlan, symbolically handed over the castle to Michael Collins, who kept him waiting seven minutes. When FitzAlan complained, Collins retorted, 'We've been waiting over 700 years, you can have the extra seven minutes.' The Castle's current role is to provide venues for grand diplomatic or state functions, and occa-sional artistic performances, such as concert recitals. The interior, including beautiful State Rooms, is operated on a pay-per-view basis, but you can wander freely around the exterior.

Whitefriar Street Carmelite Church

Whitefriar Street, off Aungier Street (475 8821/ www.carmelites.ie). Bus 16, 16A, 19, 19A, 83, 122/ Luas St Stephen's Green . **Open** 7.30am-6.30pm Mon, Wed-Fri; 7.30am-9.30pm Tue; 8.30am-7.30pm Sat; 7.30am-7.45pm Sun. **Admission** free. **Map** p251 E4.

The altar of this Byzantine-looking church is said to contain the relics of St Valentine, donated by Pope Gregory XVI in 1835, and so has a busy season with couples around the big day in February. Another treasure of the church is Our Lady of Dublin, a beautiful medieval wooden statue of the Virgin Mary. The only example of such sculpture in Dublin, it was rescued long after the Reformation was thought to have destroyed all such pieces, and is believed to have been used as a pig trough during the intervening years. At the back of the building – turn right in the antechamber just before you get to the church proper – is a very pretty little secluded garden with neat lawns, rows of rose bushes and one little bench.

Temple Bar & around

Temple Bar entered a seriously bad patch in the mid 1990s. Whether that bad patch is over yet is a moot point. Cheap flights from the UK turned it into a hot destination for rowdy stag and hen parties, and the after-dark character of the area became distinctly sleazy. Although a deliberate 'No Stags or Hens' policy by local businesses – hotels, hostels, pubs and restaurants – gradually succeeded in discouraging this kind of tourism, the area isn't out of the woods yet. These days, Temple Bar tends to feature prominently in media scare stories about teenage binge-drinking, and certainly it is still pretty unsavoury on weekend nights and exam result days. However, the good efforts of local businesses continue, and attempts to shed this louche character are beginning to pay off. Local traders are currently working on an initiative to make Temple Bar Dublin's first official Fairtrade area, so there may yet be a third act in the drama of the so-called cultural quarter. Still, during the day and early evenings, this remains one of the city's most charming neighbourhoods. The pedestrianised 18th-century cobbled streets make it ideal territory for the touristic flâneur, with enough shops, galleries, bars, cafés and general architectural diversity to keep interest alive. Old streetscapes are preserved alongside contemporary, often eco-friendly architectural projects – such as the glass-panelled Arthouse building on Curved Street, now home to the film-makers organisation Filmbase.

Sightseeing

Begin at the Dame Street end with a stroll past the Central Bank plaza where, on a Saturday, teenage Goths hang around, dressed like mini Marilyn Mansons. The **Irish Film Institute** (*see p163* and *p171*), down Eustace Street, is Dublin's only art-house cinema, showing a good range of independent and European films (there's also a café that serves reasonable food in generous portions). Opposite the IFI is No.25 Eustace Street, an Irish Landmark Trust House, available to rent overnight and a delightfully example of 18th-century domestic architecture. Behind the IFI is **Meeting House Square**, the heart of the area's cultural entertainment programme. Open-air film screenings – mainly of old classics – alternate with concerts, puppet shows, circus performers and dance events during the summer, all part of Diversions, a programme of free events co-ordinated by the Temple Bar Cultural Trust. Throughout the year, the Square is home to a hugely popular Saturday food market, which attracts faithful local foodie types and delighted visitors. Selling everything from organic chickens, vegetables and artisanal cheeses to olives, oysters and sushi, it is both a place for the weekly shopping and tapas-style grazing. Buskers playing traditional music add to the usually highly genial atmosphere. Come Sunday, the space gets transformed into a craft and furniture market, showcasing Irish and international pieces.

A small second-hand book fair on **Temple Bar Square** every Saturday and Sunday is also worth a visit – you won't find first editions or rare manuscripts, but if you're looking for vintage paperback editions of favourite classics, your chances are high. Here, too, on Sundays you will find Speaker's Square, lasting from 2pm to 6pm. This is an opportunity for anyone with a grievance, grudge or passion to get it off their chest. All are welcome, and, as with London's Hyde Park equivalent, the ranting can be top class.

The **Gallery of Photography** (*see p167*), three purpose-built levels on Meeting House Square, has a permanent collection of modern Irish photography, regular exhibitions of contemporary local work and popular touring shows; downstairs is a great collection of photography books and arty postcards. The Gallery also runs courses in photography and print techniques and rents darkroom space. Facing it across the square is the **National Photographic Archive** (*see p167*), full of excellent, often poignant photographic records of Irish life in the early part of the century. Around the corner, on Temple Bar itself, the **Original Print Gallery** (*see p169*) and **Temple Bar Gallery** (*see p167*) stand side by side. The OPG specialises in limited-edition prints, and these increasingly come from the Black Church Print Studios upstairs, making this something of a success story for an area that has a designated role in the promotion of culture. The Temple Bar Gallery, also with vast studio space upstairs and attractive shop windows, shows work that is innovative and – if not always appealing – usually local.

The distinctive **Octagon** bar (*see p129*), in the Clarence Hotel (*see p36*), is an elegant setting for an early evening gin and tonic; and the stylish **Morgan** hotel (*see p39*), at the other end of Temple Bar, does its bit too. But the older, more sophisticated crowd tends to drift away as soon as the real hordes pour in – boozy local kids and like-minded visitors.

Some of Temple Bar is becoming tentatively alternative – certainly more bo-bo (bourgeois bohemian) than authentically boho – and the mix of commerce and culture is sometimes a difficult one; many very worthy local fashion and design boutiques have failed to survive in an area that remains off the beaten track for mainstream weekend shoppers.

Opposite the Clarence Hotel, the **Project Arts Centre** (*see p167*) is currently experiencing an artistic renaissance with an eclectic and ambitious programme of theatre, comedy and art projects. However, the big blue building is not the most sympathetic of spaces, and audiences can still be elusive.

Crossing Parliament Street brings you to the Old City. Before entering it, look one way for **City Hall** (*see p67*), and the other, down on the Quays, facing Grattan Bridge, for the **Sunlight Chambers**. These hark back to the days when every Irish family had an industrial-sized bar of Sunlight soap beside the kitchen sink – 'the story of soap' is told in a delightful double bas-relief frieze that runs around the building. The Old City, although still very much a work in progress, is beginning to carve out a niche for itself as a centre for design and interiors. A Saturday fashion market (on Cow's Lane) stocks bags, clothes, jewellery and underwear by many of the country's brightest young designers, at reasonable prices. There are also some great boutiques, such as **Smock** (*see p146*), for eclectic international designers, and Beneath (*see p149*), for seriously sexy lingerie.

Further on is **Fishamble Street**, the oldest street in Dublin, where Handel's *Messiah* was first performed and where regular free open-air renditions of the piece are still staged.

The Cathedrals & around

Here you will find the intersection point of Dublin's two historic Golden Ages: the medieval period, when Dublin was a significant stop-off on the great Viking trade routes that stretched from the Baltic to North Africa; and the 18th century, when Ireland's capital briefly flowered as the second city of what was at that time the burgeoning British Empire.

Memorials in both cathedrals to the large number of Irishmen who lost their lives fighting Britain's colonial wars, the French Huguenot presence in both **St Patrick's Cathedral** (*see p70*) and in **Marsh's Library** (*see p70*), and the assortment of languages spoken in Dublin during the Middle Ages (colourfully recreated in the audio accompaniment to the **Dublinia** exhibition, *see p70*) are all proof of something that many Dubliners seem unaware of: namely, that the city experienced both periods of great wealth and large influxes of foreign nationals long before the 1990s.

As you come round the top of Lord Edward Street, **Christ Church Cathedral** (*see below*) seems less impressive than you might expect, almost dwarfed by the surrounding buildings. The best way to approach it is from the river. Just opposite the entrance to Christ Church is the **Lord Edward** pub (named after that dashing aristocrat-turned-rebel; *see p129*), with all the tattered but convivial charm of a real Dublin watering hole.

An enclosed elevated walkway crosses Winetavern Street and connects Christ Church to Dublinia. Looking west at the top of the hill,

St Audeon's church stands over the last surviving Norman gateway to the city. Open just a few months of the year, St Audeon's boasts pleasingly simple medieval architecture that makes it well worth a visit. Looking south towards the Dublin Mountains, the spire of St Patrick's Cathedral rises in surprisingly close proximity to Christ Church.

Christ Church Cathedral

Christ Church Place (677 8099/www.cccdub.ie). Bus 49, 50, 54A, 56A, 65, 77, 77A, 78A, 123. **Open** *June-Aug* 9am-6pm daily. *Sept-May* 9.45am-5pm daily. **Admission** €5; €2.50 concessions. **Credit** *Shop* MC, V. **Map** p250 D3.

Catering to a minority religion in a country where even the majority religion has seriously fallen from favour in recent years, Christ Church, like St Patrick's, relies heavily on tourism and on the services of voluntary staff to pay for its upkeep. Dubliners chiefly know it as a place to hear the bells ring out on New Year's Eve (it boasts 'the largest full-circle ringing peal in the world') and for the beautiful sung masses (Wednesdays, Thursdays and Sundays, or evensong any weekday evening at 6pm). The original Viking cathedral was put up circa 1030, but the existing Anglo-Norman building dates from the 1180s, with many subsequent restorations. Inside, it is handsome rather than spectacular; if any cathedral can be called cosy or compact, this is the one. Like so many other notable church buildings in Ireland, Christ Church suffered from some over-enthusiastic Victorian restoration, but the huge crypt that runs the full length of the cathedral dates from its first stone incarnation in the 1170s and goes

City Hall. *See p67.*

some way to representing the medieval character of the place. Many kings and conquerors worshipped here, from the Norman mercenary Strongbow to the ill-fated James II, and his rival and successor to the throne of England, William of Orange. In 1871, the whiskey-maker Henry Roe funded a restoration so thorough it left him bankrupt, and purists enraged. Keep an eye out for the heart-shaped iron box said to contain the heart of St Laurence O'Toole, and for 'the cat and the rat'. Their mummified remains were (supposedly) found in an organ pipe and were put on display in mid chase, like a single frame from a ghoulish Tex Avery animation; actually, they provide a welcome break from the austerity and pomp that characterise Christ Church. **Photo** *p66*.

Dublinia

Christ Church, St Michael's Hill (679 4611/www.dublinia.ie). Bus 49, 50, 51B, 54A, 56A, 65, 77, 77A, 78A, 123/Luas Fourcourts. **Open** *Apr-Sept* 10am-5pm daily (last admission 4.15pm). *Oct-Mar* 11am-4pm daily (last admission 3.15). **Admission** €6; €3.75-€5 concessions; €16 family; free under-5s. **Credit** MC, V. **Map** p250 D3.

The crudely interactive features of this exhibition on the world of medieval Dublin seem to date from a pre-digital age, but overall this exhibition is the best of its kind in the city. A scale model of medieval Dublin helps place the two cathedrals in their geographical context, while a reconstructed archaeological dig is probably most interesting for the newspaper clippings that accompany it – they chart the history of the noble but doomed protest to save the site of one of Viking Europe's most significant settlements at Wood Quay from destruction at the hands of Dublin Corporation. St Michael's Tower, although not a match for the Gravity Bar in the Guinness Storehouse (*see p136*), provides a fine view of the heart of old Dublin.

Marsh's Library

St Patrick's Close (454 3511/www.marshlibrary.ie). Bus 49X, 50, 50X, 54A, 56A, 77X, 150. **Open** 10am-1pm, 2-5pm Mon, Wed-Fri; 10.30am-1pm Sat. **Admission** €2.50; €1.50 concessions; free under-12s. **No credit cards**. **Map** p250 D4.

This is the oldest public library in Ireland (and the only 18th-century building still used for its original purpose). Marsh's Library stands like a miniature working version of Trinity College's Long Room. It is located just past the entrance to St Patrick's (and in comparative solitude), and the slow, steady ticking of the clock in its main room adds to the old-world atmosphere. The mitres that stand on top of the bookcases, and the wire cages (where visitors were locked in with particularly precious books, lest they be tempted to borrow them) recall the library's founder, Archbishop Narcissus Marsh.

St Audeon's Church

High Street (677 0088/www.heritageireland.ie). Bus 123. **Open** *June-Sept* 9.30am-5.30pm daily (last tour 4.45pm). **Closed** Oct-May. **Admission** free. **Map** p250 D3.

A visit to St Audeon's is well worth while, if only to escape the pomp of the two cathedrals. The only medieval parish church in Dublin still in use, it reopened to visitors in 2001, albeit only for a few months every year.

St Patrick's Cathedral

St Patrick's Close (453 9472/www.stpatricks cathedral.ie). Bus 49X, 50, 50X, 54A, 56A, 77X, 150. **Open** *Mar-Oct* 9am-6pm daily. *Nov-Feb* 9am-5pm Mon-Sat; 9am-3pm Sun. (No admission 10.45am-12.30pm, 2.45-4.30pm Sun, except for worship.) **Admission** €5; €4 concessions; €12 family. **Credit** MC, V. **Map** p250 D4.

This, the largest church in Ireland, dates from the 13th century but was founded on a far older religious site associated with St Patrick and dating from the fifth century. As a memorial to Anglo-Irish life in Ireland, it tells a more interesting tale than Christ Church, and the many plaques and monuments commemorate various celebrated figures of the Anglican Ascendancy, from Richard Boyle (Earl of Cork and 'Father of Chemistry') and John Philpot Curran (who provided the legal defence for rebel leader Wolfe Tone and fathered Sarah Curran, fiancée of the later rebel leader Robert Emmet), to former presidents of Ireland such as Erskine Childers (whose father was executed during the Irish Civil War) and Douglas Hyde (father of the Irish language revival movement). The monuments also serve as a reminder of the generations of Irishmen who served, fought and lost their lives for the British Empire: not just on the fields of France in the two World Wars (a Roll of Honour here lists the names of the 50,000 Irishmen killed fighting in the British army in WWII), but also in such far-flung places as Sudan, Burma and Afghanistan throughout the 19th century. Most consist of wordy, typically sentimental Victorian eulogies, but some are touchingly compassionate, and seem to reflect the poignant mood cast by the shadow of the tattered regimental colours that still hang from the inside wall.

All that said, St Patrick's remains most famous for its association with the celebrated writer and satirist Jonathan Swift. Most of his best-known works were written while he was dean here from 1713 to 1745. Deeply cynical and yet touched by a sort of social conscience that seems at odds with their time, Swift's savage criticisms of the cronyism and ineptitude that marked England's colonial administration of its largest island neighbour were powerful enough to bring down governments; unfortunately for him, they made him many enemies in the process, and ensured that his own career would remain somewhat stunted. Swift advocated a humane approach to the treatment of the mentally ill, and he left a large sum of money after his death to found St Patrick's Hospital; but, typically, he had prepared a caustic verse to accompany the gesture: 'He left the little wealth he had/To build a house for fools and mad/Showing in one satiric touch/No nation needed it so much.' Swift is buried here alongside his partner, friend and confidante, Stella.

St Stephen's Green & Around

It's all rather grand in this part of town.

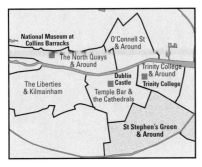

This where Georgian Dublin comes into its own: rows of stern grey townhouses lined up formally around lush green squares, leading to the quiet waters of the Grand Canal. St Stephen's Green is ideal for wandering, shopping or a cup of tea at the **Shelbourne Hotel** (*see p47*), while Merrion Square is tops for sightseeing (it seems as if every famous 19th-century Dubliner lived here). Then you can take a walk along the canal, and on to the Liffey, where it meets the sea.

St Stephen's Green

After a morning spent pushing through swarms of shoppers, the wide expanse of **St Stephen's Green** comes as a blessed relief. This elegant, beautifully designed park – always known simply as 'the Green' – was a common ground used for hangings and whippings until 1800. Today it opens out at the end of Grafton Street with tree-studded lawns, a languid pond with willows, island and stone bridge, a children's playground and formal gardens. It can fill on warm summer days, but seldom feels crowded. Entry once cost a guinea, but in 1877 Lord Arthur Guinness (in his second greatest legacy to the city) pushed through an Act of Parliament making it free – and funding the design that you see, more or less unchanged, today. Wander its paths to find the curious collection of stone circles and arguably the park's finest statue – George Moore's *WB*

Yeats. In a city where statuary realism rules with an iron fist, Moore's work stands out for its expressionistic approach – not that this means much to local yoofs, who regularly cover it with graffiti.

Other public artworks sprinkled around the green are Henry Moore's gloomy bust of Joyce, and busts of the poet James Clarence Mangan and the revolutionary Countess Marcievicz. A statue of Protestant rebel Wolfe Tone (*see p74* **Key notes**) stands ferociously on the south-western corner. In sharp contrast, the Three Fates – a gift from Germany in recognition of Irish aid in the years following World War II – slouch coolly atop a fountain at Leeson Street Gate. Other cultural park attractions include

St Stephen's Green.

Sightseeing

The glories of Dublin's Georgian architecture are clear to behold in this part of town.

outdoor art exhibitions on Saturdays, and music is played from the bandstand in summer.

If you stroll around the Green's perimeter, you can take in the historical oddity that is the **Huguenot Cemetery** on the north-east corner, as well as the illustrious Shelbourne Hotel. Once the city's most exclusive hotel, the Shelbourne is still a byword for luxury. Take a rest in one of its bars – movers and shakers favour the tiny Horseshoe Bar, but the Shelbourne Bar has more atmosphere – or have a cup of tea and a scone in its plush lobby.

The expansive green is guarded by elegant terraces of Georgian townhouses, although in recent years hotels and other newcomers have muscled in; chic shops are gaining a foothold on the Grafton Street corner. Otherwise, lovely old buildings line the streets in every direction. Yeats dismissed them as 'grey 18th-century houses', but – with all due respect – we think they're *fabulous*; as do the tourists who walk for miles to see them. Generally four storeys high, most have plain exteriors; owners expressed themselves in colourful doors and lavish door-knockers. Like well-bred aristocrats, these house keep their extravagances well

concealed: inside are spacious, beautifully proportioned rooms, sweeping staircases and ornate plasterwork. Two of the best examples of the style are on the southern side of the green in the two conjoined townhouses that make up **Newman House** (*see p73*). The outside is plain, but the elaborate interior plasterwork was so risqué that it was covered up when the building was part of the Catholic University. Also part of the university was nearby **Newman University Church** (*see p74*); Gerard Manley Hopkins was professor of classics here from 1884 to 1889, and James Joyce was a student from 1899 to 1902. Quotations from Hopkins are engraved in the church, though there's nothing from the anti-clerical Joyce; and yet, for all Joyce's contempt for the church and, in some measure, the university, a glance at the comments book shows that it's his association with the place that inspires most visitors. A room where Joyce attended classes has been lovingly restored.

Newman House backs on to the ethereally lovely 19th-century **Iveagh Gardens**, laid out by Nenian Neven and created in 1863. At first glance the gardens look private: they're ringed by high stone walls and their entrances are hidden. One door lurks behind the National Concert Hall on Earlsfort Terrace, another on Clonmel Street; a third gate has recently been created on Hatch Street, but it's usually locked. Don't be put off. Once inside you'll find long sunken lawns, a roaring waterfall, elegant stone fountains, a grotto, a rose garden and a newly planted maze: a combination that makes for one of the most graceful, beautiful parks in the city.

South of the Green, the **National Concert Hall** is a fine, imposing building, but one with several shortcomings – acoustic, in particular. On the western side of the Green rises the façade of the **Royal College of Surgeons**, elegant, imposing and still pockmarked with 1916 uprising bullet holes. Also on this terrace are the new Stephen's Green and Fitzwilliam

hotels (the expensive interiors of which deserve a look), and the glass-domed **Stephen's Green Centre** (*see p139*).

Newman House

85-86 St Stephen's Green South (716 7422). All cross-city buses/Luas St Stephen's Green. **Open** (tours only) *June-Aug* 2pm, 3pm, 4pm Tue-Fri. **Admission** €5; €4 concessions. **No credit cards**. **Map** p251 F5.

These conjoined townhouses, originally the Catholic University of Ireland and now owned by University College Dublin, are probably the finest example of 18th-century Georgian architecture open to the public. Built in 1738 for Irish MP Hugh Montgomery, No.85 has a sombre façade that hides a spacious, elegant inte-rior. When it was bought by the Catholic University in 1865, its superb plasterwork was thought too smutty for young men, so the female

Walk Georgian Dublin

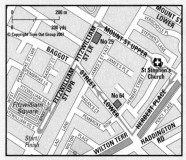

Start this ramble at the southern corner of Fitzwilliam Square, where you'll find yourself surrounded by elegant Georgian townhouses whose jaunty doorways (painted in bright primary colours) give this little enclave a festive mood. Heading north on Fitzwilliam Street, take a right on to Mount Street Upper: straight ahead is the impressive **St Stephen's Church**, more commonly known as the Pepper Canister on account of its distinctive shape. The church is certainly distinguished on the outside but rather austere within. Its prominent position in the middle of a traffic island gives it something of an iconic character, which has made it a traditionally popular choice among film location scouts (it featured three times in *Michael Collins* alone). Continue towards the church, noting as you go the discreetly positioned CCTV cameras (this, as you will know if you have ever glanced at a local

estate agent's window, is one of the most affluent neighbourhoods in the city).

Continue along past the church to Mount Street Crescent and down towards the river, passing as you go *Memories of Mount Street*, a rather lovely sculpture attached to the lamppost outside Pepper Canister House (what on earth could she be doing – swinging on it or trying to pull the thing down?). As you ponder this question, cross Herbert Place and access the towpath next to the graceful Huband Bridge. You have reached the Grand Canal. Head south-west from here along Herbert Place until you are able to turn right on to Baggot Street Lower. A little way up on the right-hand side is the **Mercy International Centre** (No.64), where Catherine McAuley founded the Sisters of Mercy in 1824 (you can see her statue at the front of the building). And just by way of contrast, juxtaposing the charitable and commercial elements of city life, the plate glass and bright modern sculpture of the Bank of Ireland's head office is a near neighbour at Nos.50-55.

As you continue up Baggot Street Lower into the parade of shops, cafés and restaurants, make sure you keep an eye open for the wrought-iron gates of **L'Ecrivain** (*see p109*), a fine place for a restorative (if somewhat pricey) meal. Then walk up to the junction with Fitzwilliam Street and turn left, taking in the view of the hills in the distance. Head for the hills and you'll end up, after just a few minutes' walk, back where you started, at Fitzwilliam Square.

nudes were covered up. Juno's curves are still hidden by a rough costume although other figures have been returned to their natural state. The house contains the famous Apollo Room, with lavish panels depicting Apollo and the Muses, and a magnificent saloon where allegories promoting prudent economy and government are framed by rococo shells and foliage. No.86 was begun in 1765 by Richard Whaley, father of notorious gambler Buck, and was later bought by the university. Head to the top of the house via the back stairs to see Gerard Manley Hopkins's spartan bedroom and study, which has been carefully preserved. Recent restoration work has improved the hall, stairs and landing at No.86.

Newman University Church

87A St Stephen's Green South (478 0616/www. universitychurch.ie). All cross-city buses/Luas St Stephens Green. **Open** 9am-5pm Mon-Fri; 9am-5.30pm Sat; 9.30am-4pm Sun. **Admission** free. **Map** p251 F5.

This church was UCD's answer to Trinity College. Now a favourite setting for society weddings, its opulent, neo-Byzantine interior found little favour when it was completed in 1856, but its impressively extravagant decor now makes it one of Dublin's most fashionable churches.

Merrion Square & around

Between St Stephen's Green and Ballsbridge is the well-preserved heart of Georgian Dublin, the wealthiest quarter of the inner city (*see p73* **Walk Georgian Dublin**). Loaded with shops, cafés and restaurants, Baggot Street is the district's main artery. The area around elegant **Merrion Square** (where a list of the former residents reads like a *Who's Who* of 19th-century Ireland) is arguably the prettiest. This is the most architecturally and culturally significant square in the district, and it seems as if every inch of space has been used for something beautiful. On its western edge is the back entrance to **Leinster House** (*see p63*), home of the Irish Parliament, flanked by the **National Gallery of Ireland** (*see p75*) and the fascinating **Natural History Museum**

Key notes Wolfe Tone

Despite his reputation as one of the leading figures of the independence movement, Theobald Wolfe Tone (to give him his full name) was in some ways an unlikely revolutionary. Born just behind Dublin Castle in St Bride's Street in 1763, he had a privileged upbringing among Dublin's Protestant elite: he was educated at Trinity College before studying law in London, and was called to the Irish bar in 1789.

As a student Tone was influenced by the radical political climate sweeping across Europe at the time (culminating, the year he became a lawyer, in the French Revolution). In the early 1790s he published a very influential series of pamphlets and essays that criticised the British-controlled administration in Dublin, and argued the need for unity across the religious divide in the independence movement. In 1791, he helped to form the United Irishmen, a political union of Catholics and Protestants.

Despite Tone's passionate advocacy for an Irish republic, the aims of the society were initially confined to parliamentary reform. When it became obvious that this would be impossible by peaceful means, the objective shifted towards armed rebellion. The society was outlawed by the British in 1794, and Tone fled to America, hoping to find support for his democratic ideals there.

But he was to be disappointed. Although he wrote in praise of the Bill of Rights, he found the young nation possessed with an 'abominable selfishness of spirit' and its people 'a churlish, unsocial race'.

Disgruntled, he set out for France in 1796. There he had better luck, as the French government offered military support for an invasion of Ireland. A force of 15,000 French soldiers set off on 15 December, but the invasion was a disaster (*see p15*). Undaunted, Tone tried to whip up support for a second attempt. When rebellion broke out in Kilkenny in 1798, the French sent a few small raiding parties to assist. This went even worse than the first attempt, and Tone was among a shipload of French soldiers intercepted by the British at Lough Swilly, County Donegal. As he was wearing the full uniform of a French adjutant-general at the time, he could hardly plead not guilty.

Like all the best heroes, Tone met with a grisly end: convicted of treason, he did not wait for the gallows, but slit his own throat with a penknife in jail. Like his stabs at invading Ireland, though, this suicide went wrong. Rather than cutting the jugular vein, he severed his windpipe, leading to a slow and agonising death eight days later. His last words are reputed to have been: 'I find I am but a bad anatomist.'

(*see p76*). It all used to look very different, as until a few years ago the Leinster Lawn ran from the road up to Leinster House, but the grass was ripped up to make way for a 'temporary' car park that is now beginning to look unpleasantly permanent. But the space is still adorned with an obelisk dedicated to the founders of the Irish Free State – Michael Collins, Arthur Griffith and Kevin O'Higgins.

Next door to the Natural History Museum is another entrance to the Parliament complex. It's quite the grandest entrance, too, although someone has saddled it with the spectacularly dull label 'Government Buildings'. This part of the complex is the last word in Edwardian bombastic opulence; once part of University College Dublin, it was neglected for years before being restored and occupied by the government in the 1990s. Its interior is just as lavish as its gleaming façade, although you'll have to take our word for that, as public tours have been suspended.

The rest of Merrion Square is occupied by offices and organisations, with small oval plaques recounting the names of each house's famous former occupants: on Merrion Square South: WB Yeats at No.82, the poet and mystic George (Æ) Russell at No.84; the horror writer Joseph Sheridan Le Fanu at No.70; and Erwin Schrödinger, co-winner of the 1933 Nobel Prize for Physics, at No.65. The hero of Catholic Emancipation Daniel O'Connell lived at No.58 – look for the plaque reading 'The Liberator'. Elsewhere around the square is the Duke of Wellington's birthplace at No.24 and the site of the British Embassy at 39 Merrion Square East – the embassy was burned down by protestors in 1972 in protest at the actions of the British army in Derry on Bloody Sunday.

The square itself has beautifully tended formal gardens, which seem labyrinthine until you get to the open space at the centre. For many years the Catholic Church planned to build a cathedral here; in fact, these plans were abandoned only in the 1970s. The square is sprinkled with art: at the southern end is a bust of Michael Collins, while at the north-western corner the figure of Oscar Wilde sprawls in multicoloured loucheness atop a rough rock and is surrounded by his favourite *bons mots*, scrawled as graffiti on two translucent columns. Perhaps inevitably, this memorial has been dubbed the 'fag on the crag'. Wilde's statue looks over at his old home at 1 Merrion Square North (now the **Oscar Wilde House**, *see p76*).

The stretch from Merrion Square East to Fitzwilliam Square was the longest unbroken line of Georgian houses in the world until 1961, when the Electricity Supply Board knocked down a row of them – 26 in all – to build a

The **Oscar Wilde House**. *See p76*.

hideous new building that mars the area's symmetry to this day. This architectural travesty was typical of local planning decisions in the 20th century: most of Dublin's finest houses were built by the British, and the developing Irish state showed a marked lack of respect for the city's colonial architecture. Only in recent years have efforts been made to protect the architectural heritage. In partial recompense for the destruction it caused, ESB tarted up **Number Twenty-Nine** (*see p76*), restoring it as a nice Georgian townhouse museum, kitted out with all the latest in circa-1800 household fashion.

Just down Fitzwilliam Street from Merrion Square, **Fitzwilliam Square** is the smallest, most discreet and most residential of the city's Georgian squares. Completed in 1825, it's an immensely charming space – even though, unfortunately, only residents have access to its lovely central garden. That square leads on to Leeson Street, a wide, long thoroughfare that slopes down to the Grand Canal.

National Gallery of Ireland

Merrion Square West (661 5133/www.national gallery.ie). Bus 5, 6, 7, 7A, 10, 44, 47, 48/DART Pearse. **Open** 9.30am-5.30pm Mon-Wed, Fri, Sat;

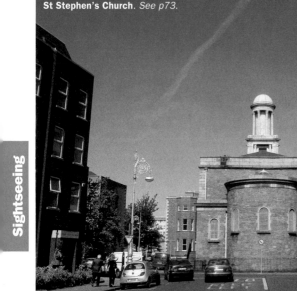

St Stephen's Church. *See p73.*

9.30am-8pm Thur; noon-5.15pm Sun. **Admission** free; donations welcome. **Map** p251 G4.

This gallery houses a small but fine collection of European works from the 14th to the 20th centuries, including paintings by Caravaggio, Tintoretto, Titian, Monet, Degas, Goya, Vermeer and Picasso. A room is also devoted to painter Jack Yeats, who developed an impressionistic style particularly suited to the Irish landscape. Look out, too, for works by Paul Henry, Roderic O'Conor, William Orpen, Nathaniel Hone and Walter Osborne. The smaller British collection is also impressive, with works by Hogarth, Landseer and Gainsborough, and every January an exhibition of Turner's watercolours draws art lovers from all over the world. The gallery's fabulous Millennium Wing has been a big draw since its opening; it provides a new entrance on Clare Street, light-drenched galleries, and the obligatory – albeit lovely – restaurant, café and gift shop. Regular changing exhibitions range in subject from Samuel Beckett's interest in fine art to the history of printmaking.

Natural History Museum

Merrion Street Upper (677 7444/www.museum.ie/ naturalhistory). Bus 7, 7A, 44, 48/Dublin City Hop On, Hop Off bus tour stop/DART Pearse. **Open** 10am-5pm Tue-Sat; 2-5pm Sun. **Admission** free. **Map** p251 G4.

Little changed since its foundation in 1857, this excellent museum owes much to the Victorian obses-

sion with exploring and collecting. It's packed with skeletons, fossils and stuffed and pickled animals from all over the world. Ireland's native wildlife is well represented, including animals extinct millennia before humans walked the land. All in all, the museum seems designed to send a tingle of delicious horror up the spine.

Number Twenty-Nine

29 Fitzwilliam Street Lower (702 6165/www.esb.ie/ numbertwentynine). Bus 6, 7, 10, 45/DART Grand Canal Dock. **Open** 10am-5pm Tue-Sat; 2-5pm Sun. **Admission** *Guided tours* €4.50; €2.50 concessions; free under-16s. **Credit** MC, V. **Map** p251 H4.

This restored 18th-century merchant house is presented as a middle-class dwelling circa 1790-1820. It stands proudly on the corner of one of the most elegant vistas in Dublin, a long neo-classical perspective stretching from Merrion Square West down Mount Street to the Pepper Canister Church (*see p73* **Walk Georgian Dublin** and *photo above*). From furniture – comfortable rather than opulent – and paintings through to toys and personal effects, the interior of this property is a treasure trove of Georgian style.

Oscar Wilde House

American College Dublin, 1 Merrion Square (676 8939/www.amcd.ie/oscar). All cross-city buses. **Open** *Guided tours* 10.15am, 11.15am Mon, Wed, Thur. **Admission** €2.50. **No credit cards.** **Map** p251 G4.

Sightseeing

At the time of writing, a programme of major refurbishment work was about to begin on this elegant Georgian house, so call ahead for details of when the property will be open again to tourists. Wilde lived here until 1876, and more than a century later the building was taken over by the American College Dublin, which has restored the ground and first floors of the house, including the surgery and Lady Speranza's drawing room. These are now open to the public by guided tour. The nominal admission fee goes towards the restoration and upkeep of the house. **Photo** *p75*.

Grand Canal & South Docks

Both Baggot Street and Leeson Street lead from St Stephen's Green down to the Grand Canal a short distance away. The canal meanders gently around the city to the south, eventually flowing into the Canal Basin in the old industrial zone of Ringsend before joining the Liffey at the south docks. Built between 1756 and 1796, it was the longest canal in Britain and Ireland, stretching from Shannon Harbour in Offaly to Dublin Bay. It has not been used commercially since 1960, and nowadays its grassy banks are a focal point for walkers, cyclists and, in summer, swimmers, who rather unwisely take to the water when the locks are full. In the winter months, great phalanxes of swans take shelter on the water and along the banks.

In recent years, the Grand Canal towpaths have been repaired along the most pleasant stretch of the canal, which runs from Grand Canal Street up to Harold's Cross Bridge, and an entirely new bridge has been constructed close to Ranelagh Bridge for the Luas tram service to run across.

The area is best explored in a walk that takes in the poignant **Jewish Museum** (*see below*), which recounts the often-neglected history of the Jews in Ireland, as well as the **birthplace of George Bernard Shaw** (*see below*), which does the man proud.

Sadly, for those who are really entranced by the canals, the Waterways Visitor Centre (which used to tell you all that you ever wanted to know about them) is now closed for good, so your only option now is to head straight over to the **Grand Canal Docks**. For centuries this area, where the Grand Canal and the Liffey join up at the bay, was the economic powerhouse that made Dublin's economy was it was. But when the economic focus shifted to mechanised, container-driven ports, this area inevitably fell by the wayside. For years, Dublin's docklands were among the most deprived areas in the city. Today, though, things are looking up, as office buildings are

beginning to line the water's edge, and developers are cracking their knuckles as they prepare to take this area on.

Already from the Financial Services Centre adjoining the Custom House east towards the bay, lots of posh new apartments are opening up, along with glittering bars and sunny cafés. Here Dublin becomes a magical city: sunshine glints on the water and bright young things sip espressos while they think of their bulging bank accounts… except at weekends, when the workers go home to the suburbs and this part of town can become disturbingly quiet.

Jewish Museum
3 Walworth Road, Portobello (450 1857 for appointments 490 1857). Bus 16, 16A, 19, 19A, 22, 22A. **Open** *May-Sept* 11am-3.30pm Tue, Thur, Sun. *Oct-Apr* 10.30am-2.30pm Sun. **Admission** free. **Map** p250 D6.
This collection of documents and artefacts relating to the Jewish community of Ireland includes a reconstruction of a late 19th-century kitchen typical of a Jewish home in the neighbourhood and, upstairs, a synagogue preserved with ritual fittings. The exhibition tells about events such as the pogroms against the Jews of Limerick in the 1920s. The museum is well arranged and has moving displays: among its exhibits is a letter, dated 1938, from the Irish Chief Rabbi to De Valera asking for six highly educated Jewish refugees (mostly doctors) to be admitted, and its almost casual rejection.

National Print Museum
Garrison Chapel, Beggars Bush, Haddington Road (660 3770/www.iol.ie/~npmuseum). Bus 5, 7, 7A, 45, 63/DART Grand Canal Dock. **Open** 10am-5pm Mon-Fri; noon-5pm Sat, Sun. **Admission** €3.50; €2 concessions; €7 family. **No credit cards**.
Surprisingly enough, this display of printing equipment isn't boring, and that is a feat in itself. The Beggars Bush building was originally a barracks, and the central garrison houses the Irish Labour History Museum, filled with documents relating to labour and industrial history. The guided tours are entertaining and informative. Recent additions to the collection include a fascinating Bookbinders' Union banner bearing the legend: 'Bind right with might'. Enough said.

Shaw's Birthplace
33 Synge Street, Portobello (475 0854/www.visit dublin.com). Bus 16, 16A, 19, 19A, 122. **Open** *May-Sept* 10am-1pm, 2-5pm Mon, Tue, Thur, Fri; 2-5pm Sat, Sun. **Admission** €6.70; €4.20-€5.70 concessions; €19 family. **No credit cards**. **Map** p251 E5.
On the plaque outside this neat Victorian house, Shaw is commemorated simply – some might say tersely – as 'author of many plays'. The house is a good example of a Victorian middle-class home, but those who aren't Shaw (or Victoriana) enthusiasts might find it all slightly tedious.

O'Connell Street & Around

Cultured and multicultural, the OC has come a long way.

In the famous brag of the 19th-century comedy Irishman: 'O'Connell Street's the widest street in the world'; even today, a few Irish websites still confidently claim it's the widest in Europe. In a city as small as Dublin, O'Connell Street is indeed wide – 46 metres (150 feet) – and its buildings are tall (for Dublin). It's the most imposing thoroughfare in the city and, though it doesn't hold the parliament, also tends to be the focal point of every political rally (see p17 **Boiling point**). But until recently it was going to seed, it had become a lucrative beat for petty criminals and junkies, its pavements mired in litter, half its fine buildings leased to burger joints, the other half knocked down.

Now all that has changed. Police (garda) patrol tirelessly, and the whole street has been placed under special planning and conservation control. Recent developments include the widening of footpaths, the removal of the old London plane trees and the planting of 200 new trees of various species, the restoration of monuments, the creation of a plaza in front of the **General Post Office** (or GPO, see p80) and, of course, the **Spire** (more commonly known as the Spike, *photo below*). All this was done to the usual barrage of criticism (people

hated the Spire, loved the old plane trees), but as the street's now looking leafy, prosperous, more pedestrianised, much tidier (litter vans trawl assiduously) – in short, much more like the main street of one of Europe's richest countries – the naysayers have quietened down.

The streets radiating off O'Connell are a cheerful, energetic mix of British high-street brands and ethnic stores (look carefully and you'll find *Hello* magazine in Russian). By the time you get to Parnell Street at the top, you're in Chinatown (see p80 **Chinatown**). Despite its chi-chi renovation, though, O'Connell Street remains a working-class hub.

O'Connell Street

O'Connell Street has its origins in the 17th-century Drogheda Street: laid out by the Earl of Drogheda, it was originally a third of the width of the current street and three-quarters as long. It was widened and lengthened in the 18th century, first by Ireland's foremost builder and millionaire, Luke Gardiner (who gave his name to Gardiner Street), and after his death by the Wide Streets Commission. On its completion in the 1790s, Sackville Street (as it was renamed) was one of the finest in Europe; Carlisle Bridge (now O'Connell Bridge) linked it to College Green and Westmoreland Street, and the whole area prospered as the city's commercial centre.

The street was such a focal point that in 1916 it was made HQ of the Easter Rising (see p16), during which many buildings were reduced to rubble. In the summer of 1922 it was the scene of fighting again, when the civil war broke out (see p19). This time it was the northern end that suffered: an entire terrace from Cathedral Street to Parnell Square was destroyed. In 1924, with the civil war now over, it was renamed O'Connell Street, and there's been no fighting since – although rallies (especially those orchestrated by Sinn Fein) still congregate outside the GPO.

It's a street of (mostly political) statues, bounded top and bottom by sculptures of Ireland's two great constitutional nationalists – Daniel O'Connell (see p82 **Key notes**) and

The **Spire**.

Charles Stewart Parnell. O'Connell's statue is the gateway to the street. Designed and built, through public subscription in the 1870s by John Henry Foley (who died before its completion), it's an imposing bronze monument of the Liberator flanked by four winged Victories. Slap-bang in the nipple of one is a bullet hole, sustained during the Easter Rising. This must have incensed the ghost of O'Connell who, in life, famously declared: 'Irish freedom is not worth the shedding of one drop of blood.'

The whole centre median of the street, lined with trees, is like an outdoor art gallery. Among the permanent statues are those to Father Mathew (the temperance apostle who, incredible to relate, had between three and four million people abstaining from drink in 1840) and Oisin Kelly's fine, vigorous statue of the great trade unionist Jim Larkin throwing his arms out wide in an explosion of energy. Other statues form temporary exhibitions – in summer 2006 Barry Flanagan's hares were leaping around madly.

The centrepiece is the **Spire** (*photo p78*), built in 2003, an enormous stainless steel shard that jabs 120 metres (396 feet) into the sky. Its nickname ('the stiletto in the ghetto') is largely one for the tourists, just as the 'floozy in the Jacuzzi' moniker for the particularly foul 1980s Joycean statue (now removed) was only used by cab drivers and tour guides. The Spire replaces Nelson's column – a pillar topped with a statue of Admiral Nelson (the twin of Trafalgar Square's) – which was blown up by the IRA in 1966, on the 50th anniversary of the Easter Rising. At first the Spire's design was bitterly opposed, but it seems to have won the city's affection (easy to see why when approaching from Henry Street on a sunny day).

The grey, columned building behind the Spire is the GPO, probably the most famous building in 20th-century Ireland. On these steps, on Easter Monday 1916, Patrick Pearse read his proclamation for a free Irish Republic: 'In every generation, the Irish people have asserted their right to national freedom and sovereignty; six times during the past 300 years, they have asserted it in arms.' He was killed by a firing squad nine days later, but five years on, Ireland was independent. Pass by today, and you'll likely find some lone socialist workers voicing protests on the newly created plaza in front of it.

The grand department store across the street from the GPO is Dublin's beloved **Clery's** (*see p138*), formerly the Imperial Hotel. Clery's balcony was the position from which Jim Larkin made a stirring speech to his supporters during the general strike in 1913. On the corner here is O'Connell Street's lone literary statue – Joyce, of course, leaning on a stick, looking (if you didn't know him) vaguely like Charlie Chaplin.

Turn into Cathedral Street, one road up, and you get to **St Mary's Pro Cathedral**, Dublin's main Catholic church, built in classical style in 1815. For a city with (give or take) 90 per cent devout church-going Catholics, it's a modest cathedral indeed, especially compared to the imposing Christ Church and St Patrick's, both of which cater to Dublin's tiny Anglican community. But after independence, both churches were careful to keep relations cordial, and Catholic bishops seem perfectly happy with the Pro Cathedral, which has seen numerous large funerals, including that of O'Connell in 1847.

Back to O'Connell Street, and the big, grand building at the top is the **Gresham Hotel** (*see p50*), which played a part in the Easter Rising many fled here to seek refuge from the battle. Apparently, the rebel leader Michael Collins evaded capture during the war of independence by hiding out here on Christmas Eve 1920. Today you can get delicious (if highly priced) afternoon tea in the lovely, old-world lobby.

Besides statues, hotels and fast-food joints (still much in evidence, though reduced), the O'Connell Street area is strong on theatres and cinemas. It's marked top and bottom by the city's two leadin theatres: the Abbey and the Gate.

The **Abbey Theatre** (*see p191*), on Abbey Street, was founded in 1904 by WB Yeats and Lady Gregory. It's Ireland's national theatre, and though it's never recaptured the glorious controversy of its opening productions, it has seen more than its share of controversy down the years, most recently with the 2005 resignation of both the artistic and managing directors. The original building was destroyed by fire in 1951; the current one, opened in 1966, is not considered one of renowned architect Michael Scott's best, and in December 2005, the government okayed a plan to move the theatre to George's Dock. This decision came after years of debate, so it may not be the very last word on where the Abbey should go. In the same building is the smaller, more avant-garde and less commercial **Peacock Theatre** (*see p191*), where you'll find more daring contemporary productions.

The **Gate Theatre** (*see p191*) stands at the other end of O'Connell Street, on the corner of Frederick and Parnell streets. It has the most elegant, best-proportioned stage in Dublin, and its antecedents are as honourable and radical as the Abbey's – it was founded in 1929 by the remarkable, flamboyant British homosexual duo, Hilton Edwards and Michael McLiammoir – and for the past five years or more, it has been winning the battle of the plays hands down, attracting world-class performers in world-class productions. The 2006 Beckett season brought the rare but comforting sight of people queuing for returns at its 18th-century doors.

At the top of O'Connell Street, beside the Gresham, the **Savoy** cinema (*see p163*) faces the old Carlton cinema. Built in 1928 as a Venetian-style theatre, then made over as 1970s kitsch, the Savoy is now, post-renovation, blandly comfortable and vacuously timeless. The Carlton has been shut for years. Though you'd hardly guess from its parlous condition, it's one of the city's most important post-Independence buildings and a rare Dublin instance of art deco design. It's boarded up, and renovation is delayed until 2012, but the O'Connell Street facelift won't be complete without it.

Until you get to Parnell Street (*see below* **Chinatown**), Abbey Street is also your best bet for a drink – the **Flowing Tide** (*see p133*) is a solid Dublin pub, frequented by locals and thespians, and everyone has a soft spot for the bar in Wynn's Hotel, so much snugger than O'Connell Street's other hotels.

General Post Office

O'Connell Street (705 7000/www.anpost.ie). All cross-city buses. **Open** 8am-8pm Mon-Sat. **Admission** free. **Map** p251 F2.
Best known as the site of the Easter Rising in 1916, the GPO remains a potent symbol of Irish independence. Designed by Francis Johnston in 1818, it was almost completely destroyed by fire during the uprising, and had barely been restored six years later when the civil war did further damage to the building. These days, the restored interior is spacious and filled with light from the street, and most of the features and fittings have been respectfully preserved. There are still bullet holes in the walls

and columns out front, and a series of paintings inside depicts moments from the Easter Rising. In a window, and visible from the outside, is the beautiful *Death of Cúchulainn*, a statue by Oliver Sheppard commemorating the building's reopening in 1929. Cúchulainn, the legendary knight of the Red Branch, is used as a symbol by both Loyalist and Republican paramilitary groups. Such terror did Cúchulainn inspire in his enemies that, even after they had succeeded in killing him, no one dared approach his body until ravens landed on his shoulders. In his poem *The Statues*, Yeats writes of how Patrick Pearse used Cúchulainn to romanticise the Irish struggle: 'When Pearse summoned Cúchulainn to his side/What stalked through the Post Office?'

Parnell Square

O'Connell Street is bookended by the bustling, multicultural Parnell Street (*see p90* **Chinatown**) and the grey and sombre **Parnell Square**, a large Georgian square made up of museums, public buildings and one very good restaurant. The imposing **Rotunda Hospital** takes up the south side of the square. Founded in 1745 by Dr Bartholomew Mosse as Europe's first maternity hospital, it has occupied its current site since 1757 in a building designed by Richard Castle, architect of Leinster House (*see p63*).

On the north side of the square, the **Garden of Remembrance** was opened on the 50th anniversary of the Easter Rising to honour those who died for Irish freedom. The garden is dominated by Oisin Kelly's huge, beautiful

Chinatown

Nowhere showcases Dublin's recent immigrant explosion quite like Parnell Street. Formerly a straggling, grey strip of down-at-heel bars and pound shops, it's been transformed into Dublin's Chinatown, or Koreatown – with a dash of Little Poland (*see also p186* **Pole acts**). Every second building on Parnell Street – and, for that matter, much of Moore Street – houses a Chinese or Korean restaurant, and nowhere in the city can you eat this well at this price. Chinese restaurants in Dublin used to be heavy, sombre, carpeted institutions, where punters paid a lot for food delivered with the decorous solemnity and creeping pace of dinner at Versailles; now, though, hordes of eager diners cram into these cheerful canteens, and freshly cooked dishes emerge swiftly from the kitchen. Most European capitals know this scene already, but it's all new to

Dublin: just when it was beginning to seem as if all good deals in this city began and ended with Ryanair, finally there's the chance of getting a delicious meals for under €10.

One Irish institution holds out on this street of world cultures, but barely. The Welcome Inn pub (corner of Parnell and Marlborough streets, 874 3227) is one of the few remaining perfect examples of 1970s architecture in the city. Go inside to be reminded of your own, your parents' or your grandparents' old wallpaper. It also plays fantastic music, and has a uniquely melancholic, friendly, twilight atmosphere – not to mention eccentric, irascible barmen. However, it's dying by inches and now opens only sporadically. It's like playing roulette on long odds – maybe every seventh try you'll find it open, but it's always worth a go (Sunday evening is probably the best bet).

sculpture of the *Children of Lir* – an enactment of an ancient Irish legend, in which four children are turned into swans by their evil stepmother.

Opposite the garden is the **Municipal Gallery of Modern Art**, also known as the Hugh Lane Gallery (*see below*), housed in the neo-classical Charlemont House. Re-opened in May 2006 after much renovation, it hosts on three floors its permanent collection of French and Irish Impressionist art, alongside changing exhibitions and Francis Bacon's London studio, which is reproduced in the gallery.

Next door to the gallery, the **Dublin Writers' Museum** (*see p82*) has an excellent collection of letters, memorabilia, photos and equipment from the city's many famous writers, and adjoins the Irish Writers' Centre, which hosts lectures, readings and literary receptions, and serves as a resource for those researching Irish literature. Recuperation from literary and artistic endeavours is provided by the excellent restaurant **Chapter One** (*see p115*) in the museum's vaulted basement.

If the Writers' Museum and Centre don't slake your literary thirst, make your way to nearby North Great George's Street, where the **James Joyce Centre** (*see p82*) dedicates itself to the eponymous giant of Irish letters. North Great George's Street is a fine street of Georgian houses, on a wonderfully steep slope. Sinead O'Connor lived here briefly, and Senator David Norris – who has the distinction of having decriminalized homosexuality in Ireland (after taking the case to the European Court of Justice in 1988) – still does. A noted Joycean, Norris was also responsible for founding the Centre. The stylish **Cobalt Café & Gallery** (*see p121*), at No.16, is an arty hangout that hosts occasional cabaret nights.

Dublin Writers' Museum

18-19 Parnell Square (872 2077/www.writers museum.com). Bus 3, 10, 11, 13, 16, 19, 22. **Open** *Sept-May* 10am-5pm Mon-Sat; 11am-5pm Sun. *June-Aug* 10am-6pm Mon-Fri; 10am-5pm Sat; 11am-5pm Sun. **Admission** €6.25; €3.75-€5.25 concessions; €17.50 family. **Credit** AmEx, MC, V. **Map** p251 E1.
It can be hard to showcase the real achievements of writers, but this small, jam-packed exhibit space does pretty well, featuring unique and well-chosen memorabilia from Swift, Wilde, Yeats, Joyce, Beckett and others. It features some unusual and intriguing artefacts, such as the phone from Beckett's Paris apartment, and playbills from the Abbey Theatre's early days. There's a great display on Brendan Behan, including a long letter he wrote from California to a friend back home in Dublin, after he made it big. He wrote of a party he'd attended with Groucho and Harpo Marx, adding, 'It was in the papers all over, but I don't suppose the Dublin papers had it. They only seem to know when I'm in jail or dying.' There's

Parnell Square, looking south.

a good café downstairs that always seems to be jammed with Italian schoolkids, and a bookstore that could use more literary memorabilia.

Hugh Lane Gallery (Municipal Gallery of Modern Art)

Parnell Square North (874 1903/www.hughlane.ie). Bus 3, 10, 11, 13, 16, 19, 22. **Open** 9.30am-6pm Tue-Thur; 9.30am-5pm Fri, Sat; 11am-5pm Sun. **Admission** *Gallery* free. *Francis Bacon Studio* €7; €3.50 concessions; free under-18s. Half-price to all 9.30am-12.30pm Tue. **Credit** MC, V. **Map** p251 E1.
The Municipal Gallery is named after Hugh Lane, nephew of Yeats's friend Lady Gregory and noted art patron who determined to leave his fine collection of French and Irish Impressionist art to the city (provided a suitable gallery was built to house it). Despite a number of vituperative poems from Yeats, Dublin Corporation did not come up with a gallery, forcing Lane to bequeath his pictures to London. At the eleventh hour he stipulated that Dublin could have them if they provided a gallery, but this codicil to his will was unwitnessed when he went down with the other passengers on the *Lusitania*, torpedoed by a German U-boat in 1915. London stuck to the letter of the law for decades, but the matter was recently settled in Irish favour (though a number of the paintings still rotate between Dublin and London).

After extensive renovations, the gallery reopened in May 2006 and now uses the full three floors. Lane's collection of Manets, Coubets and Renoirs is on the ground floor (but don't miss Irish artists Walter Osbourne and Roderic O'Conor), as are Harry Clarke's marvellous stained-glass windows, and Francis Bacon's London studio, which, in a Herculean feat of excavation, was moved piece by piece from 7 Reese

Key notes Daniel O'Connell

Daniel O'Connell's reputation can be measured by the sobriquets he acquired during his eventful spell in public life. Known variously as the Liberator and the Uncrowned King of Ireland, the politician, orator and pacifist O'Connell is famous for the belief, as he put it, that 'freedom is not worth the shedding of one drop of blood'.

Born in 1775 in County Kerry, O'Connell was part of an aristocratic Catholic family. He studied law in London from 1794 to 1796, and it was around this time that he developed an interest in the politics of Thomas Paine and Jeremy Bentham, whose radical ideas about democracy and religious tolerance struck a chord with the young man. He joined Wolfe Tone's Society of United Irishmen but was bitterly opposed to the rebellion of 1798, arguing that independence would be better achieved by political means. This was part of the reason for his withdrawal from politics over the following decade.

By the end of the 1810s, though, O'Connell was once more active in the Catholic emancipation movement and was seen by many as the natural leader of the cause. He was a founder member of the Catholic Association, which campaigned for constitutional and economic reform, particularly the repeal of the 1801 Act of Union (which officially joined Ireland to Great Britain to create the United Kingdom).

In 1828 O'Connell was elected to the British Parliament, but he was prevented by anti-Catholic legislation from actually serving as an MP. A year later, though, the government passed the Catholic Emancipation Act, allowing him to take his rightful seat in the House of Commons.

Finally able to influence policy, O'Connell became a major political player, championing causes like universal suffrage, free trade and the abolition of slavery. In 1841 he became the first Catholic Lord Mayor of Dublin.

Renewing his opposition to the Act of Union, he organised a series of mass demonstrations (known as 'monster meetings') across the country. Despite his prophetic warnings that, if ignored, the situation would lead to civil war, he won little support for the cause in Britain. Daniel O'Connell died in Genoa while on a pilgrimage to Rome in 1847, and is buried in Dublin's Glasnevin Cemetery.

Mews and reconstructed here behind glass. Visitors gape at its half-completed canvases, dirty paint-brushes, bottles of booze, books, dust, magazines and sublime filth. Bacon was born in Dublin and brought up in Wicklow. He left at the age of 16 and, ever after, even the thought of Ireland induced a panic attack, but perhaps he retained some affection for it since his heir, John Edwards, bequeathed the studio to the Hugh Lane, where it's become a major attraction. The gallery has also upped its collection of paintings by Bacon. New since the renovation is a Sean Scully Room – the only space in Ireland dedicated to this major Irish-American contemporary artist.

James Joyce Centre

35 North Great George's Street (878 8547/www.jamesjoyce.ie). Bus 3, 10, 11, 11A, 13, 16, 16A, 19, 19A, 22. **Open** 9.30am-5pm Mon-Sat; noon-5pm Sun. **Admission** €5; €4 concessions; free under-14s. **Credit** AmEx, MC, V. **Map** p251 F1.

Joyce never lived here, nor did Leopold Bloom, though a minor character in *Ulysses* – Denis Maginni – held dance classes here (but then in what building in central Dublin did a minor character in *Ulysses* not do *something* in?). How it came to be the Joyce Centre is that Senator David Norris noticed in the mid 1980s that this beautiful house was decaying, so, deciding to combine his obsession with Joyce

with his obsession with Georgian architecture, he created a trust. The house took 14 years to renovate but, through careful adherence to old photos, it now looks just as it did in 1904, when Maginni would have been holding his dance classes – the ceiling on the first floor is one of the finest in Dublin. After being run haphazardly by Joyce's nephew, the centre is now under new management and has gained greater focus. The top floor has a recreation of Joyce's room in Zurich and a touch-screen history of the publication of *Ulysses*, while the terrace holds the door of 7 Eccles Street (Bloom's house), saved from the Mater Hospital's extension in Eccles Street.

National Wax Museum

Granby Row, Parnell Square (872 6340). Bus 3, 10, 11, 13, 16, 19, 22. **Open** 10am-5.30pm Mon-Sat; noon-5.30pm Sun. **Admission** €7; €5-€6 concessions; €20 family. **No credit cards**. **Map** p251 E1.

Surely you know the drill by now – this is your basic Dublin in wax, with figures that stretch beyond the Irish borders to juxtapose subjects like Eamon De Valera with Snow White, Bart Simpson, Elvis and U2. It's probably most enjoyable for small children or those with an exaggerated appreciation of kitsch (the museum does feature some genuine oddities, not least a life-size wax replica of the *Last Supper*).

The North Quays & Around

Down by the riverside.

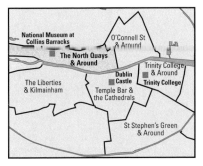

National Museum at
Collins Barracks

O'Connell St
& Around

The North Quays
& Around

Trinity College
& Around

Dublin
Castle

Trinity College

The Liberties
& Kilmainham

Temple Bar &
the Cathedrals

St Stephen's Green
& Around

The North Quays is the general name for the street that runs along the northern embankment of the Liffey. The street's actual name changes every block or so – Eden Quay, Bachelor's Walk, Ormond Quay, Inns Quay – throughout the mile-and-a-half long stretch of road. This residential area contains several markets, including the remnants of the fabled Smithfield horse-trading fair, and the city's biggest green space – Phoenix Park. It's busy, bustling and fascinating, and well worth your time.

East of O'Connell Street

After crossing the river on the O'Connell Bridge from the south side, take a sharp right along the river on to **Eden Quay**. You may be put off by the noise and fumes from the perpetual traffic jams, but music enthusiasts at least should persevere as far as 1 Eden Quay, where they will find Freebird Records in the basement of a newsagent's. This is where you'll find out about upcoming gigs, and the knowledgeable staff bring musical snobbery to *High Fidelity* heights – the contemptuous disbelief they will display at your purchases is a joy to behold, and trying to offload one's worst CDs here constitutes a popular local entertainment.

Glance up Marlborough Street to your left, and you will see both the historic **Abbey Theatre** – one of the city's most beloved and controversial theatres, whose productions once caused rioting in the streets, but now tend toward the mainstream – and the Flowing Tide bar, a mainstay of thespian Dublin, which some northsiders claim has the finest pint in the city. Dubliners tend to discuss the question of where to find the nicest stout with a dreamy intensity, while living by the motto that the best pint is the one within easy reach.

Crossing Marlborough Street, look for the **Liberty Hall Centre for Performing Arts**, which combines art with a social conscience. If this is your thing, check the adjacent ticket office to see what is coming up. On the corner is **Liberty Hall** itself, the heart of Dublin trade unionism since 1912, when it was acquired by charismatic Liverpudlian Jim Larkin and his newly formed Irish Trade and General Workers Union. Larkin became a folk hero with his stand against unfair working practices at a time when 'working on the docks' meant moving heavy objects on your back, as opposed to with the click of a computer mouse. In the early 20th

St Michan's Church. *See p86.*

Dublin Zoological Gardens. *See p88.*

century cargo ships were crucial to Dublin's economic well-being; thousands of dockers, coal carters and casual labourers were employed from the teeming tenements nearby. Dublin has often been characterised as a grand old dame, but one contemporary account described the slums as the 'suppurating ulcers covered by stinking rags under the hem of her dress'. The collapse of one tenement building led to the infamous 1913 lockout, which would become Larkin's greatest confrontation with the bosses. If you're interested in learning more, Joseph Plunkett's *Strumpet City* is an extremely readable account of the city in those times.

Beresford Place, to the left of Liberty Hall, leads to Gardiner Street, a prime example of the once-grand Georgian houses colonised by slum dwellers who lived in appalling conditions – sometimes up to 15 to a room. The street now provides considerably more salubrious accommodation to backpackers in its numerous guesthouses and hostels.

The riverside walk continues past the ugly Butt railway bridge. Just beyond it, the grand neo-classical building facing the river is the **Custom House** (*see p85*), a Dublin landmark designed by James Gandon in 1791. Its classical façade stretches for 114 metres (374 feet), with busts representing the gods of

Ireland's 14 major rivers decorating the portico. The green roof is of oxidised copper, and the extant foundations were wooden supports built on treacherous bog. One could be forgiven for seeing metaphors here for Dublin's new-found wealth, and an ideal place for such rumination is to be found on the riverbank in front of it. Benches here provide an unhindered view of the Liffey and of the new, vast and gleaming glass-fronted Ulster Bank complex across the river.

The next bridge east is Matt Talbot Bridge, named after a Dublin alcoholic who gave up the booze and wore a penitential hair shirt and chains for the rest of his days. Saint or lunatic? You decide. Here you could be in the financial district of any major international city. The glittering **International Financial Services Centre** dominates the waterfront in this area: the complex caters for 6,500 workers on any given day. At the water's edge, Rowan Gillespie's beautiful **famine sculpture** is hauntingly evocative of Ireland's tragic past, when starving emigrants poured from these docks into ships that became known as 'coffin ships' since so many passengers never made it to their destinations.

The docklands and basins that stretch east from the IFSC are slowly assuming a cosmopolitan and vibrant air. The many new

artisan dwellings stands, but a determined group of residents fought them, and ultimately stopped the whole project. There's a photogenic view from the bridge at the Point Depot, encompassing the sea in one direction and the Liffey bridges in the other. The depot itself is Ireland's biggest performance venue, and many famous names of rock and comedy have played here. Frankly, despite grandiose claims, it has the vibe of a function room at a trade show, though good acts usually overcome its dullness.

Custom House Visitor Centre

Custom House Quay (888 2375). DART Tara Street/bus 53A, 90A. **Open** *Mid March-Nov* 10am-12.30pm Mon-Fri; 2-5pm Sat, Sun. *Dec-mid March* 10am-12.30pm Mon-Fri. **Admission** €1; €3 family. **Map** p253 J4.

This centre offers access only to a small area of the building, which is worth it if you're fascinated by architecture, otherwise… hey, at least it's cheap. Displays and a video relate the history of the building, and if you enjoy them you should probably check for your pulse on the way out. Just kidding.

West of O'Connell Street

Turning left at the river after you cross O'Connell Bridge from the south, you find yourself on **Bachelor's Walk**. Its rather charming name dates back to the 18th century, when it was a favourite promenade of young men of the neighbourhood. This strip was once the centre of the city's antique and furniture trade, and such shops that remain are worth a browse.

On the wooden Liffey boardwalk here are three **Cruises Coffee Docks** – little huts manned by wonderfully grumpy staff selling coffee and sandwiches, which, weather permitting, you can enjoy alfresco on the long riverside benches.

After a few blocks, Bachelor's Walk becomes Ormand Quay Lower, and the oft-photographed **Ha'penny Bridge** stands there charmingly, waiting to be snapped. It dates to 1816 and was once a toll bridge (no prize for guessing how much it cost to cross). Once you've taken that photo, you could do worse than turn into the literary haven that is the Winding Stair (40 Ormond Quay Lower) – the best-loved of all of Dublin's many wonderful bookshops. If you'd rather get something to eat, take the turn at Liffey Street and visit Dublin's **Food Emporium** on the right – the *mollettes* in the tiny Mexican stall are gorgeous, as are the little French pastries in the adjacent stall. Back on Ormond Quay, that paragon of modern sleekness you see before you is the Morrison Hotel, where the combination of New York chic and Irish friendliness makes a perfect place for

apartment developments hereabouts are largely populated by young professionals. New shops, bars and restaurants appear constantly as the area's transformation continues. Many are part of international or national chains offering consistency rather than excellence, but the riverside D One restaurant, on North Wall Quay, is a fine place to stop for a meal.

On the water the **Jeanie Johnston famine ship** is a frail-looking replica of those ill-fated vessels. It sails the world as a kind of floating museum, and the crew are a cheery bunch who are filled with information.

If you want to get off your feet for a while, check out Mayor Street (behind the Clarion Hotel) and Excise Walk off North Wall Quay for good places to eat or drink. Depending on the time of year, a mobile cinema may also be parked here. A **farmers' market** is set up on Excise Walk Wall Quay every Wednesday from 11am to 3pm; you can stock up on local cheeses and gourmet treats, and make yourself a picnic to eat beside the river.

Along the river, an invigorating walk past cawing gulls, tall ships and navy boats brings you to the **Point Depot**, associated locally with tales of little old ladies outfoxing rampant capitalism. A few years back, there were plans to build tower blocks where the row of eight

Sightseeing

a posh cocktail, although be warned: the fatal combination of delicious drinks and luxuriant sofas might lure you away from sightseeing.

The slender and elegant bridge in front of the Morrison is the **Millennium Bridge**. Try to wander this way at night at some point, as it is strikingly lit.

Further down Lower Ormond Quay you'll pass the coffee shop **Panem**. It's a local treasure worth dropping into for coffee and for chef Ann Murphy's range of delicious soups and pastries.

The road now becomes Upper Ormond Quay. The rainbow flags flying outside Inn on the Liffey guesthouse and Out on the Liffey bar are a happy reminder that the days when Dublin's gay scene was underground are largely gone. Just before the Four Courts on Inns Quay is the **Chancery** bar, a popular 'early house', where the rough-and-ready pub life begins at 7am.

Like the Custom House, the original **Four Courts** building was designed in the 1790s by James Gandon – although it was substantially rebuilt after it was burned in the 1922 Civil War.The court building houses the Supreme and High Courts, and only the entrance hall beneath the great cupola is open to visitors. The courts have been at the centre of Dublin legal life for two centuries.

From here, turn down Church Street to visit **St Michan's Church** (*see below*), one of the oldest churches in the city. Bram Stoker always said that viewing the macabre mummified corpses in its crypt inspired *Dracula*. This is one of several churches rumoured to contain the unmarked grave of executed rebel Robert Emmet.

St Michan's Church

Church Street Lower (872 4154). Bus 25, 26, 37, 39, 67, 67A, 68, 69, 79. **Open** *Mid Mar-Oct* 10am-12.45pm, 2-4.30pm Mon-Fri; 10am-12.45pm Sat. *Nov-mid Mar* 12.30-3.30pm Mon-Fri; 10am-12.45pm Sat. **Admission** €3.50; €2.50-€3 concessions. **No credit cards. Map** p252 F4.

There has been a place of worship on this site since 1096, and the current building dates from 1686, though it was drastically restored in 1828 and again following the Civil War. Those with an interest in the macabre will love the 17th-century vaults composed of magnesium limestone, where mummified bodies – including a crusader, a nun and a suspected thief – have rested for centuries showing no signs of decomposition. You used to be able to touch one of the mummy's hands, and indeed sometimes still can if the guide is in a good mood. **Photo** *p83*.

Up to Smithfield

The road now becomes Arran Quay, and you can turn right at any point into the atmospheric **Smithfield** district. A cobbled marketplace in

the 17th century, it is now a warren of tiny Victorian streets that converge on the newly renovated Smithfield Square. This area redeems the reputation of the city's oft-maligned planning commission. The flickering light from the gas braziers adds historical authenticity to the square at night. At Christmas time it is filled with water and turned into an ice-skating rink, and there are markets here throughout the year. The monthly horse fair in Smithfield has largely been shifted to the suburbs over recent years, but it still breaks out on sporadic Sunday mornings. While you're here you can stop by the old **Cobblestone** (*see p134*) pub on North King Street (at the northern edge of the piazza) for a pint before climbing the **Smithfield Chimney** (*see below*), an observation tower at the top that offers panoramic views. There's also the **Old Jameson Distillery** (*see below*), but some say that it's a bit overrated.

Look out while on the east of the square for the Market Café, the epitome of the greasy spoon, which remains magnificently shabby despite the regeneration around it. The menu is written in marker pen on fluorescent paper and consists of breakfast, chips, or breakfast and chips, and the good thing is that you get to keep most of your money.

You might equally expect the Brown Bag Café on Coke Lane at the southern end of the square to be a place of seedy promise, but it is a perfectly respectable and reasonably priced sandwich bar. More upmarket fare can be found in Chief O'Neill's Hotel and the Kelly & Ping Asian restaurant. At night this is the new cool zone – the young and trendy should check out the **Voodoo Lounge** (*see p186*) and the **Dice Bar** (for both, *see p183*).

Old Jameson Distillery

Bow Street, Smithfield Village (872 5566/www. whiskeytours.ie). Bus 25, 26, 37, 39, 67, 67A, 68, 69, 79. **Open** 9am-6pm (last tour 5.15pm) daily. **Admission** (by guided tour only) €8.75; €7 concessions; €21 family. **Credit** AmEx, MC, V. **Map** p252 E4.

This museum is devoted to the five brand names of Irish distillers (Bushmills, Jameson, Paddy, Powers and Tullamore Dew), but it's a little short on substance. The guided tour and audiovisual presentation seem designed inter alia to tempt you to buy expensive bottles of whiskey. Still, the beautifully crafted model of distillery vessels and machines made for the 1924 World Exhibition are undeniably interesting. A tour includes a shot, but you could just as easily go to a pub.

Smithfield Chimney

Smithfield Village (817 3800/www.chiefoneills.com). Bus 25, 26, 37, 39, 67, 68, 69, 70. **Open** 10am-5pm daily. **Admission** €5; €2.50 concessions; €10 family. **Credit** AmEx, DC, MC, V. **Map** p252 E4.

The **Smithfield Chimney** has stacks of charm.

Once part of the Old Jameson Distillery, this 53m (175ft) chimney now functions as a 360-degree skyline observatory. An external glass elevator ascends to a two-tiered glass platform where you view the city, the surrounding countryside and Dublin Bay. **Photo** *p87*.

Towards Phoenix Park

Back along the river, the futuristic new suspension bridge at **Blackhall Place** was designed by Santiago Calatrava and opened in 2003. The balustrade curves down to a walkway of granite and toughened glass. In these downbeat surroundings, it is eerily postmodern, and spectacular at night.

If you head north along Blackhall Place, you arrive in **Stoneybatter**. This has some attractive pubs – notably the sensible **Walshes** at No.6, and the more raucous **Glimmerman** at No.7, in both of which Michael Collins was reputed to have hidden weapons. This area is what much of Dublin used to be like – that is to say, fairly edgy, fairly grim and fairly depressed – so if you find yourself here at night, avoid dark areas (there are quite a few) and be careful.

Back along the quays and a little further west from Blackhall Bridge is **Collins Barracks**, a branch of the splendid National Museum (*see below*). The fine renovated 17th-century building is the oldest military barracks in Europe, but these days it's put to rather more genteel use, housing the museum's decorative arts collection.

A short walk from the museum (follow Wolfe Tone Quay after it merges into Parkgate), the vast expanse of **Phoenix Park** sprawls for almost eight square kilometres (three square miles). The largest city park in Europe, it contains an invigorating blend of formal gardens, casual meadows, sports fields and wild undergrowth, as well as herds of roaming deer. Inside the park is the official residence of the Irish president, Aras an Uachtarain, a Palladian lodge that originally served as the seat of the Lord Lieutenant of Ireland.

The formal **People's Garden** opens the south-eastern entrance of the park, while across the road the huge **Wellington Monument** by Sir Robert Smirke stands guard. A short walk north-west of here, the much-improved **Dublin Zoological Gardens** (*see below*) lure you to their menagerie. Opposite the main entrance to the zoo is a lovely little wooden structure that serves excellent snacks and coffee. At the **Phoenix Monument** in the centre of the park, side roads and pathways will ultimately lead you to the **Visitors' Centre** (*see below*), the gracious 18th-century home of the American ambassador (not open to the public) and the towering **Papal Cross**, marking the spot where Pope John Paul II performed mass to the assembled multitudes during his 1979 visit.

If you don't feel up to walking back, leave by the North Circular Road entrance (at the top of Infirmary Road), and the number 10 bus will bring you back to O'Connell Street.

Dublin Zoological Gardens

Phoenix Park (677 1425/www.dublinzoo.ie). Bus 10, 25, 25A, 26, 51, 66, 67, 68, 69. **Open** *Mar-Sept* 9.30am-6pm Mon-Sat; 10.30am-6pm Sun. *Oct-Feb* 9.30am-4pm Mon-Sat; 10.30am-4pm Sun. **Admission** €13.50; €6.30-€11 concessions; €38-€47 family; free under-3s. **Credit** AmEx, DC, MC, V.

Dublin's animal house was founded in 1830, making it the third-oldest zoo in the world. It now houses 700 animals, including endangered snow leopards and golden lion tamarins. The place is run with children in mind, featuring a Pets' Corner, a Zoo Train, ample picnic facilities and play areas. But it's far from miniature in scale: the impressive African Plains is a 32-acre (13-hectare) expanse of pasture and woodland, home to (among many others) some splendid white rhinos. The zoo has received much investment in recent years and is in impressive shape. **Photos** *p84*.

National Museum of Ireland: Decorative Arts & History

Collins Barracks, Benburb Street (677 7444/www. museum.ie). Bus 25, 25A, 37, 39, 66, 67, 90, 172. **Open** 10am-5pm Tue-Sat; 2-5pm Sun. **Admission** free. **Map** p252 D4.

This branch of the National Museum of Ireland houses its collection of decoratives art. Of particular note are the extensive collections of Irish silverware and furniture. All of the exhibitions are complemented by informative, interactive multimedia displays, and frequently supplemented by workshops and talks. In addition, a new Earth Science Museum opened here in 2003, housing geological collections, fossils and even the odd chunk of dinosaur – kept well away from the china. There's also a permanent exhibition about the influential Irish designer Eileen Gray, which is excellent and well worth a look.

Phoenix Park Visitors' Centre

Ashtown Castle, Phoenix Park (677 0095/www. heritageireland.ie). Bus 37, 39. **Open** *Mid-late Mar, Oct* 10am-5.30pm daily. *Apr-Sept* 10am-6pm daily. *Nov-mid Mar* 10am-5pm Wed-Sun. **Admission** €2.90; €1.30-€2.15 concessions; €7.40 family. **No credit cards**.

Housed in the old coach house of the former Papal Nunciature, this centre explains the history of Phoenix Park and its wildlife. Admission to the centre includes a tour of nearby Ashtown Castle, a delicate 17th-century tower house. Tours also depart from the centre to Aras an Uachtarain on Saturdays throughout the year; tickets include transport to and from the Aras.

The Liberties & Kilmainham

Still independent in spirit, this is the city's feisty quarter.

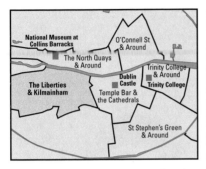

National Museum at Collins Barracks

O'Connell St & Around

The North Quays & Around

Trinity College & Around

Dublin Castle

Trinity College

The Liberties & Kilmainham

Temple Bar & the Cathedrals

St Stephen's Green & Around

Head west along the river from Christ Church, and you'll soon find your way into a lively, villagey part of Dublin, where there's plenty to distract you – this is where the black stuff is made, and where many a rebel was hanged.

The Liberties

Just beyond Christ Church, the Liberties is one of the oldest and liveliest districts of Dublin. Its markets, the vibrancy of the street life on its main artery of Thomas Street and its association with the Guinness family (see *p92* **Key notes**) all lend it character – yet it remains among the most disadvantaged areas of the city, giving the lie, incidentally, to the local cliché that the south side of the city is complacently wealthy, the north side grindingly poor.

Originally a fiercely independent self-governing district, the Liberties grew up on the high ground above the river and just west of Dublin's medieval city walls. In the 17th century it was settled by Huguenots who developed the area as a centre for silk-weaving, but the introduction of British trading restrictions in the 18th century, along with increased competition from imported cloth, signalled the area's demise. By the 19th century it was a slum bedevilled by mass unemployment and outbreaks of violence, often between the Liberty Boys (tailors' and

weavers' apprentices) and the Ormond Boys (butchers' apprentices from across the river).

In recent decades the tight-knit community has been badly scarred by the heroin trade, and gentrification, so prevalent in other parts of the city, has only recently made a few inroads here. However, the rebuilding of the **Guinness Storehouse** (see *p90*) as a tourist attraction and (perhaps more importantly) the establishment in 2000 of MediaLab Europe in the old brewery complex suggest that the pace of change may accelerate. That said, the number of refugees that have settled in the Liberties in recent years only enhances the impression that this area is a microcosm of Dublin in flux.

If the Guinness Storehouse has ensured that Thomas Street has a steady stream of daytime tourists – usually easily identifiable by their Storehouse bags – then the **Vicar Street** music venue (see *p178*) is leading the charge in making the area a popular nightspot (and one favoured especially by students from the nearby National College of Art and Design). But at the same time, Thomas Street is the centre of the city's hard-drugs trade, and it has a persistently edgy undercurrent – despite a significant Garda presence.

Off Thomas Street, Francis Street is the heart of the Dublin antiques trade, and also the site of the 18th-century **Church of St Nicholas of Myra**, which features a stained-glass window in the nuptial chapel by Harry Clarke. Meath Street, further west, hosts an old-style street market of the type that has largely disappeared from the city. If you like getting off the beaten track and want to experience a vanishing side of Dublin, this is a good place to start. At the bottom of Meath Street is the Coombe, one of the area's main thoroughfares. The maze of streets between the Coombe and South Circular Road was once the heart of the Liberties, and it boasts wonderful names like Brabazon Street, Fumbally Lane and Blackpitts. Many of the tiny brick houses here are finally being renovated, and residents must be hoping that the rising economic tide will soon lift their boats too.

At the end of Thomas Street, James's Street is synonymous in Dublin's collective imagination with the black brew. The **St James's Gate Brewery** fills all available land north and south of James's Street, right down to the river, and has been producing Ireland's world-famous Guinness for over 250 years. There had been a brewery at St James's Gate since 1670, but it was largely derelict when Arthur Guinness bought a 9,000-year lease for the site in 1759 (a bargain at £45 per annum). Guinness started by brewing ale, but soon switched to a black beer made with roasted barley and known as 'porter', due to its popularity among porters at Covent Garden and Billingsgate markets in London. The new beer proved extremely successful – by 1838 Guinness at St James's Gate was the largest brewery in Ireland, and in 1914 it became the largest in the world. It now produces 4.5 million hectolitres of Guinness Stout each year; ten million glasses are consumed around the world every day. And, although the brand and brewery have now been subsumed into the multinational Diageo drinks conglomerate, the association between Guinness and Ireland remains as potent as ever.

Although most of the complex is closed to visitors, the brewery area is impressively atmospheric: vast Victorian and 20th-century factory buildings are surrounded by high brick walls and narrow cobblestone streets, and the air is suffused with the distinctive, warming odour of hops and malt. At the heart of the complex is the fabulous Guinness Storehouse.

The Guinness Storehouse

St James's Gate (408 4800/www.guinness-storehouse.com). Bus 51B, 78A, 123/Luas James's Street. **Open** *Sept-June 9.30am-5pm daily. July-Aug*

Irish Museum of Modern Art. *See p92.*

9.30am-8pm daily. **Admission** €14; €7.50-€9.50 concessions; €30 family; free under-6s. **Credit** AmEx, MC, V. **Map** p250 B4.

No longer part of the active brewery, this 'visitor experience' is the public face of Ireland's most famous export and a celebration of the Guinness company's corporate soul. The six-storey listed building is designed around a pint glass-shaped atrium and incorporates a retail store, extensive exhibition space, function rooms, a restaurant and two bars. Much of the vast floor space is taken up with presentations on the history and making of the humble pint, which, although self-congratulatory in tone, are magnificently realised. Most entertaining, perhaps, is the advertising section – a testament to the company's famously imaginative marketing. The tour includes a complimentary pint of the best Guinness you are likely to get, and there's nowhere better to drink it than in the Gravity Bar, at the very top of the building. This circular bar has a 360-degree window and offers the kind of spectacular view over Dublin that makes the rather steep entrance fee worthwhile. (Look out for the distinctive shape of St Patrick's windmill on the other side of Watling Street.) Despite the crowds, this really is a great place in which to linger.

Kilmainham

Heading west from the brewery, you come to the Kilmainham district. If the Liberties epitomises Dublin at its most urban, Kilmainham offers a very different experience. The area is distinctly 'villagey'; the semi-rural ambience is helped by the amount of green space as well as the views across the river to the vast expanse of **Phoenix Park** (*see p88*). The main attraction here is **Kilmainham Gaol** (*see p92*), the notorious jail that housed

Key notes The Guinness family

Though most Irish people have been lectured on the dangers of the demon drink, it certainly hasn't done much damage to the Guinness family. In 1756, the founder of this Irish institution, Arthur Guinness, took out a 9,000-year lease on the St James's Gate brewery (the original document is still on display today), and the business has never looked back.

Although Arthur Guinness was the brain behind the enterprise and the black stuff itself, the man who made the huge Guinness fortune was Arthur's great-grandson, Edward Cecil Guinness. He bought out his brothers' shares in the brewery before he turned 30; a decade on, in 1886 – after he'd been made the first Earl of Iveagh – Edward Cecil made Guinness a public company, earning himself a vast personal fortune while still retaining more than 50 per cent of the shares. When he died in 1927 at the age of 80, his son Rupert took over as chairman, and was in turn succeeded by Benjamin Guinness, the third Earl of Iveagh, who died in 1992. As well as being head of the board at Guinness, Benjamin held the unique distinction of having been a senator, a member of the Oireachtas (the Irish Parliament) and a member of the House of Lords in Britain.

Although the family holding in the company – now mostly owned by drinks behemoth Diageo – has been diluted to a mere three per cent, it is still enough to establish the family as the 26th richest in Britain. With over ten million pints being sold daily, some people's thirst for Guinness seems unquenchable. The story of this family is living testament to the adage 'Guinness is good for you'.

every famous Irish felon from 1798 until 1924, when the new Free State government ordered its closure. Indeed, the list of those who spent time here reads like a roll-call of nationalist idols: Robert Emmet, John O'Leary, Joseph Plunkett, Patrick Pearse and Eamon De Valera, later the Taoiseach, who had the dubious honour of being the last ever prisoner released from here. The prison was shuttered then and has not been altered since. The boat in dry dock outside the prison is the *Asgard*, Erskin Childers's vessel, which successfully negotiated the British blockade and landed guns for the Irish Volunteers at Howth in 1912.

The other reason to head this far west is the Royal Hospital, brilliantly restored to house the **Irish Museum of Modern Art** (*see below*). The building dates from 1684 and was constructed as a hospital for military veterans.

A few minutes' walk west of the Gaol, and directly across the river from Phoenix Park, is Islandbridge, site of the **War Memorial Gardens** (entrances on Con Colbert Road and South Circular Road). Designed by Edwin Lutyens as a tribute to the 49,000 Irish soldiers who died in World War I, the gardens retain an austere beauty, with granite columns, sunken circular rose gardens, pergolas, fountains and lily ponds. Because they're slightly out of the way, they are rarely crowded, and thus make a quiet space for contemplation. The gardens slope down to the Liffey weir, where the rowing clubs of Trinity College and University College have their headquarters; and on fine days, the water is the scene of much smoothly executed coming and going.

Irish Museum of Modern Art

Royal Hospital, Military Road (612 9900/www. modernart.ie). Bus 51, 51B, 78A, 79, 90, 123/Luas Heuston. **Open** 10am-5.30pm Tue-Sat; noon-5.30pm Sun. **Admission** free.

One of the most important 17th-century buildings in Ireland, the Royal Hospital was designed by Sir William Robinson in 1684 to serve as a nursing home for retired soldiers, and, famously, he modelled it on Les Invalides in Paris. In 1991 the place was reopened as a modern art museum, with superb exhibition spaces distributed around a peaceful square. The displays are usually temporary shows, combined with a selection from the small permanent collection. The grounds include a very beautifully restored baroque formal garden. **Photo** *p90*.

Kilmainham Gaol

Inchicore Road (453 5984/www.heritageireland.ie). Bus 51B, 78A, 79, 79A. **Open** (by guided tour only) *May-Sept* 9.30am-5pm daily. *Oct-April* 9.30am-4.30pm Mon-Sat; 10am-5pm Sun. **Admission** €5.30; €2.10-€3.70 concessions; €11.50 family. **Credit** MC, V.

Although it ceased to be used as a prison in 1924, this remains the best-known Irish lock-up and one of the most fascinating buildings in Ireland. This is where the leaders of the 1916 Easter Rising, along with many others, were executed. If you harbour an interest in the 1916 Rising or, indeed, any previous rebellions in Ireland from the 18th century onwards, you'll find Kilmainham Gaol an awful lot more informative and evocative than the National Museum. Displays that document the atrocious prison conditions of the past are grimly informative, though the multimedia display on hanging may be considered by some to be a step too far.

Dublin Bay & the Coast

Where the sea air is.

Bull Island.

Dublin's great natural advantages are sea and mountains. They lend the city beauty whatever the weather and, on a good day, furnish some really stunning views. Water gives the city a great air of bustle and activity, and even though much of the maritime manoeuvring is done for leisure, not commerce, there's still plenty of vitality at quays and harbours.

The cheapest way to see the coast is still the best: take a DART from one end of the line to the other. Much of the trip is along the constantly changing seashore. The stretch from Sandycove to Bray is particularly attractive.

Northside

Clontarf

On the Northside, **Bull Island** is a fantastic nature and wildlife reserve reached by a spindly bridge off the Clontarf Road. Declared a UNESCO Biosphere in 1981, the island is barely 200 years old, formed by the gathering of sand when the Great South Wall was built in the 1700s. Sandbanks gradually became locked together by sea grass and other hardy plants, and the island's dunes and mudflats are now home to many types

of bird and plant life. There's a beach that runs the length of the island, and in the summer orchids grow here in abundance.

Opposite the Bull Island Bridge is **St Anne's Park** (833 1181), formerly the grounds of the Guinness estate, bought by Sir Benjamin G in 1832. The Clontarf Road approach is most unremarkable; in fact, it looks like scrub land. Behind, though, are splendours. Across a vast 270 acres (1.1 sq km) are straight walkways criss-crossed by little paths; and the miniature rose garden, with bower and fountain, is very pretty. Still, the large rose garden is really the thing here: hundreds of bushes, with every different colour and variety of rose; during high summer the scent is intoxicating. There's also a duck pond, tennis courts, numerous playing fields, a folly and lovely old stables. The main avenue used to sweep up to the mansion, but this burned down in 1943, and now nothing remains but a grassy knoll.

Howth

There never seems to be anyone in Howth but women, children and old people, yet there's a robust feel to the place – and not just because

Crenellations and unorthodox cultivations: that's **Talbot Botanic Gardens**. *See p96.*

of the bracing wind. Instead of the tinkle of yachts, there's the clunk of trawlers. This is a working village, not a picture postcard.

If you're in it for the long haul, jump on the No.31 bus, or walk along the shore road to the start of the five-mile (eight-kilometre) trail around the headland. The footpath cunningly avoids all the built-up areas. To the south are the Wicklow Mountains, north the Mountains of Mourne, sky above, sea below. It's desolate enough to reef you back a few centuries of civilisation. (For another walk along nearby Sutton Head, *see p95* **Walk**.)

Beside the DART station is the West Pier, the best place to buy just-caught fish. A new marina beside the harbour means the boats stay in the water all year round, rather than exposing their unsightly hulls in winter. The East Pier has a slender lighthouse at the end and rough, uneven surface; a walk along the unprotected top tier is quite exciting, and from the pier end you can make out a Martello tower and a ruined church on the rocky, uninhabited island that is Ireland's Eye. Boat trips to the island are frequent from April to October.

In the village itself is the ruined St Mary's Abbey, containing the 15th-century tomb of Christopher St Lawrence. His descendants still own Howth Castle; it's not open to the public.

National Transport Museum
Howth Castle Demesne (848 0831/832 0427/www. nationaltransportmuseum.org). Bus 31, 31B/DART

Howth. **Open** *June-Aug* 10am-5pm Mon-Fri; 2-5pm Sat, Sun. *Sept-May* 2-5pm Sat, Sun. **Admission** €3; €1.50 concessions; €8 family. **No credit cards**.
The National Transport Museum is filled with vehicles dating from the 1880s to the 1970s: trams, buses, commercial and military vehicles. Given the state of the city transport service today, it comes as a shock to discover that, a century ago, Dublin transport was among the most advanced in the world.

Malahide

The Northside's prettiest coastal village has the vast green spaces around its castle on one side and rolling ocean on the other. The Marina, where boats clink merrily at anchor, is a perfect spot for walking. The village itself has plenty of restaurants, coffee shops and boutiques, but bad parking; come by DART, rather than car.

Ardgillen Castle
Balbriggan (849 2212/www.iol.ie/~cybmanmc/). Bus 33/Balbriggan rail. **Open** *Apr-June, Sept* 11am-6pm Tue-Sun. *July, Aug* 11am-6pm daily. *Oct-Mar* 11am-4.30pm daily. **Admission** €6; €4.50 concessions; €12.50 family. **No credit cards**.
Robert Taylor, Dean of Clonfert, built this castle (it's really more of a country house with some fancy embellishment) in 1738. It stands in 194 acres (0.7 sq km) of rolling pasture, woodland and gardens, formal and freestyle. There are regular tours of the castle; of particular interest are a miniature cannon and two sad stuffed bears from America. The library has a marvellous Agatha Christie-style secret door hid-

den behind fake bookshelves; the clue to opening it is written on the spine of one of the fake books. Two coffee shops serve good cakes. But outdoors is the thing here: picnics, hide-and-seek, nature trails or romantic walks. Ardgillen is rarely too crowded; and when you've seen all you want to, a footbridge links the grounds to Barnageera beach. **Photos** *p97.*

Malahide Castle

Malahide Castle Demesne, Malahide (846 2184/www. malahidecastle.com). Bus 42/DART Malahide. **Open** *Apr-Oct* 10am-5pm Mon-Sat; 10am-6pm Sun. *Nov-Mar* 10am-5pm Mon-Sat; 11am-5pm Sun. **Admission** €6.70; €4.20-€5.70 concessions; €19 family. *Dublin Tourism combined ticket* €11.50; €7-€9.50 concessions; €32 family. **Credit** AmEx, MC, V.

The castle sits on 250 acres (0.9 sq km) – though much of it is given over to dull-looking playing fields – and the perimeter is just over two miles (three km) long; a good distance for a walk, and largely sheltered by mature trees. Historic home of the de Talbots, the castle itself is an interesting hotchpotch of architectural styles; Norman and Gothic features co-exist with beautiful period furniture. There's an extensive collection of Irish portrait paintings, and faces from history stare down at every turn; some are on loan from the National Portrait collection, others are the family's own. One in particular – Van Wyck's commemoration of the Battle of the Boyne in 1690 – is poignant, showing the 14 family members who sat down to breakfast the morning of the battle before joining King James to fight William of Orange. Not one returned. In the basement is a dimly lit self-service café that serves really good, fresh, home-made food: fish and chips, cakes and scones.

There's a model railway and doll museum, and outside is an excellent adventure playground.

Newbridge House & Farm

Newbridge Demesne, Donabate (843 6534). Bus 33B/Donabate rail. **Open** *Apr-Sept* 10am-5pm Tue-Sat; 2-6pm Sun. *Oct-Mar* 2-5pm Sat, Sun. **Admission** *House* €7; €3.50-€6 concessions; €18 family. *Farm* €3.80; €2.50-€2.80 concessions; €10 family. **Credit** MC, V.

The small house is early Georgian. Two curved wings were intended, one for either side of the front, but the plans came to nothing when the original owner, Charles Cobbe, Archbishop of Dublin, was not, as he expected, appointed Primate of Ireland. Modest as the house is, the style of furnishing is grand: lots of Portland stone, stucco by Robert West, ceiling after the Francini brothers and endless unremarkable family portraits that begin to acquire interest as stories of the dynasty unfold.

The Cobbe family was forced to sell when the state of disrepair became advanced. Fingal County Council stepped in and cut a deal that lets the family live upstairs; only the downstairs is open to the public. The official guided tour – 45 minutes – is slightly too long for what's on offer; however, the beautiful Red Drawing Room and Museum of Curiosities are well worth seeing. The latter is full of strange and sometimes ghoulish specimens: stuffed birds, bits of dusty coral, huge shells, scraps of Eastern fabrics, a tiny shoe worn by a Chinese woman with bound feet and a 'scold's bridle' – a belt to stop the mouths of witches and doomsayers.

Outside is a traditional farmyard, forge, picturesque pig sties and stables that house a huge, fantastically ornate golden coach that looks as if it must

Walk Sutton Head

Take the right-hand fork immediately past Sutton Cross, and follow the curve of the shore on to Sheil Martin Drive. Park your car and start your walk at Red Rock. The first bit runs through a very pretty meadow; scattered roof tops and a Victorian sanatorium are visible to the left; to the right is nothing but sea and sky until you pass a Martello tower. Gradually the terrain changes until you're following a narrow sandy path along the cliff edge. At times this becomes quite vertiginous, and there are occasional stone steps to scramble up and down, some in pretty bad repair. Be careful; it can get very blustery.

Below you, the cliffs give way every once in a while to stony beaches, any of which would make a good stopping place. Occasionally, you'll have to traverse one of these beaches, picking the path up again on the other side. After about 35 minutes of

walking at a decent pace, you should come to a blank-looking cottage and some walled-off land to the left. Keep walking, and cross a narrow concrete bridge across a little stream.

Around the next headland is a path down to another of the small stony beaches. This forks in two: take the left-hand branch and go down on to the beach. No, it's not much of a beach, but beyond the rock pools, immediately in front of you at the water's edge, tucked in under the left-hand cliff, is a most perfect pool. Part natural, part man-made, it fills at high tide to chest-deep and is the ideal size for a good wallow. It's all irresistibly Famous Five, so put the bottles of ginger beer to cool in one of the rock pools, strip off and take a dip.

Even if you don't quite get as far as the pool, this is an excellent walk for blowing away a few city cobwebs.

have once been a pumpkin. A café selling basic refreshments is to the right of the first courtyard.

Skerries Mill Complex

Skerries (849 5208). Bus 33/Skerries rail. **Open** *Apr-Sept* 10.30am-5.30pm daily. *Oct-Mar* 10.30am-4.30pm daily. **Admission** €6; €4.50 concessions; €12.50 family; €3 child. **Credit** MC, V.

Originally built in the 1500s, the complex has been restored, and now includes two large, working five-sail mills and one smaller four-sail watermill with bare stone walls and a thatched roof. The watermill is part of an range of stone buildings, and its many functions are outlined in different rooms such as the bakery, the weigh room and the engine room. There's a coffee shop in one of the lovely old stone buildings and a working bakery. **Photo** *p98*.

Talbot Botanic Gardens

Malahide Castle Demesne, Malahide (846 2456/ www.malahidehidecastle.com). Bus 42/DART Malahide. **Open** *May-Sept* 2-5pm daily. *Guided tour* 2pm Wed. **Admission** €4; free concessions. *Guided tour* €4. **No credit cards.**

Even when the castle is chock-a-block with curious visitors, these gardens enjoy relative tranquillity. The Walled Garden (guided tours only, Wednesdays at 2pm) has a fine collection of rare plants from Australia and New Zealand. The conservatory, designed for an old convent in the 1800s and rescued from destruction, is an excellent import. Another must-see is the old Rose Garden; though surprisingly short of these flowers, it compensates with lovely magnolias and other bright blooms. There's also a lily pond and an enclosed nursery known as the Chicken Yard. Summer is the best time to visit, but even in winter, thanks to careful and imaginative planting, there's always something to see. **Photo** *p94*.

Southside

Bray

There is a considerable amount of silly preconception in the way Bray gets sneered at by Dubliners who live in other parts of the city. Bray's reputation is somehow naff and dangerous at the same time: you might think of it as the Vinnie Jones of seaside towns. Maybe that's true if you're of cider-drinking age, but for the under-12s and sensible adults, the area makes for a perfectly jolly day out. The DART trip out will take you on a journey so beautiful that you will be in a Zen frame of mind by the time you arrive. Stroll along the promenade or stony beach, which have all the offbeat charm of an out-of-season seaside town, avoid the funfair (unless you really can't resist) and make for Bray Head. Follow the headland for a spectacular walk that takes you as far as Greystones, where you can turn and catch a DART or bus back again.

Dalkey

There's something faintly absurd in the way inhabitants still refer to this million-euro-a-millimetre area as a 'village' and cling to the conceit that it is a simple, rustic little place. And yet it's impossible to be cynical when confronted with this pretty seaside town's charm. Not for nothing have Bono, the Edge, Enya, Lisa Stansfield, Neil Jordan and plenty of hotshot businessmen chosen to buy property here. The influence of Dalkey's wealthy inhabitants can be seen in its many good restaurants, bars and delis.

Dalkey Heritage Centre (285 8366), in the restored Goat Castle on Castle Street, houses an exhibition narrated by playwright and local resident Hugh Leonard, tracing the development of the area from the Middle Ages to Victorian times. Bits of the old ruined castle are also on display, and there's a fine view from the battlements.

The real fun here is outdoors. A walk along the main drag – start on Coliemore Road, then on up Sorrento Road and finally Vico Road – gives views of a section of coastline endlessly likened to the Bay of Naples. First is Coliemore Harbour, the launchpad for boats out to Dalkey Island during the summer. (On hot summer days the tiny, uninhabited island is the only place to be guaranteed freedom from the crowds. Although it can be tricky negotiating the slippery rocks at the water's edge, it's a perfect spot for a picnic.) Past Coliemore Harbour on the left is Dillon's Park, a grassy space with views out to sea and two larger-than-life-size goat statues. Next up is Sorrento Terrace, the city's most exclusive address, on a clifftop above the sea and with views as vertiginous as a crow's nest.

From Sorrento Terrace, turn onto Vico Road. The rocky Vico bathing spot is where many of the gentlemen swimmers from the Forty-Foot (*see p98*) seem to have migrated, and it's unashamedly nudist. It's friendly and social for regulars and blow-ins alike, though the sharp rocks don't offer much scope for lounging.

From here, turn towards the upper route for Killiney Hill, on top of which stands a wishing stone and Queen Victoria's obelisk (although the proud boast of Republicans is that she never actually set foot on land to see it). From here you can explore the small forest above Burmah road, or walk (or abseil) down Dalkey Quarry.

Close to Killiney station, above the DART line, is the John Pawson-designed home of leading local art patrons Joe and Marie Donnelly. It looks like a bunker, but inside is an ultra-minimalist space housing some of the Donnelly's superb contemporary art collection:

Ardgillen Castle. See p94.

Julian Schnabel, Dorothy Cross and George Baselitz, among others. It's ostensibly open to the public on certain days of the year; visits can be arranged by calling 676 8200.

Sandymount

There are plenty of beaches to visit, though not all are for swimming. No one would dip in the flat grey waters of Sandymount strand, but if you fancy a walk in the blustery sea air, this is a good and popular spot. The hardy do the full Poolbeg Peninsula walk, taking in the Irishtown Nature Reserve, Sandymount Strand and finally the South Wall breakwater, at the end of which is a chunky red lighthouse.

Seapoint, Dun Laoghaire & Sandycove

Of the three popular year-round bathing spots on the Southside, Seapoint (the other two are the Forty-Foot and Vico) is perfect for swimming when the tide is high and laps over the two wide staircases, but the water's frustratingly shallow at low tide. Water quality is consistently good, though. On sunny days, the place is packed, mainly with families and children.

Dun Laoghaire, formerly called Kingstown in honour of the royal visit of George IV, is still mid makeover; the results so far are an excellent blend of old and new. The semi-pedestrianised main street still has its charity shops, greasy spoons and butchers, while the new Pavilion on the seafront covers the upmarket bar, stylish restaurant and fusion café end of things. What was for a long time just a satellite town around the car ferry port, filled with grotty B&Bs and hotels on hard times, has reverted to its original role as a seaside destination; weekends here are busy and crowded. The ferry depot has been rebuilt and is decent-looking and unobtrusive.

The two piers, which almost link arms around the bay, are the focus for much of the activity. The more fashionable East Pier was always popular with South Dublin matrons for the bracing two-mile (three-kilometre) there-and-back walk, but is now a weekend destination for half the city. It takes in views of Dun Laoghaire's three members-only yacht clubs and the new marina.

The less popular West Pier is quite overgrown, but has its loyal fans. If walking seems too sedate, Dublin Bay Sea Thrill (260 0949) offers high-speed boat trips lasting about 40 minutes and costing between €320 and €380.

From the East Pier, stroll along the seafront, past Teddy's ice-cream shop – which in summer has lengthy queues outside for what is reputed to be the best cone in Dublin (the secret, apparently, is using 7-Up instead of water) – to Sandycove Green. A new path takes you along the seafront, past Sandycove beach – popular with the bucket-and-spade brigade – all the way to the Forty-Foot, a year-round bathing spot once famous for being nudist men-only. It was named after the Fortieth Foot regiment, quartered in the 19th century in what is now known as Joyce's Martello tower. Battered 'Men Only' signs can still be seen, but nude bathing is increasingly unusual. Beside the Forty-Foot is Joyce's Tower, now the **Joyce Museum**.

Joyce Museum

Joyce Tower, Sandycove (280 9265/www.visitdublin. com). Bus 59/DART Sandycove. **Open** *Mar-Oct* 10am-1pm, 2-5pm Mon-Sat; 2-6pm Sun. **Admission** €6.70; €4.20-€5.70 concessions; €19 family. **Credit** AmEx, MC, V.

Famously the setting for the opening chapter of *Ulysses*, in which Joyce mocks Oliver St John Gogarty as 'stately, plump Buck Mulligan'. Gogarty must have made quite an impression; he was Joyce's host here for just one week in August 1904, before Joyce and Nora Barnacle left for Italy. Devised by Sylvia Beech in 1962, the interior has been restored to match Joyce's description of it. Exhibits are basically a collection of memorabilia – walking stick, cigar case, guitar, death mask, letters. Best of all is an edition of *Ulysses* beautifully illustrated with line drawings by Matisse. The gun platform ('Scutter!') has a great panorama of Dublin Bay.

Skerries Mills. *See p96.*

Eat, Drink, Shop

Il Baccaro. *See p103.*

Restaurants

The tuck of the Irish.

Cheap, cheerful and *molto Italiano*: **Il Baccaro**. *See p103*.

Whining after dining is a common activity in Dublin, where skyrocketing prices have been an unfortunate by-product of the country's decade-long economic transformation. But Rip-off Republic it needn't be: sure, there are pricey, even (dare we say it) overpriced restaurants around, but the Dublin public's eagerness to dine out has also promoted a good deal of healthy competition. Finally, the city's restaurateurs are realising that style over substance is an equation for short-term success only, and that good food needs integrity, not hype. As ever, the fine-dining sector is working hard (Dublin is a paradise of stellar eateries for those who have the time and funds), but the good news is that casual neighbourhood restaurants are also starting to raise standards, attracting praise from both critics and consumers. Dublin is a small city (or large town), with big aspirations and a great sense of humour, and word spreads quickly if a restaurant is not up to scratch. Snooty service, especially prevalent during the

recent boom years, has been replaced with better training and management presence. Customers have been shouting for better value, more fun and dishes they want to enjoy. Well, they're getting it all. Have faith – Dublin is becoming a lot tastier.

Around Temple Bar

French

Les Frères Jacques
74 Dame Street (679 4555/www.lesfreresjacques. com). All cross-city buses. **Open** 12.30-2.30pm, 7-10.30pm Mon-Thur; 12.30-2.30pm, 7-11pm Fri; 7-11pm Sat. **Set lunch** €17.50 2 courses; €22.50 3 courses. **Main courses** €33-€40. **Credit** AmEx, MC, V. **Map** p252 E3. ❶
The location on this busy and slightly grotty street and the cramped interior don't bother fans of this classic French old-timer. The seafood is spanking fresh, or you can always order game, another spe-

ciality. Excellent cheese plates and own-made tarts are also delicious, and a pianist at the weekend eases the pain of the prices – though lunch remains great value. One of Dublin's best French restaurants.

Le Gueleton

Fade Street (675 3708). All cross-city buses/Luas St Stephen's Green. **Open** 12.30-3pm, 6-10pm Mon-Sat. **Main courses** €9.50-€16 lunch; €12.50-€25.80 dinner. **Credit** MC, V. **Map** p252 E4. ❷
The head chef here is a current favourite among food writers – he has a knack of providing them with great foodie quotes, but there's another reason too: his cooking is a delight. Le Gueleton enjoys a very New York kind of vibe, and they don't take reservations, such is the demand for their simple, no-nonsense dishes. Occasionally, regulars complain about inconsistencies, but it doesn't seem to deter them one bit. The food and wine are keenly priced. Good fun and the perfect place for a loud and opinionated group of friends.

Indian

Jaipur

41 South Great George's Street (677 0979/www. jaipur.ie). All cross-city buses. **Open** 5-11pm daily. **Main courses** €12-€21.50. **Credit** AmEx, MC, V. **Map** p252 E4. ❸
With branches on all three sides of the city, Jaipur is in danger of becoming a chain rather than a top-class Indian, for which it has always been liked. Service is extremely courteous, and food is light and tasty. As with most Indian restaurants, vegetarians are well catered for with such tasty dishes as tandoori aloo – potatoes stuffed with bell peppers, sun-dried tomatoes, olives and spiced Indian ricotta, then grilled in a tandoor. Money has been spent on the interiors in all three branches.
Other locations: 21 Castle Street, Dalkey (285 0552); 5 St James Terrace, Malahide (845 5455).

International

The Bistro

4-5 Castle Market (671 5430/www.thebistro.ie). All cross-city buses/Luas St Stephen's Green. **Open** noon-10pm Mon; 9am-10pm Tue, Wed; 9am-11pm Thur-Sat; 1pm-9pm Sun. **Main courses** €10-€12.50 lunch; €12.50-€28.50 dinner. **Credit** AmEx, MC, V. **Map** p252 F3. ❹
Reports are mixed about the grub here, but the Bistro has two things going for it: it has the best location for people-gawping and prices are reasonable enough to be able to forgive kitchen cock-ups. Think pasta, salads (lots of them) and fish dishes, along with steak sandwiches at lunchtime. The menu is very accessible, and even if you can't bag a table outside, the upstairs room is also lovely, with cushions, bright colour scheme and banquette seating. A great spot for Saturday lunch, which you should eke out all day.

Café Bar Deli

12-13 South Great George's Street (677 1646/www. cafebardeli.ie). All cross-city buses. **Open** 12.30-11pm Mon-Sat; 2-10pm Sun. **Main courses** €7.50-€14. **Credit** AmEx, MC, V. **Map** p252 E3. ❺
The entrepreneurial owners of this cheap hotspot have described it as the Ryanair of the restaurant world. While that would be enough to put off most diners (have you ever eaten on Ryanair?), what they really mean is it's a no-fuss, no-frills type of experience. Eoin Foyle and Jay Bourke have street cred: they own a stack of bars, nightclubs and restaurants that continue to do well and survive a very fickle business. Think pizza (ten types) and pasta (rigatoni with gorgonzola, spinach, sage, cream and mascarpone). Cheap and busy.
Other locations: 52 Ranelagh Village, Ranelagh (496 1886); Bewley's, Grafton Street, Around Temple Bar (670 6755).

The best Restaurants

For cheap eats
Aya (*see p105*); **Il Baccaro** (*see p103*); **Bar Italia** (*see p113*); **Café Bar Deli** (*see above*); **The Cedar Tree** (*see p105*); **Cornucopia** (*see p111*); **Enoteca delle Langhe** (*see p113*); **Gruel** (*see p103*); **Steps of Rome** (*see p103*); **Wagamama** (*see p110*).

For fine dining
Chapter One (*see p113*); **L'Ecrivain** (*see p109*); **Restaurant Patrick Guilbaud** (*see p107*); **Shanahan's** (*see p110*); **The Tea Rooms** (*see p104*).

For first dates
Aqua (*see p115*); **La Cave** (*see p104*); **The Cellar** (*see p109*); **DAX** (*see p111*); **French Paradox** (*see p115*); **La Mère Zou** (*see p106*); **Pearl** (*see p106*); **Il Posto** (*see p109*).

For service
The Cedar Tree (*see p105*); **Fitzers** (*see p106*); **Mermaid** (*see p103*); **Mint** (*see p116*); **Pearl** (*see p106*).

For trendy dining
Bang Café (*see p109*); **Fallon & Byrne** (*see p103*); **Peploe's** (*see p111*); **Rhodes D7** (*see p112*); **The Tea Rooms** (*see p104*); **Town Bar and Grill** (*see p109*).

For vegetarians
Bar Italia (*see p113*); **Cornucopia** (*see p111*); **Jaipur** (*see above*); **101 Talbot** (*see p112*).

Eat, Drink, Shop

YOU KNOW WHO YOU ARE.

DUBLIN
12 FLEET STREET • TEMPLE BAR
+353 1 671 7777 • HARDROCK.COM

Fallon & Byrne

11-17 Exchequer Street (472 1000/www.fallonand byrne.com). All cross-city buses/Luas St Stephen's Green. **Open** 12.30-4pm, 6-10.30pm Mon-Thur; 12.30-4pm, 6-11pm Fri; 11am-4pm, 6-11pm Sat; 11-4pm, 6-10.30pm Sun. **Main courses** €8-€22.50 lunch; €12.25-€26.50 Sun. **Credit** MC, V. **Map** p252 F3. **❻**
Anyone who has been to New York's Dean & DeLuca will feel right at home at this Irish version. An awful lot of money has been pumped into converting this former telephone-exchange building into what it is now: a super-smart grocery store on the ground floor, below which is a wine bar serving and selling serious hooch. Upstairs, Parisian-style brasserie food is served at lunch and dinner. An impressive operation.

Gruel

68A Dame Street (670 7119). All cross-city buses. **Open** 11.30am-10pm Mon-Fri; 11am-10.30pm Sat, Sun. **Main courses** €4.30-€6.90 lunch; €12-€14 dinner. **No credit cards. Map** p252 E3. **❼**
Hot roast-in-a-roll sandwiches, soup served in huge bowls, pizza slices, own-made cakes and brownies are all served at great prices in this understandably popular diner. Its grown-up sister restaurant is next door (Mermaid; *see below*), but Gruel is popular with anyone looking for cheap culinary thrills. Staff may be too laid-back for high-maintenance customers, and the decor too higgledy-piggledy for design snobs, but the roast turkey with stuffing and cranberry crammed into hot home-baked rolls is what people come here for.

Mermaid

69-70 Dame Street (670 8236/www.mermaid.ie). All cross-city buses. **Open** 12.30-3pm, 6-9.30pm Mon-Sat; noon-3pm, 6-9.30pm Sun. **Set lunch** €21.95 2 courses; €25.95 3 courses. **Main courses** €18.95-€27. **Credit** MC, V. **Map** p252 E3. **❽**
Sometimes labelled trans-Atlantic just because its kitchen turns out a darned good sweet pecan pie, the Mermaid also offers fantastic salads and hearty dishes like a hand-cut fries, fried egg and béarnaise (call the cardiologist, *now*). But dishes like cod with horseradish mash and sautéed spinach or curried lamb shank showcase the kitchen's more global talents. The interior is light and breezy, as are the staff. If you're a fan of good wines and tasty food, the Mermaid is always a safe bet.

Odessa

13-14 Dame Court (670 7634/www.odessa.ie). All cross-city buses. **Open** 6-11pm Mon-Fri; 11.30am-4.30pm, 6-11pm Sat, Sun. **Main courses** €14.75-€24.95. **Credit** AmEx, MC, V. **Map** p252 E3. **❾**
Dark and mysterious, even slick, in a retro kind of way, Odessa has been here a long time. Downstairs, square armchairs can force awkward conversations – it's hard to get up close and personal – for which you may be grateful if your date starts eating too much guacamole. But some of the corner sites suit large groups. Upstairs is a bit brighter, but most of it all blends into one big fuzzy whole once the

Margaritas have taken their toll. It's good value, tasty enough and fun before a night on the razz. Houmous, rocket and walnut pesto with black olive tapenade and warm pitta bread or blackened Cajun thresher shark are typical of the globe-trotting menu.

Venue Brasserie

Anne's Lane (670 6755/www.venue.ie). All cross-city buses/Luas St Stephen's Green. **Open** noon-11pm daily. **Main courses** €9.50-€29. **Credit** AmEx, MC, V. **Map** p252 F4. **❿**
The son of two-star Michelin chef Patrick, Charles Guilbaud has opened his brasserie to mixed reviews. The menu is great – it's reasonably priced and features good fish dishes and local produce – but the ultra modern setting (in a cavernous basement) is slightly at odds with the casual food offerings. Reservations are not required and food is served all day, just a hop from Grafton Street.

Italian

Il Baccaro

Meetinghouse Square (671 4597). All cross-city buses. **Open** 5.30-10pm daily. **Main courses** €12-€20. **Credit** MC, V. **Map** p252 E3. **⓫**
This is a cute little den of a restaurant that serves tasty enough food, providing you follow some rules. Order loads of starters – the grilled mushrooms, bresaola, caponata and grilled focaccia are all tasty – because main courses can be heavy and stodgy (although, if you bring a bona fide Italian as your guest, we've noticed that the food sometimes seems to take a turn for the better). That said, this is a genuinely cheap, cheerful and fun spot before a night on the town. **Photo** *p100*.

Steps of Rome

Unit 1, Chatham Street (670 5630). All cross-city buses/Luas St Stephen's Green. **Open** noon-11.30pm Mon-Sat; noon-10pm Sun. **Main courses** €10-€14.30. **No credit cards. Map** p252 F4. **⓬**
You could be forgiven for thinking that the staff here are hideously rude. They're not – they just don't speak much English – which is fine if you speak Italian, but can be a little frustrating if you don't. Still, this lends a certain charm to a space that is otherwise light on frills (but does good square slices of pizza – the potato and rosemary variety is perfect with a couple of cold beers). Table turnover is high and customers are squashed, but it's cheap, casual and a great pit stop when shopping or wandering around Grafton Street. And if you don't fancy lingering, you can always take away.

Modern European

Bleu Bistro

Joshua House, Dawson Street (676 7015). All cross-city buses/Luas St Stephen's Green. **Open** noon-3pm, 6-11pm daily. **Main courses** €12.50-€26.95. **Credit** AmEx, MC, V. **Map** p252 F4. **⓭**

The Cedar Tree. See p105.

A rare combination of style and substance, Bleu has a sassy metropolitan look and serves high-quality casual food with a twist. Its fans rave about the fare but moan about how crowded it is – tables are close together – and the erratic service. The omelette Arnold Bennett and the fish and chips are somewhat upstaged by more ambitious fare like scallops with apple and brown butter vinaigrette.

Eden

Meeting House Square, Temple Bar (670 5372/www. edenrestaurant.ie). All cross-city buses. **Open** 12.30-3pm, 8-10pm Mon-Fri; noon-3pm, 8-10.30pm Sat, Sun. **Set lunch** €19.50 2 courses; €24 3 courses. **Brunch** €6.50-€12. **Main courses** €18-€29. **Credit** AmEx, MC, V. **Map** p252 E3. ⓴

Eden is very much a '90s-style restaurant with blue tiled interiors split over two levels and (of course) an open kitchen. Head chef Eleanor Walshe oversees the preparation of some very tasty and sensible food with nods to Irish and Italian flavours. Lunch is great if you can sit out on the square, and brunch is usually pretty busy. Roast halibut brochette, warm beetroot salad, confit of rabbit and roast magret of duck are all on offer, along with the famous smokies.

The Tea Rooms

The Clarence Hotel, 6-8 Wellington Quay (407 0813/www.theclarence.ie). All cross-city buses. **Open** 7-11am, 12.30-2.15pm, 7-10.15pm Mon-Fri; 7.30-11.30am, 12.30-2.15pm, 7-10.15pm Sat; 7.30-11.30am, 12.30-2.15pm, 7-9.15pm Sun. **Set lunch/dinner** €47.50 2 courses; €55 3 courses. **Credit** AmEx, DC, MC, V. **Map** p252 E3. ⓯

The designer Clarence Hotel *(see p36)* is home to this posh restaurant, where fine dining meets rock 'n' roll. First comes the valet parking, then killer cocktails in the louche Octagon Bar *(see p129)*, then the likes of egg custard with lobster and Sevruga caviar, seared scallop with chanterelles and white onion purée or crisp chocolate fondant in the dining room proper. Chef Anthony Ely has worked in some of the UK's best restaurants but has really honed his style here. Service is formal but accommodating, and the atmosphere, though decidedly upmarket, is never intimidating (the place is owned by rock stars, after all). And there's always a fair chance you'll find yourself next to someone famous.

Around Trinity College

French

La Cave

28 South Anne Street (679 4409/www.lacavewine bar.com). All cross-city buses/Luas St Stephen's Green. **Open** 12.30-11pm Mon-Sat; 5.30-11pm Sun. **Set dinner** €32 4 courses. **Main courses** €10.50-€13.95 lunch; €18.95-€24.50 dinner. **Credit** AmEx, MC, V. **Map** p252 H5. ⓰

One of the first wine bars in the city that was any good, La Cave feels a little seedy these days. But don't be put off – just pretend you're in Paris. It has that same louche vibe (and that same ability to rustle up a good bottle of red and a decent steak). Kind lighting and a busy atmosphere make it especially good for first dates. What's more, they serve late and are fond of wine – perfect for those customers who are too old/young for a nightclub. The menu includes fillet steak, sea bass, monkfish, mussels, and ravioli with ricotta and spinach.

Japanese

Aya
49-52 Clarendon Street (677 1544/www.aya.ie).
All cross-city buses/Luas St Stephen's Green. **Open**
12.30-10pm Mon-Fri; 12.30-11pm Sat; 1-9pm Sun.
Set dinner €30 9 courses. Main courses €10-€35.
Credit AmEx, MC, V. **Map** p252 F3. ⑰
Staff wear cute uniforms, a conveyor belt chugs along all day long and the menu contains all the usual suspects: a little yakitori, norimaki, tataki and sushi. Much of it is average, but you can enjoy decent enough beef tataki, and the noodle dishes are edible. Good deals can be had during 'twilight' hours, when there is plenty of grub to be offloaded

from the conveyor belt. The deli sells everything from not-very-Japanese egg mayonnaise sarnies to hot teriyaki dishes and lots of Japanese condiments to take home.

Middle Eastern

The Cedar Tree
11A St Andrew Street (677 2121). All cross-city
buses/Luas St Stephen's Green. **Open** 5.30-11pm
Mon-Wed, Sun; 5.30pm-midnight Thur-Sat; **Main**
courses €13.90-€25. **Credit** AmEx, MC, V. **Map**
p252 F3. ⑲
Buzzy, cosy and cute, with tasty Lebanese food, Cedar Tree is excellent value for money. Really friendly staff will guide you through a long list of options – but set menus are generously priced and serve plenty of guests. In fact, the food never stops coming, and tables turn frequently. If you're dining à deux, someone may appear to sell you roses, but no one will be offended if you say no (except maybe your date). It's also great for larger groups but insist on a large table – the vast number of courses and plates means space can be tight. **Photo** *p104.*

Vine dining

In most people's minds, the idea of meeting up for a drink in a wine bar will be forever associated with the 1980s, the era when Crockett and Tubbs were considered snappy dressers, and the sun-dried tomato the hallmark of a sophisticated dish. Or, if not that, then it conjures an image of pin-striped punters, the older ones droning about the money markets, the younger variety braying into their Blackberries. Not a pretty picture, whichever way you slice it – which is why a visit to Dublin can be such an eye-opener. Cue the unpretentious, eclectic wine bar: it's more sophisticated than a pub, and yet in no danger of vanishing up its own bottleneck; what's more, it's stocked with interesting, affordable and downright delicious wines. Plus (and it's something of a big plus), this is also where you'll find a lot of the best mid-range cooking in town.

Key players in this new master race of wine bars are **Peploe's**, **Ely** and **DAX** (for all three, *see p111*), all based in the swanky environs of St Stephen's Green. Elsewhere, among the restaurants proper, some of the best wine lists can be found at **Enoteca delle Langhe** (destination number one for fans of the Piedmont region; *see p113*), **Rhodes D7** (*see p112*), **Chapter One** (*see p113*) and **L'Ecrivain** (pictured; *see p109*).

L'Ecrivain.

Eat, Drink, Shop

Restaurant Patrick Guilbaud.

Modern Irish

Fitzers

50 Dawson Street (677 1155/www.fitzers.ie). All cross-city buses. **Open** 11.30am-11pm daily (closed 4.30-5.30pm Sat, Sun). **Main courses** €13.50-€26.95. **Credit** AmEx, DC, MC, V. **Map** p252 F4. **49**
Although part of a small family chain, this particular branch of Fitzers is the best. A professional and consistently busy operation, it has charming service, a pleasant interior and a small terrace with heaters. **Other locations**: Temple Bar Square, Temple Bar (679 0440); Millennium Wing, National Gallery, Merrion Square, Around Trinity College (663 3500).

Around St Stephen's Green

French

La Mère Zou

22 St Stephen's Green (661 6669). All cross-city buses/Luas St Stephen's Green. **Open** 12.30-2.30pm, 6-10.30pm Mon-Thur; 12.30-2.30pm, 6-11pm Fri; 6-11pm Sat; 6-9.30pm Sun. **Main courses** €19-€31.50. **Credit** AmEx, DC, MC, V. **Map** p251 F4. **20**

Belgian in origin, French by nature, La Mère Zou offers large 'tasting plates' that are a lunchtime hit with local businessmen. At night, the pretty orange room gives off a nice glow. Service has always been good, and the simple French food has always been more than acceptable, sometimes downright excellent. The rib of beef for two is a delight, mussels are done ten different ways, and the chips are the best in town. It's lovely and quiet for dinner with the family on a Sunday night, but also perfect for that romantic dinner on Saturday.

Pearl

20 Merrion Street Upper (661 3627/www.pearl-brasserie.com). All cross-city buses/Luas St Stephen's Green. **Open** noon-2.30pm, 6-10.30pm Tue-Fri; 6-10.30pm Sat, Sun. **Main courses** €21-€28. **Credit** AmEx, MC, V. **Map** p251 G4. **21**
Rarely does one find such charming staff – they have chic uniforms and serve solid French brasserie cooking. The bar area serves oysters, champagne and (during the day) delicious soup, croque monsieur and steak sandwiches. Night-time gets fancier: prawns with black pepper and mango; pan-fried foie gras with brioche; lobster with garlic butter. The couple at the helm of Pearl have lots of experience,

passion for their business and youth on their side. As a result, there is attention to detail and a desire to serve – all good qualities in a brasserie.

Restaurant Patrick Guilbaud

The Merrion Hotel, 22 Merrion Street Upper (676 4192/www.restaurantpatrickguilbaud.ie). All cross-city buses/Luas St Stephen's Green. **Open** 12.30-2.15pm, 7.30-10.15pm Tue-Sat. **Set lunch** €33 2 courses; €45 3 courses. **Main courses** €30-€80. **Credit** AmEx, MC, V. **Map** p251 G4. ㉒

It's pretty hard to beat Guilbaud's, as long as someone else is paying. Through-the-roof prices but sublime dishes (crème brulée of foie gras, ravioli of lobster), the surroundings of one of the fanciest hotels in the city and a swanky location (opposite the government buildings) keeps RPG well supplied with a moneyed clientele. That said, though, the best-value lunch in the city for haute cuisine is only €33, a pittance when you get an amuse-bouche, starter, main course, coffee and petits fours. But be warned: if you go off-piste here and start ordering cheese, dessert, and maybe that second bottle of wine, you will be forced to sell your house/partner/children to settle the bill. Although, of course, you might well consider that a fair exchange. **Photo** *above.*

International

Canal Bank Café

146 Upper Leeson Street (664 2135/www.canalbank cafe.com). All cross-city buses. **Open** 10am-11pm Mon-Fri; 11am-11pm Sat, Sun. **Main courses** €9.95-€29.95. **Credit** AmEx, MC, V. **Map** p251 G6. ㉓

This smart and easy-going café has young, sassy staff and an American-influenced menu: Cobb salad, spinach salad, pasta, omelettes, soups, burgers, steak sandwiches and quesadillas, Brooklyn meatloaf and meatballs. Get the idea? Brunch is pleasant and the menu offers all you could want to eat the morning after. Be sure to ask for a window table. There's also a sister restaurant, Tribeca (up the road in Ranelagh), which serves up a few more chicken wings but is similar in style.

Dobbins Wine Bistro

15 Stephen's Lane (661 3321/www.dobbinswine bistro.ie). All cross-city buses/Luas St Stephen's Green. **Open** noon-2.30pm, 6-10pm Mon-Fri; 6-10pm Sat; noon-3pm. **Set lunch** €19.95 4 courses. **Main courses** €18.50-€30. **Credit** AmEx, DC, MC, V. **Map** p251 H4. ㉔

wagamama

delicious noodles, rice dishes, freshly squeezed juices, wine, sake and japanese beers

wagamama dublin
south king street, dublin 2
telephone +353 (0) 1 478 2152

opening hours
mon to sat 12pm–11pm
sunday 12pm–10pm

wagamama.com

uk ı ireland ı holland ı australia ı dubai ı antwerp ı auckland ı copenhagen ı istanbul

Full of politicos and men in suits, this is one of the best places for a boozy lunch (and somewhere you could easily end up buying dinner at too – time seems to fly here…). The place reeks of money, power and property deals. The wine list is endless, and the food is all very meat and potatoes. Waiters seem to have been here forever, the location is discreet and fun is guaranteed.

Italian

Da Vincenzo

133 Leeson Street Upper (660 9906). All cross-city buses. **Open** 12.30-11pm Mon-Fri; 1-11pm Sat; 1-10pm Sun. **Main courses** €9.95-€23. **Credit** AmEx, MC, V. **Map** p251 G6. ㉕

This cosy old-timer is always busy. Try to book the snug table on the left as you walk in – it's one of the nicest spots in town. Staff are lovely enough to make you forget that the pasta dishes here are, in fact, very average. You'd do well to order pizza instead: it's well made and baked in a wood-burning oven. Keep toppings fairly plain – a simple margherita with some mushrooms and garlic is one of the best options. Food can be prepared to take away. This is one of those places you go to for the atmosphere more than anything else.

Il Posto

10 Stephen's Green (679 4769/www.ilposto restaurant.com). All cross-city buses/Luas St Stephen's Green. **Open** noon-2pm, 5.30-10pm Mon-Wed; noon-2pm, 5.30-10.30pm Thur, Fri; noon-2.30pm, 5.30-10.30 Sat; 5.30-10pm Sun. **Main courses** €12-€15 lunch; €15-€30 dinner. **Credit** AmEx, MC, V. **Map** p251 F4. ㉖

An intimate, cosy and warm basement Italian that actually serves some decent Italian grub. Lunch can be a bit disappointing (atmosphere-wise), except on a busy Friday, but dinner makes up for it. Grilled swordfish with lemon and olive oil, and fettuccini with sweet onions, grilled pancetta and parmesan cream are mighty tasty. Portions are huge, the side orders are good (not just an after-thought) and the place is usually hopping.

Town Bar and Grill

21 Kildare Street (662 4724/www.townbarandgrill. com). All cross-city buses. **Open** 10am-11pm Mon-Thur; noon-11.30pm Sat; noon-10pm Sun. **Set lunch** €20.95 2 courses, €25.95 3 courses. **Main courses** €16.95-€30.95 dinner. **Credit** AmEx, DC, MC, V. **Map** p251 F4. ㉗

Two bright young restaurateurs have created this buzzing new Dublin eaterie. Its formula is simple and (for that very reason) highly effective: the menu sets out a range of Italian dishes that appeal to sophisticated modern diners (Caprese salad, roast wild boar with red cabbage, rhubarb and ginger panna cotta), plus there's a great wine list featuring many Italian and Californian hits. Smoothly slick service rounds things off nicely. Very much the restaurant of the moment.

Modern Irish

Bang Café

11 Merrion Row (676 0898/www.bangrestaurant. com). All cross-city buses/Luas St Stephen's Green. **Open** 12.30-3pm, 6-10.30pm Mon-Wed; 12.30-3pm, 6-11pm Thur-Sat. **Main courses** €12.95-€21.50 lunch; €12.95-€27.95 dinner. **Credit** AmEx, MC, V. **Map** p251 G4. ㉘

The owners of this fashionable café have a good pedigree: restaurants and fashion have featured strongly in their lives. They drive fast cars, have pretty blondes by their sides and wisely hired an ex-chef from London's Ivy restaurant. The result is cool minimalist interiors with brash art, chandeliers and a menu that is full of dishes you want to eat. The scallops with mousseline potatoes and pancetta, along with the baked sea bass with fragrant rice, and the iced Scandinavian berries are all Ivy classics, but well translated. Cocktails are good, and all the customers seem rather fabulous. Quite possibly the most fashionable restaurant in the city.

The Cellar

Merrion Hotel, 22 Merrion Street Upper (603 0630/ www.merrionhotel.com). All cross-city buses/Luas St Stephen's Green. **Open** 7-10.30am, 12.30-2pm, 6-10pm Mon-Fri; 7-11am, 6-10pm Sat; 7-11am, 12.30-2.30pm, 6-10pm Sun. **Set lunch** €21.95 2 courses; €24.95 3 courses. **Main courses** €14-€36. **Credit** AmEx, DC, MC, V. **Map** p251 G4. ㉙

Sometimes one longs to escape the hustle and bustle of the city streets… the Cellar is just the place for that – it's an immaculate operation serving casual and contemporary classics (plum tomato and basil gallette, Caesar salad, fillet of beef and crispy fries). It is also good for more conservative folk or lovers looking for a quiet nook. You'll find no loud music or squished tables here – in other words, this is a grown-up restaurant with good facilities, but the food and prices mean it's OK to go to dinner in jeans. They also have a gorgeous terrace for al fresco dining in the warmer months.

L'Ecrivain

109A Lower Baggot Street (661 1919/www.lecrivain. com). All cross-city buses. **Open** 12.30-2pm, 7-10pm Mon-Fri; 7-11pm Sat. **Set lunch** €35 2 courses; €45 3 courses. **Main courses** €47-€53 dinner. **Credit** AmEx, MC, V. **Map** p251 H5. ㉚

Classic Irish dishes get a truly gourmet twist at this stalwart of Dublin's fine-dining scene: the oysters in Guinness sabayon are legendary. Located in the heart of the business and media district, it attracts many suits at lunch, but in the evening it's the perfect spot for a romantic dinner or family celebration. Any note of formality is truly Irish (that is, non-existent), and a good time is encouraged, often via the piano downstairs in the bar. The only drawback of this is that you may have to listen to drunken regulars singing for their supper. On a sunny day (they do happen sometimes), it is definitely worth bribing someone for a terrace table.

Eat, Drink, Shop

Local cuisine RIP

Tourists looking for a gourmet, bona fide Irish meal will be hard pressed to find it in Dublin. Globalisation has taken over the world of food, and although the finer restaurants are proud to promote Irish producers and artisan products, there is a long way to go before it can be said that Ireland's food culture is as robust as its economy. Still, consumerism has forced better quality controls, and Ireland has several schemes including the *Feile Bia* promotion, under which members guarantee traceability on products and the use of Irish ingredients. This in turn helps provide direct distribution for smaller organic farmers and cheese-makers, some of whom would go out of business if it weren't for the support of Dublin's top chefs. There are several restaurants combining Irish produce with French techniques: the charcuterie trolley at **Chapter One** (pictured; *see p113*) is an example of the amazing cured meats and terrines available in Ireland, which are silver-served to you with home-made chutneys and selections of breads – a great alternative to starters. In the country you will find simpler fare – and a greater affinity with older classics: smoked salmon, seafood chowder, oysters and grilled Dover sole. Temple Bar, the home of drunk locals, even drunker stags and sundry gullible tourists should be avoided unless you are a drunk local, gullible tourist or about to walk down the aisle. It is full of cheap and grotty restaurants masquerading as purveyors of local fare, although every now and then a decent one pops up. But on the whole, if you're looking for shamrocks and leprechauns, that's where you'll find them.

Behind the scenes at **Chapter One**.

Shanahan's

119 St Stephen's Green West (407 0939/www. shanahans.ie). All cross-city buses/Luas St Stephens Green. **Open** 6-9.45pm Mon-Thur; 6-10.30pm; 12.30-2pm Fri-Sun. **Main courses** €41-€55. **Credit** AmEx, DC, MC, V. **Map** p251 F4. ❸

Depending on who you ask, Shanahan's is either the finest restaurant in the city, or just a hideously expensive, glorified and gaudy-looking steak house with smug service and an highly expensive wine list. Fans object strongly to the latter description and wax lyrical about the famous ham and split-pea soup, the filet mignon, the onion rings and the creamed spinach (all very, very good indeed). In other words: if you love protein, and money is no object, then you will find certainly yourself in a kind of earthly paradise at Shanahan's.

Oriental

Wagamama

King Street South (478 2152/www.wagamama.ie). All cross-city buses/Luas St Stephen's Green. **Open** noon-11pm Mon-Sat; noon-10pm Sun. **Main courses** €9.25-€14.75. **Credit** AmEx, DC, MC, V. **Map** p251 F4. ❸

It may be yet another link in a long, long chain but this Dublin branch of the Wagamama noodle empire boasts really quite impressive decor. The food can be very bland, of course, but it's fast, friendly, clean and convenient. Juices, soups, skewers and noodles: it's all here. The menu is informative, with a glossary of terms that may be unfamiliar to customers not used to this type of dining. Chicken or salmon ramen and yaki soba are typical dishes on offer.

Tapas

Havana
3 Camden Market, Grantham Place (476 0046/www. havana.ie). Bus 16, 19, 122/Luas Harcourt Street. **Open** 11.30am-10.30pm Mon-Wed; 11.30am-11.30pm Thur, Fri; 1-11.30pm Sat. **Main courses** €5.95-€12.95. **Credit** AmEx, DC, MC, V. **Map** p251 E5. ㉝
A small tapas bar that's always ready for fun, Havana has pretty interiors, staff and customers. Food can be disappointing, though, but it's cheap, and the place has plenty of atmosphere. The music is hopping, and some customers tell of tables being cleared and dancing the night away. The microwave in the kitchen tells its own story, and the olives can be second rate but, as long as you aren't building up culinary expectations, you could end up having a great night here.
Other locations: George's Street, Northern Suburbs (400 5990).

Vegetarian

Cornucopia
19 Wicklow Street (677 7583). All cross city buses/ Luas St Stephen's Green. **Open** 8.30am-8pm Mon-Wed, Fri, Sat; 9am-9pm Thur; noon-7pm Sun. **Main courses** €7-€11.50. **Credit** MC, V. **Map** p252 F3. ㉞
A stalwart for vegetarians, vegans, dairy intolerants or anyone looking for healthy, wholesome grub, Cornucopia is cramped, wooden and not exactly glam. At lunch, the place is thronged with masses of earnest twentysomethings vying for a place at one of the few tables. Still, you'll be so thrilled with yourself after eating all those lentils, hearty soups and salads that you won't mind sharing your personal space with like-minded diners. For best results, though, come mid morning, when the atmosphere is more relaxed and you can dawdle over your organic porridge and freshly squeezed juice.

Wine bar

DAX
23 Upper Pembroke Street (676 1494/www.dax.ie). All cross-city buses. **Open** 12.30-2.30pm, 6-11pm Tue-Fri; 6-11pm Sat. **Set lunch** €19.50 2 courses, €24 3 courses. **Main courses** €22-€35. **Credit** AmEx, MC, V. **Map** p251 G5. ㉟
Basement restaurants have to work a lot harder than their ground-floor colleagues – they need to lure their punters with a guarantee of good food, rather than just the (all too often meretricious) promise of it through an inviting window. Here you'll find said food in the guise of French 'tapas' (if you can imagine such a thing) by the bar or more formal fare in the dining room. This new venture is already considered by many to be the city's best wine bar, with great food, charming staff and plush interiors. A welcome addition to the Dublin dining scene.

Ely
22 Ely Place (676 8986/www.elywinebar.ie). All cross-city buses/Luas St Stephen's Green. **Open** noon-3pm, 6-10pm Mon-Wed; noon-3pm, 6-10.30pm Thur; noon-3pm, 6-11pm Fri; 1-11pm Sat. **Main courses** €11-€19 lunch; €14-€27.95 dinner. **Credit** AmEx, DC, MC, V. **Map** p251 G4. ㊱
Cosy and smart, with brick walls, oversized armchairs and little nooks and crannies to sink into, Ely boasts a vast wine list that is possibly the best in the country. Thankfully, many bottles are available by the glass. The organic beef burger (sourced from the owner's organic farm), as well as some Irish classics like Kilkea oysters, bangers and mash and an Irish cheese plate, is the perfect accompaniment to oversized glasses of wine. Good fun and never dreary, due to the fact that it is often filled with glowingly successful local moguls.

Peploe's
St Stephen's Green (676 3144/www.peploes.com). All cross-city buses/Luas St Stephen's Green. **Open** noon-10.30pm Mon-Sat. **Main courses** €10.50-€27.50 lunch; €13.50-€29.50 dinner. **Credit** MC, V. **Map** p251 F4. ㊲
A truly sophisticated wine bar, Peploe's has the added advantage of what is quite possibly the best location in town. The rooms are decked out with

Chapter One. *See p113.*

wood, murals and crisp table linen, and patrolled by smartly kitted-out staff. It is fast becoming Dublin's best place for a fun Friday lunch – full of local heroes and business gurus – and has long been popular as a retreat for the city's cultured set to have their casual evening meals. The food menu has settled down into dishes like French onion soup, Caesar salad, smoked salmon with dill sauce or roast guinea fowl stuffed with sausage and lentils. The wine list is good and long, and well worth checking out, even if it's just for a glass of wine at the bar. **Photo** *above*.

North Quays & O'Connell Street

International

101 Talbot

101 Talbot Street (874 5011/www.101talbot.com). All cross-city buses/Luas Abbey Street. **Open** 5-11pm Tue-Sat. **Main courses** €13.50-€21.50. **Credit** AmEX, MC, V. **Map** p251 F2. ⑱

Casual, but serious about its vegetarian customers, this long-running restaurant nourishes wise locals who pay little attention to food fads. Don't expect any razzmatazz, just straightforward, honest cooking geared to everyone from vegans to carnivores. Dishes include marinated tomato and feta crostini, three-bean chilli burritos, and pancakes with wild mushrooms and goat's cheese. Chocoholics rave about the chocolate cake, while 101's proximity to theatreland also makes it an ideal spot pre- or post-performances.

Rhodes D7

The Capel Building, Mary Abbey (1-890 277 777/804 444/www.rhodesd7.com). All cross-city buses/Luas Jervis. **Open** noon-4pm Mon; noon-10pm Tue-Sat; noon-5.30pm Sun. **Credit** AmEx, MC, V. **Map** p252 E2. ⑲

Famous London chef Gary Rhodes has put his name to this large and buzzy 250-seater, but you won't find him at the stove. This brasserie is an exercise in branding only, with Rhodes's head chef Paul Hargreaves running the operation. The menu is full of classic Rhodes dishes (haddock rarebit, bread and butter parfait), and everything is mid priced and easy on the eye. Expect a battalion of staff, plasma screens, a thumping piano and an outdoor terrace for smokers. The location is self-consciously urban (the restaurant shares its street with sex shops, among others). But it's also right near the Four Courts, which

Peploe's. See p111.

means lunchtimes are busy with Ireland's finest lawyers; dinner, though, attracts large, noisy groups looking for pleasant food that won't break the bank.

Italian

Bar Italia

26 Blooms Lane (874 1000/) All cross-city buses/Luas Jervis. **Open** noon-10.30pm Mon-Thur; noon-11pm Fri, Sat; 1-10pm Sun. **Main courses** €8-€25. **Credit** AmEx, DC MC, V. **Map** p252 E2. ⓴
The foodies who own this Italian joint seem to have the knack of giving people what they want. The little enclave surrounding the restaurant is known locally as the Italian Quarter and is fast becoming a great place to hang out for a glass of wine or a bite to eat before catching a flick or something fancier. Pasta, grilled meats and a good supply of vegetable dishes are what turn over Bar Italia's menu. It's cheap, comfortable and friendly.

Enoteca delle Langhe

24 Ormond Quay Lower (888 0834). All cross-city buses/Luas Jervis. **Open** noon-3pm, 4pm-midnight Mon-Sat. **Main courses** €6-€15. **Credit** MC, V. **Map** p252 E3. ⓴

The owner of this lovely, bright wine bar has a penchant for Piedmont wines, Italian football and anti-Bushisms. If you are a staunch Republican, you may not want to go. But if you love beautiful Italian wine more than politics, you should get down here. The tables and chairs are well spaced, comfortable and, no doubt, very expensive. Cheese, tapenade, olives and salamis come on plates with plenty of bread (great to share, and cheap too, at about €4-€6 per person). With an Italian deli, coffee shop and two more Italian restaurants in the same development, not for nothing is this area commonly known as the Italian Quarter.

Modern Irish

Chapter One

18-19 Parnell Square (873 2266/www.chapterone restaurant.com). All cross-city buses. **Open** 12.30-2.30pm, 6-11pm Tue-Fri; 6-11pm Sat. **Set menu** €30 2 courses; €32.50 3 courses. **Main courses** €30-€33. **Credit** AmEx, DC, MC, V. **Map** p251 E1. ⓴
If you want to sample some of the most exciting food in the city, not to mention rarefied historical surroundings, then turn to Chapter One. The dining room is warm and tasteful, service is formal but

easy-going, and the food is haute cuisine yet down to earth. Considered by many to be the best restaurant in the city, Chapter One is located near to the Gate Theatre, which means that it also offers an excellent pre-theatre menu, which is reasonably priced and includes bacon and potato cakes served with pearl barley and pumpkin purée, black pudding with caramelised apple and mousseline potato, or loin of free-range pork with red cabbage. Pecan and banana strüdel with rum cream and butterscotch is just one of the tempting desserts to be had. **Photo** *p111*.

Dublin Bay & the Coast

Middle Eastern

The Olive Tree
Islamic Cultural Centre, Clonskeagh (218 5791/www. iccislam.org). Bus 11. **Open** 9am-10pm daily. **Main courses** €6.95-€7.25. **No credit cards.**
Don't expect waiter service or wines by the glass: this is essentially a canteen within the Islamic Cultural Centre. But don't be shy, either, as the owners are delighted for non-Muslims to come and sample the delicious and extremely good-value grub. It's a well-kept secret, and when you go you'll see plenty of local Irish businessmen hoping to keep the great value under wraps. Grab a tray and help yourself to tabouleh, vine leaves and various bean salads from the salad bar before venturing off for plates piled high with rice, curries, schwarma and korma accompanied by pitta bread and garlic sauce. A delicious excuse for a trip to the Bay.

Modern Irish

Nosh
111 Coliemore Road, Dalkey (284 0666/ww.nosh.ie). DART Dalkey. **Open** noon-4pm, 6-10.30pm Tue-Sun. **Main courses** €10-€13.50 lunch; €16.95-€25 dinner. **Credit** MC, V.
A day trip to Dalkey is nice for anyone, be it locals, tourists or stargazers and celebrity stalkers. It's the Beverly Hills of Dublin. The pubs do a great trade, but for something a bit more sophisticated food-wise (but still very casual), Nosh fits nicely. It's light, bright, clean and friendly. Fish and chips, steak sandwiches and the like keep the blokes happy, while salads and pasta dishes satisfy the girls. It's consistently busy and has survived in a fickle village, where many restaurants have been and gone. When you go, you'll see why.

Seafood

Aqua
1 West Pier, Howth (832 0690/www.aqua.ie). DART Howth. **Open** 1-3pm, 5.30-9.30pm Tue-Sat; 12.30-4pm, 6-9.30pm Sun. **Set menu** €29.95 3 courses. **Main courses** €17-€30. **Credit** AmEx, MC, V.

This industrial first-floor building used to be the yacht club, although when you actually see it, you'll find it looks a lot more like a factory of sorts. But its distinctly urban appearance is softened by gorgeous sea views and a very warm, cosy bar area in front of a casual, uncluttered dining room (the venue for a great Sunday lunch complete with live jazz). On bright, sunny days, leave time for a nice stroll around the harbour; at night, it's all aglow and perfect for couples, although prices get heftier. Given the coastal location, fish is the order of the day: smoked salmon, crayfish salad, seared scallops and monkfish. There's also meat for the carnivores and pasta for fussy kids.

Thai

Mao
The Pavilion, Dún Laoghaire (214 8090/www.cafe mao.com). DART Dún Laoghaire/bus 7, 7A, 46A. **Open** noon-10.30pm Mon-Wed; noon-11pm Thur; noon-11.30pm Sat; noon-10pm Sun. **Main courses** €9.95-€18.95. **Credit** AmEx, MC, V.
If the sun is shining and you want to take in some harbour air, then this restaurant is a suitably laid-back option. The Thai food is tasty, well presented and (on our visit) served by pretty, young student types. You can sit outside on the 'Metals' (a concrete plaza) and enjoy what sunshine there is while eating some very reasonably priced fish cakes, nasi goreng, chilli squid and all the usual suspects. Wash it down with bottles of Asian beer.
Other locations: Chatham Row, Around St Stephen's Green (670 4898); Dundrum Town Square, The New Dundrum Town Centre, Dundrum (296 2802).

Southern suburbs

French

French Paradox
53 Shelbourne Road, Ballsbridge (660 4068/ www.thefrenchparadox.com). DART Lansdowne/ bus 7, 45A. **Open** noon-10pm Mon-Sat. **Set lunch** €14.95 2 courses; €19.95 3 courses. **Main courses** €16-€18.95. **Credit** AmEx, MC, V.
A wine shop, deli and restaurant rolled into one, French Paradox is a joy to behold: lead-topped counters, orange leather banquettes and exposed brick walls make for a stylish backdrop. And to sharpen the appetite, platters of delicious Irish and French cheeses, cured meats and pâtés are also on display. It's mouth-watering stuff. But wine is this restaurant's true raison d'être, and advice on that subject is plentiful (and not of the hectoring, snobby variety that one all too often encounters in sommeliers of posh restaurants). The food, meanwhile, is good for picking at rather than pigging out on. An obvious fondness for artisanal products and a passion for the mighty grape override any gripes about lack of space. An adorable place.

International

Café at the Four Seasons

Four Seasons Hotel, Simmonscourt Road, Ballsbridge (269 6446). Bus 7. **Open** 3-11.30pm Mon-Thur; 3pm-12.30am Fri, Sat; 5-11.30pm Sun. **Main courses** €15-€36. **Credit** AmEx, DC, MC, V.

The dining room is split into two: the fancy Seasons restaurant and the Café, which offers casual and tasty food with sublime service. Chicken noodle soup, Caesar salad, beef and Guinness stew, stir-fried noodles with prawns and Asian greens are all typical offerings. The food in the main dining room is a good deal smarter (and costs a small fortune), but don't be ashamed of eating for a fraction of the price next door. The only drawback? There's a no-bookings policy (although some would consider that to be something of an advantage). Anyway, the hotel lobby and bars are good places to wander for 20 minutes until a table is ready.

Itsa4 Sandymount

6A Sandymount Green, Sandymount (219 4676/ www.itsabagel.com). Bus 2, 3, 18/DART Sandymount. **Open** noon-4pm, 6-10pm Mon-Fri; 11am-4pm, 6-10pm Sat; 11am-4pm, 5-9pm Sun. **Main course** €10.95-€24 lunch; €17-€28 dinner. **Credit** MC, V.

Sandymount is a posh and pretty little village on the right side of town, where the locals can be a bit demanding. And why not? They practically run the country. Itsa4 has been welcomed as a family-cum-neighbourhood restaurant serving up favourites like seared niçoise salad or ribeye steak and organic chips in the comfortable surroundings of the dining room's booths or (in warmer weather) the garden. Organic dishes and Irish suppliers are a priority here. At night, get stuck into something a little fancier: seared scallops with chilli and mango salad, sea bass with asparagus and curry oil, or rump of lamb with fresh minted peas and pancetta sit alongside a sensible kids' menu (although children are banished at 8.30pm).

Italian

Antica Venezia

97 Ashfield Road, Ranelagh (497 4112). Bus 11, 48/Luas Ranelagh. **Open** 5.30-11.30pm daily. **Main courses** €8.70-€27.95. **Credit** MC, V.

Good restaurants, good wine shops, good food shops: Ranelagh is fast becoming a little foodie nexus. Antica Venezia is staffed and (mainly) patronised by Italians – on some evenings, we have been completely surrounded by the sound of Italian being spoken (a welcome soundtrack to any meal). Food is predictable Italian fare (fresh antipasti, pastas aplenty – gamberoni, carbonara, amatriciana, arrabbiata, toscana, pesto, bolognese – and big pizzas) bolstered by a number of grilled meat dishes. Prices are quite reasonable, and the atmosphere makes for a romantic if faintly kitsch dining experience.

Modern Irish

Mint

47 Ranelagh Village, Ranelagh (497 8655). Bus 11, 11a, 18, 44, 44N, 48A, 48N/Luas Ranelagh. **Open** 12.30-2.30pm, 6.45-10.30pm Tue-Sun. **Set lunch** €31.50 3 courses. **Set dinner** €65 3 courses. **Credit** AmEx, MC, V.

Mint is the place for excellently sophisticated food served by young, confident and formal (yet relaxed) staff. Fantastic bread hints at real talent in the pastry section, but it doesn't stop there: start with the peppered tuna and go on to the sea bream with garlic potatoes or the rump of veal with cep risotto. Spanking good desserts too. A promising little restaurant with high aspirations and top service, Mint is well worth those extra few minutes spent travelling on the Luas.

Oriental

Diep Noodle Bar

Ranelagh Village, Ranelagh (497 6550/www.diep. net). Bus 11, 11A, 18, 44, 44N, 48A, 48N/Luas Ranelagh. **Open** 4-10.30pm Mon; 4-11pm Tue; 12.30-11pm Wed, Thur; 12.30-11.30pm Fri; 2-11.30pm Sat; 2-10.30pm Sun. **Main courses** €9-€11.95 lunch; €10.50-€19 dinner. **Credit** AmEx, MC, V.

To look at, this is undoubtedly the slickest Thai restaurant in Dublin – and yet, despite its chi-chi design, it somehow manages to remain entirely accessible. Most people come for the mind-blowing cocktails and the look of the place, as opposed to the grub (quality has been a bit up and down). Still, if it's sophisticated Thai dining you're after, there's always Diep Le Shaker, the (fancier) sibling restaurant in Dublin 2.

Other locations: Diep Le Shaker, 55 Pembroke Lane, Around Trinity College (661 1829/ www.diep.net).

Furama

Eirpage House, Donnybrook (283 0522/ www.furama.ie). Bus 46A. **Open** 12.30-2pm, 6-11.30pm Mon-Thur; 12.30pm, 6pm-midnight Fri; 6pm-midnight Sat; 1.30-11pm Sun. **Main courses** €12-€15 lunch; €13-€30 dinner. **Credit** AmEx, DC, MC, V.

While Chinese, Indian and Thai restaurants are a dime a dozen in Dublin, only a few of them are half decent. There's nothing unique about the look of this place or its line-up of dishes, but Furama rises above the norm by doing its food well. Dishes are light and tasty, the staff are helpful and courteous – and options like crispy duck with hoisin sauce, pancakes and spring onion, while not ground-breakingly original, are nevertheless well worth sharing. (Although you might want to keep the wonderful beef with ginger and garlic all to yourself.) Smart business types make up the bulk of the clientele here, except at more family-oriented weekends. Perhaps not worth a trip to Donnybrook, but great if you happen to be in the area.

Cafés & Coffee Shops

Louche on the Liffey.

Like apartment blocks, coffee shops in Dublin seem to be multiplying at a dizzy rate. Outlets of chains like Insomnia and Starbucks are sprouting across the city, ensuring that no matter where you go, you'll never be more than a minute's walk from a caffeine fix. You can't escape the coffee culture here, and few people would want to. Drinking a 12oz cappuccino accompanied by a complimentary handmade chocolate of choice is not to be sniffed at.

Dubliners have embraced caffeine culture like a long-lost friend. In this chapter, we have listed what we consider to be the most interesting cafés in urban Dublin. Whether it's their unique atmosphere, superior coffee or simply the fact that the staff are happy to let you linger for hours reading or chatting, Dublin's cafés provide a welcome alternative to the major chains – although, we have mentioned some of those too. Order a cup of Guatemalan Maragogype, sit down and read on.

Around Trinity College

Avoca
11-13 Suffolk Street (672 6019/www.avoca.ie).
All cross city buses/Luas St Stephen's Green.
Open 10am-5.30pm Mon-Sat; 11am-5pm Sun.
Main courses €12-€15. **Credit** AmEx, MC, V.
Map p252 F3 ❶
Avoca is a charming department store experience: quaint, classy and very Irish. They have a food hall in the basement and a modern, casual café upstairs where they serve soups (tomato and basil), pies (field mushroom and Parmesan tartlet), salads and designer sarnies. Brunch on Sunday is good: expect smooth jazz and a queue.

Beacon Cove
Powerscourt Townhouse Centre, Clarendon Street (679 7772). All cross-city buses/Luas St Stephen's Green. **Open** 8am-7pm Mon-Wed, Fri, Sat; 8am-8pm Thur; 10am-6pm Sun. **Snacks** €2.25-€6.95. **Credit** AmEx, DC, MC, V. **Map** p252 F3 ❷
This spot specialises in flavoured coffee, and it has an enormous array of exotic options. And if you require a regular caffeine fix, you can even buy one of its coffee-makers. It's a pleasant enough place, but to be honest, its cakes and pastries are something of a disappointment.

Bewley's Oriental Café
78 Grafton Street (672 7720/www.bewleys.ie). All cross-city buses/Luas St Stephen's Green. **Open** 7.30am-8pm Mon-Fri; 8am-8pm Sat, Sun. **Main courses** €6-€10. **Credit** AmEx, DC, MC, V. **Map** p252 F4 ❸
Ernest Bewley first started brewing coffee and baking sticky buns for Dubliners over a century ago, when he opened the first of his Oriental Cafés. The flagship café on Grafton Street opened its doors in 1927 and has since gone through many hands; it's now the only remaining café bearing the Bewley's name, and worth visiting – even if only to breakfast by the beauty of the original Harry Clarke windows on the ground floor.

Brown's Bar
Brown Thomas, Grafton Street (605 6666/www. brownthomas.ie). All cross-city buses/Luas St Stephen's Green. **Open** 9am-8pm Mon-Wed, Fri; 9am-9pm Thur; 9am-7pm Sat; 10am-7pm Sun. **Snacks** €5-€12.50. **Credit** AmEx, MC, V. **Map** p252 F3 ❹
As you descend the main staircase of the swanky Brown Thomas department store (*see p138*), this

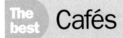

The best Cafés

Bewley's Oriental Café
Simply essential. *See left.*

Brown's Bar
To see and been seen at. *See above.*

Café Cagliostro
Tiny and fabulous. *See p121.*

Dunne & Crescenzi
The original Dublin Italian. *See p118.*

Fallon & Byrne
For choice and freshness. *See p121.*

Joy of Coffee
The name says it all. *See p119.*

La Maison des Gourmets
For sheer French panache. *See p119.*

Nude
For coffee with virtue. *See p118.*

Panem
Fun, style and river views. *See p121.*

Silk Road
Spicy, and yet tranquil. *See p120.*

Eat, Drink, Shop

Simon's Place. *See p120.*

trendy café opens up before you. It's a crowded place with people perched on small chairs beside small tables: not the most comfortable café in the world, and not exactly cheap. Still, Brown's is somewhere to see and be seen at, and it offers good coffee and pastries. Just don't get icing sugar on the suits.

Butler's Chocolate Café

24 Wicklow Street (671 0591/www.butlerschocolates. com). All cross-city buses/Luas St Stephen's Green. **Open** 8am-7pm Mon-Wed, Fri; 8am-8pm Thur; 9am-7pm Sat; 11am-7pm Sun. **Snacks** €1.80-€3.50. **Credit** AmEx, MC, V. **Map** p252 F3 ⑤

As the name suggests, this isn't simply a place to have coffee in. Alongside its excellent choice of coffee and superior cocoa, there's a luxurious range of handmade chocolates. Sadly, the sparse seating arrangement means Butler's is better suited to a quick pitstop than a long stay – however much you'd like to linger.

Other locations: Chatham Street (672 6333); 51A Grafton Street (671 0599); 19 Nassau Street (671 0772), 31 Henry Street (874 7419).

Il Caffè di Napoli

41 Westland Row, Around Trinity College (611 4831). All cross-city buses. **Open** 7am-8.30pm Mon-Fri; 9am-7pm Sat; 10am-6pm Sun. **Snacks** €3-€5. **Credit** MC, V. **Map** p251 G5 ⑥

See p120 **Take these chains.**

Other locations: throughout the city.

Dunne & Crescenzi

14-16 Frederick Street South (671 9135/www.dunne andcrescenzi.com). All cross-city buses/Luas St Stephen's Green. **Open** 8.30am-11pm Mon-Sat; noon-6pm Sun. **Main courses** €7.50-€11. **Credit** MC, V. **Map** p252 F4 ⑦

This is the original (and probably still the best) Italian café in town. Or, more accurately, Italian

cafés – for it now has two adjoining spaces on South Frederick Street. Both are small, dark and crowded, and both can feel a touch on the claustrophobic side. But the food is truly wonderful: the tasty, fresh and simple lunches include cured and smoked meats, salads and panini; there's also a full wine list and, of course, superlative coffee. **Photo** *p121.*

Fresh

Top Floor, Powerscourt Townhouse Centre, Clarendon Street (671 9669/www.cafe-fresh.com). All cross-city buses/Luas St Stephen's. **Open** 10am-6pm Mon-Wed, Fri; 10am-6pm Thur; 10am-6pm Sat. **Main courses** €4.75-€8.95. **Credit** MC, V. **Map** p252 F3 ⑧

Fresh serves excellent vegetarian and vegan food. Its menu lists a broad selection of tasty main meals, bolstered by a good choice of soups, imaginative salads and sundry sweet things. Try the apricot bran muffins early in the morning, followed by the miso soup. This is one of the best veggie spots in town.

Nude

21 Suffolk Street (677 4804/www.nude.ie). All cross-city buses/Luas St Stephen's Green. **Open** 7.30am-9pm Mon-Wed; 7.30am-10pm Thur; 8am-9pm Sat; 9am-8pm Sun. **Snacks** €4.50-€5.50. **Credit** AmEx, MC, V. **Map** p252 F3 ⑨

If you prefer your food with a dollop of virtue, this is the place: Nude specialises in freshly squeezed juices of all varieties. The menu also has excellent wraps, paninis, pre-packed salads (the chick pea and chilli is a good bet) and a small selection of snacks and sweets. It has long, canteen-style tables and hard benches, and you're not exactly encouraged to linger. But if you want some quick vitamins, and you can stomach the prices, you'll love this joint.

Other locations: 103 Lower Leeson Street (661 5650); 38 Upper Baggot Street (668 0551); BT2, 28 Grafton Street (672 5577).

Eat, Drink, Shop

La Corte

Top Floor, Powerscourt Townhouse Centre, William Street South (633 4477). All cross-city buses/Luas St Stephen's Green. **Open** 10am-6pm Mon-Sat. **Main courses** €7-€10. **Credit** MC, V. **Map** p252 F3 ⑬
Part of a new wave of good Italian cafés, La Corte's biggest attraction is its location – high up on the top floor of the Powerscourt, far from the madding crowd. It offers excellent coffee and lunches of panini and antipasti. Ingredients are simple and excellent, and the service swift and pleasant.
Other locations: Epicurean Food Hall, Liffey Street (873 4200); International Financial Services Centre, Custom House Square, North Quays (672 1929).

LaraLu

George's Street Arcade, South Great George's Street (087 990 8003). All cross-city buses/Luas St Stephen's Green. **Open** 10.30am-6pm Mon-Sat. **Snacks** €3.40-€5.60. **No credit cards. Map** p252 E3 ⑭
Welcoming you to the bizarre delights of the George's Street Arcade, Lara Lu has no seating, but is handy if you want to assemble a picnic lunch. It sells terrific sandwiches, picnic foods and fresh, healthy soups; stay away from the hotpots though – they can be a bit on the greasy side.

Lemon Crêpe & Coffee Company

66 William Street South (672 9044/www.lemonco. com). All cross-city buses/Luas St Stephen's Green. **Open** 8am-7.30pm Mon-Wed, Fri; 8am-9pm Thur; 9am-7.30pm Sat; 10am-6.30pm Sun. **Snacks** €5-€10. **No credit cards. Map** p252 F3 ⑮
Amid the tyranny of ciabatta and panini, a café specialising in crêpes is a relief. Come here for tasty sweet and savoury pancake-based snacks; and if you really want a sandwich, they can do that, too. The café is small and usually crowded, so you might prefer a table outside: it's a good spot from which to watch trendy young things stroll past.
Other locations: 60 Dawson Street (672 8898).

La Maison des Gourmets

15 Castle Market (672 7258). All cross-city buses. **Open** 8am-7pm Mon-Fri; 8am-6pm Sat. **Main courses** €9.50-€13. **Credit** AmEx, MC, V. **Map** p252 F3 ⑯
This charming French pâtisserie sits above an excellent bakery of the same name, and has recently had a much-needed revamp. The tiny dining room, kitted out in off-whites and cool grey banquettes, is sunny and welcoming, and the food is superb: french toast with bacon for breakfast, savoury tarts for lunch, and cakes all day long. Service can be slow and less than charming; but if you want the best of French pastries and coffee, this is the place.

Queen of Tarts

4 Cork Hill, Dame Street (670 7499). All cross-city buses. **Open** 7.30am-6pm Mon-Fri; 9am-6pm Sat; 10am-6pm Sun. **Main courses** €5-€8. **No credit cards. Map** p252 E3 ⑰
The Queen of Tarts reigns supreme as one of Dublin's quality cafés, and the food that's served

West Coast Coffee Company

2 Lincoln Place, Around Trinity College (661 4253). All cross-city buses. **Open** 7am-6pm Mon-Fri; 9am-5pm Sat; 10am-3pm Sun. **Snacks** €1-€5. **No credit cards. Map** p251 G5 ⑩
See p120 **Take these chains.**
Other locations: throughout the city.

Around Temple Bar

Joy of Coffee

25 East Essex Street, Temple Bar (679 3393/www. joyofcoffee.ie). All cross-city buses/Luas Jervis. **Open** 9am-11pm Mon-Thur; 9am-11.30pm Sat; 10am-10pm Sun. **Main courses** €5-€8.50. **No credit cards. Map** p252 E3 ⑪
This is probably the pick of the crop in Temple Bar. Joy of Coffee is small and often crowded, and its seats are none too comfortable; but it offers a decent menu and really takes its brews seriously. Even better, nobody will annoy you if you just want to sit down and have a long read of the paper – all of which makes it popular with the trendy crowd.

Kaffe-Moka

39 William Street South (679 8475). All cross-city buses/Luas St Stephen's Green. **Open** 8am-midnight Mon-Fri; 10am-midnight Sat, Sun. **Main courses** €7.50-€12. **Credit** MC, V. **Map** p252 E5 ⑫
One of Dublin's first continental-style cafés, the Kaffe-Moka mini-chain got it right from the beginning, with a winning mix of big windows, dozens of teas and coffees and a relaxed atmosphere. They serve no fewer than 40 different types of coffee, all ground to order. Chess games and newspapers are available; upstairs is a bit calmer and has squashy sofas – perfect for a lazy afternoon.
Other locations: Epicurean Food Hall, Middle Abbey Street, Around O'Connell Street (872 9078).

here is suitably regal. We're talking terrific grub: breakfasts might be potato cakes or scones with raspberries or mixed fruit; the lunchtime savoury tarts are light, flaky and delicious. Everything is baked on the premises. For most people, though, the real glory is the wide range of cakes, crumbles, brownies and meringues.

Other locations: City Hall, Dame Street (672 2925).

Silk Road
Chester Beatty Library, Dublin Castle (407 0750/ www.cbl.ie). All cross-city buses/Luas Jervis. **Open** May-Sept 10am-5pm Mon-Fri; 11am-5pm Sat; 1-5pm Sun. Oct-Apr 10am-5pm Tue-Fri; 11am-5pm Sat; 1-5pm Sun. **Main courses** €8.50-€11. **Credit** AmEx, MC, V. **Map** p252 E3 ⓭

Silk Road is set inside the fabulous Chester Beatty Library (*see p66*), and carries the museum's Eastern and Islamic theme into its menu. Come here for spice and heat, or the excellent value coriander-flecked salads, as well as for tall glasses of mint tea and honey-soaked baklava. The place tends to be pleasantly tranquil; nab a table beside the long, gleaming pool in the museum's atrium, and relax.

Simon's Place
George's Street Arcade, South Great George's Street (679 7821). All cross-city buses/Luas St Stephen's Green. **Open** 8.30am-5.15pm Mon-Sat. **Snacks** €3.60-€4.20. **No credit cards. Map** p252 E3 ⓯

Simon says: sometimes simplicity is best. Great soups, good coffee, vast sarnies and a casual vibe are the trademarks of this popular café. The layout is a little chaotic and uninspiring – it's certainly not designed to please – but the atmosphere is warm and busy. If you want to find out what's going on around town, this is the place to come to: there are fliers and posters everywhere. Get here late morning to sample the sublime cinnamon buns. **Photos** *p118*.

Around St Stephen's Green

Café Java
145 Leeson Street Upper (660 0675). Bus 11, 11A, 46A. **Open** 7.15am-3.45pm Mon-Fri; 9am-3.45pm Sat; 10am-3.45pm Sun. **Snacks** €4.95-€9.50. **Credit** MC, V. **Map** p251 G6 ⓴

Café Java has been around for ages and ages, and it still seems to be holding its own against newer competitors. The secrets of its ongoing popularity are breakfast, lunch and coffee, and its clever mix of light food – bagels, poached eggs, sandwiches with a twist – is handled well in simple but stylish surroundings. Staff are sweet, too.

Other locations: 5 Anne Street South (670 7239).

Café Sol
58 Harcourt Street, Around St Stephen's Green (475 1167/www.cafesol.ie). All cross-city buses. **Open** 7am-6pm Mon-Fri. **Snacks** €3-€4. **No credit cards. Map** p251 F6 ㉑

See below **Take these chains**.

Other locations: Throughout the city.

National Gallery of Ireland Café & Fitzer's Restaurant
Merrion Square West (663 3500/www.fitzers.ie). All cross-city buses. **Open** 9.30am-5.30pm Mon-Wed, Fri, Sat; 9.30am-8.30pm Thur; noon-5pm Sun. **Main courses** €10-€11.50. **Credit** AmEx, DC, MC, V. **Map** p251 G4 ㉒

The National Gallery's Millennium Wing houses two lovely cafés. The smaller one, occupying a bright, white, funkily furnished room on the second level, offers coffee, tea, scones and snacks. The Fitzer's Restaurant in the Winter Garden is flooded with light from a glass roof and serves stylish (although uneven) main meals. Both spots are worth a visit for the surroundings alone.

Take these chains

It's hardly a secret that Dubliners really love their coffee, and the competition to provide them with a daily fix intensifies with every passing week. The city's coffee shop chains range from huge multinational brands (yes, US behemoth Starbucks has branches in Dublin) to smaller, more individual and more enjoyable operations. Below are three of our favourites – reliable outfits, all.

Café Sol
Sol has a branch, shop or vendor on every corner, it seems. The sandwiches and muffins are not bad, both for choice and quality. This particular branch (*see above*) enjoys a great location right next to the dreamy Iveagh Gardens.

Il Caffe di Napoli
The best takeaway coffee in the city (*see p118* – and this branch is conveniently close to both Pearse Station and Merrion Square. The coffee, pastries and sandwiches are excellent; service is snappy and courteous. **Hunger's Mother** is a nearby branch – it's a little bigger, with seats, and excellent food (11-14 Fenian Street, 639 8884, closed weekends).

West Coast Coffee Company
The comfy sofas and excellent menu of paninis, pastries and light meals draw you irresistibly in. The coffee is always good, and this branch (*see p119*) is handy for Trinity College and Merrion Square.

Dunne & Crescenzi. *See p118.*

Relax

*Habitat, 7 St Stephen's Green North (674 6624).
All cross-city buses/Luas St Stephen's Green.* **Open**
10am-5pm Mon-Wed, Fri; 10am-7pm Thur; 9.30am-
5pm Sat; noon-5pm Sun. **Snacks** €7.95-€16.95.
Credit MC, V. **Map** p252 F3 ㉔
In spite of its woeful name, this café upstairs in
Habitat is cool, sleek and fashionable – if a tad loud.
Habitat furniture and design are used throughout,
Rothko prints adorn the walls and the food runs
from coffee and pastries to soups and pasta.

Around O'Connell Street

Café Cagliostro

*Bloom's Lane, 24 Ormond Quay Lower (888 0860).
All cross-city buses/Luas Jervis.* **Open** 7am-6pm Mon-
Fri; 8am-6pm Sat; 9am-6pm Sun. **Snacks** €5.50.
Credit MC, V. **Map** p252 E2 ㉒
Tiny and fabulous, Café Cagliostro is one of the main
tenants in the Bloom's Lane courtyard, just off the
quays. It features plain, stylish furniture and offers
excellent coffee and hot chocolate, as well as a chaste
but tasty selection of Italian sandwiches and desserts.

Cobalt Café

*16 North Great George's Street (873 0313). All cross-
city buses.* **Open** 10am-11pm Mon-Sun. **Snacks**
€5.20-€7.80. **Credit** MC, V. **Map** p251 F1 ㉕
Housed in a skilfully restored Georgian house, this
handsome place is popular with local arty types and

office workers. On the arts side, Cobalt doubles as a
gallery, and hosts the occasional cabaret night. The
food can be hit and miss. But if you're after style and
a relaxed atmosphere, look no further.

Expresso Bar

*6 Custom House Quay, IFSC (672 1812). Bus
90A/Luas Busaras.* **Open** 7am-5pm Mon-Fri; 10am-
5pm Sat, Sun. **Main courses** €11-€17.50. **Credit**
AmEx, MC, V. **Map** p251 G2 ㉖
The Expresso Bar serves good food in stylish surroundings. The bright white dining room and huge
white plates are nice, and the food – pancakes and
bacon drenched with syrup (breakfast), warm salads and elegant pasta dishes (lunch) and cinnamon-
dusted bread-and-butter pud (all day) – is a winner.
Other locations. 1 St Mary's Road, Ballsbridge
(660 0585).

Fallon & Byrne

*11-17 Exchequer Street (472 1010/www.fallonand
byrne.com). All cross-city buses/Luas St Stephen's
Green.* **Open** 8am-10pm Mon-Fri; 9am-9pm Sat;
11am-7pm Sun. **Main courses** €3.50-€6. **Credit**
MC, V. **Map** p252 E3 ㉗
A recent addition to Dublin's ever burgeoning gas-
tro revolution, Fallon & Byrne serves a wide range
of food from its long, well-stocked counters. Plain
sandwiches are given a dramatic twist, and the hot
food is sumptuous: pleasingly fresh vegetables, say,
or perfectly cooked Thai green curry.

Govinda's

*4 Aungier Street, (475 0309) All cross-city buses/
Luas St Stephen's Green.* **Open** noon-9pm Mon-Sat.
Snacks €2.95-€9.30. **Credit** AmEx, MC, V. **Map**
p252 E4 ㉘
This place is run by the Dublin Hare Krishna
branch. Even if you're not vegetarian, you'd be hard
pressed not to be tempted by something on the wide
ranging menu: dahl and rice, samosas and salads.

Munchies

*19-22 Lord Edward Street (670 9476/
www.munchies.ie). All cross-city buses.* **Open** 7am-
7pm Mon-Sat; 9am-6pm Sun. **Main courses** varies.
Credit AmEx, MC, V. **Map** p252 D/E3. ㉙
Thank goodness, Munchies hasn't lost any of its
charm after its recent refurbishment. Excellent breakfasts still vie for precedence over such classics as the
Munchie Brunchie and one of the best club sandwiches in town; the place is hectic at lunch. The down-
side is the mark-up you have to pay for eating in.

Panem

*21 Ormond Quay Lower (872 8510). All cross-city
buses/Luas Jervis.* **Open** 9am-6pm Mon-Sat; 10am-
4pm Sun. **Snacks** €2.80-€4.20. **No credit cards**.
Map p252 E2 ㉚
Panem is the real thing in a world of fakes. True, the
space is tiny and the menu not extensive, but what
it does, it does brilliantly: fine coffees, good soups,
filled focaccias, freshly baked bread, savoury pasties
and a couple of daily pasta dishes – all served up in
a fun, stylish room overlooking the river.

Pubs & Bars

It's not all pint-sized, you know.

The 'Dodgy Few' no more: Temple Bar's **Foggy Dew** has remade itself in style. *See p127.*

Dublin writer Brendan Behan called himself 'a drinker with a writing problem'. Oscar Wilde, once a resident of Merrion Square, reckoned 'work is the curse of the drinking classes'. And on one occasion, Tipperary-born actor Richard Harris claimed he'd formed 'a new group called Alcoholics Unanimous. If you don't feel like a drink, you ring another member and he comes over to persuade you'.

Yes, when it comes to the Irish and drinking, this is the city that launched a thousand quips. Booze-related quotes, jokes and clichés fall like rain on the Liffey around here, but we've got a newsflash for you: it's a myth. You've been had.

In Ireland, the fields really are emerald green and the people genuinely friendly; but there are no leprechauns, no one says 'top o' the mornin', and the citizens of Dublin do not spend their days slouched on barstools waiting for you to walk in so they can entertain you.

Once you've filed all that neatly away under 'marketing strategy', though, you can still go out and discuss it over a fine pint of Guinness. For there are plenty of excellent pubs and entertaining bars in Dublin in which you

can while away your own days and nights. The nightlife here probably won't blow away somebody familiar with New York or London, but it's thoroughly enjoyable all the same. As long as you don't smoke, that is. Smoking in bars and restaurants was banned in a sweeping, California-style edict that came into effect in 2004 (*see p131* **Ave pariah**).

Now, would the fun-loving, cigarette-waving, pint-chugging Irish people you've heard about all your life do a thing like that? Never. They're a myth, we tell you.

WHERE TO DRINK

If what you're looking for is a pub with a bit of *craic*, as they rarely say around here (another myth), you almost cannot go wrong. Any part of town will do. But here are a few pointers to get you started: south of the river is where Dublin's more fashion-conscious drinkers like to rest their Prada bags and sip Cosmopolitans, while the area north of the river is associated with more old-fashioned, down-to-earth pubs. Still, that demographic is changing somewhat, particularly along the North Quays, where edgy and interesting new bars are luring of trendsters across the river in growing numbers. Temple Bar is famed for being packed with particularly drunk, particularly boring British people (Americans: think 'frat party'), while the joints around Trinity College can, at times, attract middle-aged tourists by the busload.

But there are countless exceptions to every one of these rules, so we suggest you pick a bar from our list that sounds like your kind of place and go there, regardless of where it happens to be located. And once you've found it, take a moment to raise a glass to Brendan. That Irishman really could drink.

Around Trinity College

AKA
6 Wicklow Street (670 4220). All cross-city buses/Luas St Stephen's Green. **Open** 3pm-1am Mon-Thur; 3pm-3am Fri, Sat. **Credit** MC, V. **Map** p252 F3 ①
Leather beanbags are among the recent refurbishment's new ideas, but this subterranean bar is still weak on atmosphere and strong on loud music and expensive drinks – and past its prime. Still, it's a reasonably stylish place in which to down a pre-club cocktail or post-prandial bevvie.

Bailey
2 Duke Street (670 4939). All cross-city buses/Luas St Stephen's Green. **Open** noon-11.30pm Mon-Thur, Sun; noon-12.30pm Fri, Sat. **Credit** AmEx, MC, V. **Map** p252 F3 ②
Aching to be hip, thoroughly self-conscious: this is not the original Bailey of lore. Before it was torn down years back, the old one featured in *Ulysses* (Leopold Bloom lived at 7 Eccles Street, which used to be one of the entrances to the bar) and was a vital organ in Dublin's literary life. Today, the new one has decor and drinks prices in step with the chic clientele, though the outdoor seating area is a great spot at which to while away an afternoon watching Dubliners walk past. Bring a well-stuffed wallet.

Ba Mizu
Powerscourt Townhouse Centre, 59 William Street South (674 6712/www.bamizu.com). All cross-city buses. **Open** noon-11.30pm Mon-Wed; noon-2.30am Thur-Sat; 12.30-11pm Sun. **Credit** MC, V. **Map** p252 F3 ③
Richly decorated in dark wood and some decidedly odd art, Ba Mizu is one of Dublin's better 'new' watering holes. Subdued lighting and plush leather armchairs make the lobby bar perfect for a nocturnal rendezvous, while the back bar offers brighter and busier surroundings. Take a look underfoot and you'll notice there's a river running through the bar.

The Bank
20-22 College Green (677 0677/www.bankoncollege green.com). All cross-city buses. **Open** 9.30am-midnight Mon-Wed; 9.30am-1am Thur; 9.30am-1.30am Fri, Sat; 9.30pm-midnight Sun. **Credit** AmEx, DC, MC, V. **Map** p252 F3 ④

No prizes for guessing what type of transaction used to be carried out here. The central bar dominates the spacious lounge, and professional types sprawl on the surrounding seating area. There are some beautiful design features, but the atmosphere isn't exactly marvellous.

Bruxelles
7-8 Harry Street, off Grafton Street (677 5362). All cross-city buses/Luas St Stephen's Green. **Open** 10.30am-1.30am Mon-Wed; 10.30am-2.30am Thur-Sat; noon-1.30am Sun. **No credit cards.** **Map** p252 F4 ⑤
Bruxelles is one of those Dublin institutions that somehow manage to appeal to almost every punter – especially chin-stroking music fans, students and tourists. The rockers and mods bar downstairs plays a weird mix of tunes; upstairs is for those who just fancy a good pint and a chat. Although it needs a lick of paint, the place has pots of charm – and a useful outside seating area.

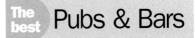
The best Pubs & Bars

The Cobblestone
Trad music downstairs, top bands upstairs, and as cosy as they come. *See p134.*

The Foggy Dew
Because it's as popular with the locals as it is with tourists. *See p127.*

The Hairy Lemon
For the name. *See p136.*

JJ Smyths
As a boozer it's fair, but as a jazz venue it's simply tops. *See p132.*

Life Café-Bar
For pure relaxation. *See p134.*

The Long Hall
This ornate Victorian gin hall is still one of Dublin's unmissable boozers. *See p129.*

Octagon Bar
OK, it's painfully hip; but it's also friendly, and the cocktails are fab. *See p129.*

The Palace
Oldest bar in town and still fine. *See p130.*

The Porterhouse
When you've had enough of the black stuff, try this microbrewery. *See p130.*

Ron Blacks
It looks like a gentleman's drinking club. What more needs to be said? *See p127.*

Café en Seine

40 Dawson Street (677 4567/www.capitalbars.com).
All cross-city buses/Luas St Stephen's Green.
Open 11am-2.30am daily. **Credit** AmEx, MC, V.
Map p252 F4 ⑥

One of Dublin's first superpubs, Café en Seine has a decadent art deco theme reminiscent of 19th-century Paris. It's big enough to get lost in, so overcrowding is never a problem. The place is an after-work favourite among Dawson Street professionals, and is rumoured to have had the most expensive refurbishment in Dublin – which might explain the sky-high cost of a drink. **Photos** *opposite.*

Cocoon

Royal Hibernian Way, off Grafton Street (679 6259/www.cocoon.ie). All cross-city buses/Luas St Stephen's Green. **Open** 11.30am-3pm Mon, Thur, Fri, Sat; 11.30am-11.30pm Tue, Wed; 4-11.30pm Sun.
Credit MC, V. **Map** p252 F4 ⑦

Owned by Ireland's own international playboy Eddie Irvine, Cocoon is one of Dublin's swankiest bars. As the saying goes, 'it's for men who want to be Eddie Irvine, and women who want to sleep with him.' Beautiful staff serve expensive cocktails to beautiful yuppies, but there are a few detectable signs of wear and tear. **Photo** *p126.*

Dakota

9 William Street South (672 7696/www.dakota bar.ie). All cross-city buses/Luas St Stephen's Green. **Open** noon-11.30 Mon-Wed, Sun; noon-2am Thur; noon-2.30am Fri, Sat. **Credit** AmEx, MC, V. **Map** p252 F3 ⑧

Dimmed lighting and half-moon leather booths make Dakota one of Dublin's coolest and (predictably) busiest late-night bars. The long bar ensures you're never waiting too long for a drink, although it can get a bit hectic at the weekend. It's a great place for a sociable drink with friends (try to grab one of those booths) and reliably quiet during the day, with a cool warehouse feel.

Davy Byrne's

21 Duke Street (677 5217/www.davybyrnes.com).
All cross-city buses/Luas St Stephen's Green. **Open** 11am-11.30pm Mon-Thur; 11am-12.30am Fri; 9am-12.30am Sat; 11am-11pm Sun. **Credit** AmEx, MC, V.
Map p252 F4 ⑨

In *Ulysses*, Leopold Bloom stops here for a gorgonzola sandwich and a glass of burgundy. 'He raised his eyes and met the stare of a bilious clock. Two. Pub clock five minutes fast. Time going on. Hands moving. Two. Not yet.' The clock is said to be kept a five minutes fast, and the bar is now a regular for well-dressed Dubliners. Seating can be scarce, and the place is better suited to conversation than raucous revelry.

The Duke

9 Duke Street (679 9553). All cross-city buses/Luas St Stephen's Green. **Open** 11am-11.30pm Mon-Thur; 11.30pm-12.30am Fri, Sat; noon-11pm Sun. **Credit** AmEx, MC, V. **Map** p252 F3 ⑩

If you feel daunted by the prospect of the hyper-trendy pubs nearby, the Duke offers something less pretentious. There's plenty of room on its two floors, the drinks are reasonable and the carvery lunch is one of the best in town.

4 Dame Lane

4 Dame Lane (679 0291/www.8sws.com). All cross-city buses/Luas St Stephen's Green. **Open** 5pm-2.30am Mon-Sat; 5pm-1am Sun. **Credit** AmEx, MC, V. **Map** p252 F3 ⑪

Though no longer as popular as when it first opened late in 2000, the two-floor 4 Dame Lane still brings plenty of people to its brazier-flanked doors. The eclectic mix of music and minimalist surroundings pulls a bohemian crowd. The addition of booths hasn't made much difference, as the punters prefers to mingle and jive on the dancefloor.

Grogan's Castle Lounge

15 William Street South (677 9320). All cross-city buses/Luas St Stephen's Green. **Open** 10.30am-11.30pm Mon-Thur; 10.30am-12.30am Fri, Sat; 12.30-11pm Sun. **No credit cards. Map** p252 F3 ⑫

Grogan's has a relaxed, shabby charm, great Guinness and great toasted sandwiches: three good reasons for its customers – old regulars and a number of more youthful rogues – to drop in. It's the perfect bolt-hole in which to escape the hustle and bustle of Grafton Street. The sometimes bizarre artworks on the walls are for sale, often put there by punters.

International Bar

23 Wicklow Street (677 9250). All cross-city buses/Luas St Stephen's Green. **Open** 10.30am-11.30pm Mon-Thur; 10.30am-12.30am Fri, Sat; 12.30-11pm Sun. **No credit cards. Map** p252 F3 ⑬

Refreshingly laid back, the International's long bar is always lined with Guinness-drinking regulars. An interesting crowd spills out on to the street in fine weather to sit on stools and swap stories. There are also regular comedy nights with some of Dublin's more notable comics occasionally dropping in.

Kehoe's

9 South Anne Street (677 8312). All cross-city buses/Luas St Stephen's Green. **Open** 10.30am-11.30pm Mon-Thur; 10.30am-12.30am Fri, Sat; 12.30-11pm Sun. **Credit** MC, V. **Map** p252 F4 ⑭

If you suffer from a fear of small spaces, avoid the lavatories in Kehoe's. Designed with Lilliputians in mind, they are (literally) a low point in a pub that is otherwise rich with old-style character and delightful snugs. Friendly staff serve beautifully creamy Guinness, and the upstairs bar has changed little since John Kehoe died many years ago. At busy times a crowd gathers around the stairs, giving it the feeling of a convivial house party.

Long Stone

10 Townsend Street (671 8102/www.thelongstone.com). All cross-city buses/DART Tara. **Open** noon-11.30pm Mon-Thur; noon-12.30am Fri; 2pm-2.30am Sat; 3-11pm Sun. **Credit** AmEx, MC, V. **Map** p252 G3 ⑮

Café en Seine.

Cocoon. *See p124.*

The Long Stone is a fairly run-of-the-mill pub whose main attraction is that it's handy for a drink after a visit to the Screen on D'Olier Street (*see p164*). The place can get madly crowded, but the *craic*'s good, even if the interior isn't up to much.

McDaid's

3 Harry Street, off Grafton Street (679 4395). All cross-city buses/Luas St Stephen's Green. **Open** 10.30am-11.30pm Mon-Thur; 10.30am-12.30am Fri, Sat; 12.30-11pm Sun. **No credit cards. Map** p252 F4
Popularly known as the Brendan Behan bar, McDaid's was once a haunt of the literary avant-garde, but is now more likely to be packed out with bus loads of people in search of a 'real' Dublin pub. It can get seriously busy on Saturday night, when the Guinness fans jostle for space in the compact main bar.

Messrs Maguire

1-2 Burgh Quay (670 5777/www.messrsmaguire. com). All cross-city buses/Luas Abbey Street. **Open** 10.30am-12.30am Mon, Tue; 10.30am-1.30am Wed; 10.30am-2am Thur; 10.30am-2.30am Fri, Sat; noon-midnight Sun. **Credit** AmEx, MC, V. **Map** p251 F2
This quayside spot tries really hard, but never quite seems to get there. Downstairs has dark flooring, wood stools and affable barmen, while upstairs there's more ambience – despite the fact that it's obviously going for an old-school vibe. Still, it has

its own microbrewery, so if you're tiring of the black stuff, you know where to make for.

Mulligan's

8 Poolbeg Street (677 5582/www.mulligans.ie). DART Tara Street. **Open** 10.30am-11.30pm Mon-Thur; 10.30am-12.30am Fri, Sat; 12.30-11pm Sun. **Credit** MC, V. **Map** p252 G2
This legendary Dublin boozer really comes into its own on a Sunday afternoon, when you can sit back and watch the Guinness settle. Mulligan's first opened its doors in 1782, and the tobacco-stained ceilings, glassy-eyed octogenarians and a no-mobiles policy mean it retains authenticity and is gloriously unpretentious. Things get seriously packed on weekday evenings as workers from nearby offices flood in for their daily jar. **Photo** *p132*.

Neary's

1 Chatham Street (677 8596). All cross-city buses/Luas St Stephen's Green. **Open** 10.30am-11.30pm Mon-Thur; 10.30am-12.30am Fri, Sat; 12.30-11pm Sun. **Credit** MC, V. **Map** p252 F4
Rich mahogany tones, plush seating, heavy curtains and disaffected thespians from the nearby Gaiety Theatre give Neary's a unique atmosphere. The friendly barmen lovingly serve an excellent pint of plain (even skimming the head for the aesthetes among us). The upstairs lounge is open at weekends and offers a livelier scene.

Eat, Drink, Shop

O'Neill's
2 Suffolk Street (679 3671/www.oneillsbar.com). All cross-city buses. **Open** 10.30am-11.30pm Mon-Thur; 10.30am-12.30am Fri, Sat; noon-11pm Sun. **Credit** AmEx, MC, V. **Map** p252 F3 ⑳
O'Neills is the kind of place you wander into at 6pm and take seven hours to find your way out of. Yup, it's labyrinthine and chaotic, and there are enough pleasant nooks and crannies to make it an intimate spot, despite its substantial size; but it can be blighted by hordes of beer-swilling weekenders. The meat-and-two-veg lunch from the carvery is highly regarded by the hungover looking for soakage.

Ron Blacks
37 Dawson Street (672 8231/www.ronblacks.ie). All cross-city buses/Luas St Stephen's Green. **Open** 10.30am-11.30pm Mon-Wed; 10.30am-2.30am Thur, Fri; noon-2.30am Sat; noon-11pm Sun. **Credit** AmEx, MC, V. **Map** p252 F4 ㉑
This looks like a gentleman's drinking club, with dark mahogany panelling and voluptuous leather seats – and, indeed, seems to be frequented by the type of chap who doesn't mind being waited on. If you can get over the guffawing professionals, it's actually an attractive place in which to have a quiet drink (albeit an expensive one). Not to be confused with its more fun-loving neighbour: Ron Black's Dawson Lounge, the smallest bar in Dublin.

Samsara
La Stampa Hotel, 35 Dawson Street (671 7723/www.lastampa.ie). All cross-city buses/Luas St Stephen's Green. **Open** noon-12.30am Mon-Thur; noon-2.30am Fri, Sat; noon-1.30am Sun. **Credit** AmEx, MC, V. **Map** p251 F4 ㉒
North African-influenced superpub Samsara, like nearby Café en Seine (*see p124*), is astonishingly long, as you discover when you try to find the loos. It's smart and determined to be thoroughly sophisticated, but it should be avoided by anyone whose idea of hell is standing behind 17 people at the bar.

Sheehan's
17 Chatham Street (677 1914). All cross-city buses/Luas St Stephen's Green. **Open** 11am-11.30pm Mon-Thur; 11am-12.30am Fri, Sat; 12.30-11pm Sun. **Credit** MC, V. **Map** p252 F4 ㉓
This is a pleasant, glass-fronted bar that tends to attract your basic central-city crowd of lawyers, writers and a few other business/media types.

Around Temple Bar

The Auld Dubliner
24 Anglesea Street (677 0527/www.thesmithgroup.ie). All cross-city buses/Luas Jervis. **Open** 10.30am-11.30pm Mon-Thur; 10.30am-12.30am Fri, Sat; 12.30-11pm Sun. **Credit** (minimum €10) AmEx, MC, V. **Map** p252 F3 ㉔
If you're up for a laugh and a sing-song, and you're happy to drink with dewy-eyed tourists enthusing about the traditional music being played onstage, this place, smack-bang in the heart of Temple Bar,

is for you. There are bands playing traditional music upstairs, decent pints at the bar and coddle (a traditional Dublin sausage, bacon and potato stew) on the lunch menu. It can get very packed at weekends.

The Brazen Head
20 Bridge Street Lower (679 5186/www.brazenhead.com). Bus 21, 21A/Luas The Four Courts. **Open** 10.30am-12.30am Mon-Sat; 12.30pm-12.30am Sun. **Credit** DC, MC, V. **Map** p250 C3 ㉕
Although it's a bit hard to find (across the river from the Four Courts), the Brazen Head is worth the effort. It claims to be Ireland's oldest pub, and may well be; it's been in operation since 1198, and the rebel Robert Emmett planned an uprising here in 1802. Today it offers trad music, real fires and the tastiest warm bar nuts in the country. Thinking positively, the high quota of tourists adds to its 'good time' atmosphere.

Dragon
64 South Great George's Street (478 1590/www.capitalbars.com). All cross-city buses. **Open** 5-11.30pm Mon-Wed; 5pm-2.30am Thur-Sat; 5-11pm Sun. **Credit** AmEx, MC, V. **Map** p252 E3 ㉖
From the street, this mostly gay bar looks small, but get inside the former bank building and you'll find that it stretches back and back. Expect cool young things drinking bottled beer, Japanese prints, enormous fish tanks and pale wood aplenty. A great venue if there's a gang of you.

Farrington's
27-29 Essex Street East (671 5135/679 8372/www.thesmithgroup.ie). All cross-city buses/Luas Jervis. **Open** 10.30am-11.30pm Mon-Thur; 10.30am-12.30am Fri, Sat; noon-11pm Sun. **Credit** MC, V. **Map** p252 E3 ㉗
You get two bars for the price of one here. On the ground floor, thick wooden ledges, ornate mirrors and darkly lit spaces provide an idea of what an old Irish pub must have looked like; take the stairs and it's as if Habitat's chief designer had been let loose with an unlimited budget. Despite its location in Temple Bar, Farringdon's tends to be quieter than its neighbours – though you'll still get the ubiquitous Temple Bar hen-night pub crawlers popping in, along with inquisitive tourists.

The Foggy Dew
1 Fownes Street Upper (677 9328). All cross-city buses/Luas Jervis. **Open** noon-11.30pm Mon, Tue; 11am-12.30am Wed; 11am-1am Thur; 11am-2am Fri, Sat; 1pm-1am Sun. **No credit cards**. **Map** p252 E3 ㉘
Sitting adjacent to the looming Central Bank and named after an old Irish ballad, this is one of those rare pubs in Temple Bar that draws a healthy mix of tourists and Dubliners; indeed, since its refurbishment, it has attracted the very jokers who once dubbed it the 'Dodgy Few'. You'll hear the best of Irish and international alternative music playing throughout the night. Get here early and lay claim to one of the charming snugs. **Photo** *p122*.

OUR CLIMATE NEEDS
A HELPING HAND TODAY

Be a smart traveller. Help to offset your carbon emissions from your trip by pledging Carbon Trees with Trees for Cities.

All the Carbon Trees that you donate through Trees for Cities are genuinely planted as additional trees in our projects.

Trees for Cities is an independent charity working with local communities on tree planting projects.

www.treesforcities.org   Tel 020 7587 1320

Trees for Cities
Charity registration number 1032154

The Front Lounge
33-34 Parliament Street (670 4112). All cross-city buses. **Open** noon-11.30pm Mon, Wed, Thur; noon-1am Tue; noon-2am Fri; 3pm-2am Sat; 3pm-11.30pm Sun. **Credit** MC, V. **Map** p252 E3 ㉙
A comfortable distance from the madding crowd of Temple Bar, the Front Lounge offers a relaxed atmosphere for refined drinking: velvet couches, black marble tables and lots of beautiful people. The Back Lounge to the rear is a gay fave; check out the karaoke on Monday nights, Dublin's top camp event.

The Globe
11 South Great George's Street (671 1220/www.the globe.ie). Bus 12, 16, 16A, 55/Luas St Stephen's Green. **Open** 3pm-2.30am Mon-Sat; 5pm-12.30am Sun. **Credit** AmEx, MC, V. **Map** p252 E3 ㉚
Populated with students writing theses, fashion victims in vintage Dior tank tops and the odd celebrity (Robbie Williams comes here, apparently, when he's in town), the Globe is nothing if not varied. Sit yourself down at one of the long wooden tables, order a pint and a chunky sandwich and do what everyone else is doing: people-watch. A wide range of foreign beers and an eclectic mix of music spun by in-house DJs enhance the experience.

Hogan's
35 South Great George's Street (677 5904/www. hoganscafebar.com). Bus 12, 16, 16A/Luas St Stephen's Green. **Open** 1pm-11.30am Mon-Wed; 1pm-1am Thur; 1pm-2.30am Fri, Sat; 4-11pm Sun. **No credit cards**. **Map** p252 E4 ㉛
Despite first impressions, this isn't a poseur's paradise. As befits the trendy Village Quarter, Hogan's is a lively bar filled with a hip and stylish twentysomething crowd, listening to the hippest indie sounds. The upstairs bar can sometimes get uncomfortable, but thankfully there's the downstairs dancefloor to escape to.

The Long Hall
51 South Great George's Street (475 1590). All cross-city buses/Luas St Stephen's Green. **Open** 4-11.30pm Mon-Wed, Sun; 1-11.30pm Thur; 1pm-12.30am Fri, Sat; 1-11pm Sun. **No credit cards**. **Map** p252 E4 ㉜
This ornate Victorian gin palace has it all: jovial barman, old bloke at the bar with a pint of Guinness, smattering of characterful regulars. Indeed, the whole place looks as if it's been carved out of thick mahogany. From its antique chandeliers to its mirrored bar, the Long Hall has survived the recent neighbourhood renovations and is still regarded as one of Dublin's unmissable boozers.

The Lord Edward
23 Christchurch Place (454 2158). All cross-city buses. **Open** 11am-11.30pm Mon-Thur; 11am-12.30am Fri; noon-12.30am Sat; 12.30-11pm Sun. **Credit** AmEx, MC, V. **Map** p250 D3 ㉝
After a visit to Christ Church Cathedral, cross the road and enter the calming Lord Edward. The round bar on the lower level is a typical old-fashioned boozer selling good Guinness, while the lounge upstairs is cosy and relaxed. The staff add to the pleasant atmosphere, as does the excellent porter; indeed, it's a fine spot in which to read the paper and enjoy that *craic* you've been hearing so much about.

The Market Bar
Fade Street, off South Great George's Street (613 9094/www.marketbar.ie). All cross-city buses/Luas St Stephen's Green. **Open** noon-11.30pm Mon-Thur; noon-12.30am Fri, Sat; 4-11pm Sun. **Credit** AmEx, MC, V. **Map** p252 E3 ㉞
This little piggy went to market… The Market Bar was once a pig abattoir, and the grates in the floor used to flow with blood. The only thing flowing these days, though, is beer and plenty of it: this is one of Dublin's most popular bars. There's a no music policy, so the noisy chatter of conversation wafts through the lofty space; be prepared to shout. Staff are cool but polite, and the tapas menu is good value and worth sampling; a creative smoking area has been rigged up under cover by the door.

Octagon Bar
Clarence Hotel, 6-8 Wellington Quay (670 9000/ www.theclarencehotel.ie). All cross-city buses/Luas Jervis. **Open** 11am-11.30pm Mon-Thur; 11am-12.30am Fri, Sat; noon-11pm Sun. **Credit** AmEx, MC, V. **Map** p252 E3 ㉟
There are only a few bars in Dublin that can honestly be described as painfully hip, and Octagon is one of them. Situated in the sleek Clarence Hotel (*see p36*), this eight-sided bar has been seen some very famous bums on its black leather stools and in its sleek, contemporary booths. For all its trend factor, though, the staff are friendly and good at what they do; even when it's crowded, you'll soon have a generous, well-made cocktail in hand. It's a bit expensive, but some things are worth paying for.

Oliver St John Gogarty
58-59 Fleet Street (671 1822/www.gogartys.ie). All cross-city buses. **Open** *Bar* 10am-2am Mon-Thur, Sun; 10am-3pm Fri, Sat. *Lounge* 6pm-2.30am Mon-Thur; 3pm-2.30am Fri-Sun. **Credit** AmEx, MC, V. **Map** p252 F3 ㊱
Named after the man parodied as Buck Mulligan in *Ulysses*, this place got its bar counter from the green room in the once-famous Theatre Royal. As well as that, there's an authentic flagstone floor and a large oatmeal grinder; the style here is nothing if not eclectic. Bands play traditional music nightly, and the seafood in the upstairs restaurant is very good. This is a great place to wind up in at the end of a Dublin pub crawl.

O'Shea's Merchant
12 Bridge Street Lower (679 3797). Bus 21, 21A/ Luas The Four Courts. **Open** 10.30am-11.30pm Mon-Wed; 10.30am-2am Thur-Sat; 12.30pm-2am Sun. **Credit** AmEx, MC, V. **Map** p250 D3 ㊲
There's something strange about having an Irish theme bar in Ireland. If you've never been to Ireland before, the place offers everything Irish you could

ever want – Irish dancing, traditional Irish music, Irish football on the telly, decent Irish food and intriguing Irish 'country nights' on Wednesdays. Enjoy yourself, but remember that the real Ireland is waiting for you right outside the door.

The Palace

21 Fleet Street (bar 677 9290/lounge 679 3037/ www.palacebardublin.ie). All cross-city buses/Luas Abbey Street. **Open** *Bar* 10.30am-11.30pm Mon-Thur; 10.30am-12.30am Fri, Sat; 12.30-11pm Sun. *Lounge* 7-11.30pm Tue; 5-11.30pm Wed, Thur; 5pm-12.30am Fri; 6.30pm-12.30am Sat; 6-11pm Sun. **Credit** MC, V. **Map** p252 F3 ⑳

The oldest bar in Dublin to have kept its original form, the grand old Palace deserves a place on everybody's pub crawl. If it's authenticity you're after, this place delivers, with its aged marble counter, mirrored alcoves and a reputation as a writers' hangout. Indeed, the walls are adorned with many famous literary faces. This is a pub that rarely gets uncomfortably busy.

Peter's Pub

1 Johnston's Place (677 8588). All cross-city buses/Luas St Stephen's Green. **Open** 10.30am-11.30pm Mon-Thur; 10.30am-12.30am Fri, Sat; 1-11pm Sun. **Credit** MC, V. **Map** p252 E4 ⑳

This is, quite simply, an oasis in a metropolitan desert. Located just off increasingly fashionable William Street South, the small modern pub offers a decent sandwich, a legendary pint of plain and a glimpse into the lives of Dublin's citizens. The small interior is reminiscent of someone's living room and, accordingly, the emphasis is on polite conversation.

The Porterhouse

16-18 Parliament Street (679 8847/www.porterhouse brewco.com). All cross-city buses/Luas Jervis. **Open** 11.30am-11.30pm Mon-Wed; 11.30am-2am Thur; 11.30am-2.30am Fri; noon-2.30am Sat; 12.30-11pm Sun. **Credit** MC, V. **Map** p252 E3 ⑳

Dublin's oldest microbrewery pub sprawls casually over three storeys. Its wooden decor may be excessively rustic, but the Porterhouse makes up for that with the quality of the beer. It sells only its own label, but its stouts, lagers and ales are better than any mass-produced beer; the Oyster Stout, made on the premises with real oysters, is very good. The pub also serves excellent pub food at reasonable prices, and its Irish stew and bangers and mash will fill you up without breaking the bank.

The Stag's Head

1 Dame Court, off Dame Street (679 3687). All cross-city buses/Luas St Stephen's Green. **Open** 10.30am-11.30pm Mon-Thur; 10.30am-12.30am Fri, Sat; noon-11.30pm Sun. **Credit** MC, V. **Map** p252 E3 ⑳

The Stag's Head is hidden away on Dame Court, but easily found thanks to the pavement mosaic on Dame Street that points punters to its hallowed door. Inside it's all mahogany, stained glass and mirrors; enjoy the intimate Victorian smoking room while the gigantic stag's head hanging above keeps a vigilant

watch over proceedings. The Stag's is a favourite among students of Trinity College, and film buffs may like to know that *Educating Rita* was shot here.

Temple Bar

48 Temple Bar (672 5286/www.templebarpubdublin. com). All cross-city buses/Luas Jervis. **Open** 11am-12.30am Mon-Sat; noon-12.30am Sun. **Credit** MC, V. **Map** p252 E3 ⑳

Two words sum up this bar: always packed. That's excellent news for the owners, but punters may find the hunt for a seat offputting. One unusual feature is the outdoor area in the middle of the large bar – a good place for a cigarette break. Traditional music and singalongs make this a haven for foreign accents: don't expect to hear much Irish lilt.

Thomas Read

1 Parliament Street (671 7283/www.thomasread.ie). All cross-city buses/Luas Jervis. **Open** 10.30am-11.30pm Mon-Thur; 10.30am-2.30am Fri, Sat; 11am-12.30am Sun. **Credit** AmEx, MC, V. **Map** p252 E3 ⑳

Opposite the grandeur of City Hall sits Thomas Read, a bustling modern bar offering a varying choice of scenes. The main bar is trendy and modern, while downstairs is a mecca for young indie rockers, with regular free gigs. Pass through a back corridor and you're in the neighbouring pub, The Oak, which has an intriguing history; check out the frames around the walls.

Turk's Head

27-30 Parliament Street (679 9701/www.paramount hotel.ie). All cross-city buses/Luas Jervis. **Open** noon-1am Mon, Tue, Sun; noon-2.30am Wed-Sat. **Credit** AmEx, MC, V. **Map** p252 E3 ⑳

If you're in town for shallow, meaningless… discourse with someone of the opposite sex, the Turk's Head has your name on the door. Popular with twentysomethings, this pub/club (you decide) is huge, with two levels of bars and a large dancefloor. The Gaudi-inspired walls add to the impression of drinking in a cavern of Turkish delight, and nubile bellydancers gyrate on Tuesdays.

Around St Stephen's Green

The Bleeding Horse

24 Camden Street Upper (475 2705/www.thebleeding horse.com). Bus 16, 16A, 19, 19a, 49n 83/Luas Harcourt. **Open** noon-12.30am Mon-Wed; noon-1am Thur; noon-2am Fri, Sat; noon-11.30pm Sun. **Credit** MC, V. **Map** p251 E5 ⑳

The Bleeding Horse has occupied this prominent Camden Street site for two centuries. These days it attracts a pleasant crowd of local regulars and an energetic student group in almost equal proportions. The bar sprawls over several levels: the connecting rooms downstairs are covered with heavy beams and a dark, medieval atmosphere, and there's a fairly good restaurant upstairs. The place can get busy at weekends, when a younger crowd jams in before heading on to the nearby Harcourt Street clubs.

Ave pariah

Two years after the Irish government outlawed smoking in public places, tobacco fans have become pariahs, woefully short of a place that lets them hold a pint in one hand and a cigarette in the other. The good news, of course, is that far fewer people wake up the next day reeking of ashtray, and the air is cleaner. Still, if a fag's your bag, here's a list of a few places that welcome smokers.

Right beside the Grand Canal, the **Barge** (Charlemont Bridge, 475 1869) is a nice place at which to while away an afternoon. In sunny weather the area outside pulls droves of people shirking work and trying to suntan.

Dicey's Garden (21-25 Harcourt Street, 478 4066) has picnic tables, a balcony section with its own bar and patio heaters for chillier evenings. In all, it's a very pleasant smoker's sanctuary.

At the **Odeon** (see p133), you can stand on the spacious, heated terrace and watch the fun unfurl before you: drunk people plus a tram line equals endless entertainment. Get there early, though; the last Luas leaves at 12.30am.

The **Pavilion** bar in Trinity College (see p59) has the biggest smoking area in Dublin: a cricket pitch. Spend a leisurely afternoon on the grass, sipping cool beer and watching a game of cricket get interrupted by streakers.

Whelan's (see p133) is the ideal place to go to if you've run out of smokes. Don't bother trying to bum a cigarette: just stand near a group of smokers, breathe deeply, and reap the benefits of passive smoking.

Odeon. *See p132.*

Corner Stone

40 Wexford Street (478 9816). Bus 55, 61, 62, 83/Luas St Stephen's Green. **Open** 11am-11.30pm Mon-Thur; 11am-2.30am Fri; 4pm-2am Sat. **Credit** AmEx, MC, V. **Map** p251 E5 **46**

The façade on this corner building has been restored in recent years and now forms a pleasing introduction to the (also remodelled) bar inside. The decor is contemporary but not ultra-fashionable, with subdued lighting and leather seats in cool shades. Lunches here are tasty, and the upstairs lounge hosts live music and late drinking at weekends.

Dawson Lounge

25 Dawson Street (671 0311/www.dawsonlounge.ie). All cross-city buses/Luas St Stephen's Green. **Open** 12.30-11.30pm Mon-Thur; 12.30pm-12.30am Fri, Sat; 4-11pm Sun. **Credit** AmEx, MC, V. **Map** p251 F4 **47**

A tiny downstairs bar at the bottom of a corkscrew staircase, the Dawson Lounge markets itself as the smallest bar in Dublin. Unsurprisingly, it's cosy in winter and summer. If you're at all claustrophobic, stay at street level; otherwise, climb down (and be careful negotiating the stairs on the way back up).

Doheny & Nesbitt

5 Baggot Street Lower (676 2945/www.dohenyand nesbitt.com). Bus 10, 11, 11A/Luas St Stephen's Green. **Open** 10.30am-12.30am Mon-Thur; 10.30am-12.30am Fri, Sat; 12.30-11pm Sun. **Credit** AmEx, DC, MC, V. **Map** p251 G4 **48**

At weekends, this glorious old pub is packed to the gills with lawyers getting squiffy and quoting Blackstone and law gossip at each other. If this doesn't appeal – and why would it? – you'll be pleased to know it's at its best during the week, when all is quiet, you can gaze at your reflection in the polished wood and enjoy a pleasant, contemplative drink. In summer and on rugby days it's mayhem again, with hordes of drinkers spilling out on to the street.

Dowling's

13 Upper Baggot Street (667 7156). Bus 10, 11.
Open 11am-midnight Mon-Thur; 11am-1pm Fri-Sun.
Credit MC, V. **Map** p251 H5 ⑭

After a shaky beginning, Dowling's has polished up its act and is now one of the best wine bars on the south bank, with an excellent wine list and a small but adequate selection of food. The bar is small and narrow, with exposed brick walls and a coal fire; the staff are pleasant and well informed; and the coffee is excellent. If you're out on the canal or mooching around the Georgian town, this is a good retreat.

Ginger Man

40 Fenian Street (676 6388). All cross-city buses.
Open 11am-12.30am Mon-Thur; 11am-1.30am Fri, Sat; 5-11pm Sun. **Credit** MC, V. **Map** p251 H4 ⑮

This small, old-fashioned pub is just round the corner from Merrion Square, and great for a pint or two after a jaunt around the museums. The regular pub quizzes are good fun, the atmosphere is always relaxed – and you can dine until 9pm if you choose.

JJ Smyths

12 Aungier Street (475 2565/www.jjsmyths.com).
Bus 16, 16A, 19, 19A, 83/Luas St Stephen's Green.
Open 10.30am-11.30pm Mon-Thur; 10.30am-12.30am Fri, Sat; 12.30-11pm Sun. **No credit cards**. **Map** p252 E4 ⑯

Downstairs, this is just a regular, unassuming old-fashioned Dublin boozer – and very nice with it. But it's also a famous jazz bar – head upstairs to hear some of the city's top jazz every night of the week (Thurdays and Sundays are best). The musical associations don't end there: a plaque commemorating Thomas Moore, noted poet and recorder of Ireland's oral music tradition, is mounted beside the front door – this was his local. *See also p176.*

Ocean Bar

The Millennium Tower, Charlotte's Quay Dock, off Ringsend Road (668 8862/www.oceanbar.ie). Bus 1,2,3/DART Grand Canal Dock. **Open** noon-11.30am Mon-Thur; noon-12.30am Fri, Sat; 12.30-11pm Sun.
Credit MC, V.

This upmarket dockside establishment claims to have Dublin's only waterfront public licence. We don't know about that, but the patios overlooking the canal basin are ideal for drinking if there's even a hint of sunshine – though the wind off the water can be positively brisk – and the bistro serves decent food until 10pm. Ocean was once very much on its own here, but the cranes bristling on the other side of the water are evidence of the area's development.

Odeon

57 Harcourt Street (478 2088/www.odeon.ie). Bus 14, 15, 16/Luas Harcourt. **Open** noon-11.30pm Mon-Wed; noon-12.30am Thur; noon-2.30am Fri, Sat; noon-11pm Sun. **Credit** AmEx, MC, V. **Map** p251 F5 ⑯

Take a Luas to the old Harcourt Street station. The impressive façade of the Odeon is a sign of what to expect once inside. There aren't too many seats, but nobody really cares: people come here to see and be seen on a sea of polished floorboards under vaulted ceilings. It's not cheap by any means: you pay for the atmosphere and the style. Odeon is especially pleasant on Sunday, when you can deliciously fritter the afternoon away with free newspapers or watch a classic film showing on the big screen. **Photo** *p131.*

Dublin authenticity in spades (switch off your mobile): that's **Mulligan's**. *See p126.*

O'Donoghue's

*15 Merrion Row (660 7194/lounge 676 2807/www.
odonoghuesbar.com). All cross-city buses/Luas St
Stephen's Green.* **Open** 10.30am-11.30pm Mon-Thur;
10.30am-12.30am Fri, Sat; 12.30-11pm Sun. **Credit**
AmEx, MC, V. **Map** p251 G4 ⓼

Impromptu jam sessions are a staple here, and outfits like the Dubliners play regularly. While the
music really pulls in the tourists, O'Donoghue's really pulls in all sorts of customers: genuine locals and
visitors, young and old. While the pub itself can be
a little claustrophobic (especially mid session)
there's an excellent back-alley smoking area, where
you can (after a fashion) catch your breath.

O'Neill's

37 Pearse Street (671 4074). DART Pearse. **Open**
noon-11.30pm Mon-Thur; noon-12.30am Fri, Sat.
Credit AmEx, MC, V. **Map** p251 G3 ⓼

Pearse Street can feel a little quiet and desolate at
night, but O'Neill's is one good reason to venture
down this way. It's only a few minutes from College
Green (but still well away from the crowds) and it's
a fine bar in general, with lots of separate rooms and
big glowing fires. Gaggles of besuited folk drink
here, but don't be put off: there are plenty of seats
for all – and good pub grub, too.

Solas

*31 Wexford Street (478 0583). Bus 16, 16A, 19,
19A, 23/Luas St Stephen's Green.* **Open** 11am-
12.30am Mon, Tue; 11am-1.30am Wed-Sat; noon-
12.30am Sun. **Credit** AmEx, MC, V. **Map** p251 E5 ⓼

An attractive spot to come to before hitting the clubs
along the Camden Street strip, Solas is trendy yet
easy-going. It's an attractive place: the orange globe
lamps are warm, the crimson banquettes plush, and
the cherry wood tables glossy. It also serves reasonably priced pub food, and the menu leans vaguely towards spice, with dishes like Szechuan beef and
chicken enchiladas. In general, it's cosy, inviting and
well worth a visit.

Smyth's

10 Haddington Road (660 6305). Bus 10. **Open**
10am-11.30pm Mon-Thur; 10.30am-12.30am Fri, Sat;
12.30-11pm Sun. **Credit** MC, V. **Map** p251 H5 ⓼

Close to the banks of the Grand Canal, Smyth's is a
real neighbourhood pub with a disarmingly laid-
back atmosphere. Though an ill-considered renovation a few years back did its best to garble the
atmosphere, it only partly succeeded, and Smyth's
remains a quiet, snug and comfortable boozer. If
you're strolling on the canal towpath, drop in.

Toner's

*139 Baggot Street Lower (676 3090). Bus 10, 11,
11A/Luas St Stephen's Green.* **Open** 10.30am-11.30pm
Mon-Wed; 10.30am-12.30am Thur-Sat; 12.30-11pm
Sun. **Credit** AmEx, MC, V. **Map** p251 G4 ⓼

Toner's is an authentic Dublin pub that has survived
being tarted up over the years: the character that
made it popular to begin with still remains, the bar
itself is still pleasing, and the tarting up was done

with a mercifully light hand. At weekends Toner's
is packed to the rafters, but if you find yourself on
Baggot Street on a wet afternoon, there are few better places in which to take refuge. It also holds the
honour of being the only pub visited by WB Yeats.
How could you doubt his judgement?

The Village

*26 Wexford Street (475 8555/www.thevillagevenue.
com). Bus 16, 16A. 19, 19A/Luas Harcourt.* **Open**
11am-2.30am Mon-Fri; 5pm-2.30am Sun. **Credit**
AmEx, MC, V. **Map** p251 E5 ⓼

The Village is one of Dublin's newest and best music
venues, catering to a wider and more diverse crowd
than Whelan's next door (*see below*). The success of
its nightly gigs, however, tends to distract attention
from the bar itself, which is attractive and agreeable
in its own right. The striking modern frontage of the
building allows lots of natural light to flood the front
room, and this then gives way to the subdued red
and orange lights and cool atmosphere of the main
bar. You can eat here at any time of the day, and eat
well; Sunday brunch is accompanied by jazz bands.

Whelan's

*25 Wexford Street (478 0766/www.whelanslive.com).
Bus 16, 16A, 19, 19A, 122/Luas Harcourt.* **Open**
10.30am-1.30am Mon-Wed; 10.30am-2.30am Thur-
Sat; 2pm-1.30am Sun. **Credit** AmEx, MC, V. **Map**
p251 E5 ⓼

While the front bar is admirably good-humoured
and the staff are always attentive, the main attraction here is the gig venue (*see p178*), admission to
which is gained from an alleyway around the corner. Whelan's is one of Dublin's best-loved music
venues, and it has played host to many famous
names before they hit the big time. The new smoking area has been a welcome addition.

Around O'Connell Street

Flowing Tide

*9 Abbey Street Lower (874 4106). All cross-city
buses/Luas Abbey Street.* **Open** 10.30am-11.30pm
Mon-Thur; 10.30am-12.30am Fri, Sat; noon-11pm
Sun. **Credit** MC, V. **Map** p251 F2 ⓼

A recent renovation has converted the much-loved
Tide from a reliable Dublin boozer with a raffish
edge into a trendy place with polished wood floors
and sleek chrome details. Perhaps the new look is
not to all tastes, but the essentials remain the same:
the staff and Guinness are as decent as ever, and the
bar's location means it still attracts a crowd of actors
and audience from the nearby Abbey Theatre.

The Isaac Butt Café Bar

*Opposite Busáras Station, Store Street (819 7636).
All cross-city buses/Luas Busaras.* **Open** 5-11.30pm
Mon-Wed, Sun; 5pm-2.30am Thur-Sat. **Credit** MC, V.
Map p251 G2 ⓼

A range of techno club nights first made this bar
popular among Dublin students and backpackers
from nearby hostels, but the emphasis has recently

Eat, Drink, Shop

shifted to live indie music. The warren-like bars provide comfortable refuge from the cares of the world, and there's a big screen for football matches. Beware, though: many unsuspecting voyagers have dropped in from the adjacent bus station 'for a quick one', only to find themselves tarrying long after the 5.11 to Cork has gone.

Kiely's
37 Upper Abbey Street (872 2100). All cross-city buses/Luas Abbey Street. **Open** 10.30am-11.30pm Mon-Wed, Sun; 10.30am-12.30am Thur; 10.30am-2am Fri, Sat. **Credit** AmEx, MC, V. **Map** p251 E2 ⬤
This is two very different bars in one. The Abbey Street entrance leads to a snug, old-style dark wooden bar that's good for quiet pints or watching football in peace. The back of the pub – with the Liffey Street entrance – is 'K3' and couldn't be more different. It's a large, trendy space with a cheery twentysomething crowd. The juxtaposition shouldn't work as well as it does – but one thing both areas have in common is excellent and well-priced food.

Life Café-Bar
Irish Life Centre, Abbey Street Lower (878 1032/ www.lifebar.ie). All cross-city buses/Luas Abbey Street. **Open** 9am-11.30pm Mon-Thur; 2pm-1.30am Fri, Sat. **Credit** AmEx, MC, V. **Map** p251 G2 ⬤
Life is elegant and slightly pricier than the average, with a fine range of beers and excellent coffees. It's all about chilling out, so there are comfortable sofas dotted invitingly around the place. Its proximity to Busáras and to Connolly Station makes it a popular break spot for modish travellers, but most style-conscious locals don't bother; this can be a good or a bad thing, depending on your point of view.

Patrick Conway
70 Parnell Street (873 2687). All cross-city buses/ Luas Abbey Street. **Open** 10am-11.30pm Mon-Thur; 10am-12.30am Fri, Sat; noon-11pm Sun. **No credit cards. Map** p251 F1 ⬤
A thoughtful pick of interior mood-setters, including candlelight and drapes, gives this Victorian pub a cosy, relaxed atmosphere. Plentiful seating in lovely booths, an unpretentious bunch of punters and friendly bar staff are its biggest attractions. If you fancy a quiet pint, this civilised place will fit the bill very nicely indeed. **Photos** *p135.*

Pravda
35 Liffey Street Lower (874 0076/www.pravda.ie). All cross-city buses/Luas Jervis. **Open** noon-11.30pm Mon, Tue; noon-2.30am Wed-Sat; 12.30-11pm Sun. **Credit** AmEx, MC, V. **Map** p252 E2 ⬤
To be perfectly honest, an abundance of cyrillic script stencilled on the walls does not an authentic Russian bar make; but Pravda pulls off the ersatz Eastern European thing pretty well. The building is large and rambling, and the atmosphere is chilled during the day and vibrant at night. It's a particularly nice place for an afternoon hot toddy, with its view of the Ha'penny Bridge and the shoppers streaming past; but after 10pm the volume of the

music will drown out your inner monologue. The place could do with a lick of paint, too.

The Woolshed
Parnell Centre, Parnell Street at Capel Street (872 4325/www.woolshedbaa.com) All cross-city buses/ Luas Jervis. **Open** noon-11.30pm Mon-Wed; noon-1am Thur, Fri, Sun; 10.30am-1am Sat. **Credit** AmEx, MC, V. **Map** p251 E2 ⬤
This place proudly proclaims itself home from home for 'Aussies, Kiwis and Saffas'. Drinking pints, playing pool and watching sport on TV fill up the day, while at night bands of decidedly mixed quality line up to crank up the volume (on the basis, apparently, that if it can't be good, it might as well be loud). Nearly always fun, though.

Around the North Quays

The Cobblestone
77 King Street North (872 1799/www.imro.ie). Bus 25, 26, 37, 39, 67, 67A, 68, 69, 79/Luas Smithfield. **Open** 4-11.30pm Mon-Thur; 4pm-12.30am Fri, Sat; 1-11pm Sun. **No credit cards. Map** p250 C2 ⬤
This place is a gem. The musicians' corner downstairs attracts traditional players whom you would pay to see elsewhere, and the paying venue upstairs rarely books a duff band (lo-fi, trad and folk tend to dominate). Overall it's cosy, while eschewing unnecessary frills; if you want to avoid excessive paddywhackery in favour of genuine traditional Dublin pubbery, come here. *See also p176.*

Dice Bar
Queen Street, off Arran Quay (633 3936). All cross-city buses/Luas Smithfield. **Open** 5-11.30pm Mon-Thur; 5pm-12.30am Fri, Sat; 3.30-11pm Sun. **Credit** MC, V. **Map** p250 C2 ⬤
A red neon sign reading 'Phat Joint' protrudes from the downbeat wall outside, and the bar itself has a vaguely illicit, Noo Yawk street vibe, courtesy of owner Huey from the Fun Lovin' Criminals. We could reel off a list of the rock stars who've dropped in here for a snifter, but the Dice is not about being star-struck. Best thing about it? Possibly the cool tunes, the laid-back crowd or the post-goth decor illuminated by dozens of church candles; but for us it's the bouncer's afro, a work of tonsorial art worthy of a preservation order.

Hughes' Bar
19 Chancery Street, off Church Street (872 6540). All cross-city buses/Luas The Four Courts. **Open** 7am-11.30pm Mon-Thur; 7am-12.30am Fri, Sat; 7-11pm Sun. **Credit** AmEx, MC, V. **Map** p250 D2 ⬤
Hughes sits next to the law courts. Some argue there's a rough edge to it, but its excellent trad music sessions make it worth a visit. Actor Brendan Gleeson pops in from time to time and Bob Dylan's backing band joined the house musicians recently for the type of unplanned and informal gig for which the pub is becoming known.

Patrick Conway. *See p134.*

Jack Nealons

*165 Capel Street (872 3247). All cross-city buses/
Luas Jervis.* **Open** noon-11.30pm Mon-Thur, Sun;
noon-12.30am Fri, Sat; **Credit** AmEx, MC, V. **Map**
p252 E3 ⓐ

Popular with pre-clubbers, Nealons is stylish but
relaxed. The downstairs bar is usually less hectic
than upstairs, but at weekends you take a seat where
you can find it. If the drinks seem slightly on the
pricey side, the happily braying customers don't
object. Look out for the juggling barmen, whose
cocktail expertise may tempt you towards something more adventurous than a pint of plain.

Morrison Hotel Bar

*Morrison Hotel, Ormond Quay Lower (887 2400/
www.morrisonhotel.ie). All cross-city buses/Luas
Jervis.* **Open** 10.30am-11.30pm Mon-Thur; 10.30am-
12.30am Fri, Sat; noon-11.30pm Sun. **Credit** AmEx,
MC, V. **Map** p252 E2 ⓐ

This place is pure class. With an interior designed
by fashion guru John Rocha, the Morrison's extremely stylish bar has plenty of comfy black couches on
which you can sip cocktails and dreamily peer out
at the silvery Liffey mist. What's particularly good
about the place is its combination of the aforementioned quality with some of the friendliest bar staff
in the city. If you've got the cash, there's truly no
more salubrious spot at which to spend an evening.
Dress to impress and arrive early.

O'Reilly Bros aka The Chancery

*1 Inns Quay (677 0420). All cross-city buses/Luas
The Four Courts.* **Open** 7.30am-11.30pm Mon-Sat;
noon-11pm Sun. **No credit cards. Map** p252 D3 ⓐ

At first glance, the Chancery is a spit-and-sawdust
local with little to recommend it. It is, however, worthy of note as one of Dublin's early houses – bars
that are legally allowed to open at 7.30am to service
market traders and those who work nights. For that
reason, it's a popular final port of call for clubbers.
It can be an odd (some would say dispiriting) experience to enter a bar so early and find people behav-
ing as if it were the top of Saturday night, but it's
certainly worth knowing about.

Voodoo Lounge

*39 Arran Quay (873 6013). All cross-city buses/Luas
Smithfield.* **Open** noon-1am Mon-Wed; noon-3am
Thur, Fri; 4pm-3am Sat; 4pm-1am Sun. **No credit
cards. Map** p250 C2 ⓐ

Voodoo is a happening bar-club with garage bands
seven nights a week and DJs at weekends. (A black-
board in the window communicates each week's musical line-up.) Inside, the masks, beads and other scary
paraphernalia are dimly lit by candles and complemented by eerie murals on supernatural themes.
Happily, the likeable staff ensure that the vibe remains
positive. Plenty of bottled beers, yummy pizza slices
and an old Space Invader machine make it worth
trekking up the quays for a bit of black magic.

Zanzibar

*36 Ormond Quay Lower (878 7212/www.zanzibar.ie).
All cross-city buses/Luas Jervis.* **Open** 5pm-2.30am
Mon-Thur, Sun; 3pm-2.30am Sun. **Credit** AmEx,
MC, V. **Map** p252 E2 ⓐ

Few bars provoke such divisive reactions as this vast
booze jungle. Inside are palm trees and 'African' dec-
orations; outside are queues of teens and early twen-

tysomethings shivering in their finery. It's clear why some dismiss Zanzibar as a meat market. And that's why, even though the bouncers are heavyhanded and staff are narky, the place continues to pack 'em in. Its customers just don't know any better.

Northern suburbs

The Clarendon
4 Chatham Row (679 2909). All cross-city buses/ Luas St Stephen's Green. **Open** noon-11.30pm Mon-Thur; noon-2am Fri, Sat; noon-1am Sun. **Credit** AmEx, DC, MC, V.
With its glass front, the Clarendon could be accused of being a place for blatant posing; but in reality it's simply a great bar. While a number of beautiful and sometimes famous people can be seen here, the pleasant staff and comfortable seating make for an enjoyable bar. Try to get the seats beneath the stairs: a cosy and quiet spot in the middle of a busy bar.

Flannery's
Camden Street (478 2238). All cross-city buses/Luas Harcourt. **Open** noon-2.30am Mon-Fri; 1pm-2.30am Sat, Sun. **Credit** AmEx, MC, V.
Unashamed of its less-than-appealing exterior, Flannery's is at its busiest on the weekend, when a crowd of nurses, teachers and Gardai pack out the bar. Ideal for a night out with single friends before heading on to Copper Face Jacks down the road.

Gravity Bar
James Street, the Liberties (471 4527/www. guinnessstorehouse.com). Bus 51B, 78A, 123/Luas James's Street. **Open** (admission with tour only) *Jan-Mar, Oct-Dec* 9.30am-5pm daily. *Apr-Sept* 9.30am-7pm daily. **Credit** MC, V.
The Guinness Storehouse is one of the most popular tourist attractions in Dublin. Not surprising, considering the highlight of the tour is the experience offered by the Gravity Bar. Set at the top of a converted grain house, this very special bar commands a 360° view of Dublin from floor-to-ceiling windows. With the Guinness making the shortest journey in the world from vat to glass, the beer is great, too.

Hairy Lemon
42 Lower Stephen Street (671 8949). All cross-city buses/Luas St Stephen's Green. **Open** 10.30am-11.30pm Mon-Thur; 10.30am-12.30pm Fri, Sat; 12.30-11pm Sun. **Credit** MC, V.
While the decor may seem a little quirky, don't be put off spending an evening in this great little pub. The Lemon's popular any time of the week, and it can be hard to find a seat; but if you do, you're in for a fun night out. The music isn't the usual safe chart hits, either – a pleasant change from the soundtrack at many of the more popular bars in the area.

Kavanagh's
1 Prospect Square, Glasnevin (830 7978). Bus 13, 19, 19A. **Open** 10.30am-11.30pm Mon-Thur; 10.30am-midnight Fri, Sat; 12.30-11pm Sun. **No credit cards.**

Way off the beaten track, Kavanagh's is a Dublin institution and thus, for many, worth the trek. Owing to its location next door to Glasnevin cemetery, this famous boozer is better known as 'The Gravediggers'. It has hardly changed in its 150-year history, and one of its chief attractions is that you can bring your pints out to the square on sunny days. Loved by many (ask Brad Pitt) for its spit-and-sawdust simplicity, it can be a little hard to find but definitely worth the effort.

Lobby Bar/Crawdaddy
Old Harcourt Station, Harcourt Street (476 3374/ www.pod.ie). Bus 14, 14A, 15A, 15B, 48A/Luas Harcourt. **Open** 5pm-12.30am Mon-Thur; 5pm-2.30am Fri, Sat. **Credit** MC, V.
The Lobby Bar is sandwiched between the famous POD nightclub and new live music venue Crawdaddy. Vaulted arches give the place a spacious atmosphere, and the funky seating adds to the decadent atmosphere. It can get busy when there are gigs next door, but is usually quiet at other times. The smoking area out front, where you can watch space-age trams shuttle back and forth while you dream of the future, is excellent.

Searson's
42-44 Baggot Street Upper (660 0330/www. searsons.ie). Bus 10. **Open** 10am-11.30pm Mon-Thur; 12.30pm-1.30am Fri, Sat; 4-11pm Sun. **Credit** AmEx, MC, V.
While all around it, pubs bow to the pressure to refurbish and change direction, Searson's sticks to its guns and its rather lovely classic Victorian decor. Punters are professionals, regulars and twentysomethings, and there's an ample smoking area out the back. A visit to Searson's before and/or after a rugby game at Lansdowne Road is a must: the atmosphere is usually hilarious.

Sin é
14-15 Ormond Quay (878 7078). All cross-city buses/Luas Jervis. **Open** 11.30am-12.30am Mon-Wed; 11.30am-2.30am Thur, Fri; 1pm-2.30am Sat; 1pm-12.30am Sun. **Credit** MC, V.
Located on the north side of the quays, Sin é is a diamond in the rough. Great music and a brazen crowd make for wild, wild nights. The only gripe would be the early closing of the smoking area to the rear; for the rest of the evening, smokers have to trudge through the sweaty crowd to get to the entrance.

Traffic
54 Middle Abbey Street (873 4800). All cross-city buses/Luas Abbey Street. **Open** 3-11.30pm Mon-Wed; 3pm-2.30am Thur-Sat; 4-11.30pm Sun **Credit** MC, V.
Traffic appeared shortly after the arrival on Abbey Street of the nightclub Spirit. While its decor is stylish and trendy, its glory days as a style bar seem to have passed. However, it's now becoming a favourite venue for aspiring DJs and a good place at which to spot emerging talent or down a quick one before moving on to Spirit.

Shops & Services

Cut to the purchase.

Birkenstock. *See p149.*

Dublin is currently one of the most fashionable cities in Europe, and it shows. The retail industry is thriving here, and the choice of shops runs from smart, cosmopolitan delis to neat indie record stores. While the city now holds its own against other European capitals, with plenty of big chain stores and heavyweight designers, Dublin still retains an independent edge: check out its seductive little boutiques and Irish labels to see what we mean.

Part of Dublin's appeal is its handy size. It's compact and navigable, so walking from one shopping area to another is a pleasure; and if you weary of the urban scene, you can jump on a Luas and hang out with the suburbanites at the mammoth **Dundrum Town Centre** (*see p139*).

In the city, a good place to start south of the River Liffey is Grafton Street. A smart pedestrianised thoroughfare, it draws eager consumers and hopeful buskers in equal measure, and is lined with a good selection of chain stores and shoe shops. Avoid it mid afternoon at the weekend, though, unless you particularly enjoy elbowing your way through huge crowds. For a taste of upmarket Dublin, try the exceptionally elegant **Brown Thomas** (*see p138*), a super-chic department store devoted to the world's most exclusive labels.

Nearby **William Street South**, **Castle Market** and **Drury Street** offer a hipper, trendier slice of retail life, with independent boutiques and a slower pace, while the pleasant jumble of **George's Street Arcade** is ideal for unearthing unusual second-hand gear, from books to bell-bottoms. Head down to the Old City at the northern edge of Temple Bar, and you'll find the fashionable **Cow's Lane Market** (10am-5pm Sat), and hip little stores.

North of the river lies the long, busy and shop-filled **Henry Street**, the **Jervis Centre** (*see p139*) and the faded **ILAC** (*see p139*), a run-down shopping centre that's finally being given a much-needed renovation. Vastly less pretentious than the southside, the northside has a different atmosphere, and Moore Street, with its old-school market traders, offers a glimpse into pre-Celtic Tiger Dublin.

NEED TO KNOW

Shops are generally open from 9am to 6pm Monday to Saturday, and from around noon to 6pm on Sunday. Almost all stores stay open late on Thursday – usually until 8pm or 9pm.

MasterCard and Visa credit cards are widely accepted; AmEx and Diners Club cards are generally only accepted in the bigger stores.

Sales tax (VAT) is 21 per cent; visitors from outside the EU can get a refund at the airport.

One-stop shopping

Department stores

Arnotts

12 Henry Street, Around O'Connell Street (805 0400/www.arnotts.ie). All cross-city buses/Luas Jervis. **Open** 9am-6.30pm Mon, Wed, Fri, Sat; 9.30am-6.30pm Tue; 9am-9pm Thur; noon-6pm Sun. **Credit** AmEx, DC, MC, V. **Map** p251 F2.

Secret Book & Record Shop. *See p140*

Back in the '90s, Arnotts was an uninspiring department store better known for school uniforms than stylish clothing; but thanks to a huge overhaul, it's now a vast, gleaming, modern behemoth focusing on affordable rather than expensive labels. You'll find a vast array of women's and men's concessions, including Tommy Hilfiger, Mango and Diesel.

Brown Thomas

88-95 Grafton Street, Around Trinity College (605 6666/www.brownthomas.com). All cross-city buses/ Luas St Stephen's Green. **Open** 9am-8pm Mon, Wed, Fri; 9.30am-8pm Tue; 9am-9pm Thur; 9am-7pm Sat; 10am-7pm Sun. **Credit** AmEx, MC, V. **Map** p251 F4.
Plush, elegant and painfully fashionable, Brown Thomas is the only place in Dublin you can pick up Louis Vuitton luggage, a Hermès scarf or a pair of Christian Louboutin shoes. Popular with travelling celebs, Dublin rich kids and the local glitterati, BTs (as it's colloquially known) is lined with wall-to-wall designer labels, including Marni, Marc Jacobs and Dolce & Gabbana. There's a substantial, and pricey, menswear collection in the basement, plus homewares, two cafés and designer handbags galore.

Clery & Co

18-27 Lower O'Connell Street, Around O'Connell Street (878 6000/www.clerys.com). All cross-city buses/Luas Abbey Street. **Open** 9am-6.30pm Mon-Wed, Sat; 9am-9pm Thur; 9am-8pm Fri; noon-6pm Sun. **Credit** AmEx, DC, MC, V. **Map** p251 F2.
You'd expect a bit more style from Dublin's longest-standing department store, especially after its €20-million revamp; but it still exudes a traditional charm. It's housed in an elegant building that boasts a smart shopfront and some beautiful staircases, but it's the stock that sets Clery apart from its peers: high-street labels like Sisley and Topshop, and MOR ranges from Gerry Weber and Bianca.

Dunnes Stores

Henry Street, Around O'Connell Street (872 3911/ www.dunnesstores.ie). All cross-city buses/Luas Jervis. **Open** 8.30am-7pm Mon-Wed; 8.30am-9pm Thur; 8.30am-8pm Fri; noon-6pm Sun. **Credit** AmEx, MC, V. **Map** p251 F2.
Dunnes Stores holds a special place in the hearts of Dubliners, thanks to its good-value, no-nonsense gear. It's exceptionally inexpensive, carries a good range of babies' and children's clothes, and is great for well-priced homewares that can be surprisingly stylish. Some of the larger stores also sell groceries. **Other locations**: throughout the city.

Marks & Spencer

15-20 Grafton Street, Around Trinity College (679 7855/www.marksandspencer.com). All cross-city buses/Luas St Stephen's Green. **Open** 9am-8pm Mon-Wed, Fri; 9am-9pm Thur; 8.30am-7pm Sat; noon-6.30pm Sun. **Credit** MC, V. **Map** p251 F4.
Occupying an enviable spot in a beautiful building on Dublin's Grafton Street, M&S draws a mix of shoppers, from slipper-seeking pensioners to fashion-conscious types after something from the trend-

driven Autograph and Limited Collection ranges. Prices are reasonable and quality is high.
Other locations: 24-29 Mary Street, Around North Quays (872 8833).

Roches Stores
54-62 Henry Street, Around O'Connell Street (873 0044/www.roches-stores.ie). All cross-city buses/Luas Jervis. **Open** 9am-6.30pm Mon-Wed, Fri, Sat; 9am-9pm Thur; 11am-6pm Sun. **Credit** AmEx, MC, V. **Map** p251 F2.
A few years ago, Roches Stores was where you'd go to buy a duster or some pillows. Now it's been unrecognisably (and successfully) transformed into a choice department store, with a vast range of accessories and beauty products, as well as Dublin's only branch of Spanish label Zara.
Other locations: throughout the city.

Shopping centres

Dundrum Town Centre
Sandyford Road, Dundrum (299 1700/www.dundrum.ie). Bus 17, 44C, 48A, 48N, 75/Luas Balally. **Open** 9am-9pm Mon-Fri; 9am-7pm Sat; 10am-7pm Sun. **Credit** varies.
Fifteen minutes outside the city centre is the goliath of Dublin shopping malls, the Dundrum Town Centre. This pristine place is an unashamed temple to consumerism and gets packed out with hungry suburban shoppers at weekends. Midweek it's much quieter and more pleasant, although you'd still need a good few hours to scout it out. As well as the usual range of well-known chain stores, there's a dinky but disappointing boutique branch of Harvey Nichols and a decent-sized House of Fraser. There are several cafés and restaurants, as well as a cinema.

ILAC Shopping Centre
Henry Street, Around O'Connell Street (704 1460). All cross-city buses/Luas Jervis. **Open** 9am-6pm Mon-Wed, Fri, Sat; 9am-9pm Thur; noon-6pm Sun. **Credit** varies. **Map** p251 F2.
Tatty, tawdry and thoroughly unpleasant, this horrid 1980s vintage shopping centre is finally treating itself to a much-needed revamp. The Henry Street entrance is now bright and airy, with a branch of H&M heralding better things to come.

Jervis Centre
Jervis Street, Around O'Connell Street (878 1323/www.jervis.ie). All cross-city buses/Luas Jervis. **Open** 9am-6pm Mon-Wed, Fri, Sat; 9am-9pm Thur; noon-6pm Sun. **Credit** varies. **Map** p251 E2.
There's little that's quintessentially Irish about this bright, modern shopping centre; instead, you'll find big UK stores like Dixons, Argos, Debenhams and M&S. It's an airy and pleasant place to wander around, though, with a fair selection of clothes stores such as Topshop, Dorothy Perkins and Next.

Powerscourt Townhouse Centre
59 William Street South, Around Temple Bar (671 7000/www.powerscourtcentre.com). All cross-city

buses/Luas St Stephen's Green. **Open** 10am-6pm Mon-Wed, Fri, Sat; 10am-8pm Thur; noon-6pm Sun. **Credit** varies. **Map** p251 F3.
Despite a location bang in Dublin's bullseye, the Powerscourt Townhouse Centre is a remarkably calm, quiet and elegant spot. With impressive plasterwork, exposed brickwork and an imposing staircase, it's one of the city's best 18th-century Georgian buildings. Enjoy classical piano music in the background, sip a frothy cappuccino in a café overlooking the light-filled courtyard, or browse through a good selection of antiques and curios, shoe shops, a photography store and branches of French Connection and All Saints. The Design Centre, home to some of Ireland's best-known designers, is right up on the top floor.

Stephen's Green Centre
St Stephen's Green West (478 0888/www.stephensgreen.com). All cross-city buses/Luas St Stephen's Green. **Open** 9am-6pm Mon-Wed, Fri, Sat; 9am-9pm Thur; noon-6pm Sun. **Credit** varies. **Map** p251 F4.
Looming over Grafton Street on the edge of St Stephen's Green, this massive shopping centre looks and feels like an overblown conservatory. Bright and breezy, it's a nice enough spot with a wide selection of shops on three floors, and extensive parking.

Antiques

On the face of it, Dublin shopping attractions are bright, modern and mainstream; but scratch the surface, and you'll find a city with a thriving antiques trade. The area around Thomas Street and the Liberties has been marked out for redevelopment as Dublin's new Soho (south of Heuston Station, amusingly), but it's also where you'll find a rake of atmospheric, dusty and interesting antiques. **Francis Street**, near St Patrick's Cathedral, is where it all happens. Lined from top to bottom with a good selection of long-established stores, it's where Dublin's serious antiques hunters come to for a fix. Prices can range from reasonable to exorbitant, so it's a good idea to know your stuff; this place might look easygoing but it's all about experienced dealers and big business.

A little further south in the same area, **Clanbrassil Street** also has a scattering of smaller, cheap antiques and junk shops – the kind of places where you can spend a late sunny afternoon browsing around before going home with something that you never really wanted in the first place.

For jewellery, Dublin is well supplied – but prices are high. **Rhinestones** (*see p148*) is a great spot for the amateur enthusiast, and John Farrington's on East Essex Street is ideal for those with more serious intentions: vintage Cartier watches, say, and Edwardian diamond necklaces. **Anne Street South**, near Trinity

College, is well provided with small silver jewellers; here you'll also find **Cathach Books**, purveyor of antique books and prints. At the **Powerscourt Townhouse Centre** (*see p139*) there's a jumbled selection of antique stores pleasantly arranged inside the very attractive Georgian building, selling cameos and silver spoons.

Books

Short of reading matter? Try the excellent second-hand stalls in the **George's Street Arcade**, which tend to have a little bit of everything, from Kafka to Stewart Home. And at a fraction of the price of the larger, high-street stores.

General

Books Upstairs

36 College Green, Around Trinity College (679 6687/ www.booksirish.com). All cross-city buses/Luas St Stephen's Green. **Open** 10am-7pm Mon-Fri; 10am-6pm Sat; 1-6pm Sun. **Credit** MC, V. **Map** p251 F3.
Books Upstairs retains an independent feel, with a notable stock of Irish literature as well as drama, philosophy, psychology, history and gay and lesbian titles. There's a regular array of bargain titles.

Eason's

40 O'Connell Street, Around O'Connell Street (858 3800/www.easons.ie). All cross-city buses/Luas Abbey Street. **Open** 8.30am-6.45pm Mon-Wed, Sat; 8.30am-8.45pm Thur; 8.30am-7.45pm Fri; noon-5.45pm Sun. **Credit** AmEx, MC, V. **Map** p251 F2.
Relentlessly busy, this long-established shop won't win any prizes for atmosphere, but it has a good selection of books over four floors.
Other locations: throughout the city.

Hodges Figgis

56-58 Dawson Street, Around Trinity College (677 4754). All cross-city buses/Luas St Stephen's Green. **Open** 9am-7pm Mon-Wed, Fri; 9am-8pm Thur; 9am-6pm Sat; noon-6pm Sun. **Credit** AmEx, MC, V. **Map** p251 F4.
Wall-to-wall books over three tightly packed floors. There's a good selection of special offers on throughout the year and an extensive stock.

Hughes & Hughes

Stephen's Green Centre, St Stephen's Green (478 3060/www.hughesbooks.com). All cross-city buses/ Luas St Stephen's Green. **Open** 9.30am-6pm Mon-Wed, Fri, Sat; 9.30am-8pm Thur; noon-6pm Sun. **Credit** AmEx, MC, V. **Map** p251 F4.
This chain has a decent selection of Irish and international popular fiction, as well as small sections on history, cookery and self-help. It also has a handy branch in Dublin Airport, should you suddenly find yourself short of in-flight reading material.
Other locations: throughout the city.

Waterstone's

7 Dawson Street, Around Trinity College (679 1260/ www.waterstones.co.uk). All cross-city buses/Luas St Stephen's Green. **Open** 9am-7pm Mon-Wed, Fri; 9am-8pm Thur; 9am-6.30pm Sat; 11am-6pm Sun. **Credit** AmEx, MC, V. **Map** p251 F4.
Waterstone's layout gives this branch of the big UK chain a quirky appeal, and you could easily spend several hours in the small specialist rooms. There's a good selection of titles on offer, with readings and signings throughout the year.
Other locations: Jervis Centre; *see p139*.

Second-hand & rare

Cathach Books

10 Duke Street, Around Trinity College (671 8676/ www.rarebooks.ie). All cross-city buses/Luas St Stephen's Green. **Open** 9.30am-5.45pm Mon-Sat. **Credit** AmEx, MC, V. **Map** p251 F3/4.
Many a pleasant afternoon can be spent thumbing through the dusty, yellow-paged gems that fill the shelves of this charming shop. It's not cheap, but there's an admirable pick of first editions and signed copies from the likes of Beckett, Joyce, Yeats and Wilde. Cathach also sells rare maps and prints.

Greene's

16 Clare Street, Around St Stephen's Green (676 2554/www.greenesbookshop.com). All cross-city buses. **Open** 9am-5.30pm Mon-Fri; 9am-2.30pm Sat. **Credit** AmEx, DC, MC, V. **Map** p251 G4.
Set near the National Art Gallery, Greene's is now one of Dublin's bookish landmarks. An impressive number of literary giants have walked through its door over the years, including Brendan Behan, WB Yeats and Beckett. Greene's is well known for its good selection of new, second-hand and antiquarian books. The storefront has changed little since 1917.

Secret Book & Record Shop

15A Wicklow Street, Around Trinity College (679 7272). All cross-city buses. **Open** 11am-6.30pm daily. **No credit cards**. **Map** p251 F3.
This is a great second-hand bookshop with a bit of everything: a few out-of-print paperbacks, recently remaindered titles and even LPs. Despite its rather tongue-in-cheek name, it's not much of a secret, but still worth nosing out. **Photo** *p138*.

Specialist

Connolly Books

7 Bloom Lane, Around O'Connell Street (874 7981/ www.communistpartyofireland.ie/cbooks/index.html). All cross-city buses/Luas Jervis. **Open** 9.30am-6pm Mon-Sat. **Credit** DC, MC, V. **Map** p251 E2.
Temporarily exiled across the river from its usual spot in Temple Bar, Connolly Books takes its name from James Connolly, Ireland's socialist pioneer. As you might expect, it stocks contemporary leftist writing, plus books on Irish history, feminism and philosophy. It's popular with Gaelic speakers, too.

Louise Kennedy. *See p147.*

Style and the suburbs

Blackrock

While it could never be described as hip, Blackrock has a good range of small designer stores, interiors shops and cutesy children's boutiques that make it a good spot to spend a few hours. Just beside the sea along the south coast, its focal point is the small main street, while a bright but boring little shopping centre offers a reasonable selection of book and clothes shops. Gentlemen Please (47 Main Street, 278 8788) is for blokes bored with slim pickings in the city centre, with labels like Strellson, Day by Birger & Mikkelsen and Nicole Fahri; women with a lust for designer labels should head to Khan (15 Rock Hill, Main Street, 278 1646), a Blackrock mainstay with consistently good stock. For some Scandinavian designs to take home, try Nordic Living (57 Main Street, no phone), which stocks excellent furniture, rugs, textiles, accessories and gifts.

Dundrum

Dundrum used to be a drab, soulless village until the excessively hyped Dundrum Town Centre (*see p139*) arrived to save the inner-city suburb from death by dullness. Crammed with shops, from children's bookstores to sleek designer boutiques, the centre is a vast temple to consumerism. It also has a good range of cafés, restaurants and a cinema. Check out House of Fraser, which has an excellent beauty section and a good selection of women's clothing. The centre's branch of Harvey Nichols, meanwhile, might be disappointingly small but it still manages to stock a good line of designer pieces and posh shoes.

Glasthule

This pretty little village is set on the southern coast, and has a great smattering of clothes, accessories and shoe shops jumbled up with the butchers, newsagents and dry-cleaners. Caviston's (59 Glasthule Road, 280 9120) is a friendly deli with excellent sandwiches, salads, gourmet pastas and organic produce, as well as a famed fish section. At Soul (2 Glasthule Terrace, 280 8895) you'll find a sublime collection of designer shoes, with gloriously sculpted heels from European greats like Pedro Garcia. Jewellery store Halo (4 Glasthule Road, 284 5922) is well worth a look, while designer fashion gets a boho twist at the local branch of the Dublin boutique Rococo (20 Glasthule Road, 230 0686).

Ranelagh

Ranelagh is near the city centre but still has a chilled-out village vibe, with plenty of cafés and restaurants between the shops. One excellent reason for making the short trip here is the small but super-chic boutique Kelli (45 Ranelagh Village, 497 0077), which sits unassumingly on the main street. This stylish shop has a breezy feel and a well-picked collection from labels like See by Chloe and Nocturne, as well as some very desirable accessories. Pregnant women with an eye for design should head for Bella Mamma (The Triangle, 496 8598) – one of the earliest maternity boutiques in Dublin to offer an alternative to dowdy dungarees, with pieces from Gharani Strok and Noppies. For unusual blooms and all things floral, try the beautiful (and wonderfully fragrant) Blooming Amazing (38 Ranelagh Village; 491 0233).

Forbidden Planet

6-7 Crampton Quay (671 0688). All cross-city buses. **Open** 10am-7pm Mon-Fri; 10am-6pm Sat; 11am-4pm Sun. **Credit** AmEx, MC, V. **Map** p251 F2.

Elbow your way among teenage geeks and comic freaks, and you'll find a good selection of science fiction and fantasy. There are also books, mags, videos, toys, action figures and posters from across the globe.

CDs & records

Big Brother Records

4 Crow Street, Around Temple Bar (672 9355/www. bigbrotherrecords.com). All cross-city buses/Luas Jervis. **Open** 11am-7pm Mon-Wed, Fri; 11am-8pm Thur; 11am-6pm Sat. **Credit** MC, V. **Map** p251 E3.

The friendly staff are what makes Big Brother so pleasant. And they know their stuff, with a great independent selection of vinyl and CDs that covers all the bases from tech-house to punk-funk. It's a good place to catch up on club news, and the store has a nifty location in the heart of Temple Bar.

Borderline Records

17 Temple Bar (679 9097). All cross-city buses/Luas Jervis. **Open** 10am-9pm Mon-Fri; 10am-6pm Sat; 2-6pm Sun **Credit** MC, V. **Map** p251 E3.

Local uni students flock here for the good range of affordable titles and for the unpretentious staff and generally relaxed vibe. Those in the know say it is especially strong on rare releases, although to the untrained eye, it just seems like a pretty decent all-rounder.

Eat, Drink, Shop

Celtic Note

12 Nassau Street, Around Trinity College (670 4157/www.celticnote.com). All cross-city buses/Luas St Stephen's Green. **Open** 9am-6.30pm Mon-Wed; 9am-8am Thur; 9am-7pm Fri, Sat; 11am-6pm Sun. **Credit** AmEx, MC, V. **Map** p251 H5.
If you're after Irish stuff, then this is the place to come to (note those big posters of Irish artists in the window). Helpful staff are on hand to answer any queries, and the stock also includes a decent pick of British and American folk artists.

Claddagh Records

2 Cecilia Street, Around Temple Bar (677 0262/ www.claddaghrecords.com). All cross-city buses/Luas Abbey Street. **Open** 10.30am-5.30pm Mon-Fri; noon-5.30pm Sat. **Credit** MC, V. **Map** p251 E3.
Irish music die-hards will delight in Claddagh's excellent and extensive stock of traditional and folk tunes. There's everything here from early traditional 1960s recordings to the most recent releases. It's a great spot at which to pick up a rare folk album, find out about traditional concerts or just catch up on what's happening in Irish music.

Golden Discs

31 Mary Street, Around O'Connell Street (872 4211/ www.goldendiscs.ie). All cross-city buses/Luas Jervis. **Open** 9.30am-6pm Mon-Wed; 9.30am-8pm Thur; 9.30am-6.30pm Fri; 9am-6.30pm Sat; noon-6pm Sun. **Credit** AmEx, MC, V. **Map** p250 D2.
Golden Discs is increasingly becoming overshadowed by larger international chains, which may be in part because of its dedication to MOR stock. It's not a bad record store, just not that inspiring. **Other locations**: throughout the city.

HMV

65 Grafton Street, Around Trinity College (679 5334/www.hmv.co.uk). All cross-city buses/Luas St Stephen's Green. **Open** 8.30am-7pm Mon-Wed, Fri, Sat; 8.30am-9pm Thur; 10am-7pm Sun. **Credit** AmEx, MC, V. **Map** p251 F4.
Cross the threshold of this three-level megastore on a Saturday afternoon, and you'll get blasted with ear-drumming pop, as well as having to fight your way through a wall of teenagers. At other times, it's a good if unatmospheric shop for the latest releases, DVDs and other entertaining gear. You can also buy gig tickets here. **Other locations**: throughout the city.

Road Records

16B Fade Street, Around St Stephen's Green (671 7340/www.roadrecs.com). All cross-city buses/Luas St Stephen's Green. **Open** 10am-6pm Mon-Wed, Fri, Sat; 10am-7pm Thur; 2-6pm Sun. **Credit** MC, V. **Map** p251 E4.
Vinyl junkies should head to Road Records, an old-school music store that has a chilled-out vibe and a great selection of left field tunes. There are great staff, a small but perfectly formed interior and good tunes on the stereo; it's a good spot for stuff from Irish independent artists.

Design Yard at Whichcraft. *See p148.*

Selectah Records

4 Crow Street, Around Temple Bar (616 7020/www. selectahrecords.com). All cross-city buses/Luas Jervis. **Open** 11am-7pm Mon-Wed, Fri; 11am-8pm Thur; 11am-6pm Sat; 1-5pm Sun. **Credit** MC, V. **Map** 251 E3.
Selectah stocks titles from a wide range of international and home-grown dance acts. The shop specialises in vinyl but also sells CDs.

Tower Records

16 Wicklow Street, Around Trinity College (671 3250/www.towerrecords.co.uk). All cross-city buses/Luas St Stephen's Green. **Open** 9am-9pm Mon-Sat; 11.30am-7.30pm Sun. **Credit** AmEx, MC, V. **Map** p251 F3.
Another chain, but thankfully this one has a good array of alternative and world music, plus jazz, traditional and country. It also sells music mags and foreign newspapers.

Children

Clothing

Although Dublin does have a reasonable selection of dedicated children's clothes stores, it's worth exploring the children's departments in **Next**, **Zara**, **Roches Stores**, **Dunnes**, **Marks & Spencer** and **Arnotts**. If you want to pamper your little, head to super-posh **BT2**.

Toys

Banba Toymaster
48 Mary Street, Around North Quays (872 7100).
All cross-city buses/Luas Jervis. **Open** 9.30am-6pm
Mon-Wed, Fri; 9.30am-8pm Thur; 9am-6pm Sat;
noon-6pm Sun. **Credit** MC, V. **Map** p250 D2.
The young and young-at-heart are likely to lose their
heads in this colossal pantheon of play. The tightly
packed aisles roar with every big brand name you
can think of, as kids cluster around the latest toys.

Early Learning Centre
3 Henry Street, Around O'Connell Street (873 1945/
www.elc.co.uk). All cross-city buses/Luas Abbey Street.
Open 9.30am-6pm Mon-Wed, Fri; 9.30am-8.30pm
Thur; 9am-5.30pm Sat; 1-5pm Sun. **Credit** MC, V.
Map p251 F2.
A well-known chain that's known for its bright, fun
and educational toys, all designed to stimulate and
engage babies, toddlers and youngsters.

Pinocchio's
5 Westbury Mall, Westbury Hotel, off Grafton Street,
Around Trinity College (677 7632). All cross-city
buses/Luas St Stephen's Green. **Open** 10am-6pm
Mon-Wed, Fri, Sat; 10am-7pm Thur. **Credit** AmEx,
MC, V. **Map** p251 F4.
If you're fed up of the plastic horrors of mainstream
toy shops, then the folksy appeal of Pinocchio's
offers a good alternative. You'll find wooden toys,
furry puppets, old-fashioned teddy bears and cutesy
bits and bobs.

Crafts & gifts

If you're after upmarket crafts, walk the area
around **Cow's Lane** and **Temple Bar**; for
traditional knitware, contemporary Celtic
jewellery and Waterford Crystal, try **Nassau
Street** near Trinity College.

Modern crafts

Avoca Handweavers
11-13 Suffolk Street, Around Trinity College (677
4215/www.avoca.ie). All cross-city buses/Luas St
Stephen's Green. **Open** 10am-6pm Mon-Wed, Fri,
Sat; 10am-8pm Thur; 11am-6pm Sun. **Credit** AmEx,
DC, MC, V. **Map** p251 F3.
Avoca is always ferociously busy at the weekends.
As well as a good selection of clothing, the three-
floor store bursts at the seams with pretty jewellery,
unusual and wacky gifts, cute children's clothing
and cookbooks from its famous County Wicklow
café. Downstairs you'll find a small café and deli
with delectable breads and tempting sweets.

Design Yard
Cow's Lane, Around O'Connell Street (474 1011/
www.designyard.ie). All cross-city buses/Luas Jervis.
Open 9am-6pm Mon-Sat; 11am-6pm Sun. **Credit**
AmEx, DC, MC, V. **Map** p251 E3.

Ann Summers. *See p149.*

A far cry from the tatty craft shops that choke up
Dublin's city centre streets, elegant Design Yard
takes a contemporary approach with wares from
modern Irish artists. The selection of jewellery is
extensive and excellent.

Traditional crafts

Blarney Woollen Mills
21-23 Nassau Street, Around Trinity College (671
0068/www.blarneywoollenmills.ie). All cross-city
buses/Luas St Stephen's Green. **Open** 9am-6pm Mon-
Wed, Fri, Sat; 9am-8pm Thur; 11am-6pm Sun.
Credit AmEx, MC, V. **Map** p251 F3.
Blarney Woollen Mills is slightly chintzy but good
for hand-woven items like throws, sweaters and
scarves. If you're after souvenirs, you can choose
from Waterford Crystal and Belleek china, as well
as some traditional linen and Celtic jewellery.

Kilkenny Shop
6 Nassau Street, Around Trinity College (677 7066/
www.kilkennygroup.com). All cross-city buses/Luas St
Stephen's Green. **Open** 8.30am-7pm Mon-Wed, Fri;
8.30am-8pm Thur; 9am-6.30pm Sat; 11am-6pm Sun.
Credit AmEx, DC, MC, V. **Map** p251 F3.
Kilkenny has a stylish atmosphere and offerings
from a selection of eclectic designers. As well as contemporary jewellery and glassware from the likes of
John Rocha and Louise Kennedy, there's pottery
from Stephen Pearce, and hip handbags from inter-

nationally renowned designer Orla Kiely. The café upstairs serves indulgently creamy cakes and wholesome salads.

Louis Mulcahy

46 Dawson Street, Around Trinity College (670 9311/www.louismulcahy.com). Bus 10, 46A/Luas Stephen's Green. **Open** 10am-6pm Mon-Wed, Fri, Sat; 10am-8pm Thur. **Credit** AmEx, MC, V. **Map** p251 F4.

It might be impossible to cram one of Mulcahy's oversized vases into your suitcase, but there's also smaller stuff here, including his trademark fine porcelain and hearty stoneware.

Woollen Mills

41 Lower Ormond Quay, North Quays (828 0301). All cross-city buses/Luas Jervis. **Open** 9am-5pm Mon-Wed, Fri; 9am-7pm Thur; 9.30am-6pm Sat. **Credit** AmEx, MC, V. **Map** p251 E2/3.

It's a full-on wool fest at this 1888 store, with Aran, cashmere, merino and mohair items in profusion: a pleasing array of sweaters, capes, scarves and cardies to keep out the bitter winter winds. Not exactly cutting edge but not dowdy, either.

Electronics

Cameras

Camera Centre

56 Grafton Street, Around Trinity College (677 5594/www.cameracentre.ie). All cross-city buses/Luas St Stephen's Green. **Open** 9am-6pm Mon-Wed, Fri, Sat; 9am-8pm Thur; 1-5.30pm Sun. **Credit** AmEx, DC, MC, V. **Map** p251 F4.

As well as the usual cameras, camcorders, binoculars and telescopes, Camera Centre also offers a one-hour film-processing service.

Camera Exchange

9B Trinity Street, Around Trinity College (679 3410/www.cameraexchange.ie). All cross-city buses/ Luas St Stephen's Green. **Open** 9am-6pm Mon-Wed, Fri, Sat; 9am-7pm Thur. **Credit** AmEx, MC, V. **Map** p251 F3.

Camera Exchange has new and used camera equipment – a good place if you're shopping on a budget.

Computer parts & repairs

Beyond 2000

2 Chatham Row, Around Temple Bar (677 7633). All cross-city buses/Luas St Stephen's Green. **Open** 9.30am-6pm Mon-Sat. **Credit** AmEx, MC, V. **Map** p251 F4.

A good, central place for PC-related gizmos.

Maplin Electronics

Unit 1-4, The Smyth's Building, Jervis Street, Around O'Connell Street (878 2388/www.maplin. co.uk). All cross-city buses/Luas Jervis. **Open** 9am-6pm Mon-Wed, Fri; 9am-8pm Thur; noon-6pm Sun. **Credit** AmEx, MC, V. **Map** p251 E2.

Maplin is a reliable store for computer parts and equipment. It's the kind of place you tend to be unaware of until your modem stops working, at which point it becomes the most vital shop in town.

Fashion

While Dublin is packed with smart little boutiques, the city's shopping streets also throng with every possible chain store. Both ends of the market, in other words, are fairly comprehensively covered. Among the better mid-range UK chains in the city centre are **Jigsaw** (Grafton Street), **Reiss** (St Stephen's Green), **All Saints** (Powerscourt Townhouse Centre) and the Danish label, **Noa** (Westbury Mall). The new **Topshop** at St Stephen's Green is a mecca for Dublin's young and fashionable, from perky teens to trend-conscious thirtysomethings; while **French Connection** (Powerscourt Townhouse Centre), **Oasis** (Henry Street and Grafton Street), **Warehouse** (Grafton Street), **H&M** (Henry Street) and **Zara** (Jervis Centre) also draw the teeming masses. Keep your eye open for the perennially excellent bargains at Irish stores such as **A-Wear** and **Penneys**.

Boutiques

Ave Maria

38 Clarendon Street, Around Trinity College (671 8229). All cross-city buses/Luas St Stephen's Green. **Open** 10am-6pm Mon-Wed, Fri, Sat; 10am-8pm Thur; 1.30-5.30pm Sun. **Credit** AmEx, MC, V. **Map** p251 F4.

This cheeky little boutique carries eclectic, very fashionable designs and a broad range of labels, from the super-expensive to the almost affordable. The interior is swanky without being over-the-top and the sales assistants are pleasant and helpful. It also stocks glitzy accessories and shoes.

Chica Day

Unit 25, Westbury Mall, Clarendon Street entrance, Around St Stephen's Green (671 9836). All cross-city buses/Luas St Stephen's Green. **Open** 10am-6pm Mon-Wed, Fri, Sat; 10am-7pm Thur. **Credit** MC, V. **Map** p251 F4.

Chica has a good-quality range of ornate, sparkly clothes that err on the conservative side of boho. You can choose from two pink-fronted shops in the Westbury Mall: one is for day and the other for night, but both are filled with riotously pretty stuff.

Costume

10-11 Castle Market, Around Temple Bar (679 4188). All cross-city buses/Luas St Stephen's Green. **Open** 10am-6pm Mon-Wed, Fri, Sat; 10am-7pm Thur. **Credit** AmEx, MC, V. **Map** p251 F3.

You'll find all kinds of very cool designer togs here. *See p148* **Boutique chic.**

Eat, Drink, Shop

Rococo

Westbury Mall, Westbury Hotel, off Grafton Street, Around Trinity College (670 4007). All cross-city buses/Luas St Stephen's Green. **Open** 10am-6pm Mon-Wed, Fri, Sat; 10am-8pm Thur; 1-5pm Sun. **Credit** AmEx, MC, V. **Map** p251 F4.
Roxanna Allen's dinky bohemian boutique is well worth a look. *See p148* **Boutique chic**.

Smock

20-22 Essex Street West, Around Temple Bar (613 9000). All cross-city buses/Luas Jervis. **Open** 10.30am-6pm Mon-Sat. **Credit** MC, V. **Map** p251 F3.
Perfectly picked designs *See p148* **Boutique chic**.

Tulle

28 George's Street Arcade, Around Temple Bar (679 9115). All cross-city buses. **Open** 10am-6pm Mon-Wed, Fri, Sat; 10am-7.30pm Thur; 1-5pm Sun. **Credit** MC, V. **Map** p251 E3.
Tulle is something of an anomaly in George's Street Arcade, with its tumbling, eclectic stalls and second-hand stores. Heralded by a pink neon sign, the shop has a simple understated interior filled with a strong collection of small hip designers.

International designers

As well as the shops listed here, **Brown Thomas** (*see p138*) is great for big-name designers, **Urban Outfitters** (Cecelia House, Temple Bar) has quirky offbeat labels and **Costume** (Castle Market) has an impressive range of European names. **Richard Alan** (South King Street) and **Pia Bang** (Grafton Street) have a good selection of prestigious but lesser-known designer labels.

Alias Tom

Duke House, Duke Street, Around Trinity College (671 5443). All cross-city buses/Luas St Stephen's Green. **Open** 9.30am-6pm Mon-Wed, Fri, Sat; 9.30am-8pm Thur. **Credit** AmEx, MC, V. **Map** p251 F4.
Top men's designer togs. *See p148* **Boutique chic**.

BT2

28-29 Grafton Street, Around Trinity College (605 6666). All cross-city buses/Luas St Stephen's Green. **Open** 9am-8pm Mon-Wed, Fri; 9am-9pm Thur; 9am-7pm Sat; 10am-7pm Sun. **Credit** AmEx, MC, V. **Map** p251 F4.
Chirpy, colourful and with a good range of expensive high-street labels and designer jeans, BT2 is an offshoot of the more upmarket Brown Thomas. There are shoes downstairs, with a decent men's collection; children's clothes are on the top floor.

Louis Copeland

39-41 Capel Street, North Quays (872 1600/www. louiscopeland.com). All cross-city buses/Luas Jervis. **Open** 9am-5.30pm Mon-Wed, Fri, Sat; 9am-8pm Thur. **Credit** AmEx, DC, MC, V. **Map** p251 E2.
Ireland's most famous tailor has been kitting out the chaps for over a century. As well as Copeland's own brand, the store carries designs from Ralph Lauren, Versace and Paul & Shark.

Richard Alan

58 Grafton Street, Around Trinity College (616 8906). All cross-city buses/Luas St Stephen's Green. **Open** 10am-6pm Mon-Wed; 10am-8pm Thur; 9.30am-6pm Fri, Sat; noon-6pm Sun. **Credit** AmEx, DC, MC, V. **Map** p251 F4.
This plush store drips with luxurious clothes that are breathtakingly expensive.

Rhinestones. *See p148.*

Irish designers

Claire Garvey

*6 Cow's Lane, Around Temple Bar (671 7287/www.
clairegarvey.com). All cross-city buses/Luas Jervis.*
Open 10am-5.30pm Tue-Sat. **Credit** AmEx, MC, V.
Map p251 E3.

If you feel a theatrical moment coming on, try Claire
Garvey's Temple Bar shop. Garvey's designs are
unashamedly flamboyant and decadent – but emi-
nently wearable, all the same.

Design Centre

*Powerscourt Townhouse Centre, 59 William Street
South, Around St Stephen's Green (679 5718/www.design
centre.ie). All cross-city buses/Luas St Stephen's
Green.* **Open** 10am-6pm Mon-Wed, Fri; 10am-8pm
Thur; 9.30am-6pm Sat; noon-6pm Sun. **Credit**
AmEx, MC, V. **Map** p251 F3.

The Design Centre is an institution on the Dublin
shopping scene, although it's a tough climb to its
airy location at the top of the Powerscourt
Townhouse Centre. The shop stocks cutting-edge
international labels but is also the best place to keep
abreast of the cream of Irish design.

Jen Kelly

*50 North Great George's Street, Around O'Connell
Street (874 5983). All cross-city buses.* **Open**
9am-5.30pm Mon-Fri. **Credit** AmEx, MC, V.
Map p251 F1.

Haute couturier Jen Kelly designed the costumes for
Riverdance, but don't let that put you off. His opulent
creations are famed for their rich use of velvet, fur,
satin, Chantilly lace and lavish embroidery, while his
refurbished Georgian manor revives bygone elegance. Costly stuff, but worth every penny.

Louise Kennedy

*56 Merrion Square, Around St Stephen's Green (662
0056/www.louisekennedy.com). Buses 44, 48/DART
Pearse.* **Open** 9am-6pm Mon-Sat. **Credit** AmEx, MC,
V. **Map** p251 G4.

Famed throughout the world for her exquisitely tai-
lored suits and her opulent eveningwear, Louise
Kennedy is popular with a diverse range of women
from Samantha Mumba to Cherie Blair. Her stunning Georgian salon and home showcase her desirable designs as well as her exclusive collection of
Tipperary crystal glasses, bowls, candlesticks and
decanters. **Photo** *p141.*

Tyrrell Brennan

*13 Lower Pembroke Street, Around St Stephen's
Green (670 4178/www.tyrrellbrennan.com). All cross-
city buses.* **Open** by appointment. **Credit** AmEx,
MC, V. **Map** p251 G5.

Affable design duo Niall Tyrrell and Donald
Brennan have broken the rigorous fashion mould
with bold designs for real women. Don't expect any
fuddy-duddy fashions here: this talented pair does
a fine line in stylish ready-to-wear and made-to-order
gear that's a big hit with Ireland's media types.

Jewellery & accessories

Powerscourt Townhouse Centre (*see p139*)
is home to all kinds of jewellers ranging from
straightforward silversmiths to an assortment
of eccentric antiques shops. **Johnson's Court**
(off Grafton Street), on the other hand, is a good
spot for small independent jewellers, but you'll
also find the big posh emporiums here. All you
need to bring is your credit card.

Appleby's

5 Johnson's Court, Around Trinity College (679 9572/www.appleby.ie). All cross-city buses/Luas St Stephen's Green. **Open** 9.30am-5.30pm Mon-Wed, Fri; 9.30am-7.30pm Thur; 9.30am-6pm Sat. **Credit** AmEx, MC, V. **Map** p251 F4.

Expect strictly upmarket diamond rings, pearls and watches by Longines, Hermès and Van Cleef & Arpels.

Costelloe & Costelloe

14A Chatham Street, Around Trinity College (671 4209/www.costelloeandcostelloe.com). All cross-city buses/Luas St Stephen's Green. **Open** 10am-6pm Mon-Wed, Fri, Sat; 10am-8pm Thur; 1.30-5pm Sun. **Credit** AmEx, MC, V. **Map** p251 F4.

With its dazzling selection of sparkly handbags and glistening jewellery, this pretty little accessories shop looks much more expensive than it actually is.

Design Yard at Whichcraft

Cow's Lane, Around Temple Bar (474 1011/www. whichcraft.com). All cross-city buses. **Open** 9.30am-6.30pm Mon-Wed, Fri, Sat; 9.30am-8pm Thur; 10am-6pm Sun. **Credit** AmEx, MC, V. **Map** p251 E3.

Quality is high at this modern, sleek jewellery concession housed within a larger crafts store. Expect chic pieces from cutting-edge European and Irish designers. **Photo** *p143*.

Paul Sheeran

7 Johnson's Court, off Grafton Street, Around Trinity College (635 1136). All cross-city buses/Luas St Stephen's Green. **Open** 9.45am-5.45pm Mon-Wed, Fri, Sat; 9.45am-7.45pm Thur. **Credit** AmEx, MC, V. **Map** p251 F4.

Don't be surprised if you bump into a celeb at this glamorous temple to all that glistens. Stocking some of the world's most exclusive brands, Sheeran's is a colossal emporium that oozes wealth and prestige.

Rhinestones

18 St Andrew's Street, Around Trinity College (679 0759/www.rhinestones.ie). All cross-city buses/Luas St Stephen's Green. **Open** 9.30am-6pm Mon-Wed, Fri, Sat; 9.30am-8pm Thur; noon-6pm Sun. **Credit** AmEx, MC, V. **Map** p251 F3.

Rhinestones is nothing short of stunning, with its wonderful collection of sumptuous art deco and antique jewellery. But check the tag before you fall in love with that precious 1930s necklace: some of the prices are breathtaking. **Photo** *p146*.

Vivien Walsh

24 Stephen Street Lower, Around St Stephen's Green (475 5031/www.vivienwalsh.com). All cross-city buses/Luas St Stephen's Green. **Open** 11am-6pm Mon-Wed, Fri; 11am-7pm Thur; 10am-6pm Sat. **Credit** MC, V. **Map** p251 E4.

Walsh is Ireland's top costume designer, and this pretty store is like a jewellery box filled with pieces to mesmerise and seduce, from sumptuous little handbags to extravagant necklaces and earrings. Prices range from affordable to expensive.

Weir's

96 Grafton Street, Around Trinity College (677 9678/www.weirandsons.ie). All cross-city buses/Luas St Stephen's Green. **Open** 9.30am-6pm Mon-Wed, Fri, Sat; 9.30am-8pm Thur. **Credit** AmEx, MC, V. **Map** p251 F4.

Boutique chic

Alias Tom

Men draw the short straw when it comes to Dublin boutiques – the exception, of course, being Alias Tom (*see p146*). With wall-to-wall designer labels and suitably snooty sales staff, this long-established store manages to retain its cool – and prices that will make most shoppers blanch. Expect lots of Gucci and sleeker-than-thou suits.

Costume

The rails at Costume (*see p145*) can be packed a little too tightly for comfort, but that's the only complaint about this pretty store. Some of the prices are sky high, but there's plenty of variety, and plenty of the latest designs from top European and international names. Light floods in through the large main window, making this a very pleasant shop in which to spend time browsing on a sunny afternoon.

Rococo

Rococo (*see p146*) eschews predictable labels and severe designs in favour of something a little more creative. Bohemian without being excessively theatrical, this tiny boutique just beside the Westbury Hotel bursts at the seams with colourful fashions from a good selection of labels from around the world. Prices can be a little high – but what else would you expect from a store that Britney Spears has been seen in?

Smock

If the bright lights and disposable clothing of chain stores turn you off, you may well find sartorial solace at Smock (*see p146*). This diminutive boutique has been at the heart of the fashion scene for the past five years, with a fantastic array of designers from Australia, New York and Belgium. Staff are friendly and stock is très chic.

Schuh. *See p150.*

Weir's doesn't have the clean, contemporary lines of many of Dublin's top jewellery stores, and it's all the better for it: time has stood still in its wonderfully faded and atmospheric interior. Come here for quality jewellery, silverware and watches.

Lingerie

Ann Summers

30-31 O'Connell Street (878 1385/www.ann summers.com). All cross-city buses/Luas Abbey Sreet. **Open** 9.30am-6.30pm Mon-Wed, Sat; 9.30am-9pm Thur; 9.30am-7pm Fri; noon-6pm Sun. **Credit** MC, V. **Map** p251 F2.

Looking for an edible thong or a naughty nurse outfit? Ann Summers is for you. Proud purveyor of sex toys, kinky lingerie, bondage gear, potions and lotions, this cheeky sex store presents its erotic wares in a bright, sleaze-free environment. Fun, but not for all the family. **Photo** *p144.*

Beneath

1 Cow's Lane, Temple Bar (674 5983/www.beneath.ie). All cross-city buses/Luas Jervis. **Open** 10.30am-6pm Tue, Wed, Fri, Sat; 10.30am-7pm Thur. **Credit** AmEx, MC, V. **Map** p251 E3.

This pleasant lingerie store stocks a good collection of smalls from international brands like Calvin Klein, Lejaby, Fantasie and Pureda.

Susan Hunter

Westbury Mall, Around Trinity College (679 1271/ www.susanhunter.ie). All cross-city buses/Luas St Stephen's Green. **Open** 10am-6pm Mon-Wed, Fri, Sat; 10am-7pm Thur. **Credit** AmEx, DC, MC, V. **Map** p251 F4.

This pint-sized shop is supposedly the oldest lingerie shop in town, and it's hugely popular with women after high-end luxury labels like La Perla, Lejaby and Aubade. Indulge yourself with 1940s starlet-style silk dressing gowns, French knickers and slips.

Shoes

Try department stores **Arnotts** and **Brown Thomas** or **BT2** Grafton Street is also a good place to look for shoes, with branches of **Nine West** and **Office**.

Birkenstock

36 Wicklow Street (675 3766/www.birkenstock. co.uk). All cross-city buses/Luas St Stephen's Green. **Open** 9.30am-6pm Mon-Wed; 9.30am-7.45pm Thur; 9.30am-5.30pm Fri; 9.30am-6pm Sat. **Credit** MC, V. **Map** p251 F3.

Expect the trademark comfort and design at this large Birkenstock emporium. **Photo** *p137.*

Camper

10 Wicklow Street, Around Trinity College (207 409 3103/www.camper.com). All cross-city buses/Luas St Stephen's Green. **Open** 10.30am-7pm Mon-Sat. **Credit** MC, V. **Map** p251 F3.

Dublin's new Camper store stocks a good range of designs from the hip Majorcan shoe company. It's a relatively small space, but shoes are well laid out, with men's on one side, and women's on the other.

Cherche Midi

23 Drury Street, Around Temple Bar (675 3974). All cross-city buses/Luas St Stephen's Green. **Open** 10am-6pm Mon-Wed, Fri, Sat; 10am-8.30pm Thur; 1-6pm Sun. **Credit** MC, V. **Map** p251 E3.

Eat, Drink, Shop

With its beautiful black-and-pink interior and gilded mirrors, Cherche Midi looks like it should be selling French knickers instead of high-end shoes. The seriously fashionable footwear isn't cheap, but these heels are crafted by top international designers. And what a lovey environment to shop in.

Schuh

47 O'Connell Street, Around O'Connell Street (872 3228/www.schuh.ie). All cross-city buses/Luas Abbey Street. **Open** 9.30am-6.30pm Mon-Wed, Fri, Sat; 10am-8pm Thur; noon-6pm Sun. **Credit** AmEx, MC, V. **Map** p251 F2.

The environment (and some of the shoes) might be a little garish for some, but this busy and popular shoe store has a vast selection of footwear, with trainers from the likes of Evisu, Puma and Converse, as well as some rather sexy heels. **Photo** *p149*.

Other locations: throughout the city.

Vintage clothing

Jenny Vander

50 Drury Street, Around Temple Bar (677 0406). All cross-city buses. **Open** 10am-5.45pm Mon-Sat. **Credit** MC, V. **Map** p251 E3.

There's nothing fusty about this exquisite vintage clothing store, which carries an elegant range of carefully selected threads, hats, jewellery, shoes and accessories. It has become something of a firm favourite among Dublin's style cognoscenti, and it's an absolute must-visit for anyone in search of that truly original find.

Wild Child

61 South Great George's Street, Around Temple Bar (475 5099). All cross-city buses. **Open** 10am-6pm Mon-Wed, Fri, Sat; 10am-7pm Thur; 1-6pm Sun. **Credit** MC, V. **Map** p251 E3.

Not so much vintage as second-hand, this shop is the kind of place people look to for tongue-in-cheek '70s kitsch or florid '50s shirts. There's a lot of tat here, but persist and you may find a gem.

Laundry & dry-cleaning

Grafton Cleaners

32 William Street South, Around Temple Bar (679 4309). All cross-city buses/Luas St Stephen's Green. **Open** 8.30am-6.30pm Mon-Wed, Fri; 8.30am-7pm Thur; 8.30am-5pm Sat. **Credit** AmEx, MC, V. **Map** p251 F3.

You can expect a reliable service from this conveniently located laundry.

Food & drink

Bakers & pâtisseries

The Bakery

Pudding Row, off Essex Street, Around Temple Bar (672 9882). All cross-city buses. **Open** 7am-5pm Mon-Fri. **No credit cards. Map** p251 E3.

Creamy cakes and sticky delights are laid out for your delectation at this no-nonsense bakery. Put the diet on hold for a few minutes.

La Maison des Gourmets

*15 Castle Market, Around Temple Bar (672 7258).
All cross-city buses.* **Open** 8am-7pm Mon-Fri; 8am-
6pm Sat. **Credit** AmEx, DC, MC, V. **Map** p251 E3.
A recent change of ownership had Dublin's pastry
lovers quaking in their boots, but La Maison des
Gourmets still sells rich, buttery croissants, wonderfully crafted breads and exquisite cakes. Linger
over a pastry and coffee at one of the outdoor tables.

Delicatessens

The **George's Street Arcade** is also a handy
purveyor of tasty olives, Moroccan sandwiches
or super-strong Spanish coffee.

Fallon & Byrne

*Exchequer Building, 11-17 Exchequer Street, Around
Temple Bar (472 1010/www.fallonandbyrne.com).
All cross-city buses/Luas St Stephen's Green.* **Open**
8am-10pm Mon-Fri; 9am-9pm Sat; 11am-8pm Sun.
Credit MC, V. **Map** p251 E3.
Young, fashionable professionals who fancy them-
selves as Manhattanites flock to this chic new deli.
You can shop for miso soup, sip coffee, feast on
gourmet sarnies at an Italiano coffee bar or indulge
in some truffles. Housed within a beautiful building,
it's already a hit with its bright and modish feel.
There's a restaurant and s wine cellar; *see also p103.*

Magills

*14 Clarendon Street, Around Trinity College (671
3830). All cross-city buses/Luas St Stephen's Green.*
Open 9.30am-5.45pm Mon-Sat. **Credit** MC, V.
Map p251 F4.
The steady popularity of this relentlessly busy deli
is a testament to the quality of its produce. Fresh
breads line the counter, salamis hang from the ceiling and expensive pastas fill the shelves. The staff
are exceptionally knowledgeable and helpful.

Sheridan's Cheesemongers

*11 Anne Street South, Around St Stephen's Green
(679 3143/www.sheridanscheesemongers.com). All
cross-city buses/Luas St Stephen's Green.* **Open**
10am-6pm Mon-Fri; 9.30am-6pm Sat. **Credit** MC, V.
Map p251 F4.
Ireland's artisan cheese producers have a strong reputation throughout the country, and Sheridan's
stocks the cream of the crop. Yes, this tiny store can
overwhelm the nose, but it's the best purveyor in the
city of locally produced and European cheeses.
Other locations: markets throughout the city.

Health food

On top of the establishments below, you'll find
spacious branches of health-food stockist **Tony
Quinn Health Stores** throughout Dublin.

Nature's Way

*ILAC Centre, Parnell Street, Around O'Connell
Street (872 8391/www.hollandandbarrett.com). All
cross-city buses/Luas Jervis.* **Open** 9am-6pm Mon-
Wed, Fri, Sat; 9am-8pm Thur; noon-6pm Sun.
Credit MC, V. **Map** p251 E1.
What sets Nature's Way apart from Dublin's many
booming health-food stores is its staff. You'll find
knowledgeable assistants ready to find the right
remedy for your complaint.
Other locations: throughout the city.

Nourish

*GPO Arcade, Henry Street, Around O'Connell Street
(874 3290/www.nourishonline.ie). All cross-city
buses/Luas Abbey Street, Jervis.* **Open** 9am-6pm
Mon-Wed, Fri, Sat; 9am-8pm Thur. **Credit** AmEx,
MC, V. **Map** p251 F2.
There's no messing about here: this modern, practical shop does what it should with a decent range of
health foods, vitamins and pick-me-ups.
Other locations: throughout the city.

Wine & alcohol

For a city so in love with potable pleasures,
Dublin is surprisingly devoid of good off-
licences. The George's Street branch of **Dunnes
Stores** is alright if you're stuck for a six-pack,
but wine lovers are far better served, with good
spots like **Vaughan Johnson's** (11 Essex
Street, Temple Bar), **Claudio's Wines**
(George's Street Arcade) and **Berry Bros
& Rudd** (4 Harry Street).

Whelans

*23 Wexford Street, Around St Stephen's Green
(475 2649/www.whelanslive.com). All cross-city
buses/Luas Harcourt Street.* **Open** 10.30am-10.30pm
Mon, Tue; 10.30am-11pm Wed; 10.30am-11.30pm
Thur-Sat; 12.30-11pm Sun. **Credit** AmEx, MC, V.
Map p251 E5.
You might get distracted by the cracking pub of the
same name next door, but *this* Whelan's is a reliable,
fairly central off-licence.

Health & beauty

Cosmetics

Don't miss the vast, luxurious and sleek beauty
counters at **Brown Thomas** and **Arnotts**, as
well as the more affordable and diverse ranges
at **Roches Stores**.

Body Shop

*82 Grafton Street, Around Trinity College (679
4569/www.thebodyshop.com). All cross-city buses/
Luas St Stephen's Green.* **Open** 9.30am-6.30pm Mon-
Wed, Fri, Sat; 9.30am-8.30pm Thur; noon-6pm Sun.
Credit AmEx, MC, V. **Map** p251 F4.
The big beauty chain is as popular as ever, with its
good lip balms, massage oils and body butters.
Other locations: throughout the city.

Face 2/Make-up ForEver

*40 Clarendon Street, Around Trinity College (679
9043/www.face2.ie). All cross-city buses/Luas St*

Eat, Drink, Shop (side tab)

Stephen's Green. **Open** 9.30am-6pm Mon-Wed, Fri, Sat; 9.30am-7pm Thur. **Credit** AmEx, MC, V. **Map** p251 F4.

Make-up ForEver was opened by a local professional make-up artist and is now a fixture on the beauty scene. Make-up's the name *and* the game.

Nue Blue Eriu

9 William Street South, Around Temple Bar (672 5776/www.nueblueeriu.com). All cross-city buses/ Luas St Stephen's Green. **Open** 10am-6pm Mon, Fri, Sat; 10am-8pm Tue-Thur. **Credit** MC, V. **Map** p251 F3.

If mainstream beauty brands leave you cold, you might find inspiration at this chic emporium filled with cult beauty products. Splurge on scents from E Coudray, skincare from Prada and make-up from Shu Uemura in a cool, stylish environment. There are also treatment rooms to the rear of the shop.

Hairdressers

The Natural Cut

34 Wicklow Street, Around Trinity College (679 7130). All cross-city buses/Luas St Stephen's Green. **Open** 10am-6pm Mon-Sat. **No credit cards.** **Map** p251 F3.

If you're scared of sulky hairdressers wielding hair-straighteners and bottles of noxious gunk, try this soothing alternative. The salon also forgoes the shampoo and blow-dry route for a spray-and-snip technique. A cut starts at €60.

Peter Mark

St Stephen's Green Centre, Around St Stephen's Green (478 0362/www.petermark.ie). All cross-city buses/Luas St Stephen's Green. **Open** 9am-5.30pm Mon-Wed, Sat; 9am-7pm Thur; 9am-6pm Fri. **Credit** AmEx, MC, V. **Map** p251 F4.

Peter Mark is better priced than most city-centre hairdressers, but it's hectic. On the plus side, it's one of the few city centre hairdressers where you might be able to get seen to without booking in advance. **Other locations**: throughout the city.

SitStil

17 Drury Street, Around St Stephen's Green (616 8887/www.sitstil.com). All cross-city buses/Luas St Stephen's Green. **Open** 9.30am-6pm Tue, Wed; 9.30am-8pm Thur; 9.30am-7pm Fri; 9am-5pm Sat. **Credit** MC, V. **Map** p251 E3.

Relaxed and tastefully decorated with antique-style furnishings, this small, chic salon has a calm vibe: they even throw in an Indian head massage with every appointment. Cut and blow-dry starts at €60. **Photo** *p150.*

Opticians

You can get eye examinations (and purchase good-quality budget eyewear) at branches of **Specsavers** (www.specsavers.com) all over the city. Check the website for details.

Optika

1 Royal Hibernian Way, Dawson Street, Around Trinity College (677 4705). All cross-city buses. **Open** 9.30am-6pm Mon-Wed, Fri, Sat; 9.30am-6.30pm Thur. **Credit** MC, V. **Map** p251 F4.

This hip optician stocks desirable and costly shades from the likes of Dolce & Gabbana and YSL.

Pharmacies

There are branches of the reliable UK pharmacy chain **Boots** throughout the city.

Hickey's

21 Grafton Street, Around Trinity College (679 0467/www.hickeyspharmacies.ie). All cross-city buses/Luas St Stephen's Green. **Open** 8.30am-8pm Mon-Wed, Fri; 8.30am-8.30pm Thur; 8.30am-7.30pm Sat; 11am-6pm Sun. **Credit** AmEx, MC, V. **Map** p251 F4.

A small but decent pharmacy with a great location. **Other locations**: throughout the city.

Sports & outdoor equipment

For a more specialist selection of outdoor equipment, follow your compass to Capel Street, where there are several good shops. **Lowe Alpine** (17-18 Temple Lane) is the place to trek to for skiers, rock climbers, alpinists and mountain bikers.

Foot Locker

28 Henry Street, Around O'Connell Street (872 1417/www.footlocker-europe.com). All cross-city buses/Luas Abbey Street. **Open** 10am-6.30pm Mon-Wed, Fri; 10am-8pm Thur; 9.30am-6.30pm Sat; noon-6pm Sun. **Credit** MC, V. **Map** p251 F2.

Booming music and wall-to-wall sports gear make this heavyweight chain a massive hit with teens. Block out the loud Euro-pop and focus on the stock: from swimwear to specialist trainers. **Other locations**: throughout the city.

Millets Camping

26 Mary Street Little, Around North Quays (873 3571/www.gelert.com). All cross-city buses/Luas Jervis. **Open** 9am-6pm Mon-Wed, Fri, Sat; 9am-7.30pm Thur; noon-6pm Sun. **Credit** MC, V. **Map** p251 E2.

An extensive range of high-quality tents and camping equipment at competitive prices.

Patagonia

24-26 Exchequer Street, Around Temple Bar (670 5748/www.patagonia.com). All cross-city buses. **Open** 10am-6pm Mon-Wed, Fri; 10am-8pm Thur; 9.30am-6pm Sat; 1-5pm Sun. **Credit** AmEx, MC, V. **Map** p251 E3.

This environmentally aware, inspirationally 'right-on' store stocks all the gear you could want for a range of outdoor activities. Need an organic cotton shirt? A wind-proof fleece? Well, fear not, you've come to the right place.

Arts & Entertainment

The Gate. *See p193.*

Festivals & Events

This city certainly knows how to have a good time.

It's important not to be misled by the fact that Dublin is stocked with great pubs, which are in turn stocked with great Guinness, which is drunk in large volumes by everyone from rowdy stags to urbane professionals. Yes, this is a party town, famously so; but what you need to remember is that it's also a pretty conservative city in an equally (if not considerably more) conservative country. All we're saying is, don't expect the gay abandon of Sydney or the adventurousness of New York, and you'll have a good time.

There are quite a few annual events worth knowing about before you book your holiday. First, of course, there's **St Patrick's Day** (*see below*), still by far the biggest entry in the Dublin calendar. It's now celebrated with plentiful pints of the black stuff the world over, but Dublin is the fun's epicentre. As long as you can cope with the crowds, the weather and the queues, there's no better place to enjoy it.

Calmer heads prevail in the summer at the excellent **Dublin Writers Festival** and the **Bloomsday Festival** (for both, *see p154*): the latter celebrates the works of James Joyce, while the former pulls in some of the world's best writers. That sort of thing would bore the bejaysus out of most of the people packed into the stands for the **Six Nations** rugby tournament (*see below*) each spring, of course. But then, to each his own.

Winter

Christmas Eve Vigil

St Mary's Pro-Cathedral, Marlborough Street, Northside (874 5441). DART Connolly Station. **Admission** free. **Map** p251 F1. **Date** 24 Dec.
The majority of Christmas events here still focus on the religious festival itself. A Christmas vigil is held in St Mary's Pro-Cathedral by the Archbishop of Dublin, with the beautiful sounds of the Palestrina Choir at 9.30pm. Mass follows at 10pm.

Christmas Day & St Stephen's Day

Date 25, 26 Dec.
On Christmas Day, shops, pubs, restaurants and public transport all close down. On St Stephen's Day (known as Boxing Day in the UK, and in the US as 'the day after Christmas') most pubs reopen; there's little public transport; and the day ends with a big party. St Stephen's Day also sees the start of the Christmas Racing Festival at Leopardstown Racecourse.

Jameson International Dublin Film Festival

Information: 13, Merrion Square, St Stephen's Green & Around (661 6216/www.dubliniff.com). **Tickets** phone for details. **Date** Feb-Mar.
Rising from the ashes of the much-maligned Dublin International Film Festival, this new event seems to be succeeding where the other failed. It celebrates the best of Irish and world cinema in screenings across the city, backed up by events that let fans meet Irish screenwriters, directors and actors.

Six Nations Rugby

Croke Park, Jones Road, Drumcondra, Northern suburbs (836 3222/www.crokepark.ie). Bus 3, 11, 11A, 16, 16A, 51A. **Open** Office 9.30am-5.30pm Mon-Fri. **Tickets** €10-€110. **Credit** AmEx, DC, MC, V. **Date** (at Croke Park) 11, 24 Feb.
This rugby competition between England, Ireland, Scotland, Wales, France and Italy is one of the biggest events in the Irish sporting calendar. Home games are played at Croke Park (*see p188*), and the atmosphere of a big match affects the whole city. Even when Ireland are not playing at home, match days are so partytastic that fans have been known to travel to Dublin solely to watch the game in a Dub pub. Accommodation is almost impossible to find.

Spring

St Patrick's Day Parade & Festival

Information 676 3205/www.stpatricksfestival.ie. **Date** 17 Mar.
It's the world's best excuse for a drink or seven: the feast day of a Welshman who ran the snakes out of Ireland. Over the past few years, the day has been comprehensively glammed up. The parade still forms the core of the celebrations, with some of Europe's brightest street performers and some of the world's loudest pyrotechnics. There's also a four day festival of world-class entertainment including concerts, exhibitions, street theatre, deafening fireworks and general frivolity. Pubs and bars are packed to the rafters from morning to night.

Convergence Festival

Information: 15-19 Essex Street West, Around Trinity College (674 6396/www.sustainable.ie/convergence). Tickets prices vary, phone for details **Date** mid April. **Map** p251 E3.
This week-long event favours a simple, ethical approach to the business of urban living. Its programme features conferences, theatre, film screenings and exhibits, and themes that include slow food, sustainability, eco-design and plant medicine.

A real 'we are the world' event: the **Festival of World Cultures**. *See p156*.

International Dance Festival Ireland

Information: 26 South Frederick Street, Southside (679 0524/www.dancefestivalireland.ie). **Tickets** phone for details. **Date** May.

This innovative and often provocative event was launched in 2002, and brings the best international dance companies to perform in the Abbey and the Project. Despite a rocky start (when an audience member sued the festival for programming a show that featured nudity and urination), the festival has been a success. From 2006 it will be held every year.

Summer

Dublin Writers Festival

Tickets 881 9613/www.dublinwritersfestival.com. **Tickets** prices vary, phone for details. **Date** June.

Drawing together 50-odd writers and poets from all over the world, this increasingly high-profile literary event dishes up a banquet of readings, discussions and public debates. Programmes tend to be adventurous, with readings from heavyweights like Julian Barnes sitting comfortably beside an introduction to contemporary Arab writing. Try not to miss the Rattlebag poetry slam, where members of the public compete for a prize.

Bloomsday Festival

Information: James Joyce Centre, 35 North Great George's Street, Around O'Connell Street (878 8547/ www.jamesjoyce.ie). **Tickets** prices vary, phone for details. **Date** 16 June.

Held every year around 16 June, the date on which *Ulysses* is set, and taking its name from the novel's central character, the Bloomsday Festival commemorates Bloom's 'walking out' with a week-long celebration. Readings from Joyce, performances, excursions and meals help recreate the atmosphere of 1904 Dublin. Booking is strongly advised.

Diversions on the Square

Meeting House Square, Around Temple Bar (677 2255/www.templebar.ie). All cross-city buses/Luas Jervis. **Admission** free. **Map** p251 E3. **Date** June-Aug.

All summer, a wide variety of free open-air events takes place in the heart of Temple Bar. There are lunchtime and evening concerts, innovative dance performances and family events every Sunday afternoon. Film buffs should look out for the IFI's Saturday night outdoor screenings of classic movies.

Music in the Park

Information 222 5441/www.dublincity.ie. **Admission** free. **Date** June-Aug.

The sun is shining, there's laid-back jazz in the background and all is right with the world. Dublin City Council's free open-air concerts and recitals in the city's parks have been a huge success. Brass and swing bands can be heard most afternoons at venues like the Civic Offices Park on Wood Quay, Merrion Square Park and St Stephen's Green. **Photo** *p156.*

Pride

Information: Outhouse, 105 Capel Street (873 4932/ www.dublinpride.org). **Date** June.

Highlights of this week-long gay festival include a gay *céilidh*, drag contests, workshops, readings and theme nights in gay-friendly venues. The flamboyant centrepiece, however, is the Pride march itself, which troops from the Garden of Remembrance at the top of O'Connell Street to the grass-covered amphitheatre beside the Civic Offices at Wood Quay.

Dublin Jazz Festival

Information: 670 3885/877 9001/www.esb.ie/jazz. **Date** early July.

Organised by the Improvised Music Company, the Dublin Jazz Festival offers a sassy mix of international and local jazz, with a bit of world music

Festival of World Cultures

thrown in. As well as the many gigs at venues across town, including Vicar Street (*see p178*) and the NCH (*see p181*), there are movies, workshops and exhibitions. Tickets are available from the Dublin Jazz Week box office in Tower Records (*see p143*).

Women's Mini-Marathon

Information: 293 0984/www.womensmini marathon.ie. **Tickets** €13 walking or jogging; €20 running. **Date** early June.

The annual Women's Mini-Marathon is the largest event of its kind in the world, attracting upwards of 30,000 participants (not all of them female). It's less a competition than an opportunity to raise money for charity, and the vast majority of people walk rather than run the 10km (six-mile) course.

Oxegen

Information: www.mcd.ie/www.oxegen.ie. **Tickets** check website for details. **Credit** AmEx DC, MC, V. **Date** mid July.

Filling the gap left by the much-missed Witness festival, Oxegen was Ireland's only multi-stage music festival of 2004. Staged over two days at the Punchestown Racecourse in County Kildare (*see p189*), the 2006 line-up included the Who, Franz Ferdinand, the Strokes, Goldfrapp and Red Hot Chilli Peppers. Check local listings or the website for the next one. *See also p157* **A breath of air**.

Dublin Horse Show

Royal Dublin Society, Anglesea Road, Ballsbridge, Southern suburbs (668 0866/www.rds.ie/horseshow). Bus 7, 45/DART Lansdowne Road. **Open** 9am-6.30pm Wed-Sun. **Admission** €28-€47; €23-€42 concessions. **Credit** AmEx, MC, V. **Date** early Aug.

Offering some of the richest prizes in the world, this five-day showjumping event attracts high-profile visitors and competitors. The famous Nations' Cup, where international teams compete for the prestigious Aga Khan Trophy, is traditionally held on a Friday; Thursday is Ladies' Day.

Festival of World Cultures

Venues across the city (271 9555/www.festivalof worldcultures.com). **Date** 24-26 Aug.

This annual arts and music festival is as international in scope as its name would suggest (more than 50 countries take part). It may have a worthy aim (namely, promoting respect, understanding and awareness between different cultures) but it's also a really good laugh. **Photos** *p155, above*.

Liffey Swim

Rory O'More Bridge to Custom House Quay (information 833 2434). **Date** late Aug/early Sept.

Attempted generally by the very brave or the very stupid, this annual swimming race begins at the Rory O'More Bridge (near the Guinness Brewery) and ends 1.5 miles (2km) downstream at the Custom House (*see p85*). It was first done by a handful of cold water enthusiasts in 1920, and these days it attracts about 500 swimmers.

Autumn

All-Ireland Hurling & Football Finals

Croke Park, Jones Road, Drumcondra, Northern suburbs (836 3222/www.gaa.ie). Bus 3, 11, 11A, 16, 51A. **Tickets** prices vary, phone for details. **No credit cards.** **Date** *Hurling* 2nd Sun in Sept. *Gaelic football* 4th Sun in Sept.

The north side of the city traditionally grinds to a halt on the second and fourth Sundays in September, as fans of Gaelic football and hurling travel from all over the country to Croke Park for their respective finals. *See also p188.*

Dublin Fringe Festival

Information: 677 8511/www.fringefest.com. **Tickets** prices vary, phone for details. **Credit** MC, V. **Date** late Sept-early Oct.
The Fringe is such an established event it hardly deserves the term 'fringe'. It's usually a mixed bag, but it has its moments. The festival is dedicated to providing a focus for new companies, though it also acts as a test bed where veteran companies can try out new material. The emphasis is on the unusual, and performances are innovative. The huge demand for venues during the event has sometimes forced companies to adapt quickly: previous performances have taken place in public toilets and parked cars.

Dublin Theatre Festival

Information 677 8439/www.dublintheatrefestival. com. **Tickets** €15-€35. **Credit** MC, V. **Date** 27 Sept-13 Oct.
This has been a showcase for the best of Irish and world theatre since its foundation in 1957. It not only provides a stage for emerging local talent, but also attracts international productions. Most of the city's theatrical venues host festival events, and the pro-gramme is usually varied; sometimes it follows a specific theme. Be sure to book in advance.

Adidas Dublin City Marathon

Information 623 2250/2159/entry form hotline 626 3746/www.dublincitymarathon.ie. **Credit** MC, V
Date 29th Oct.
Ever since it first ran in 1980, the Dublin City Marathon has been hugely successful, attracting thousands of runners to the city's streets. The 26-mile (42km) course starts and finishes at the top of O'Connell Street and traces a route through Dublin's historic streets and suburbs. It starts at 8.30am, and you can cheer on the finishers a couple of hours later. Those hoping to compete should submit their entry form at least three weeks before the race.

Samhain Festival (Hallowe'en)

Information: Dublin Tourism, Suffolk Street, Around Trinity College (www.visitdublin.com). **Date** 31 Oct.
Hallowe'en in Dublin is based on the traditional pagan festival of Samhain (pronounced: 'sow in'), a celebration of the dead that signalled the end of the Celtic summer. Dublin's Samhain Festival is one of Ireland's largest night-time events, attracting up to 20,000 people as the Hallowe'en Parade winds its way through the city from Parnell Square to Temple Bar and Wood Quay. The fireworks display afterwards is worth staying up for.

A breath of air

It might be stretching it a little to describe the Oxegen music festival as Ireland's answer to Glastonbury or Roskilde; Scotland's T In The Park is a more apt comparison, especially the two events usually feature more or less identical line-ups. Still, the two-day, six-stage extravaganza, held in Punchestown in County Kildare, has earned its reputation as Ireland's largest annual live music event. Acts who have appeared in recent years include The Strokes, James Brown, The Who and Snoop Dogg.

It wasn't always this way of course. The festival's appearance in 2000 (it was called Witness until 2004) was nothing if not timely. Irish music fans had long been hankering for something on a bigger scale than the annual shindig at Slane Castle (where MOR headliners like Robbie Williams and Bryan Adams had ruled the roost). And, with the economy booming, they were happy to pay through the nose to get it.

The exorbitant prices charged on site at Oxegen are the stuff of legend; a ride on the Big Wheel, for example, cost €8 in 2006. But, to its credit, the festival has done more than just line the pockets of its promoters. Its multi-stage format has afforded valuable exposure to dozens of hitherto unknown local acts each year: Rodrigo Y Gabriela in 2002 and Republic of Loose in 2004 are among those to benefit. (In Slane, the best such acts could hope for would be the lunchtime slot, when most of the crowd are still swilling cider in the car park.)

Lately, though, the gloss has begun to fade. Allegations that tents were burned and campers terrorised in the drunken aftermath of Oxegen 2006 prompted organisers to pull the plug on the official message board. Meanwhile, a slew of copycat festivals – specialising in everything from dance and hip-hop to country – has emerged to challenge its once unrivalled supremacy. Leading the charge is the Electric Picnic, which has so far managed to pull in much cooler headliners (Nick Cave, Kraftwerk and the Flaming Lips in 2005) and far fewer hoards of drunken teenagers than its longer established adversary.

For Ireland's long suffering music fans, such rivalry can only be good news.

Children

Where to go with the kids in tow.

Dublin society as a whole is becoming more child-aware and child-friendly. Although Dubliners won't actually cross roads to pinch your youngster's chubby cheeks, they're no longer quite so likely to start moving breakables out of reach. Most restaurants now extend a warm welcome to families and are starting to provide decent kiddy menus. There's a welcome inclination to update parks and playgrounds, and the city's many festivals are now genuinely family-focused in a way that only enhances the fun for everyone else.

The seaside is still the surest bet, and Dublin has plenty of nearby beaches where sand castles can be built, kites flown and balls kicked. Parks are another thing the city does well. And, of course, the wide open spaces of the countryside are just a hop, skip and a jump away.

INFORMATION

The 'Ticket' supplement with Friday's *Irish Times*, its Saturday magazine, and the *Sunday Independent*'s 'Living & Leisure' section, are all good sources of information, particularly for festivals, family days and other one-offs. The Dublin Tourism Centre's *Family Fun in Dublin* brochure has more long-term options, and www.dublinks.com has a good and comprehensive 'Kids' link.

For children's shops, *see p143*.

Arts & crafts

These days, you can't swing a paintbrush in most local museums without splattering a child-oriented cultural programme or interactive display – everything from art lessons to workshops and junior lectures. **Collins Barracks** (*see p88*) and the **Natural History Museum** (*see p76*) both hold events designed to teach kids about art and history; or you could book them into the **Ark Children's Cultural Centre** for an immersion in the art world.

Ark Children's Cultural Centre

11A Eustace Street, Around Temple Bar (670 7788/www.ark.ie). All cross-city buses/Luas Jervis. **Open** *information/box office* 10am-5pm Mon-Fri; 1am-5pm Sat. **Admission** free. **Map** p253 G4/5. The Ark is good fun. This is the only purpose-built cultural centre in Europe devoted to children, and it has fantastic amenities: an indoor theatre, outdoor amphitheatre, gallery spaces and a workshop where the young can learn how to build their own musical instruments, stage their own plays, productions and much more. **Photo** *p160*.

Babysitting

This is still a difficult city in which to find good babysitting for visitors. Few nurseries allow drop-ins, and those that do tend to be small and in shopping or leisure centres, so they're only really good for an hour or two. However, many hotels offer childcare.

Eating out

Dublin is full of fast-food joints, from McDonald's to the home-grown Supermac, but in these health-conscious times many parents feel that even burgers should be good quality. The best organic burger in town is to be found at **Odessa** (*see p103*), though the restaurant is slightly too trendy to be child-friendly after dark. Round the corner on George's Street, **Café Bar Deli** (*see p101*) is fuss-free, no-booking and large-party-friendly for pizza and pasta. The name notwithstanding, the **Bad Ass Café** (9 Crown Alley, 671 2596) and **Elephant & Castle** (18 Temple Bar, 679 3121), both in Temple Bar, provide all the staples that children insist upon: pizzas, burgers, chips and omelettes. **Gotham Café** (8 South Anne Street, 679 5266) is a teenage heaven.

For something a little more exotic, try **Wagamama** (*see p110*) and **Yamamori Noodles** (71 South Great George's Street, 475 5001), both of which do reliable Japanese fare at long tables in a good-humoured atmosphere.

The **Vaults** (605 4700), a cavernous café-restaurant underneath Connolly Station, runs regular family days, with food, face-painting and magic shows.

Bewley's Café (*see p101*) may be trying to shed its casual image in favour of something a bit fancier, but it is still good for unfussy meals.

Sightseeing & tours

City centre

A wander through Temple Bar at the weekend will usually unearth plenty of fun, even if it is only sampling the wares of the **market** in

Meeting House Square, or wandering into one of the centre's many museums. One of the most popular museums for children is **Dublinia** (*see p70*), but it's looking a little tattered around the edges these days and is less amusing and educational than it ought to be. On a rainy day, make your way over to the **Natural History Museum** (*see p76*) – a genuine old-school Victorian museum, with not an interactive display in sight, just cramped glass cases full of skeletons, pickled creatures and stuffed animals. The ground floor of this fine old building houses the fauna of Ireland under the skeleton of a gigantic fin whale suspended from the ceiling. Upstairs (note, there's no lift, so prams and buggies must be left with the attendant downstairs) are creatures of the rest of the world. It's a dusty, old-fashioned and yet magical place – an archetype of museums as they once were. Children are fascinated by things like the sheer size of the giraffe or the strangeness of sea creatures and the ferocity of grizzly bears.

If it's a sunny day and you want to spend some time outside, **St Stephen's Green play area** is well equipped and orderly, with plenty of ducks to feed nearby, while **Trinity College** is spacious and pleasant for walks, although there are too many 'Keep Off the Grass' signs about. Still, the cricket greens, when not in use, provide plenty of space for charging around.

O'Connell Street & the North Quays

O'Connell Street has had a makeover. The Luas tramline is in place, the trees have been replanted and a general clear-up has been effected: it's now a pleasant place for a stroll. The boardwalk that runs along the north side of the Liffey, from O'Connell Street down towards Capel Street Bridge, is another. Up at the top of O'Connell, the **National Wax Museum** (off Parnell Square, 872 6340, *see p82*) isn't the most sophisticated of museums but it has a children's world of fairytale and fantasy, crazy mirrors, secret tunnels and a chamber of horrors.

Not far from there, **Smithfield Chimney** (817 3800, *see p86*) has a glass lift up to an enclosed viewing platform that gives panoramic views of the city, and Smithfield itself has its famed horse-trading market, which falls on occasional Saturdays.

Beyond Smithfield, the vast expanse of **Phoenix Park** offers much to do in good weather, including the ever-distracting **Dublin Zoo** (*see p88*). The years have been kind to the zoo, which has regenerated into a jolly spot with increasing emphasis on conservation and safari-

Natural History Museum. *See p76*.

style attractions. New enclosures for many of the animals mean it is possible to observe them in something closer to their natural habitat. Phoenix Park's visitors' centre has an exhibition on the park's nature and wildlife.

Close by are a number of stables that make good use of the park – **Pony Camp** (868 7000) will take children from five years and up, either in the paddock or around the park, depending on their experience.

Southern suburbs

Airfield Trust
Upper Kilmacud Road, Dundrum (298 4301). Bus 44, 48A, 75/Luas Dundrum. **Open** 10am-5pm Tue-Sat; 11am-5pm Sun. **Admission** €5; €4 concessions; €3 children; free under-3s. **Credit** MC, V.
The Airfield Trust was once the home of the eccentric, benevolent Overend sisters. Now a private charity, it's run as an educational and recreational resource. As well as the house itself, there's a working farm, Victorian greenhouse, walled garden and orchard. The Overends were car-mad, so there is a car museum, and the vintage Rolls-Royce is a beauty. There is a strong show-and-tell aspect to Airfield, which is very popular with school trips, but you can go on a family day out and simply wander around very enjoyably. There's an on-site restaurant with good home-cooked food.

Ark Children's Cultural Centre. *See p158.*

Around Dublin Bay

The scenic coastal villages or towns – **Dalkey**, **Dún Laoghaire**, **Howth** or **Malahide** (*see pp93-98*) – all make for excellent day-trips destinations, but in most cases the beaches are pebbled. **Balbriggan Beach** on the northside is pretty, picturesque and has a sandy beach. Closer in, **Sandycove** (*see p98*) fulfils this role on the southside, though it can be crowded on warm days.

Malahide Castle

See p95 for listings.
The castle is exciting enough all on its own, and then there's the Fry Model Railway and Tara's Palace to make this a perfect junior his 'n' hers day out. The model railway features detailed replicas of Heuston and Cork railway stations, and a range of tiny, working trains that runs from vintage 1920s models to streamlined modern variants. Tara's Palace is a dolls' house built in the style of an 18th-century mansion. The basement café is excellent, and there's a wooden adventure playground.

National Sealife Centre

Strand Road, Bray, Co Wicklow (286 6939/www. sealife.ie). DART Bray. **Open** *Summer* 10am-5.30pm daily. *Winter* 11am-4pm Mon-Fri; 10am-5pm Sat, Sun. **Admission** €9.75; €6.95-€8 concessions; free under-3s; €31-€37 family. **Credit** MC, V.
This aquarium is constructed on a fairly humble scale, so there isn't much in the way of child-friendly wow factor. However, the wide variety of marine species, most of them native to these shores, means there's plenty to see, while the emphasis on conservation is commendable. There are baby sharks, seahorses and more. All in all, the National Sealife Centre is a great place to explore.

Newbridge House & Farm

See p95 for listings.
An old-style cobbled farmyard with stables, a forge, hen coops, pig sties, cow byres and sheep pens, bits of old farm machinery and a varied collection of animals – Newbridge has it all. There are about 15 different types of hen alone. Peacocks wander with a gang of lesser fowl, and there are a couple of albino versions. The café seems surprisingly stern to parents and kids: 'No Prams or Buggies' says one of many tart signs, while another warns, 'Table for Two ONLY'. Still, it will furnish the basics; don't let them spoil your fun.

Out of town

Harap Farm & Butterfly House

Magillstown, Swords (840 1285/www.butterfly ireland.com). **Open** *May-Aug* 10am-5.30pm Tue-Sat; noon-5.30pm Sun. **Admission** €8; €4-€5 concessions; €20 family. **No credit cards.**
Thirty degrees of heat and 85 per cent humidity: the Butterfly House is like a small tropical rainforest, complete with banana plants, exotic flowers and a pool full of fat carp. Canaries flit about freely, and are scarcely bigger than the amazing butterflies. These come in an extraordinary variety of colours – black-and-white striped, electric blue, bright orange – many with weird and wonderful markings. To get there, take the airport road, follow signs towards Swords. Once there, look for signs, or find the Balheary Road – the Butterfly House is 3km (two miles) down this road.

Reynoldstown Animal Farm

Reynoldstown (841 2615). **Open** *Apr-Sept* noon-5pm daily. **Admission** €6. **No credit cards.**
This is a working organic farm, so less cute than Newbridge, but the miniature horse (the size of a big dog) more than compensates. Most breeds here are

more hardy than showy, but there are plenty of smaller creatures, like rabbits and chicks, to be petted and fed. To get there, take the M1 until you see a sign for Naul – about 19km (12 miles) – north of the airport. Reynoldstown is about 3km (two miles) down the road. Follow signs from there – the maroon and white gate lodge can be seen from the road.

Organised tours

Dublin Bus Ghost Tour

Starts from Dublin Bus offices, 59 Upper O'Connell Street, Around O'Connell Street (703 3028/www.dublinbus.ie). **Tours** 8pm Mon-Fri; 7pm, 9.30pm Sat, Sun. **Tickets** €25. **Credit** AmEx, MC, V.

This one is really for the teenagers, since it's not recommended for children under 14. (For younger kids, Dublin Bus does a variety of good tours, including the hop-on, hop-off city bus tour around the city. Call the number above for more details.) If you've got itchy teens, though, they'll probably love this spooky trip that fills you in on the best of Dublin's haunted houses, the life of Bram Stoker and body-snatching in St Kevin's graveyard.

Dublin Sea Safari

Embarks from Dublin City Moorings at the IFSC on the North City Quays, or from Malahide Village Marina in Dublin Bay (806 1626/www.seasafari.ie). DART Malahide. **Prices** €25-€30 per person, depending on group size. **Credit** MC, V.

This organisation makes good use of the city's top attraction: the sea. Departing from opposite Jury's Inn on Custom House Quay, or from Malahide Marina, its all-weather inflatable lifeboats seat seven for an exhilarating whirl round the bay. Youngsters of any age can go, but the wetsuits only fit eight years and up. Choose from the Eco Safari (which covers wildlife around Skerries, Lambay Island and Ireland's Eye), the Thrill Seeker (for high-speed junkies, and unsuitable for younger children) or the Leisure Safari (for those kids who want to learn about culture and heritage).

Viking Splash Tour

Information 707 6000/www.vikingsplashtours.com. Starts from Bull Alley Street, by St Patrick's Cathedral. **Tours** *Feb 2nd-Mar 8th* (every 30mins) 10am-4pm Wed-Sun. *Mar 9th-Oct 31st* 9.30am-5pm daily. *Nov* Tue-Sun 10am-4pm. **Tickets** €16-€18.50; €8.95-€9.50 concessions; €52-€60 family (up to 3 children). **Credit** MC, V.

One of the best ways to see the city, and not just for children, this tour company trucks people around in yellow canopied vehicles called 'ducks' dating from World War II. They're amphibious, so when you've finished touring by land, they trundle into the Grand Canal Basin and churn about the bay. The driver and guides keep up a merry flow of information. Ten tours a day depart from Bull Alley Street beside St Patrick's Cathedral, but note that they cannot take prams. Tours sell out, so booking in advance is advised. Viking helmets are optional.

Sport & activities

If your children like the noise and excitement of karting, Dublin has a good racing venue. **Kart City** in Santry (*see below*) has petrol-driven go-karts that really *go*, and are virtually impossible to flip over. Kids from six years and up can whizz around, but must be accompanied by an adult. The Stillorgan **Leisureplex** (*see below*) is the site of endless pre-teen birthday parties. Bowling, Quasar, bouncy castles, adventure playgrounds… you won't see them for hours. And the **Ramp 'n' Rail Skatepark** (*see below*) is where to go if they have reached the skateboard and rollerblade years.

Horse riding and water sports, each in their own way, make use of the city's best attributes: its littoral location and Dubliners' equine enthusiasms. **Oldtown Riding Stables** (Wyestown, Oldtown, Co Dublin, 835 4755) has the advantage of being located near a lovely stretch of rural Ireland, which makes for some very pleasant cantering and trotting. The **Irish National Sailing School** (*see below*) will instruct children over eight in water activities like sailing and windsurfing.

Kart City

Old Airport Road, Cloghran, Northern suburbs (842 6322/www.kartcity.net). Bus 33, 41, 41B, 41C, 230, 746. **Open** noon-late daily. **Rates** *Adult track* €20 for 15mins. *Junior track* €15 for 15mins. **Credit** MC, V.

Three tracks are available for four-wheel jeeps, kiddie karts and adult karting. Karting is not recommended for children under 12.

Leisureplex

Old Bray Road, Stillorgan, Southern suburbs (288 1656). Bus 46A. **Open** 24hrs daily. **Admission** €1. **Credit** MC, V.

This noisy amusement chain offers all the usual activities like bowling, Quasar laser games and adventure play areas. At the Stillorgan centre kids can design and paint ceramics at Pompeii Paints, while Blanchardstown has dodgems for that old-fashioned fairground experience.

Other locations: Blanchardstown Centre, Northern suburbs (822 3030); Malahide Road, Coolock, Northern suburbs (848 5722); Village Green Centre, Tallaght, Southern suburbs (459 9411).

Ramp 'n' Rail Skatepark

96A Upper Drumcondra Road, Northern suburbs (837 7533). Bus 3, 11, 13, 33, 41. **Open** *May-Aug* noon-9pm daily. *Sept-Apr* noon-9pm Tue-Sun. **Admission** €6.50-€8. **Credit** MC, V.

Slightly off the beaten track in Drumcondra, this skatepark is bright and colourful. The kiddies' area keeps the little ones away from their more adventurous older siblings. Speaking of which – only helmets and the ramps are provided; boards, blades, pads are your own.

Film

The reel Dublin.

In 2006, Ken Loach's *The Wind that Shakes the Barley,* about the Irish war of independence and civil war in the 1920s, took the Palme d'Or at Cannes and ignited a media row, with British papers accusing Loach of making a 'repulsive' film that 'drags the reputation of our nation through the mud'. Though many suspected the French of indulging in their national pastime of Brit and Yank bashing (the film drew clear parallels to the current situation in Iraq), scooping the top prize proved that Irish history could be a crowd-puller. It also placed Loach in the distinguished line of British directors (Alan Parker, Stephen Frears, John Boorman) who have made authentically Irish films with Irish casts, as opposed to using the gorgeous scenery and the tax breaks to make blockbusters set in Camelot or the Time of the Dragons.

However, even more interesting than Loach's prize were two other recent films that also scooped awards, if not the golden palm: *Pavee Lackeen (see p165* **Key notes)** and *Adam & Paul.* What got Irish cinema buffs excited about these two was not only the fact that the scripts, locations, cast and directors were all home-grown (*Pavee*'s director, Perry Ogden, is British but he's lived in Dublin for over ten years), but that both were partly financed by the Irish Film Board and both dealt with marginalised sectors of society – *Pavee* with travellers, and *Adam and Paul* with drug addicts. They were a refreshing antidote to the recent slew of romantic comedies – *About Adam, Goldfish Memories, When Brendan Met Trudy* – that make Dublin look bright, upbeat, metrosexual, feel-good… and not remotely like Dublin. Both were also low-budget and, hopefully, they have blazed the trail for other low-budget, independent Irish films. Film in Ireland is still a nascent art, and the industry is tiny, but low-cost techniques should help directors experiment and keep control of their material. And maybe the rest of the country will get a look-in one day – now that Hollywood's love affair with the west of the country (*The Quiet Man, Ryan's Daughter*) seems to be over, all Irish films begin and end in Dublin (or Belfast).

Meantime, Ireland's popularity as a film location continues – the government fought off competition from Eastern Europe, where labour is much cheaper, by raising the percentage of expenditure eligible for tax relief to 80 per cent for all films, up from pre-2006 levels of 55 per cent or 66 per cent. So 2006 saw the welcome return of loads of big-budget international projects, including *Becoming Jane* (about Jane Austen) and the *History of the Tudors.*

The **Irish Film Institute** on Eustace Street is an excellent starting point for an exploration of Ireland's film heritage – classic films to watch out for are Robert Flaherty's *Man of Aran* (1934), Brian Desmond Hurst's *Playboy of the Western World* (1961), John Davies' and Pat Murphy's *Maeve* (1982) and Alan Clarke's *Elephant* (1989). The **Screen** on d'Olier Street is the other place to catch the maverick and offbeat. The other city-centre cinemas – **Savoy, Cineworld** – are multiplexes offering the usual fare. Sadly, the tiny Stella in Rathmines, last bastion of the local cinemas that used to pepper the 'burbs, has finally closed down, leaving only multiplexes outside the centre.

The city plays host to a number of festivals throughout the year, including the cleverly titled Dublin Film Festival, the Dublin Gay and Lesbian Film Festival, and the Dark/Light Festival (www.darklight-filmfestival.com) in May or June, which emphasises digital films by up-and-coming filmmakers. A recent addition is the Jameson International Dublin Film Festival, which started in 2004 and offers a great mix of Irish, international, mainstream and offbeat pictures. For all festivals, *see pp154-157.*

GENERAL INFORMATION

New films open on Fridays, and movie listings appear daily in the *Irish Times* and the *Evening Herald.* The IFI also publishes its own guide, which you'll find in many cafés and bars, as well as at the cinema itself. Ticket prices vary, hovering around €8-€10 for new releases.

Cinemas

Cineworld

Parnell Centre, Parnell Street, Around O'Connell Street (information 872 8444). All cross-city buses. **Open** 11.20am-9.30pm Mon-Thur, Sun; 11.20am-11.50pm Fri, Sat. **Tickets** €7; €4-€5.50 matinées; €4-€4.50 concessions. **Credit** AmEx, MC, V. **Map** p251 F1.
Since it opened about eight years ago, this multiplex has been through more names than Prince (Virgin, UGC) but through each name change, it has remained exactly the same: the latest releases on the

How Long Is Forever at the
Dark/Light Festival. *See p162.*

best screens, crystal-clear sound, chairs you can fall asleep in and super-sized tubs of popcorn. Definitely the best way to enjoy blockbusters' special effects, and there are so many screens that you can sometimes catch a rare indie too. The queues are horrendous most of the time, so be sure to book or come well in advance.

Irish Film Institute

6 Eustace Street, Around Temple Bar (679 3477/ www.irishfilm.ie). All cross-city buses. **Open** noon-9.30pm daily. **Tickets** €6.50-€7; €5.50 matinées. **Credit** MC, V. **Map** p251 E3.
The starting point for Irish cinema, the IFI is in a wonderfully converted 17th-century building in Temple Bar and has two screens, a bookshop and an enormous public film archive; there's also a busy bar, which serves decent food and is a popular hangout in its own right. On offer is what you'd expect from a serious, non-commercial film buffs' centre: arthouse, indie, foreign-language, experimental, documentary, classic; in short, everything that you won't find anywhere else in Dublin. The IFI operates a membership system at the box office,

although in practice this means that only films that have not obtained a censor's certificate (usually those not on release elsewhere) are closed to the general public. Don't let this put you off: at just €15 per year, or €1.20 per week, the cost of joining is hardly prohibitive. During the summer months, check out the IFI's annual programme of outdoor screenings in Meeting House Square.

Savoy

16-17 O'Connell Street Upper, Around O'Connell Street (874 8487). All cross-city buses. **Open** 1.30-9pm daily. **Tickets** €6 before 6pm; €8 after 6pm; €5-€6 concessions. **Credit** MC, V. **Map** p251 F1.
The Savoy, long a fixture of shabby 1970s chic that perfectly complemented the litter-strewn O'Connell Street has, like the street itself, finally had its facelift. These days, it's in a timewarp of wood panelling and fake chandeliers, and has gone from atmospheric to anodyne, but the seats are definitely more comfortable and the box office more responsive, so many will accept the trade-off. The Savoy no longer has the largest screen in the city so isn't guaranteed the premières, but its location is prime, and it still

Arts & Entertainment

Screen snacks.

trades on years of affection, so it remains integral to the festivals. Expect the usual mainstream blockbuster and rom-com programming.

Screen

D'Olier Street, Around Trinity College (672 5500). All cross-city buses. **Open** 2-9pm daily. **Tickets** €7.50; €5 concessions; €5 matinées. **Credit** MC, V. **Map** p251 F3.

Just round the corner from Trinity College, the Screen is scuffed, tatty, eternally studenty, and its programme is exactly what you'd expect: offbeat without being obscure; a mix of second-run, limited-release, foreign-language and arthouse pictures that can pack them in at busy times. Two of the three screens have seats for couples, so take someone you'd like to know better. **Photos** *above.*

Out-of-town multiplexes

With the Stella gone, the 'burbs have nothing in the way of quaint, unusual or independent cinemas. So here, instead, is the best of the rest.

IMC Lower George's Street

Dún Laoghaire, Dublin Bay (information 280 7777/booking 230 1399/www.imc-cinemas.com). Bus 7, 7A, 45A, 46A, 46X, 59, 75, 111, 746. **Open** 1-8pm Mon-Fri; noon-8pm Sat, Sun. **Tickets** €8; €5-€6 concessions; €6 matinées. **Credit** MC, V.

Ormonde Stillorgan

Stillorgan Plaza, Kilmacud Road, Northern suburbs (278 0000/www.ormondecinemas.com). Bus 46, 46B, 63, 84, 84X, 86. **Open** 11.30am-7.30pm daily. **Tickets** €7.70; €4.70-€6.25 concessions; €4.70 matinées. **Credit** AmEx, MC, V.

Santry Omniplex

Old Airport Road, Santry, Northern suburbs (842 8844). Bus 16, 16A, 33, 41, 41B. **Open** noon-8.30pm Mon-Fri; 11am-8.30pm Sat, Sun. **Tickets** €8; €5.50-€5 concessions; €6 matinées. **Credit** MC, V.

UCI Cinemas

Malahide Road, Coolock, Northern suburbs (848 5122/www.uci.ie). Bus 20B, 27, 42, 42B, 43, 103, 104, 127, 129. **Open** 12.30-8.30pm daily. **Tickets** €8; €5.50-€6.25 concessions; €4-€6.25 matinees. **Credit** MC, V.

Other locations: Blanchardstown Shopping Centre, Blanchardstown, Northern suburbs (1-850 525 354); The Square, Tallaght, Southern suburbs (459 8400).

Vue

Liffey Valley Shopping Centre, Clondalkin, Southern suburbs (08712 240 240/1520 501000/ www.myvue.com). Bus 78A, 210, 239. **Open** 11.30am-10.30pm Mon-Thur, Sun; 11.30am-midnight Fri, Sat. **Tickets** €8.50; €6.30-€5.50 concessions; €6.50 matinées. **Credit** AmEx, MC, V.

Key notes Perry Ogden

Perry Ogden's debut *Pavee Lackeen* (2005) was one of Irish cinema's big recent success stories, winning awards, critical acclaim and worldwide screenings. Featuring mainly non-professional actors, it follows a few months in the life of Winnie, a ten-year-old traveller girl whose large family lives in a caravan, which is plonked unceremoniously by the side of a thoroughfare near the North Quay. It's an episodic, unsentimental, naturalistic film, made powerful by the performance of its protagonist Winnie – sweet, poignant and funny – and its sympathy for characters like Winnie's mother, who maintains a cool dignity throughout. Travellers are, many would say, Ireland's most maligned community, and the film caused much soul-searching in a country where the huge wealth accumulated in the past ten years has yet to trickle down.

When we catch up with Ogden in his marvellous studio on Capel Street, in Dublin's north side, he is just back from a fashion shoot in Italy. He began his career as a fashion photographer and was (and is) hugely successful, doing shoots for *Vogue*, *Arena*, *The Face* et al. Even now he still does fashion shoots 'to help finance' his films.

An Englishman (he was born in Shropshire, though his mother is Irish), Ogden has lived in Dublin for over ten years. He first visited in 1983, 'loved the light', then moved over 'for a girl'. The rest of Dublin first heard of him in the late 1990s, when his extraordinary photos of traveller kids riding bareback around Dublin estates were exhibited in the

then down-at-heel Smithfield (*see p86*). These photos were gathered into a book, *Pony Kids* (1997), which drew the attention of Hollywood. At meetings with producers, Ogden realised he'd gone as far as he wanted to with ponies but did want to go on exploring the kids' lives. So he sold the rights to the book and with the money embarked on his own independent film – *Pavee Lackeen* was self-financed until the completion stage, when the Irish film board stepped in. Shot over ten months, it evolved organically from an initial rough 24-page script, incorporating a lot of suggestions from Winnie and her family (the family in the film is her real family).

Ogden currently has three projects in development stage, which he doesn't want to talk about yet, but he's determined to keep control of his material. Ireland, he says, 'is a potentially great environment' for an independent filmmaker. (Mind that 'potentially'.) What's great is that people are 'very talented and enthusiastic' – his crew worked long hours for little pay on *Pavee* and all were excited and committed. But film is still in its early stages in Ireland, confidence and assurance are hard to come by, and Ogden feels the tendency is 'to look too much to Hollywood and America – the most successful directors make Irish stories to a Hollywood model; the less successful ones make Hollywood stories to an Irish model.' But there are signs of coming of age – Ogden's favourite recent Irish film is Mark O'Halloran's and Lenny Abrahamson's *Adam & Paul* (2004). A film about two junkies trying to score, *Adam and Paul* portrayed a recognisable (if comically heightened) Dublin. Ogden admires it because, like *Pavee*, it eschews the tried-and-tested Hollywood narrative arc, and has a more organic feel. Both films were made on low budgets, but benefited from Irish Film Board money. If they herald the new direction of Irish film, the next decade should be very interesting.

Arts & Entertainment

Galleries

Where to hang in Dublin.

Gallery of Photography. See p167.

The Irish art market is buoyant. With a seemingly unending stream of post-Celtic Tiger gazillionaires investing in home-grown art, records are made and broken at every auction, and the market is showing no sign of slowing down.

The pre-Celtic Tiger market was confined to four or five serious millionaire buyers, who bought conservatively in the 1980s and early '90s – mostly 18th-century landscapes and works by the late 19th- and early 20th-century artists Jack Yeats, Sir John Lavery and Sir William Orpen. But now, not only are there hundreds of new buyers, but tastes have moved on, and there's a strong market at auction in 20th-century and contemporary work. Sotheby's and Christie's have their annual Irish sales in London in May each year and, reflecting the changing market, Sotheby's hosted its first every Contemporary Irish Sale in Dublin in autumn 2006.

However, the tastes of Irish millionaires remain fairly conservative, making the cutting-edge work offered in contemporary commercial galleries like **Green on Red** (see p168) extremely difficult to sell on the auction market. But such zeitgeist galleries are the exception rather than the norm – most galleries go for the solid and well established. The market is also

insular – Ireland is, after all, an island, and the Irish like to buy Irish. Apart from Lavery, Orpen, William Scott, and one contemporary, Sean Scully, most – if not all – of the Irish artists doing well in Dublin are virtually unheard of on the international markets.

Public galleries have benefited from the strong economy and increased public spending on arts – the **National Gallery** (see p75), the **Chester Beatty Library** (see p66) and the **Irish Museum of Modern Art** (see p92) are all beautifully housed and host excellent temporary exhibitions as well as their own permanent collections, while the **Hugh Lane Gallery** (Municipal Gallery of Modern Art; see p167 and 81) re-opened in May 2006, after a complete renovation – it now has three floors of exhibition rooms and new Sean Scully and Francis Bacon rooms.

The commercial galleries are mostly clustered round two areas in the centre: Temple Bar, which also houses two of the city's most innovative and challenging non-commercial spaces, the **Project Arts Centre** (see p194) and the **Temple Bar Gallery and Studios** (see p167); and Grafton Street and St Stephen's Green, where you'll find the **Kerlin** (see p168) and the **Rubicon** (see p169) for contemporary art, and the excellent **Gorry** (see p168) and

Solomon (*see p169*) for more traditional work. But do stray off the beaten track for the adventurous Green on Red, tucked behind Trinity College, and **Kevin Kavanagh Gallery** (*see p168*), on the North Quays. And if you want a democratic street art fair, go to Merrion Square on Sunday afternoon – all and sundry are out, displaying their magnum opi. Most of the work runs from anodyne to garish to kitsch, but some of it is fine, and you can always haggle your way to a bargain.

Exhibition spaces

Douglas Hyde Gallery
Arts Building (entrance Nassau Street Gate), Trinity College (608 1116/www.douglashydegallery.com). All cross-city buses. **Open** 11am-6pm Mon-Wed, Fri; 11am-7pm Thur; 11am-4.45pm Sat. **Admission** free. **Map** p251 F3.
The Douglas Hyde Gallery (named after the first president of Ireland, a Gaelic scholar but not, confusingly, an artist) was co-founded by Trinity College and the Arts Council in 1978 and is housed in basement premises in the college. Its fare is exemplary, innovative Irish and international artists, including Gabriel Orozco, Luc Tuymans, Dorothy Cross, Felix Gonzalez-Torrez, Marlene Duma and Richard Billingham. It's consistently ahead of the pack and plays neither parochial nor safe. The space is chilling, uncompromising, cavernous and now smacks just a bit too much of 1970s utilitarian minimalism. There's no natural light, and you never feel very comfortable, but you do feel up to the mark and virtuous.

Gallery of Photography
Meeting House Square, Around Temple Bar (671 4654/www.irish-photography.com). All cross-city buses. **Open** 11am-6pm Tue-Sat; 1pm-5pm Sun. **Admission** free. **Map** p251 E3.
A gem of a space in the heart of Temple Bar. This gallery's permanent collection of 20th-century Irish artworks is run in conjunction with monthly exhibitions by Irish and international photographers. The bookshop is well stocked. **Photo** *left*.

Hugh Lane Gallery (Municipal Gallery of Modern Art)
Parnell Square North, Around O'Connell Street (874 1903/www.hughlane.ie). Bus 3, 10, 11, 13, 16, 19, 22/Luas Abbey Street. **Open** 10am-6pm Tue-Thur; 10am-5pm Fri, Sat; 11am-5pm Sun. **Admission** *Gallery* free. **Credit** MC, V. **Map** p251 G3. *See p81.*

Irish Museum of Modern Art
Royal Hospital, Military Road, Kilmainham (612 9900/www.modernart.ie). Bus 51, 51B, 78A, 79, 90, 123/Luas Heuston. **Open** 10am-5.30pm Tue-Sat; noon-5.30pm Sun. **Admission** free.
It may seem a contradiction to house a museum of modern art in a 17th-century building, but it's a conceit that works well here. The Royal Hospital, once

a nursing home for retired soldiers, sits on a hill with sweeping views of formal gardens. In 2003 director Enrique Juncosa took the helm, and he has put on a number of superb exhibitions, most notably British artist Howard Hodgkin in 2006, for which the usually stark white walls of the hospital were painted in mint and gold under the artist's instructions. The gallery showcases mostly conceptual and abstract work and reserves one wing for works from the vast permanent collection.

National Photographic Archive
Meeting House Square, Around Temple Bar (603 0371/www.nli.ie). All cross-city buses. **Open** 10am-5pm Mon-Fri; 10am-2pm Sat. **Admission** free. **Map** p251 E3.
Just across the square from the Gallery of Photography (*see above*), the Archive has a wonderful permanent collection of historic Irish photographs from the late 19th to early 20th centuries, as well as changing exhibits of Irish photography.

Project Arts Centre
39 East Essex Street, Around Temple Bar (box office 881 9613/administration 679 6622/www.project.ie). All cross-city buses. **Open** *Box office* 11am-7pm Mon-Sat. **Credit** MC, V. **Map** p251 E3.
A conglomeration of custom-designed theatre and performance spaces as well as a gallery, the PAC was founded in 1966 but has been in its present premises less than ten years. Probably the most adventurous space in the city, and the only one where Tracey Emin could show her bed, it has been criticised as overly conceptual and isolationist – but surely every capital city needs a venue that can keep the flag of ultra-modernism flying?

Royal Hibernian Academy
15 Ely Place, Around St Stephen's Green (661 2558/www.royalhibernianacademy.com). DART Pearse/all cross-city buses/Luas St Stephen's Green. **Open** 11am-5pm Tue, Wed, Fri, Sat; 11am-8pm Thur; 2-5pm Sun. **Admission** free. **Map** p251 G4.
Down a lovely cul-de-sac just off St Stephen's Green, the RHA, founded in 1830 as a counterpart to London's Royal Academy, is wonderfully housed and situated. Four large, well-proportioned galleries on two floors, with plenty of natural light, show both Irish and international artists. Its scale means this is the natural choice for larger exhibitions. Touting itself as artist-based and orientated, its annual exhibition in May features over 1,000 exhibits selected by jury, and is the best showcase for emerging artists. Affordable prices and well worth a visit.

Temple Bar Gallery and Studios
5-9 Temple Bar (671 0073/www.templebargallery.com). All cross-city buses. **Open** 11am-6pm Tue, Wed, Fri, Sat; 11am-7pm Thur. **Credit** MC, V. **Map** p251 E3.
TBG & Studios is arguably the most covetable artists' studios in Dublin, with a decent contemporary gallery space at ground-floor level in the heart of Temple Bar. If you like what you see in the

gallery, you can schedule a studio visit and meet the artists, 30 of whom work upstairs. This is a purely non-commercial affair, and displays here are always challenging and uninhibited.

Commercial galleries

Apollo Gallery

51C Dawson Street, Around Trinity College (671 2609/www.apollogallery.ie). All cross-city buses/Luas St Stephen's Green. **Open** 10.30am-6pm Mon-Wed, Fri, Sat; 10.30am-8pm Thur; 1-6pm Sun. **Credit** MC, V. **Map** p251 F4.

From the sublime to the ridiculous – alongside a chance lovely portrait by Louis le Brocquy is the kind of kitsch you find in Sunday's open-air Merrion Square market. 'Eclectic' is the best description for the Apollo, but there really is something for everyone, and it's probably the only gallery in Dublin where you can still haggle, making it absolutely worth a visit.

Cross Gallery

59 Francis Street, The Liberties (473 8978/ www.crossgallery.ie). Bus 51B, 78A, 123. **Open** 10am-5.30pm Tue-Fri; 11am-4pm Sat. **Credit** MC, V. **Map** p250 D3/4.

If you happen to be in the Liberties, don't miss this gallery. The space, reminiscent of spaces on New York's Lower East Side, holds mostly abstract pieces. Its young director has a flair for choosing some of the best emerging Irish painters around, including Siobhan McDonald, Sonia Shiel and Brigid Flannery.

Gorry Gallery

20 Molesworth Street, Around Trinity College (679 5319/www.gorrygallery.ie). All cross-city buses/Luas St Stephen's Green. **Open** 11.30am-5.30pm Mon-Fri; 11am-2pm Sat (during exhibitions). **No credit cards.** **Map** p251 F4.

This gallery is a lovely space, where an old-world atmosphere is combined with some wonderfully eccentric touches. The Gorry sells Irish art from the 18th to the 21st centuries, and also specialises in painting restoration work.

Graphic Studio Gallery

Through the Arch, off Cope Street, Around Temple Bar (679 8021/www.graphicstudiodublin.com). DART Tara Street/all cross-city buses. **Open** 10am-5.30pm Mon-Fri; 11am-5pm Sat. **Credit** AmEx, MC, V. **Map** p251 F3.

Another Temple Bar gem, GSG's works on paper by Irish and international contemporary printmakers are displayed on two levels, in both group and solo shows. After taking in the good temporary displays, you can spend some time perusing a permanent selection of affordable works in folders, with prices starting at a very reasonable €60. This is an atmospheric space that offers affordable pieces by Louis le Brocquy, William Crozier and Tony O'Malley, alongside consistently strong work by local artists such as Cliona Doyle, John Graham and James O'Nolan.

Green on Red

26-28 Lombard Street East, Around Trinity College (671 3414/www.greenonredgallery.com). DART Pearse/all cross-city buses. **Open** 10am-6pm Mon-Fri; 11am-5pm Sat. **Credit** MC, V. **Map** p251 H3.

It may be a little off the beaten track, beyond Pearse Street DART station, but this gallery is well worth seeking out, as many consider it to be one of the city's best. The high industrial ceiling complements the sparse contemporary works inside. Prices are a bit high as well, but the collection of works on paper will suit those on a budget. The gallery represents some of the best local and international contemporary artists, including Fergus Feehily, Mark Joyce, Gerard Byrne, Paul Doran, Eilis O'Connell, Alice Maher and Corban Walker.

Hallward Gallery

65 Merrion Square, Around O'Connell Street (662 1482/www.hallwardgallery.com). DART Pearse/all cross-city buses. **Open** Sept-June 10.30am-5.30pm Mon-Thur; 11am- 5pm Fri; 11am-3pm Sat. *July, Aug* 10.30am-5.30pm Mon-Thur; 11am-3pm Sat. **Credit** MC, V. **Map** p251 H4.

Despite being tucked into a Georgian basement, this space is surprisingly bright. Works here tend to be contemporary Irish art of the tried and tested variety. The quality is always very high, with many well-established artists on show – expect names such as John Kelly RHA, John Behan RHA, Eithne Carr and David King.

Hillsboro Gallery

3 Anne's Lane, Anne Street South, Around St Stephen's Green (677 7905/www.hillsboro fineart.com). All cross-city buses/Luas St Stephen's Green. **Open** 10.30am-6pm Mon-Fri; 10.30am-4pm Sat. **No credit cards.** **Map** p251 F4.

A very welcome new addition to the city-centre galleries, Hillsboro moved in 2003 from the suburbs of Drumcondra to this airy space off Grafton Street. It specialises in contemporary Irish and British artists, but leaves a bit of space for modernism. Strong on the 'St Ives artists' – Sandra Blow, William Scott, Roger Hilton and Nancy Wynne Jones. **Photo** *right.*

Kerlin Gallery

Anne's Lane, Anne Street South, Around St Stephen's Green (670 9093/www.kerlin.ie). All cross-city buses/Luas St Stephen's Green. **Open** 10am-5.45pm Mon-Fri; 11am-4.30pm Sat. **No credit cards.** **Map** p251 F4.

This gallery's focus is on conceptual, minimal and abstract work, and it has some of the country's most successful contemporary artists in its stable: people like Felim Egan, Mark Francis, Callum Innes, Brian Maguire, Fionnuala Ni Chiosain, Sean Scully and Sean Shanahan.

Kevin Kavanagh Gallery

66 Great Strand Street, Around North Quays (874 0064/www.kevinkavanaghgallery.ie). All cross-city buses/Luas Jervis. **Open** 10.30am-5.30pm Mon-Fri; 11am-5pm Sat. **No credit cards.** **Map** p251 E2.

Just north of the Liffey, behind the Morrison Hotel, this industrial space primarily exhibits works by good contemporary Irish artists. Its emphasis is more on painting than on installation, and it regularly features works by noted local artists such as the inimitable Paul Nugent, Gary Cole, Mick O'Dea, Dermot Seymour, Michael Boran and Stephen Loughman.

Oisin Art Gallery

44 Westland Row, Around Trinity College (661 1315/www.oisingallery.com). DART Pearse/all cross-city buses. **Open** 9am-5.30pm Mon-Fri; 10am-5.30pm Sat. **Credit** MC, V. **Map** p251 G3.

This central, popular gallery recently moved to this beautiful new space right next door to its former home on Westland Row, and now it has a bit more room – there's even a spacious courtyard. Oisin deals in traditional and contemporary artists, including John Skelton, Katy Simpson, Ronan Goti, Cecil Maguire and Alan Kenny.

Original Print Gallery

4 Temple Bar, Around Temple Bar (677 3657/www. originalprint.ie). DART Tara Street/all cross-city buses/Luas Jervis. **Open** 10.30am-5.30pm Mon-Fri; 11am-5pm Sat; 2-6pm Sun. **Credit** MC, V. **Map** p251 E3.

Next door to the Temple Bar Gallery and Studios (*see p167*), the OPG is a brightly lit space that is as much a showcase for printmakers as an opportunity to flick through folders of both international and Irish works. Look out for Siobhan Cuffe, Anthony Lyttle, Cliona Doyle and John Graham.

Peppercanister Gallery

3 Herbert Street, Around St Stephen's Green (661 1279). DART Pearse/bus 7A, 8, 10. **Open** 10am-5.30pm Mon-Fri; 10am-1pm Sat. **Credit** MC, V. **Map** p251 H5.

In a basement space just off Mount Street, this gallery is a family-run affair with an informal yet highly polished atmosphere. Its artists (mainly Irish) are usually contemporary or early 20th century – names like Anne Donnelly, Neil Shawcross, Liam Belton and Breon O'Casey.

Rubicon Gallery

10 St Stephen's Green North (670 8055/www. rubicongallery.ie). All cross-city buses/Luas St Stephen's Green. **Open** noon-6pm Tues-Sat. **Credit** MC, V. **Map** p251 F4.

Overlooking the treetops of St Stephen's Green, the Rubicon focuses on Irish and British contemporary artists in all media. Its most recent trend shifts have been towards more conceptual work. Its curatorial approach is innovative, and its artists vary from traditional superstar Hughie O'Donoghue to groundbreaking artists like Nick Miller, Blaise Drummond, Tom Molloy, Ronnie Hughes, Eithne Jordan and Donald Teskey.

Solomon Gallery

Powerscourt Townhouse Centre, William Street South, Around Trinity College (679 4237/www. solomongallery.com). All cross-city buses/Luas St Stephen's Green. **Open** 10am-5.30pm Mon-Sat. **Credit** MC, V. **Map** p251 F3.

The Solomon is located in a beautiful 18th-century Georgian drawing room and is one of Dublin's leading art galleries and dealers in Irish 20th-century and contemporary paintings. Regular exhibitions of work by Peter Collis RHA, Hector McDonnell, James Hanley RHA and Brian Ballard are held alongside annual 'Collectible' shows of important works by Louis le Brocquy, William Scott and Jack B Yeats. The Solomon is also strong on sculpture, representing Rowan Gillespie, Patrick O'Reilly, Imogen Stuart and the estate of FE McWilliam.

Taylor Galleries

16 Kildare Street, Around St Stephen's Green (676 6055). DART Pearse/bus 10, 11, 13/Luas St Stephen's Green. **Open** 10am-5.30pm Mon-Fri; 11am-3pm Sat. **Credit** MC, V. **Map** p251 G4.

This beautiful gallery fills an entire Georgian townhouse. There's a feeling of real elegance to the space, which shows some of Irish modernism's heavyweights – figures such as Louis le Brocquy, William Crozier, Tony O'Malley and Brian Bourke – yet also hosts occasional shows by innovative younger artists.

Hillsboro Gallery. *See p168.*

Gay & Lesbian

Here's to you, Mrs Robinson.

Gay visitors to Dublin might like to offer up thanks to Mary Robinson and Senator David Norris. While in presidential office, Mrs Robinson was a key figure in the wave of liberalism that brought about the decriminalisation of male homosexuality in 1993; Mr Norris was another. With legalisation came an increase in the quantity and quality of gay and gay-friendly venues in the city.

The mid 1990s saw a gay boom in Dublin, with the opening of bars, clubs, newspapers, magazines and several political organisations. Although the pink explosion didn't last, the gay and lesbian scene in Dublin still has plenty going for it. You may be surprised to see how few entirely gay venues are on offer for a city of Dublin's size; but the number of gay-friendly venues more than makes up for it.

Sadly, all is not entirely equal. To date, there is not a single wholly lesbian bar in the city. In the past, a room in a bar was rented out and flyers handed around in the city's mainstream gay bars. These days, though, the lack of a lesbian bar scene means that venues such as the **George** and **GUBU** (for both, *see p171*) tend to attract both gays and lesbians, and the result is a friendly, mixed vibe that you won't find in many other cities.

Another advantage of the mixed scene is the entertainment. Drag queens sporting ridiculously high heels battle it out with kings lip-synching Elvis songs. The volume of gay talent on the city's glittering stages has been made possible by the absence of a 'gay men only' or 'lesbian only' door policy. If you can, try to incorporate a Sunday night into your stay in the capital as many of the gay club one-nighters are kept especially for then. To hell with Monday morning.

The Front Lounge. *See p171.*

Note this: unlike other international cities, the gay scene in Dublin is spread out over many streets. This means that visitors will find themselves trekking from one part of the city centre to another in search of homo havens, and it's unfortunately true that gay couples are rarely seen holding hands in public.

It's not all bad news, though. Most 'straight' bars are gay-friendly. Some are home to gay nights and welcome both gay and lesbian customers. The same can be said for most restaurants and hotels, where gay and lesbian bookings are part of the norm. The days of requesting a twin room are long gone.

One of the best times to meet gay and lesbian locals is during the year's big gay events. These include the Alternative Miss Ireland contest, a Lesbian Arts Festival, Pride and the Gay and Lesbian Film Fest in the summer.

GAY NEWS

Media information on gay life in the capital is easier to come by than ever before. *Gay Community News* (or *GCN*) is Ireland's monthly gay and lesbian magazine, and it is free in most gay bars and clubs and a handful of bookshops. Two mini-mags for the Dublin scene have also

emerged: *Free!* and *Scene City*. Both contain pocket-sized city maps with the gay venues highlighted. There are no glossy gay or lesbian magazines published here, but *Gay Times*, *Attitude* and *Diva* are widely available. Two superb and up-to-date gay Irish websites are www.gcn.ie and www.queerid.com.

Bars

The Front Lounge

33-4 Parliament Street, Around Temple Bar (670 4112). All cross-city buses. **Open** noon-11.30pm Mon-Thur; noon-12.30am Fri, Sat; 4-11.30pm Sun. **Credit** MC, V. **Map** p250 E3.
As sleek as a Porsche's bumper, The Front Lounge is a large, gay-friendly bar. Clientele-wise, expect hordes of handsome guys in suits and stubble and a gaggle of oh-so-interesting Sauvignon Blanc sippers. This is a mixed bar, and the queerest part is the raised section at the back, where local drag super-sister, Miss Panti, hosts Casting Couch, a karaoke extravaganza on Tuesday nights. **Photo** *opposite*.

The George

89 South Great George's Street, Around Temple Bar (478 2983/www.capitalbars.com). All cross-city buses. **Open** 12.30-11.30pm Mon, Tue; 12.30pm-2.30am Wed-Sat; 2.30pm-1am Sun. **Credit** AmEx, MC, V. **Map** p251 E3.
With a recent makeover, huge crowds at weekends and a multitude of theme nights, The George still has what it takes to be one of the biggest and best gay venues in the city. It's a hotbed most nights, especially on Sundays, when Shirley Temple-Bar hosts a notorious bingo session. During the day, it's a relaxed hangout, but late at night it transforms into a tightly packed nightclub with in-house DJs and a central dancefloor with a raised stage to dance on. If you're gay and visiting Dublin, it's inevitable you'll end up here at some point.

The Globe

11 South Great George's Street, Around Temple Bar (671 1220/www.theglobe.ie). Bus 16, 16A, 19, 19A, 55. **Open** noon-11.30pm Mon-Thur; noon-11.45pm Fri, Sat; 4pm-1am Sun. **Credit** AmEx, DC, MC, V. **Map** p251 E3.
Populated by thesis-preparing students, fashion victims clad in the latest Gucci tank tops and the odd celebrity, the Globe is nothing if not varied. The crowd is mixed, but also very gay-friendly. Take a seat at one of the long, wooden tables, order a pint and a chunky sandwich and do what everyone else is doing – namely, making sure that as many people as possible are watching them.

GUBU

7-8 Capel Street, North Quays (874 0710). All cross-city buses. **Open** 5-11.30pm Mon-Thur; 5pm-12.30am Fri, Sat; 4-11.30pm Sun. **Credit** MC, V. **Map** p251 E2.
Its name might stand for 'Grotesque, Unbelievable, Bizarre, Unprecedented', but don't be fooled by that.

'Straight-friendly' GUBU is a long, slender bar that has recently ditched its restrained modernist design, opting instead for a softer quilted suburban feel. Located over the river from its sister bar, the gay-friendly Front Lounge, GUBU attracts a trendy, predominantly male, professional crowd who either wants a quiet chat or to be entertained, depending on the time of day. Wednesday's hilarious all-singin', all-dancin' drag show is recommended. **Photos** *below*.

Company

27 Ormond Quay Upper, North Quays (872 2480). All cross-city buses. **Open** noon-11.30pm Mon-Thur; 10am-2.30am Fri; 11am-2.30am Sat; 12.30-11.30pm Sun. **No credit cards. Map** p251 E2/3.
This long, darkly concealed bar has recently attempted to revamp its waning 'out on the Liffey' image. Once the main competitor to the George, it's rarely packed now, except on men-only Saturday nights. But a recent renovation has slowly won over some dedicated followers. The absence of a dress code makes the bar a refuge for hardcore party-goers spiling over from the previous night.

The Dragon

64 South Georges Street, Around Temple Bar (478 1590). All cross-city buses. **Open** 5pm-2.30am Mon; 5-11.30pm Tue, Wed; 5pm-2.30am Thur-Sat; 5- 11pm Sun. **Credit** MC, V. **Map** p251 E3.
Formerly a cavernous dive, the Dragon has been completely revamped, with over-the-top theatrical touches and an extravagant entrance flanked by red leather couches. On weekend nights the long main bar heaves with young gay guys and their gal pals. There's a dancefloor and a welcoming outdoor courtyard that usually ends up as a talking house. Regular in-house DJs play an assortment of funk, electro and house every night, but it can quieten down midweek. The Dragon is immensely popular (not to mention cruisey).

Irish Film Institute Bar

6 Eustace Street, Around Temple Bar (administration 679 5744/www.irishfilm.ie). All cross-city buses. **Open** 9.30am-11.30pm Mon-Thur, Sun; 10am-12.30am Fri, Sat. **Credit** MC, V. **Map** p251 E3.
The IFI Bar occupies the same building as an art-house cinema. It's a sympathetic renovation of the old Quaker meeting house, with an extended bar that encloses a large bright glass-roofed courtyard. It has a significant gay and lesbian presence, and the institute is home to the city's annual Gay and Lesbian Film Festival in August.

Club nights

Glitz

Breakdown, below Break for the Border, Lower Stephen Street, Around Trinity College (478 0300/www.capitalbars.com). Bus 16, 16A, 19, 19A. **Open** 11pm-2.30am Tue. **Admission** €7; €8 after midnight. **No credit cards. Map** p251 E4.

Glitz is all about commercial dance music, supplied by the fabulous DJ Fluffy. The club itself has a central dancefloor surrounded by plentiful seats (ideal for a spot of people-watching); UK acts are regularly flown over to keep the beats going.

KISS

The Shelter at Vicar Street, 99 Vicar Street, Kilmainham & West (454 6656). Bus 78A, 123. **Open** third Sat, last Fri of mth. **Open** 10.30pm-3am. **Admission** €10. **No credit cards. Map** p250 C3.
Recently launched as a monthly club for 'gay girls and their male friends', KISS has quickly established itself as one of the best gay clubs in town. The women tend to be more femme than butch, which might explain the club's most unusual feature – the slow sets. Chart remixes prevail for most of the time.

Shift

64 Dame Street, Around Temple Bar (675 3971). All cross-city buses. **Open** 5pm-4am daily (Shift every Monday). **Admission** varies. **Credit** MC, V. **Map** p251 E3.
Another new gay night in yet another newly refurbished venue, Shift knocks the Monday blues into a cocked hat. The ubiquitous DJ Karen provides the funky electro house, the sound system is excellent, and the dancefloor is cosy. Shift is mostly popular with tourists and students; there are regular drinks and flyers promotions.

Tease

Temple Bar Music Centre, Curved Street, Around Temple Bar (www.clubtease.net). All cross-city buses. **Open** 10pm-2am 1 Sat a mth. **Admission** €12. **No credit cards. Map** p251 E3.

Tease is held one Saturday a month at the mammoth Temple Bar Music Centre. It's a huge gay event stocked with hot young things in skimpy attire, leggy men in wigs and DJs in drag. The indie club Q+A sometimes hijacks Tease, so check the local gay press for details before strapping on your heels.

Saunas

The Boilerhouse

12 Crane Lane, Around Temple Bar (677 3130/ www.the-boilerhouse.com). All cross-city buses. **Open** 1pm-5am Mon-Thur; 1pm Fri-5am Mon. **Admission** €20. **Credit** AmEx, MC, V. **Map** p251 E3.

Dublin's biggest sauna is equipped with a steam room, whirlpool, solarium, gym and even a café.

The Dock

21 Ormond Quay Upper, Around North Quays (872 4172). All cross-city buses. **Open** 9am-4am Mon-Thur; 9am Fri-5am Mon. **Admission** €15 Mon-Thur; €20 Fri-Sun. **Map** p251 E2/3.

Sitting right beside the Inn on the Liffey on the river's North Quays, the Dock is a bit smaller than the Boilerhouse, but that only makes it more intimate. Best of all, if you've nothing planned for the weekend, it's open the entire 48 hours.

Information & advice

Gay Men's Health Project

19 Haddingdon Road, Ballsbridge, Southern suburbs (660 2189/www.gaymenshealthproject.ie). Bus 10. **Open** 6.30-8pm Tue; 6-7.30pm Wed.

A drop-in sexual-health clinic for gay and bisexual men. The Gay Men's Health Project offers a service that is free, friendly and entirely confidential.

Gay Switchboard Dublin

872 1055/www.gayswitchboard.ie. **Open** 8-10pm Mon-Fri, Sun; 3.30-6pm Sat.

Help and information for the gay community.

Lesbian Line

872 9911. **Open** 7-9pm Thur.

An advice and information line.

Outhouse

105 Capel Street, Around North Quays (873 4932/ www.outhouse.ie). All cross-city buses. **Open** noon-6pm Mon-Fri; 1-6pm Sat, Sun; women's night 6-11pm Thur; men's night 6-11pm Fri. **Map** p251 E2.

A useful lesbian and gay meeting place, with social activities like book, youth and travelling clubs.

GUBU. *See p171.*

Arts & Entertainment

Music

From brash beats to suave strings, this town has a rich musical mix.

Irish music could be divided into two eras: BT and AT, or Before Them and After Them. Confused? It's simple, really: modern music in Ireland began in the mid 1960s, when Van Morrison and a group of his friends formed a trailblazing R&B outfit called Them.

Dublin saw the Belfast band's success and produced two acts that mined the rich heritage of Irish trad music: Thin Lizzy and Horslips. At the same time, a 1960s folk revival led by the Chieftains and the Dubliners reached its apotheosis in the early '70s with the trad supergroup Planxty, featuring Christy Moore. Then, in the wake of the punk upheaval in Britain, Dublin got its own collection of angry young men. Bob Geldof's Boomtown Rats voiced their frustration with political and cultural stagnation in Ireland, only to be kicked around by a bunch of blokes with big hair: U2. After them came Sinead O'Connor and Kevin Shields (the eclectic genius behind My Bloody

Valentine), and with the grizzled addition of Shane MacGowan's Pogues, Dublin's place in the pantheon of international stars was set.

Then it all went quiet. On walls across town, the graffito 'Dublin is Dead' became the standard assessment of the Irish music scene. But recently, things have been looking up. The last few years have seen a burst of live music in the capital, and the hunger for new tunes has revitalised the city's music scene.

Venues like the International Bar (*see p176*) have helped promote quality acts like Gemma Hayes, Adrian Crowley and Paddy Casey. The DIY punk scene brewing for so many years in small clubs around Dublin (such as JJ Smyth's and Ballroom of Romance) has delivered Redneck Manifesto, Large Mound and Republic of Loose; the electronica and dance scene has spawned Herv, Si Schroeder and Ti Woc; while the Future Kings of Spain, Turn and La Rocca take inspiration, and make plenty of lolly, from the US rock scene. Other 'breakthrough' bands of the recent past include fashion-obsessed, pop devotees the Chalets and the more considered guitar sounds of Crayonsmith and Mumblin' Def Ro. For fans of straight-up rock, the Immediate and Humanzi are two rising bands worth lending an ear to; and all manner of electronica, from ambient to evil, has sprung up of late, thanks in part to the hard work of independent labels like Alphabet Set, Go Away recordings and Trust Me I'm A Thief. With the recent success of Damien Rice's *O* in Britain and the US, Dublin's music scene may also have a new superstar.

Meanwhile, traditional Irish performers still knock out some of the best and most exciting music the country has to offer. The last decade has seen the emergence of a whole new generation of such acts (Lunasa, Solas, Martin Hayes and Dennis Cahill, Karen Casey and North Cregg, say), while bands like Kila combine Irish trad with the world music styles of Africa, the Far East and South America.

Ticket sales are fuelled by enterprises like Road Records and Claddagh Records (for both, *see p143*), which help acts convert local success to national and international acclaim; then there's the crop of new venues that host the bands, such as the Village, Liberty Hall and Crawdaddy (*see p177*) – all supplying a hungry local audience with new sounds.

The Cobblestone. *See p176.*

Temple Bar Music Centre. See p178.

Still, newest isn't always best, and most music fans agree that Whelan's (*see p178*), one of the most prestigious venues in the city, remains the best place at which to hear Dublin's brightest up-and-coming stars.

INFORMATION

To find out what's happening in town, pick up local free sheet the *Event Guide* for full listings of concerts in Dublin. You can find it in bars, cafés and record shops.

TICKETS

While places like the Point (*see p180*), Whelan's and Olympia (*see p180*) have their own box offices, other major venues and such smaller but established names as Vicar Street (*see p178*) rely on agencies for ticketed concerts. You can get tickets at **Ticketmaster** (0818 719 300/from outside Ireland 456 9569/ www.ticketmaster.ie) in the St Stephen's Green

shopping centre, which deals with just about every big event. The reservation service in the Tourism Centre on Suffolk Street can make credit card bookings (605 7729/ www.visitdublin.com), and tickets can often be bought at record shops like Road Records and Big Brother Records (*see p142*). Check our listings or call the venues directly to find out the best source of tickets.

WHERE TO GO

Most band venues are, conveniently enough, located in or around the city centre. A few of them, such as the Helix (*see p177*) and the National Stadium (*see p179*), are deep in the suburbs – but even those are only 30 minutes from the centre by bus. Larger-scale rock concerts are occasionally held in outdoor venues like Punchestown racecourse, Croke Park (now the default venue while Lansdowne Road is being renovated) and the RDS (*see p180*).

Bars & small venues

Ballroom of Romance

The Lower Deck, 1 Portobello Harbour, Around St Stephen's Green (475 1423). Bus 16, 16A, 19, 19A, 122/Luas Charlemont. **Open** varies. **Admission** €10. **Credit** MC, V. **Map** p251 E6.

This monthly alternative live music club, taking place in an old man's pub, has showcased talented new indie acts. It's a pick 'n' mix – you could get the static noise of (retards) – that's brackets retards brackets – one night and the bubblegum pop of the Chalets on the next. As a starting point for Irish alternative music, though, Ballroom of Romance is an essential venue.

Bleu Note

61-63 Capel Street, Around O'Connell Street (0872 878 755/878 3371). All cross-city buses/Luas Jervis. **Open** varies Thur-Sun. **Admission** *Thur, Sun* free. *Fri, Sat* free before 10pm; €6 after. **Credit** MC, V. **Map** p251 E2.

A brand-new pub and live music venue, with the main floor completely dedicated to jazz, Blue Note is a welcome addition to the city's live music scene. The second floor plays an eclectic mixture of blues, soul funk and Latin every Thursday to Sunday night; there are classic jazz movies on Monday nights (with free popcorn, to boot).

Bruxelles

7-8 Harry Street, off Grafton Street, Around Temple Bar (677 5362). All cross-city buses/Luas St Stephen's Green. **Open** 10.30am-1.30am Mon-Wed; 10.30am-2.30am Thur-Sat; noon-1.30am Sun. **No credit cards. Map** p251 F3.

The musical quality here can vary, but even so, this is a great pub: you'd do well to pop in for a drink anyway. Local blues acts play upstairs early in the week; there's dancing late at night down in the Zodiac Bar, and you'll be served a loud of helping of classic rock in the Heavy Metal Bar (which feels a good deal like *Wayne's World*, except without the irony). *See also p123.*

The Cobblestone

77 King Street North, North Quays (872 1799/ www.musiclee.com). Bus 25, 26, 37, 39, 67, 67A, 68, 69, 79/Luas Smithfield. **Open** 4-11.30pm Mon-Thur; 4pm-12.30am Fri, Sat; 1-11pm Sun. *Bar music* from 9pm daily. *Back bar venue* from 9pm Thur-Sat. **Admission** *Bar* free. *Back bar venue* €10-€15. **No credit cards. Map** p250 C2.

Overlooking the vast square at Smithfield, this is an old-fashioned, friendly boozer that hosts trad music in its back bar. Upstairs is a surprisingly comfortable and intimate space that specialises in more serious gigs by good traditional and roots groups, as well as the odd rock act. *Photo p174.*

Eamonn Doran's

3A Crown Alley, Around Temple Bar (679 9114/ www.eamonndorans.com). All cross-city buses. **Open** noon-3am daily. *Live music* phone for details.

Admission varies depending on acts; call for further details. **Credit** AmEx, MC, V. **Map** p251 E3.

Eamonn Doran's replaced the once-famous Rock Garden when its star dimmed in the late '90s. Owner Dermott Doran kept the metallic decor in the basement venue and refurbished the upstairs bar. Doran's is slowly gaining prominence as a starting point for such young Irish rock acts as Halite, the Things and the Republic of Loose.

The Hub

24-25 Eustace Street, Around Temple Bar (635 9991/www.thehubmezz.com). All cross-city buses/ Luas Jervis. **Open** *Live music* from 8pm daily. *Music club* 11pm-3am daily. **Admission** varies. **Credit** MC, V. **Map** p251 E3.

A new, small-scale rock venue in the city centre, this basement bar (below the Mezz Bar) has a small stage, which puts the musicians and audience pretty much face to face. Acts here tend to be local rock bands on the way up, plus a few low-key international acts. Dublin needs small venues like this to give smaller bands a chance, but the atmosphere is not high class, and the sound tends to be woolly.

International Bar

23 Wicklow Street, Around Trinity College (677 9250). All cross-city buses/Luas St Stephen's Green. **Open** 10.30am-11.30pm Mon-Thur; 10.30am-12.30am Fri, Sat; 12.30-11pm Sun. *Live music* from 9pm Tue-Sun. **Admission** varies. **No credit cards. Map** p251 F3.

The International is a quaint old pub with a small but charming venue upstairs. In recent years, it has become more of a comedy space, with four nights of stand-up each week; but it still does jazz on Tuesday nights, experimental music with Lazy Bird on Sunday nights, and two trad sessions in the bar on Sunday afternoons and evenings.

JJ Smyth's

12 Aungier Street, Around St Stephen's Green (475 2565/www.jjsmyths.com). Bus 16, 16A, 19, 19A, 83/ Luas St Stephen's Green. **Open** *Live music* from 9pm Mon, Tue, Thur-Sun. **Admission** varies. **No credit cards. Map** p251 E4.

One of the city's oldest jazz and blues venues, Smyth's does good music every night bar Wednesdays. There's an acoustic open-jam session on the first Tuesday of every month, and fine jazz is the order of the night on Monday, Thursday and Sunday. The keen, friendly crowd and cheap pints are added bonuses. *See also p132.*

O'Shea's Merchant

12 Bridge Street Lower, Liberties (679 3797). Bus 21, 21A/Luas The Four Courts. **Open** 10.30am-11.30pm Mon-Wed; 10.30am-2am Thur-Sat; 12.30pm-2am Sun. *Live music* from 9.30pm daily. **Admission** free. **Credit** AmEx, MC, V. **Map** p250 C/D3.

This sprawling pub and restaurant hosts live trad music and set dancing every night. It can be good fun with the right crowd but tends to attract large coach tours looking for that Oirish vibe.

Crawdaddy.

Medium-sized venues

The Ambassador

Top of O'Connell Street, Around O'Connell Street (0818 719 300/www.mcd.ie/ ambassador). All cross-city buses/Luas Abbey Street. **Open** varies. **Admission** varies. **Credit** *Ticketmaster* AmEx, DC, MC, V. **Map** p251 F1.

The Ambassador was a theatre, then a woefully underused cinema. As a rock venue, it keeps many of its old trappings: decor, balcony and a large stage. It's a big stage to fill, and it takes loud rock bands like the Lost Prophets or charismatic indie acts like Beck to put the place to best use. The management has pretty much cornered the Dublin market in nu metal and hard indie rock; an acoustic act would be lost in this 1,200-seat venue.

Crawdaddy

Hatch Street Upper, off Harcourt Street, Around St Stephen's Green (478 0166/www.crawdaddy.ie). Bus 15A, 15B, 86/Luas Harcourt Street. **Open** varies. **Admission** varies. **Credit** *Ticketmaster* AmEx, MC, V. **Map** p251 E5.

Medium-sized Crawdaddy is an exciting new venue that meets the demand for live music with an impressive roster of contemporary jazz, world music and rock. It can hold about 300 people, and ticket prices tend to be higher than average; but the place has the atmosphere of an intimate jazz club, and draws acts of the calibre (not to mention considerable, genre-busting diversity) of Courtney Pine, the Fall and Talvin Singh. **Photos** *above*.

The Helix

DCU, Collins Avenue, Glasnevin (700 7000/www.the helix.ie). Bus 11, 13A, 16, 16A, 19A. **Open** varies. **Admission** varies. **Credit** AmEx, MC, V.

Part of Dublin City University's building complex, the Helix is a multi-venue arts centre in the leafy suburb of Glasnevin. Its three venues – Mahony Hall, the Theatre and the Space – cover the range from small gigs to bigger concerts. The smaller venues have fielded some of the bigger acts from Dublin's music scene, and recently hosted Van Morrison and Lou Reed. The only drawback is the distance – a good half-hour trip – from the city centre.

Liberty Hall Theatre

33 Eden Quay, Around O'Connell Street (872 1122/www.libertyhall.ie). All cross-city buses/Luas Abbey Street. **Open** varies. **Admission** varies. **Credit** AmEx, MC, V. **Map** p251 F2.

This theatre and music venue sits inside Ireland's main union hall, the famous Connolly Hall. It was very popular in the '70s (Paul Brady has released a live album he recorded here in 1978), but fell into disuse. The recent renovation turned its fortunes around, and the place now offers a refreshing programme of world music, jazz and rock. Long may its popularity continue.

The Sugar Club

8 Leeson Street Lower, Around St Stephen's Green (678 7188/www.thesugarclub.com). Bus 46A/Luas St Stephen's Green. **Open** 8pm-midnight Mon-Thur; 8pm-3am Fri-Sun. **Admission** €10-€15. **Credit** AmEx, MC, V. **Map** p251 G6.

One of Dublin's most stylish venues, the Sugar Club has the feel of a hip US jazz bar. The audience gazes down on the musicians from tiered seats with tables, and never needs lift a finger: waiters bring booze from a large bar at the back. The programme ranges from cabaret and rock to jazz or singer-songwriter sets. Weekday crowds are mainly suits; keep an eye on listings for the likes of KT Tunstall and Crazy P.

Temple Bar Music Centre

Curved Street, Around Temple Bar (670 9202/ www.tbmc.ie). All cross-city buses. **Open** *Live music* 7.30pm (check for days). **Admission** varies. **Credit** MC, V. **Map** p251 E3.

Temple Bar Music Centre has been undergoing a bit of a makeover in the last few years. It was once seen as home to hard-rock bands, where sound quality and atmosphere mattered less than beer and decibels; but new owners have turned it into a quality venue. Improvements have been made to the seating, sound system and look of the place, and its line-up has widened to include traditional Irish groups like Lunasa and Dervish, as well as American roots artists like Guy Clark. **Photo** *p175*.

Vicar Street

99 Vicar Street, off Thomas Street West, Around North Quays (information 454 6656/tickets from TicketMaster/www.vicarstreet.com). Bus 123. **Open** *Live music* from 7.30pm daily. **Admission** varies. **Credit** *Ticketmaster* AmEx, DC, MC, V. **Map** p250 C3.

A modern venue with an old-style feel, Vicar Street has comfortable seating, sensitive lighting and a great sound system. It was recently expanded to hold 1,000 punters, but has lost none of its intimate atmosphere. The spacious pub in the front and the little bars hidden in the corridors are handy, too. Acts include Bob Dylan, Kanye West, Rufus Wainwright, Calexico and Al Green, as well as big-name jazz and comedy acts and top local musicans.

The Village

26 Wexford Street, Around St Stephen's Green (475 8555/www.thevillagevenue.com). Bus 16, 16A. 19, 19A/Luas Harcourt. **Open** 11am-2.30am Mon-Fri; 5pm-2.30am Sun. **Admission** varies. **Credit** AmEx, MC, V. **Map** p251 E5.

This shiny venue opened in 2003 on the same site as the underperforming Mean Fiddler. The good people at Whelan's (*see below*) took it on and gave it a thorough makeover; the redesign and revamped sound system made it a cosy and enjoyable spot. It now has some of the most interesting musical offerings in town – the likes of Sufjan Stevens and Clap Your Hands Say Yeah.

Whelan's

25 Wexford Street, Around St Stephen's Green (478 0766/www.whelanslive.com). Bus 16, 16A, 19, 19A, 122/Luas Harcourt. **Open** *Live music* from 8.30pm Mon-Sat. **Tickets** €9.50-€25. **Credit** *TicketMaster* AmEx, MC, V. **Map** p251 E5.

One of Dublin's most prestigious venues, Whelan's has built an unassailable reputation among Dublin music fans. It's the stomping ground for most of the city's up-and-coming bands: Damien Rice, David Kitt, the Frames, Paddy Casey and Gemma Hayes all made their first appearances here. With a line-up that takes in Irish trad, English folk and American roots, this is a vital Dublin venue. *See also p133*.

The Gaiety. *See p179*.

Arts & Entertainment

Doyle on troubled waters

At one point during Roger Doyle's 1978 composition *Thalia*, a little girl's voice with a strong Dublin accent emerges from a swarm of metallic noise and says, rather scoldingly, 'What do you think you're doing?' This is more or less what Doyle has been hearing from critics and audiences for much of his career. 'God help the future of music if Mr Doyle has anything to do with it,' read a review of *Thalia* in Irish MOR weekly *Hot Press*. Little did they know that their fears – to some extent, at least – were to be realised. It's only in recent years, with acts like Matmos, Merzbow, Christian Fennesz and William Basinski exploring similar territory, that Doyle's compositions finally seem to have some sort of context. Even today, though, it's easy to see why his early work was greeted with such bafflement. It's certainly not for everyone – even listeners who consider themselves adventurous.

Doyle has long been one of Ireland's most ambitious musicians, and is seen as

something of an electronic music pioneer. In his early twenties he played drums in various jazz and rock groups, until he discovered the possibilities of tape technology and began to experiment with *musique concrète*. He was invited to study at the Institute of Sonology at Utrecht in 1974, where he established himself as a significant player in the field of experimental sound collage. He released his first LP, *Oizzo No* ('I don't know' pronounced with a heavy Dublin accent – anticipating, no doubt, the puzzlement with which the music would be greeted) in 1975.

Today, Doyle's highly respected for his innovations, but little heard of outside avant-garde music circles. Oddly enough, he's probably most widely known for the incidental music he composed for Steven Berkoff's production of Wilde's *Salomé* at the Gate – music that is not especially characteristic of the uncompromising, often abrasive work he has been producing since the mid '70s. His magnum opus, *Babel*, is an expansive musical depiction of a city of towers that maps out its locations one room at a time. In 2004, Doyle was commissioned to provide the music for the 'Proteus' installation at the National Library's centenary exhibition for Joyce's *Ulysses* – an apt enough choice, given that both Joyce and Doyle have a similar predilection for creating swirling, multiform and imposing works of competing voices and wandering perspectives. It seems unlikely, though, that the city will ever celebrate any centenaries of Doyle's oeuvre: despite the kudos from the avant-garde inner circle, it's difficult to imagine the likes of Bertie Ahern or Michael Flatley professing their love of his music.

Large venues

The Gaiety
King Street South, Around St Stephen's Green (677 1717/www.gaietytheatre.com). All cross-city buses/ Luas St Stephen's Green. **Open** *Live music* noon-4am Fri, Sat. **Admission** €12 Fri; €15 Sat. **Credit** MC, V. **Map** p251 F4.
The Gaiety is a spacious, old-time concert hall whose main trade is opera and theatre, but it has given space to rock performers like the Divine Comedy and Lambchop. A few years ago, it opened its lofty corridors to club nights, with live music and DJs in different rooms. Late nights at the Gaiety are also a draw; open till 4am, it has the latest licence in town

(making it, for obvious reasons, one of the most popular places in town…). Fridays feature Latin, salsa and world music, and Saturday nights revolve around funk, soul and groovy jazz. **Photos** *left*.

National Stadium
145 South Circular Road, Southern suburbs (information 453 3371). Bus 19, 22. **Open** *Office* 9am-4pm Mon-Fri. **Tickets** varies. **Credit** *Ticketmaster* AmEx, MC, V.
The National Stadium was a popular venue in the 1970s and '80s, with everyone from Led Zeppelin to Van Morrison playing here. It holds a seated audience of 2,200 and has a large stage, but has never had a great sound system. Gigs here are now quite rare; it has largely returned to being a sports venue.

Olympia

72 Dame Street, Around Temple Bar (679 3323/ tickets 0818 719 330/www.mcd.ie/olympia). All cross- city buses/Luas Jervis. **Open** *Box office* 10.30am- 6.30pm Mon-Sat. *Music usually 8pm, midnight Tue-Sun; phone for details.* **Tickets** *varies.* **Credit** AmEx, MC, V. **Map** p251 E3.

The Olympia is one of Dublin's old music halls. It's a fabulous place, with red velvet seats and theatre boxes on either side of the stage; the design is per- fect for music and the acoustics are excellent. Famed for its late-night gigs, it's become more of an estab- lished music venue in recent years, hosting the likes of Radiohead, Bowie and Blur. These days late-night gigs only happen on Saturdays and usually feature tribute bands like the Australian Doors.

Amphitheatres

The Point

East Link Bridge, North Wall Quay, Around North Quays (tickets 836 6777/www.thepoint.ie). Tara Street or Connolly DART/rail. **Open** *Box office* 10am-6pm Mon-Sat. **Tickets** *varies.* **Credit** AmEx, DC, MC, V.

With its capacity of 8,500, the Point is one of Dublin's biggest indoor venues. Visitors have included Eric Clapton, Pearl Jam and the Rolling Stones, and big musical shows like *Riverdance* and *Les Misérables*. Still, the echo-ey acoustics and its sheer size mean performers are dwarfed – but it remains the venue that big shows and big stars pre- fer to play in.

RDS Showgrounds

Ballsbridge, Southern suburbs (668 0866/www. rds.ie). Bus 5, 7, 7A, 8, 45/DART Lansdowne Road. **Open** *varies.* **Tickets** *varies.* **Credit** *TicketMaster* AmEx, MC, V.

One of the city's main sites for festival-size concerts, these sprawling grounds have hosted the Red Hot Chili Peppers and the re-routed Lisdoonvarna festi- val. It has a capacity of 40,000, but while this is one of Dublin's longest-standing open-air venues, its main activity is showjumping, so food and drink facilities depend on each gig's promoters. Seats in the stands provide the best view, but standing on the grass in front of the stage means better sound.

Classical music

Though Dublin music buffs are fond of the fact that Handel's *Messiah* had its première here in 1742, the city's contribution to classical music is largely undistinguished. The city has no opera house, and despite the occasional success of productions such as *Salomé* and *Tosca* at the Gaiety, Dublin really doesn't compare with other European cities.

Still, the situation is far from hopeless. Though classical music doesn't have the high profile of other art forms here, there's still

plenty being made. The **National Concert Hall** is home to the **RTÉ Concert Orchestra** and the **National Symphony Orchestra**. Performances by contemporary chamber ensembles such as Vox 21, the **Crash Ensemble** and popular choir **Anúna** can often be seen at the likes of the **Project Arts Centre** and the **Helix**.

Other regular events around town include the **RTÉ Proms** (208 3434/www.rte.ie), a feast of international music held each May, and the triennial **Dublin International Organ & Choral Festival**. And yes, there's an annual performance of the *Messiah* in commemoration of its debut here every Easter Tuesday at 1pm, on Fishamble Street.

Opera companies

Opera Ireland

The Schoolhouse, 1 Grantham Street, Around St Stephen's Green (478 6041/www.operaireland.com). Founded in 1941, Opera Ireland is as close as Ireland gets to a national opera company. Guest performers have included Placido Domingo, José Carreras and even Luciano Pavarotti, who made his internation- al debut with the company in a 1963 production of *Rigoletto*. After transforming itself in the 1980s into a more eclectic outfit, the company is as much at home with Verdi and Shostakovich as with Mark- Anthony Turnage's *Silver Tassie*. Its two short sea- sons at the Gaiety Theatre are in autumn and spring.

Opera Theatre Company

Temple Bar Music Centre, Around Temple Bar (679 4962/www.opera.ie). Founded in 1986, this company is the national tour- ing company of Ireland. In addition to producing four tours a year, it also runs the Opera Theatre Studio, a training facility for young singers. It has achieved national and international success with baroque and early classical operas, as well as 20th- century works. It occasionally commissions new operas by Irish composers.

Orchestras, choirs & ensembles

Anúna

Information 283 5533/www.anuna.ie. Best known for its association with the Riverdance group, this gifted Celtic choir has toured worldwide. Founder and artistic director Michael McGlynn has been at the helm since 1987; the choir's intricately arranged vocal harmonies sell CDs by the truckload. Anúna performs regularly in Dublin; check listings.

Crash Ensemble

The O'Reilly Theatre, Belvedere College, Great Denmark Street (information 858 6644/www.crash ensemble.com).

National Concert Hall.

Largely responsible for putting cool back into classical, this outfit fuses the likes of Philip Glass and Steve Reich with dance, video and electronica. It regularly commissions and performs works by new Irish composers.

National Chamber Choir

Information 700 5665/www.dcu.ie/chamber.
Based on the Northside campus of Dublin City University, this professional choir puts on many concerts throughout the year. Its repertoire runs from Seiber and Thompson to Handel, and in summer and winter it can be heard every second Thursday at the National Gallery of Ireland.

RTÉ Concert Orchestra

Information 208 3347/www.rte.ie/music/rteco.
Considerably less ambitious than its big sister the NSOI, the RTÉ Concert Orchestra is defined by its broadcasting remit. It has the largest audience of any Irish classical music outfit, thanks to Ireland's winning streak in the Eurovision Song Contest in the 1990s, when the orchestra was called upon to play to TV audiences of 300 million.

RTÉ National Symphony Orchestra

Information 208 3347/www.rte.ie/music.
The National Symphony Orchestra was founded in 1926 to provide music for radio broadcasts, and it's still run by radio and TV network RTÉ. The NSOI has developed greatly over the past few years.

Venues

In addition to the venues listed below, concerts are often held in the city's theatres (*see pp191-195*). The O'Reilly Hall (858 5665) at Belvedere College is sometimes used for concerts by the RTÉ orchestras, and the Irish Museum of Modern Art in Kilmainham (612 9900/ www.modernart.ie) occasionally rents

out its impressive annexe hall to independent ensembles. There are also beautifully sung daily services and choral concerts at St Patrick's Cathedral and Christ Church Cathedral. Finally, don't miss Latin mass at St Mary's Pro Cathedral, sung by the Palestrina Choir every Sunday at 11am.

Municipal Gallery of Modern Art (Hugh Lane Gallery)

Parnell Square North, Around O'Connell Street (874 1903/www.hughlane.ie). Bus 3, 10, 11, 13, 16, 19, 22/Luas Abbey Street. **Open** 10am-6pm Tue-Thur; 10am-5pm Fri, Sat; 11am-5pm Sun. **Admission** free. **Credit** MC, V. **Map** p251 E1.
This ample hall in the Hugh Lane Gallery hosts the long-running and stylish Sunday at Noon concerts. The series features jazz, contemporary and classical music from Ireland and abroad, and runs from October to June.

National Concert Hall

Earlsfort Terrace, Around St Stephen's Green (475 1572/www.nch.ie). All cross-city buses. **Open** *Box office* 10am-7pm Mon-Sat. **Credit** AmEx, DC, MC, V. **Map** p251 F5.
Dublin's main venue for orchestral music was established in 1981, in the Great Hall of what was then University College Dublin. It retains the bland flavour of a lecture theatre, though its acoustics are generally considered excellent. Its annexe, the John Field Room, hosts performances of chamber, jazz, traditional and vocal music. **Photos** *above*.

RDS Concert Hall

Royal Dublin Society Showgrounds, Ballsbridge, Southern suburbs (information 668 0866/www.rds.ie). Bus 7, 45, 84. **Credit** *TicketMaster* AmEx, MC, V.
This overly large but fairly serviceable hall is set in Ireland's main showjumping arena. In its favour, the venue is large enough to accommodate a modestly sized opera company, but it lacks a certain cosiness.

Nightlife

The highs and lows of Dublin's dancefloors.

It's all about who's watching you at **Spy**. See p184.

In case you haven't noticed, things have changed around here. In the space of a decade, Dublin has gone from having no scene at all to having a notoriously drunken scene – and from there to, most recently, gradually developing a scene that might turn out to be quite cool. It's enough to make a clubber dizzy.

It all started with that EU cash infusion in the early 1990s. A few clubs opened up, and it wasn't long before the word spread that there was cheap booze to be had in Dublin. Suddenly, people were coming from all over the planet to check out 'Europe's new party capital'. More clubs and bars opened to satisfy demand, causing word to spread further. Dublin was hot.

It was too good to last, of course, and by the end of the 20th century, Dublin's bars and clubs had reached critical mass. The city was awash with 'booze tourists', fun-loving types who took advantage of the cheap budget flights, the favourable exchange rates and that famous Irish hospitality (which, in truth, was beginning to wear a bit thin under the non-stop onslaught

of drunken international stag parties). Temple Bar was becoming a no-go area for locals and sane tourists, particularly at weekends. There was vomit on the pavement and syringes in some of the lavatories. Still, huge new bars were opening all over town, most of them designed with partying tourists, rather than character, in mind. At the same time, prices were skyrocketing: the price of a pint almost doubled in just a few years. It seemed like the party might be over. For Dubliners, staying in became the new going out.

But these things happen in cycles, and as the crowds thinned, the people who had made Dublin's party reputation in the first place began to resurface, and the party started up again. These days Dublin's nightlife is geared towards more discerning patrons, and the city offers a dynamic variety of venues, but you need to know where to look to find the best.

Most of them are within ten minutes' walk from the banks of the Liffey. On the south side, the best concentration of bars and clubs is around George's Street and Wicklow Street. On the north side, the layout is a little more random, but Abbey Street, just off O'Connell Street, has some of the hottest new bars and clubs. One thing that didn't survive, though, is Temple Bar. Once the centre of the clubbing universe, it's largely dead now. These days, locals only recommend Temple Bar to the sort of tourists they don't want to see in their favourite clubs.

A final note. Not to keep harping on about it, but Ireland has banned smoking just about everywhere, including nightclubs. Some think this has cleared the air a bit too much (it turns out the worst thing you can smell in a club isn't smoke after all). Others think it's fabulous (at least your clothes won't smell like a bonfire the morning after). But whichever side you're on, don't even think about lighting up.

Clubs & dance bars

Ballroom

Fitzsimmon's Hotel, Around Temple Bar (677 9315/www.fitzsimmonshotel.com). All cross-city buses. **Open** 11pm-2.30am Mon-Thur; 10.30pm-3am Fri, Sat; 11pm-1.30am Sun. **Admission** €5-€8 Mon-Thur, Sun; €10-€13 Fri, Sat. **Credit** AmEx, MC, V. **Map** p251 F3.

Since it's in the centre of Temple Bar, the Ballroom is popular with tourists and plays chart hits. The large basement club gets very crowded at weekends, and most of the crowd seems to have wound up here by accident, or because they aren't familiar enough with the city to pick a triendier place. Turn up drunk.

Carnival

11 Wexford Street, Around St Stephen's Green (405 3604). Bus 16, 16A, 19, 19A, 122. **Open** noon-midnight daily. **Admission** free. **No credit cards.** **Map** p251 E5.

Owned and run by Eamon Dorans – the same crowd that looks after the Dice Bar (*see below*) – Carnival is the top spot on the Camden Street 'strip' if you like your bar music to be funk and jazz, your lighting moody, and your things young and pretty. One drawback is that the bar tends to go from yawningly empty on a weeknight to packed by 8pm on a weekend. If you're coming on a Friday, get in early.

Dice Bar

Queen Street, off Arran Quay, North Quays (872 8622). All cross-city buses. **Open** 5-11.30pm Mon-Thur; 5pm-12.30am Fri, Sat; 3.30-11pm Sun. **Admission** free. **Credit** MC, V. **Map** p250 C2.

Small, dark and tricky to get to, this is the best DJ bar in town. The music is never less than exceptional, with different resident DJs every night, and there's a selection of beers from local microbreweries to choose from. On a good night the walls sweat; then there are the really great nights, but no one can actually remember them.

Gaiety

King Street South, Around Trinity College (677 1717/www.gaietytheatre.com). All cross-city buses. **Open** midnight-4am Fri, Sat. **Admission** €9-€14 Fri; €14 Sat. **Credit** MC, V. **Map** p251 F4.

One of the city's oldest and largest theatres by day and a mega club by night, this big, Victorian place has several spaces for bands, DJs and films. There are lots of bars in a variety of sizes, and the warren-like structure of this beautiful old building means you almost need a map (or at least a local guide) to find your way around. The Gaiety is a particularly good destination for fans of Latin and jazz.

The George

89 South Great George's Street, Around Temple Bar (478 2983/www.capitalbars.com). All cross-city buses. **Open** 12.30-11.30pm Mon, Tue; 12.30pm-2.30am Wed-Sat; 2.30pm-1am Sun. **Admission** €8 after 10pm. **Credit** AmEx, MC, V. **Map** p251 F4.

This is the gayest gay club in Dublin, but it's still straight-friendly: on a good night the George is as much fun as any straight club will be. If you're in town on a Sunday at about 6pm, check out the George's famed drag bingo and cabaret.

GUBU

7-8 Capel Street, North Quays (874 0710). All cross-city buses. **Open** 5-11.30pm Mon-Thur; 5-12.30am Fri, Sat; 4-11.30pm Sun. **Admission** free. **Credit** MC, V. **Map** p251 E2.

This is a new-school gay bar – which means, apparently, that you can't really tell that it's a gay bar: GUBU is more about post-modern interior design than camp and cross-dressing. As with most gay-friendly bars, the music is the best pop party tunes. However, Tuesday nights host the excellent jazz ensemble the Company. GUBU is a DJ bar, rather than a club, although it certainly attracts a clubby late-night clientele.

The Hub

23 Eustace Street, Around Temple Bar (670 7655/ www.thehubmezz.com). All cross-city buses. **Open** 11pm-late daily. **Admission** €7-€12. **Credit** MC, V. **Map** p251 E3.

This basement club and live music spot is the least tourist-oriented venue in Temple Bar. In fact, the average tourist would probably find the Hub a little unnerving. It does live music until 11pm, then turns into a club. The vibe depends on what bands have played that night, but if you like it messy and rock 'n' roll, you won't be disappointed. Keep an eye on local listings and gig posters.

Lillie's Bordello

Adam Court, Grafton Street, Around Trinity College (679 9204/www.lilliesbordello.ie). All cross-city buses. **Open** 11.30pm-late Mon-Sat. **Admission** €15 for non-members. **Credit** AmEx, MC, V. **Map** p251 F4.

You have to be 'somebody' to get in and, once inside, there are lots of reserved areas to negotiate. It looks to us like the crowd is just a bunch of hairdressers who think they're VIPs. If there are any celebs in here, they're safely tucked away in one of the reserved suites, being bored to death by Dublin's self-appointed elite. Staff are precious, and although the music can be good, everyone's far too worried about striking a pose to really let their hair down.

Dame Lane

4 Dame Lane, Around Temple Bar (679 0291). All cross-city buses. **Open** 5pm-2.30am Mon-Sat; 5pm-1am Sun. **Admission** free. **Credit** AmEx, DC, MC, V. **Map** p251 E3.

Pitching itself somewhere between a DJ bar and a nightclub, Dame Lane is a two-level, New York loft-style space, popular with club kids during the week and a hip, more professional crowd at the weekend. The bar downstairs is ideal for a quiet-ish drink, while upstairs is good for an incredibly loud drink. Neither really has a dancefloor, but that never seems to stop people, and as the night progresses, every inch of floor fills up. It can get claustrophobically crowded, but then, let's face it, so can pretty much everywhere else.

Pravda

35 Lower Liffey Street, Around O'Connell Street (874 0090). All cross-city buses/Luas Jervis. **Open** 4-11.30pm Mon-Wed; 4pm-2.30am Thur, Fri; noon-2.30am Sat; 12.30-11pm Sun. **Admission** free. **Credit** MC, V. **Map** p251 E2.

One of the more consistent spots on the north side of Dublin's River Liffey, this Russian-themed bar has comfy seating and a fine selection of vodkas, all surrounded by Soviet iconography. The bar hosts numerous themed music nights during the week, from funk to live bands; their latest offering, La République, combines short films, art and live music on Thursday nights.

Red Box

Old Harcourt Street Station, Harcourt Street, Around St Stephen's Green (478 0225/0166/www.pod.ie). All cross-city buses. **Open** varies; 10pm-3am most nights. **Admission** €5-€25. **Credit** MC, V. **Map** p251 E5.

Red Box has the biggest dancefloor in the city centre, so you can freak out with room to spare. It's all designed to create an explosive atmosphere, especially on nights when big-name guest DJs visit: keep an eye open for special events.

Ri Ra

Dame Court, off South Great George's Street, Around Temple Bar (677 4835/www.rira.ie). All cross-city buses. **Open** 11.30pm-2.30am daily. **Admission** €5-€10. **Credit** AmEx, DC, MC, V. **Map** p251 E4.

This place is a safe bet seven days a week. Mondays are particularly busy with Strictly Handbag (soul and '80s dancefloor fillers). Ri Ra has been in business for almost a decade and has acquired a small army of regulars who set a friendly if somewhat messy tone. The music policy varies, but the general theme is 'tunes to party to'. The door policy and dress code are relaxed.

Rogue

64 Dame Street, Around Temple Bar (675 3971). All cross-city buses. **Open** 5pm-4am daily. **Admission** varies. **Credit** MC, V. **Map** p251 E3.

Pitching itself against the hordes of super-bars that have sprung up all over Dublin in the last few years, Rogue is sister to the cosy New York bar of the same name (located in the fashionable Chelsea district of Manhattan). Its recently renovated downstairs hosts the hugely popular Bodytonic outfit, which mixes up some of the city's best-loved dance DJs with some fine international guest names.

Solas

31 Wexford Street, Around St Stephen's Green (478 0583). Bus 55, 61, 62, 83. **Open** 10.30am-12.30am Mon-Thur; 10.30am-1.30am Fri; 11.30am-1.30am Sat; 4pm-midnight Sun. **Admission** free. **Credit** AmEx, MC, V. **Map** p251 E5.

One of the city's first DJ bars, Solas is still a good spot at which to kick off your night. 'Smoking gardens' have sprung up in many bars around town since the indoor smoking ban, and this bar's recently furnished rooftop provides one of the best ones going. The music starts earlier than in many other bars, and it often seems to lean towards the jazzy-funky side of things. It's a fun place, but its principal drawback is a tendency to get absurdly crowded at weekends.

Spirit

57 Abbey Street Middle, Around O'Connell Street (877 9999/www.spiritdublin.com). All cross-city buses. **Open** 11pm-5am Thur-Sun. **Admission** varies. **Credit** MC, V. **Map** p251 F2.

In an attempt to bring Dublin's club culture to international level, Spirit has divided itself into three zones: Mind, an underground chillout area that lays on massage, holistic healing and beds; Body, the main bar; and Soul, a dance area with funky soul music. This place is for clubbers who realise that it's not all about drinking and dancing (though these activities are still encouraged). Spirit has a sister club in New York, but the Dublin branch has become rather naff.

Spy/Wax

Powerscourt Townhouse Centre, William Street South, Around Temple Bar (677 0014/www.spydublin.com). All cross-city buses. **Open** 6pm-3am daily. **Admission** *Spy* free Mon-Fri; €8 non-members after midnight Sat. *Wax* €5-€8 Mon-Sat. **Credit** MC, V. **Map** p251 F3.

Two flash, upmarket clubs in one: Spy upstairs, Wax downstairs. Spy is for those who like to watch and be watched rather than sweat on the dancefloor; Wax is all about the dancefloor, it's more of a weekend club, and the music is predominantly house and hip hop. This is an ideal spot for showing off, and the cocktails are fab. Spy has a dress code and a fairly strict door policy, but Wax goes the other way: if Spy is haute couture, Wax is jeans. The two clubs have separate entrances, but they connect inside. **Photo** *p182.*

Traffic. *See p186.*

Temple Bar Music Centre

Curved Street, Around Temple Bar (670 9202/www.tbmc.ie). All cross-city buses. **Open** varies, check local listings. **Admission** varies. **Credit** AmEx, MC, V. **Map** p251 E3.
One of the city's better music venues until 11.30pm, then a nightclub, this 1,000-capacity venue hosts a wide selection of club nights: indie to salsa to house to hip hop.

Traffic

54 Abbey Street Middle, Around O'Connell Street (873 4800/www.traffic54.net). All cross-city buses. **Open** 11pm-3am Fri, Sat. **Admission** €8 Fri; €10 Sat. **No credit cards. Map** p251 F2.
Traffic's glamorous decor might have you believe you've just walked into an uptight cocktail lounge. But this boozer attracts a serious clubbing crowd. **Photo** *p185.*

Twenty One

D'Olier Street, Around Trinity College (671 2089). All cross-city buses. **Admission** free. **Credit** MC, V. **Map** p251 F3.
Geared for the student crowd, week nights feature drinks promotions and schoolgirl outfits. Weekends are toned-down versions of the same.

Village

26 Wexford Street, Around St Stephen's Green (475 8555). Bus 16, 16A, 19, 19A. **Open** 11am-2.30am Mon-Sat; noon-1am Sun. **Admission** varies. **Credit** AmEx, MC, V. **Map** p251 E5.
The bar at Village is a focal point in the bustling Wexford Street area, with its late hours, free admission and a wildly eclectic music policy. It's no surprise that it pulls in the crowds – indeed, there's never a quiet night here, and although the Saturday crowds can be a touch suburban, it's one of Dublin's best bets for a wild night out.

Voodoo Lounge

39 Arran Quay, North Quays (873 6013). All cross-city buses. **Open** noon-12.30am Mon-Thur; noon-2am Fri, Sat; noon-1am Sun. **Credit** MC, V. **Map** p250 C2.
Voodoo is co-owned by NY rockers Fun Lovin' Criminals, who set the tone by hanging out here whenever they're in town. This is a popular late-night spot, and a good choice for signing off your pub crawl. The crowd is mixed, and the music slanted towards heavy rock and punk.

Whelan's

25 Wexford Street, Around St Stephen's Green (478 0766/www.whelanslive.com). Bus 16, 16A, 19, 19A, 122. **Open** 11pm-2.30am Thur-Sat. **Admission** €5 Thur; €7 Fri, Sat. **Credit** AmEx, MC, V. **Map** p251 E5.
Though more of a music venue than a nightclub, Whelan's still hosts some of the best indie and alternative club nights in town. Crowds here are a ragtag bunch, with only a love of music and beer in common. There's hardly a musician in the city who hasn't done time on Whelan's stage and at its bar. This place is a gem: perfect, even, if you don't want to go clubbing but still want to stay out late.

Pole dancing

With three separate Polish-language publications launched in Dublin in the past six months, it's become undeniably clear that there are a whole lot of Poles here. Such a large and sudden foreign influx may tend to provoke hostility, but these enterprising young immigrants have hit on a winning solution that has helped Irish people settle in all over the world: the pub.

Two Polish bars in particular are working the charm like Dubliners thought only they could. **Zagloba** (98 Parnell Street, 814 8648) leads the way. The bar's friendly atmosphere challenges the best of Irish shebeens. With live music and jazz throughout the week, Zagloba attracts a mixed crowd of Poles and natives and serves an interesting, if limited, menu of Polish fare prepared fresh daily. During daylight hours, the bar attracts mostly Poles looking for a taste of home, but at night it pulls in patrons from all over the city eager to sample the next big thing to hit the Dublin scene.

Then there's **Kanal** (15 Capel Street, 874 5850), which opened in 2005. It's notable as much for the food it serves as for anything else; the pork knuckles in beer sauce and the dumplings are highlights, best washed down with Leech beer or a home-brewed vodka. Armed with a penchant for steady daylight drinking, Poles have found themselves quite at home here in the alcohol stakes. However, the similarities between our two cultures go far beyond stews and booze. As the regular karaoke nights prove, the punters like to belt out a good tune too.

In a mirror image of the 'Brain Drain' from '80s Ireland, young Polish economists, dentists and vivisectionists have come here to find jobs. And the value of this new cultural influx goes far beyond public houses. But like Irish bars all over the world in the heyday of emigration, these provide a network for the emigrant population, as well as an atmosphere where both cultures can mingle and share their favourite pastime.

Sport & Fitness

Good, clean fun.

The fact that Dublin is a keen sporting city with a decent range of facilities is often overlooked (that is, when the Six Nations and other big tournaments are not in town). But, from a visitor's point of view, sport can provide a fast track into an area of Dublin life that's refreshingly free of tourist gloss. Racing, rugby, soccer and the indigenous games of Gaelic football and hurling are all popular and accessible spectator sports.

The most talked-about element of Dublin sporting life (in recent times, anyway) has been the regeneration of the **Lansdowne Road Stadium** (*photo p190*). At the time of writing, the necessary planning permission seemed to have been acquired, and the scheduled start date for regeneration work was January 2007. The duration of the work has been set at two years – supposing, of course, that every detail goes to plan.

To find out what's going on while you're in town, check the *Irish Times*, which prints a detailed daily sports diary. If you want in-depth knowledge of Irish sporting culture, two books by the country's top sports journalists, Tom Humphries' *Laptop Dancing and the Nanny Goat Mambo* and Con Houlihan's *More Than a Game*, are both superbly written.

Spectator sports

Gaelic football & hurling

Gaelic football is a cross between rugby and soccer, while hurling most closely resembles hockey. Both games are fast, furious and not for the faint of heart – as Ireland's national games, they're both treated with reverence.

The rules are fairly simple: in both games, teams of 15 players compete on a playing field with both rugby goalposts and soccer nets. Getting the ball in the net is worth three points (a goal), while putting it over the crossbar earns one. How each sport achieves this, however, is decidedly different.

Gaelic football's closest living relative is Australian-rules football – like soccer on speed – while hurling is also one of the world's fastest field sports. In hurling games the ball, or *sliothar*, is hit or carried along by a hurley stick; the clash of the ash and the aggressive momentum of the game make it incredibly

exciting to watch. Fragments of the ancient Brehon Laws show that hurling was played (and regulated) as early as the eighth century. It was banned by the English Crown in the 12th century, but when the British weren't looking the game continued to thrive. Today it vies with Gaelic football as the country's biggest sport.

Games are run by the **Gaelic Athletic Association** (*see p188*), an amateur organisation that holds a unique place in Irish life. There are GAA clubs in every parish, and the top players of each are selected for inter-county competition. Counties play for the league in winter and the more important **All-Ireland Championship** in summer. Big games are quintessentially Irish occasions that bring colour and passion to the streets and pubs, and if you see a preponderance of sky-blue football shirts with the three-castle city crest, you'll know that the local favourites are doing the business.

Dublin play some matches at **Parnell Park**, but the big games are played at the home of the GAA, **Croke Park** (*photo below*). Also, until the regeneration work at Lansdowne has been completed, Croke Park will be hosting all **Six Nations** matches, as well as various other rugby and soccer matches.

Croke Park. *See p188.*

Field of greens

The Irish National Baseball Field is not quite as grand as it sounds. There are no bleachers or stands, no popcorn vendors or beer stalls. Nobody sells those big foam 'We're Number 1' hands for you to wave around. Instead, the team plays in a public park and the fans sit on grassy banks around the field. There aren't too many of them.

This is a team that plays for itself and for pride. And, amazingly, it wins. It all started in 1996, when a cocky amateur softball team decided to try for the big time. The team made up of expat Americans and Irish business executives, teachers and shopkeepers who played weekends and after work, had never played on a real baseball diamond, never used a professional bat or glove, hadn't even hit a baseball (softballs are bigger and... softer). Still, they thought, how hard could it be? And they entered themselves in the European Championship. And they got whupped.

They lost their first game (against the Czech Republic) 23-2. Then they lost again. And again. In the end, they managed to score a total of 18 points, while their opponents succeeded in racking up a collective total of 77 points.

Croke Park

Jones Road, Drumcondra, Northern suburbs (836 3222/www.crokepark.ie). Bus 3, 11, 11A, 16, 51A. **Open** *Office* 9.30am-5.30pm Mon-Fri. **Tickets** €20-€30; €15 concessions. **No credit cards**.

Gaelic Athletic Association

Croke Park, Jones Road, Drumcondra, Northern suburbs (836 3222/www.gaa.ie). Bus 3, 11, 11A, 16, 51A. **Open** 9.30am-5.30pm Mon-Fri.

Parnell Park

Clantarkey Road, Donnycarney, Northern suburbs (831 0066/www.hill16.ie). Bus 20, 27, 27B, 42, 42A, 42B. **Tickets** €20-€60; €15 concessions. **No credit cards**.

Greyhound racing

The greyhound tracks at Harold's Cross and Shelbourne Park have bars and reasonable food offerings, as well as (between them) racing events six nights a week. Further information can be obtained from the **Greyhound Board** (Bord na gCon) at Shelbourne Park (*see below*).

Harold's Cross Racetrack

151 Harold's Cross Road, Harold's Cross, Southern suburbs (497 1081/www.igb.ie). Bus 16, 16A. **Open** *Racing* 6.30-10.30pm Mon, Tue, Fri. **Tickets** €10; €5 concessions. **No credit cards**.

Shelbourne Park

Lotts Road, Ringsend, Southern suburbs (668 3502/www.igb.ie). Bus 2, 3. **Open** *Racing* 6.30-10.30pm Wed, Thur, Sat. **Tickets** €8; €4 concessions. **Credit** MC, V.

Horse racing

The saying goes that all men are equal over and under the turf, and at Dublin's year-round horse races, the atmosphere in the stands, betting rings and bars is hard to beat. The **Curragh** racecourse (*see p189*) is the home of flat racing, hosting classic races, including the prestigious Irish Derby each summer. Steeplechasing is the major focus of racing in Ireland, though, and the Grand National takes place in April at **Fairyhouse** (*see p189*) in County Meath. Then there's the National Hunt Festival each spring

But they won one game (against then war-torn Yugoslavia), and that's what they hung on to.

They raised some money, they practised some more, they got some new team members, and in 2000 they headed back to the European Championships, this time in Croatia. They arrived, but their luggage didn't, so they attended the opening ceremony in flip-flops and shorts, while everyone else wore freshly pressed baseball uniforms. Then they lost brutally to Denmark, Finland and Croatia before finally eking out a 10-9 win against Hungary.

Inspired by this single victory, they practised some more, and in 2004 they astonished the crowds by winning the bronze medal at the same championships where they had been beaten twice before.

Now, they say, with no money and a great deal of faith, they are going for the gold in 2008.

Visitors to Dublin in the spring or summer can watch them play and admire their optimism at the National Fields (known universally as the Field of Dreams) at Corkagh Park in the west Dublin suburb of Clondalkin. For schedules and information, visit www.baseballireland.com.

at **Punchestown** (*see below*), while the four-day Leopardstown Festival, starting the day after Christmas at Leopardstown (*see below*), is one of the country's social highlights.

For race-day transport call **Dublin Bus** (873 4222, www.dublinbus.ie) for Leopardstown, and **Bus Éireann** (836 6111, www.buseireann.ie) or **Iarnród Éireann** (836 6222, www.irish rail.ie) for the others.

Curragh Racecourse
Curragh, Co Kildare (045 441 205). **Open** *Race times usually* 2.15pm or 2.30pm Sat, Sun; phone for details. **Tickets** €15-€50. **Credit** AmEx, DC, MC, V.

Fairyhouse Racecourse
Ratoath, Co Meath (825 6167/www.fairyhouse racecourse.ie). **Open** *phone for details.* **Tickets** €12-€25; €8-€20 concessions. **Credit** MC, V.

Leopardstown Racecourse
Foxrock, Co Dublin (289 3607/www.leopards town.com). Bus 46A/DART Blackrock then 114 bus/concessionary bus from the Luas on race days. **Open** *phone for details.* **Tickets** €14-€55; free under-14s. **Credit** MC, V (for pre-bookings).

National Stud
Tully, near Kildare, Co Kildare (045 521 617/ www.irish-national-stud.ie). **Open** *Feb-Nov* 9.30am-6pm daily. Closed Dec, Jan. **Admission** €9; €7 concessions; €20 family; €4.50 child; free under-5s. **Credit** MC, V.

Punchestown Racecourse
Naas, Co Kildare (045 897 704/www.punchestown.com). **Open** *phone for details.* **Tickets** €15; €8 concessions; free under-14s. **Credit** MC, V.

Rugby union

Rugby in Dublin was usually associated with the city's elite private schools, but the recent swing to professionalism has widened its appeal; provincial rugby in particular has really taken off. Leinster compete at Donnybrook in the **Inter-Provincial Championship** and the **Celtic League** (against teams from Scotland and Wales), but it's the hugely successful European cup contest that has been getting the most attention lately.

At the international level, the **Six Nations Championship** (Jan-Mar; *see p164*) is the highlight of the rugby year, and match weekends inspire cheerful debauchery among the sheepskin-and-hip-flask brigade. The national side will now play at Croke Park while Lansdowne Road is being regenerated. Contact the **Irish Rugby Football Union** (668 4601, www.irishrugby.ie) for more details.

Lansdowne Road Stadium
62 Lansdowne Road, Ballsbridge, Southern suburbs (668 4601/www.irishrugby.ie). DART Lansdowne Road. **Open** Call for details; for Six Nations tickets, contact Croke Park (*see p188*).

Soccer

When the national soccer team is doing well, their matches can bring the city to a standstill. On a local level, check out the **Eircom League**, where crowd enthusiasm and gritty passion take precedence over the ostentatious glamour and self-indulgence that is so often associated with top English sides these days. Your best bet for atmosphere and facilities is **Dalymount Park** in Phibsborough, home to Bohemians FC.

Contact the **Football Association of Ireland** (676 6864, www.fai.ie) for information about fixtures.

Bohemians FC
Dalymount Park, Phibsborough, Northern suburbs (868 0923/www.bohemians.ie). Bus 10, 19, 19A, 38, 120. **Tickets** €15; €5-€8 concessions. **No credit cards.**

Arts & Entertainment

Shamrock Rovers

35 Boyne House, Greenmount Office Park, Harold's Cross (709 3620/www.shamrockrovers.ie). **Tickets** €15; €5-€10 concessions. **No credit cards.**
Following a recent relegation, the Rovers now find themselves in the reduced circumstances of the First Division of the Eircom League (the Premier Division is where they fell from). Games are still great fun, though, and well worth turning up to. At the time of writing, plans were to relocate to 9 Centre Point Business Park, Oak Road, Dublin 12. But check the website, just to be sure.

Shelbourne FC

Tolka Park, Richmond Road, Drumcondra, Northern suburbs (837 5536/www.shelbournefc.ie). Bus 3, 11, 11A, 13, 16, 16A. **Tickets** €15; €6 concessions. **No credit cards.**

Active sports & fitness

Golf

More than 60 golf courses sprawl across County Dublin, including some of the finest links in the world. Most accept visitors, but green fees vary greatly. Corballis near Donabate has two decent cheap courses: **Corballis Links** (843 6583, www.golfdublin.com), which is always in good nick and has the potential to reduce any golfer to tears, and the **Island** (843 6205, www.the islandgolfclub.com), which is one of the city's

Lansdowne Road Stadium. *See p189.*

most dramatic golfing venues. **Hollystown** (820 7444, www.hollystown.com) in Mulhuddart is pleasant but deceptively simple, and it boasts a lovely clubhouse. **Grange Castle** (464 1043, www.pgasportmanagement.com), 20 minutes from the city centre near Clondalkin, is set in the grounds of Kilcarberry House; it's slightly busier and more expensive than the others, but the cost is reflected in the quality of the course.

The upmarket **Portmarnock Hotel and Golf Links** (846 0611, www.portmarnock.com) is superb; equally impressive is the adjacent and slightly controversial **Portmarnock Golf Club** (846 2968, www.portmarnockgolfclub.ie), which has hosted many Irish Opens. The **K Club** in Straffan is also excellent. Expect to pay up to €200 for a game at these.

Contact **Dublin Corporation** (222 2222, www.dublincity.ie) for details of cheaper courses and prices (including pitch-and-putt). A complete list of private courses can be obtained from the **Golfing Union of Ireland** (Glencar House, 81 Eglinton Road, Donnybrook, Dublin 4, 269 4111, www.gui.ie).

Gyms & fitness centres

Contrary to any popular misconceptions about their Guinness consumption, the Irish are as into physical fitness, gyms and workouts as anybody else, so there are plenty of modern, well-equipped workout facilities in Dublin.

Crunch Fitness

UCD Campus, Belfield, Southern suburbs (260 3155). Bus 10, 11, 46A. **Open** 7am-10pm Mon-Fri; 10am-5.30pm Sat, Sun. **Rates** €12 per visit; €6.50 student. **Credit** MC. V.
The University College health centre is fully equipped with CV machines and free weights, and it hosts regular aerobics classes.
Other locations: The Pavilion, Marine Road, Dun Laoghaire (280 1299).

Markievicz Leisure Centre

Townsend Street, Around Trinity College (672 9121/www.dublincity.ie). DART Tara Street/all cross-city buses. **Open** 7am-9.45pm Mon-Thur; 7am-8.45pm Fri; 9am-6pm Sat; 9am-4pm Sun. **Rates** €5.50-€6.60 per visit. **Map** p251 G3.
This centre, which is run by the Dublin Corporation, is relatively inexpensive; it has a fully equipped gym, swimming pool and sauna.

YMCA Gym

Aungier Street, Around Temple Bar (478 2607/ www.ymca.ie). Bus 16, 16A, 19, 19A. **Open** 7.30am-10pm Mon-Fri; 9.30am-4.30pm Sat. **Rates** €5 per visit. **Credit** MC, V. **Map** p253 E4.
This place is conveniently central, and the great advantage for visitors who want to work off the holiday weight is that anyone can use its small fitness classes on a pay-as-you-go basis.

Theatre & Dance

Dublin's performance arts have a glorious past and a thriving present.

If Ireland has a reputation for literature, it's mostly down to its dramatists. There's one Irish lion among novelists – Joyce – and one among the poets – Yeats – but it's only when you get to the stage that the names start tripping off the tongue: Sheridan, Wilde, Shaw, O'Casey, Beckett, Behan, Friel, McDonagh. We could go on. From 1771 (Goldsmith's *She Stoops to Conquer*) to 1913 (Shaw's *Pygmalion*), most of the comedies written for the London stage were by Irishmen. Since Shaw, Irish plays have tended to be regional and idiomatic (with the great exception of Beckett), and they need Irish actors. Admittedly, Synge's *Playboy of the Western World* was performed to great acclaim in Chinese in Beijing in March 2006, but it's impossible to think of O'Casey, Behan or Friel being performed in any but Irish accents.

Theatre

Classics from the Irish canon – *The Importance of Being Earnest, Waiting for Godot* and the like – are performed with steady regularity and varying quality by the country's two most venerable theatres, the **Abbey** and the **Gate**. Every decade or so, Dublin audiences are treated to an iconic performance of one of these, which then proves an impossible act to follow.

The best bets for new, avant-garde work are the **Peacock** and the **Project**, which host independent experimental companies such as **Coisceim** and **Rough Magic** (for both, *see p194*). A number of classy, state-of-the-art theatres – the **Helix**, the **Draoiocht**, the **Civic** – have recently gone up in the Northside suburbs. They generally act as receiving houses for touring productions.

Tickets & information

The *Dublin Event Guide* and Thursday's *Irish Times* both contain listings and reviews; the *Dubliner* is more selective but carries intelligent reviews of the bigger productions. Most Dublin theatres and companies produce their own leaflets, generally found in tourist centres, hotels and cafés. In addition, the *Golden Pages* phone directory has a particularly useful theatre information section.

THE GATE THEATRE

All set at **The Gate**. See p193.

Tickets for some theatres are available through **TicketMaster** at HMV on Grafton Street, though it charges a booking fee (0818 719 300, from outside Ireland 456 9569, www.ticket master.ie). Other tickets should be bought directly from the individual theatres.

Theatre venues

The Abbey

26 Abbey Street Lower, Around O'Connell Street (box office 878 7222/www.abbeytheatre.ie). All cross-city buses. **Open** *Box office* 10.30am-7pm Mon-Sat. **Tickets** €15-€30; €9.50 concessions Mon-Thur, Sat matinée; €15 previews. **Credit** MC, V. **Map** p251 G2.
Established by WB Yeats and Lady Gregory in 1904 to further the nationalist cause, the Abbey opened to glorious controversy – Synge's *Playboy of the Western World* (1907) and O'Casey's *Plough and the Stars* (1926) were considered so shocking in conservative Dublin (in particular Synge's use of the word 'shift' to mean knickers) that they were met with riots. Contemporary playwrights would kill for that kind of publicity, but unfortunately things haven't been so exciting since, though the Abbey still gets loads of column inches, mostly from people railing against its creative mire – 'Abbey-bashing' is a favourite national pastime, and very tedious it is too. OK, the Abbey's not what it was in the days of Synge, Yeats and O'Casey, and its record on discovering new talent would make an A&R man in the Midlands look good, but could we move on, please? It's had its moments – most notably in furthering the careers of Brian Friel and Tom Murphy – and presumably will again. Admittedly, now is not one of those moments… For the past five years or so, the national theatre has been in the doldrums, with a long, procrastinated row over where it should be relocated (this seems to be solved – it's going to the Docklands) and the resignation in 2005 of the artistic and managing directors. It's still struggling – the 2006 programme falls back on the tried and tested (Wilde and Sheridan) – and needs an injection of dynamism if it wants to fill its seats with anything other than the passing trade of tourists.

Andrew's Lane Theatre

9-17 Andrew's Lane, off Exchequer Street, Around Temple Bar (679 5720/www.andrewslane.com). All cross-city buses. **Open** *Box office* 10.30am-7pm Mon-Sat. **Tickets** varies. **Credit** AmEx, MC, V. **Map** p251 E/F3.
One of only a few specifically commercial theatres in Dublin, Andrew's Lane hosts a variety of touring provincial companies and international acts offering both dramatic and musical works. It usually goes with crowd-pleasers like the *Vagina Monologues*, but the small studio upstairs shows more experimental stuff. The building itself isn't the most comfortable – run-down, featureless and cold in winter – but the atmosphere is easy-going and audiences are clearly out to enjoy themselves.

Bewley's Café Theatre

Grafton Street, Around St Stephen's Green (information 086 878 4001). All cross-city buses. **Open** *Shows* 1.10pm Mon-Sat. **Tickets** (at the door) €12 incl soup & sandwiches. **No credit cards.** **Map** p251 F4.
Dublin's only year-round venue for lunchtime drama, this café theatre is an elegant and intimate space that has a reputation for staging exciting, innovative productions of classics and new Irish works. In addition to the lunchtime shows, evening productions take place here from time to time, and it really comes into its own during the fringe festival (*see p195* **Fringe benefits**). **Photo** *right.*

Civic Theatre

Tallaght Town Centre, Tallaght, Southern suburbs (462 7477/www.civictheatre.ie). Bus 49, 49A, 50, 54A, 56A, 65, 65B, 77, 77A. **Open** *Box office* 10am-6pm Mon-Sat. **Tickets** *Main auditorium* €18-€20; €12 concessions. *Studio* €15; €12 concessions. **Credit** MC, V.
The windy suburbs of Tallaght may be a far cry from theatreland, but trekking out to this 350-seater – a bright state-of-the-art space with a studio, restaurant, bar and gallery – can be rewarding. This is primarily a receiving house for established provincial and international touring productions.

Draiocht

Blanchardstown Centre, Blanchardstown, Northern suburbs (885 2622/www.draiocht.ie). Bus 38, 38A, 39, 39X, 236, 237, 239, 270. **Open** *Box office* 10am-6pm Mon-Sat. **Tickets** varies. **Credit** MC, V.
This well-appointed suburban theatre also has studio space, an art gallery and a handy bar. Like the Civic, Draiocht acts as a receiving house, playing host to a broad range of performing and visual arts, both national and international, from stand-up comedy, dance and children's shows to music recitals and dynamic contemporary theatre.

Focus

6 Pembroke Place, off Pembroke Street Upper, Around St Stephen's Green (676 3071). Bus 10, 11, 13, 46A. **Open** *Box office* 10am-5pm Mon-Fri; noon-5pm Sat. **Tickets** €12-€16. **No credit cards.** **Map** p251 G5.
Tiny, high-minded, and the only Stanislavsky theatre in Dublin, the Focus was the brainchild of Irish-American actress/director Deirdre O'Connell, who came to Dublin in the 1960s, married Luke Kelly of the Dubliners, founded this theatre with its affiliated actors' studio and was for 40 years a Dublin legend. Since her death in 2001, the theatre has been run by Joe Devlin and continues, in the tradition of its founder, to show avant-garde, experimental plays with its Stanislavsky-trained actors.

Gaiety

King Street South, Around St Stephen's Green (677 1717/www.gaietytheatre.com). All cross-city buses. **Open** *Box office* 11am-7pm Mon-Sat. **Tickets** €20-€35 plays; €32-€78 opera. **Credit** AmEx, MC, V. **Map** p251 F4.

Bewley's Café Theatre. *See p192.*

The Gaiety is a lovely Victorian chocolate box-style theatre that hosts the Christmas pantos and the spring opera season. It also caters for classic Irish plays and West End shows during the theatre festival. Problem is that if you've been brought up going to the panto every Christmas, you can't take any other production at the Gaiety seriously – 'Oh no, he didn't!' you want to shout as soon as you settle into those velvet seats, never mind that it's Hamlet's ghost, not the Ugly Sisters on stage… For the past eight years it's also hosted a weekend club, so now the stench of beer and memories of last night's revellers mingle with the panto catcalls.

The Gate

1 Cavendish Row, Around O'Connell Street (874 4045/www.gate-theatre.ie). All cross-city buses. **Open** *Box office* 10am-7pm Mon-Sat. **Tickets** €23-€25; €16 previews. **Credit** AmEx, MC, V. **Map** p251 F2.
The Abbey's misfortune is the Gate's opportunity. While the national theatre has been foundering since the start of the millennium, its younger, sassier rival has gone from strength to strength. The year 2006 was triumphant, opening with Ralph Fiennes and Ian McDiarmuid in Friel's classic *The Faith Healer*, then moving seamlessly into a Beckett season – showcasing John Hurt, Michael Gambon and Barry McGovern – to celebrate the writer's centenary. The Gate's director, Michael Colgan, runs a shrewd operation, mixing international stars with local greats in quality productions that have them queuing for returns. He's helped by having the most elegant, spacious theatre in the city and by a rambunctious, cosmopolitan legacy. The Gate was founded in 1928 by the flamboyant, legendary, homosexual duo Hilton

Edwards and Micheál MacLiammóir (both English, MacLiammóir gaelicised his name), who for forty years fed an eager public with an uncompromising diet of avant-garde experimental Irish and international plays. That cosmopolitan legacy allows Colgan to cast his net wide, unlike the poor Abbey, which, as the 'national theatre', seems condemned to unadulterated Irish fare. **Photos** *p191.*

The Helix

Dublin City University, Collins Avenue, Glasnevin, Northern suburbs (700 7000/www.helix.ie). Bus 11, 13, 19A. **Open** *Box Office* 10am-6pm Mon-Sat. **Tickets** varies. **Credit** MC, V.
This performance space on the northern campus of Dublin City University is home to three separate venues, and hosts a wide variety of theatre, music and popular entertainment. Programming is eclectic: the Helix has hosted everything from big bands to ballet, while gigs by heavyweights like Van Morrison and Lou Reed have bolstered the venue's reputation even further. In short, the Helix is a fine and much-needed addition to the arts scene in the north of the city.

Olympia

72 Dame Street, Around Temple Bar (679 3323/ tickets 0818 719 330/www.mcd.ie/olympia). All cross-city buses. **Open** *Box office* 10.30am-6.30pm Mon-Sat. **Tickets** varies. **Credit** AmEx, MC, V. **Map** p251 E3.
This old-style variety theatre – it was Dublin's first music hall – retains its physical characteristics (many of them authentically grimy) but has largely parted company with straight theatre. It's an occa-

Dance Theatre of Ireland.

spaces host theatre, dance, video and film, contemporary and popular music, cultural debates and performance pieces, making this Dublin's main venue for the new, the innovative and the cutting-edge.

Samuel Beckett Centre
Trinity College, Around Trinity College (608 2266/www.tcd.ie/drama). All cross-city buses. **Open** *Box office (during show)* 11am-6pm Mon-Fri. *Week before a show starts* 11am-6pm Mon-Fri; 10am-5pm Sat. **Tickets** varies. **Credit** MC, V. **Map** p251 F3.
Built in the mid 1990s for Trinity College's drama course, the Samuel Beckett Centre is a neat, wooden building housing a small, technically superb stage. Ideal for small productions – especially those written by its eponymous author because you can easily snuff out all natural light – it caters mainly for Trinity students, but roving theatre and dance companies occasionally pitch camp here as well.

Tivoli
135-138 Francis Street, Around Kilmainham (454 4472). Bus 50, 78A. **Open** *Box office (during show)* 10am-6pm Mon-Sat. **Tickets** varies. **Credit** MC, V. **Map** p250 D4.
This place hosts all manner of live entertainment, from serious drama to musicals. Irish and international shows feature in equal measure, but don't expect to see anything radical.

Dance

There's *Riverdance* and then there's dance in Ireland. And dance companies in Ireland have suffered, and continue to struggle. Why? Because, while the Irish like their small daughters to hop around in embroidered skirts, and might even join a set themselves if sufficiently drunk, there's no tradition of sitting still on seats watching dancers move through a narrative. A short-lived national ballet company dissolved in 1989 and there hasn't been one since. In its stead, a few small, dedicated and talented companies keep the art of dance alive.

Dance companies

Coisceim
14 Sackville Place, Around O'Connell Street (878 0558/www.coisceim.com).
This inventive ensemble – its name is Gaelic for 'footstep' – owes much of its success to the stylish choreography of artistic director David Bolger. Founded in 1995, Coisceim has collaborated with theatre companies such as Rough Magic and the Peacock. A good number of its shows are original pieces written by Bolger.

Dance Theatre of Ireland
Bloomfields Centre, Lower Georges Street, Dún Laoghaire, Dublin Bay (280 3455/www.dance theatreireland.com).

sional venue for well-known international stand-up comedians, but these days its cavernous auditorium usually reverberates with the sound of big-name rock and pop acts.

The Peacock
26 Abbey Street Lower, Around O'Connell Street (box office 878 7222/www.abbeytheatre.ie). All cross-city buses. **Open** *Box office* 10.30am-7pm. **Tickets** varies. **Credit** MC, V.
The Peacock is the experimental arm of the Abbey and has a small stage in the vaults of that larger theatre. It seems to escape all the scandals and carping directed at the Abbey and is a happier, more relaxed place. You'll see some excellent small productions here – but it has to be said that, for a theatre set up to showcase new Irish talent, it doesn't seem to have discovered anyone since Frank McGuinness in 1986. All the new crop, Martin McDonagh, Marina Carr, Conor McPherson et al, got their start elsewhere.

Project Arts Centre
39 Essex Street East, Around Temple Bar (box office 881 9613/administration 679 6622/www.project.ie). All cross-city buses. **Open** *Box office* 10am-6pm Mon-Sat. **Tickets** €10-€20; phone for details of preview and concession prices. **Credit** MC, V. **Map** p251 E3.
Project began 35 years ago as a visual arts project in the foyer of the Gate (*see p193*), and settled into these refurbished premises in 2000. The building's three multi-functional performance and exhibition

Arts & Entertainment

Known for the arresting visual quality of its work, this group performs material devised by its two artistic directors, Robert Connor and Loretta Yurick. Recently, the dancers have added a multimedia dimension to their performances, with interactive digital technology and fantastic backdrops. The company's Centre for Dance offers public classes in contemporary, jazz and salsa. **Photo** *p194*.

Irish Modern Dance Theatre

23 Upper Sherrard Street, Northern suburbs (874 9616/www.irishmoderndancetheatre.com)
Performing ambitious new works to original music by young composers, the Irish Modern Dance Theatre, run by John Scott, collaborates frequently with artists such as the playwright Tom MacIntyre and photographer Chris Nash, and it has strong links with international dance companies.

Traditional Irish dance

Traditional Irish dancing is still a big thing, but not in Dublin. If you're keen on it, you'll need to make the trip further west to Clare, Galway or Limerick, which hosts the Blas Summer School of Irish Traditional Music

and Dance (www.ul.ie/~iwmc/blas/). However, if you are confined to Dublin, you can still stumble across the odd impromptu session. You're guaranteed a set at the two venues listed below, but they're smoothly touristic, rather than spontaneous. Still, if it's your first experience of the genre, you may well find it highly entertaining.

Cultúrlann na hÉireann

32 Belgrave Square, Monkstown, Dublin Bay (280 0295/www.comhaltas.com). Bus 7, 8. **Open** *Dancing* 9pm Fri. **Admission** €8. **No credit cards.**
Cultúrlann na hÉireann (the Irish Cultural Institute) hosts popular large ceilidhs or communal dances, just like in the good old dance-hall days. They attract a mix of committed locals and curious tourists.

O'Shea's Merchant

12 Bridge Street Lower, Around North Quays (679 3797). Bus 21, 21A. **Open** *Dancing* 9pm-12.30am daily. **Admission** free. **Credit** AmEx, MC, V. **Map** p250 D3.
This atmospheric pub not only offers trad music and set dancing seven nights a week – you can also get a nice pint and relax here.

Fringe benefits

In 2005, on its tenth anniversary, Dublin's Fringe came of age. Formerly tied to the city's main Theatre Festival like a whining smaller brother, it has now cut loose and set up shop alone. It takes place in September in the fortnight before the festival, is entirely separate, uses different venues and has a different ethos. Where the festival is purist (only theatre allowed) and extremely rigorous in selection – just 22 shows in 2005 – the Fringe is eclectic and wide-ranging, with 130 shows in 2005, covering theatre, music, dance, visual arts and comedy.

From 2006, however, Fringe director Wolfgang Hoffmann wanted to concentrate and streamline: there were be 100 shows over two weeks, instead of the three weeks the Fringe used to run for. Highlights included a **Lantern Trail**: all along the Liffey from Grattan Bridge to George's Dock (about a mile) lanterns of all shapes and sizes, made by 100 different artists, illuminated the city. This annual event will be the visual face of the Fringe. The **Spiegeltent** (a large, ornate, mirrored style of tent, first used in Weimar Germany in the 1930s), which since 2001 has been a focal point of the Fringe, was set up again in George's Dock, catering

specifically for music acts. After midnight it became the Fringe Club (artists performing in the Fringe got in free – everyone else paid just a fiver to party till 2.30am).

Other Fringe venues include the **Project Arts Centre**, the **Samuel Beckett Centre** and **Bewley's Café Theatre** – all the small, funky venues the city has to offer, in other words. The bigger theatres are reserved for the festival proper. About half of the acts are international, the other half Irish. The dance acts – in the Project and the Samuel Beckett – are a rare chance to see dance in Ireland that isn't *Riverdance*. Hoffmann, a former dancer himself, wants to establish in Dublin a tradition of watching contemporary dance.

The way to enjoy the Fringe is to go to as many shows as possible and end up as many nights as possible in the Spiegeltent after hours. The more you see, the more you get into the whole thing – the atmosphere is informal and relaxed; possibilities for mingling with actors, musicians, writers and directors are excellent; you start recognising people from shows the night before; and Dublin begins to feel like a small village. This is the last event of the year before autumn draws in – give yourself over to it.
The Fringe (8171 677/www.fringefest.com).

Time Out
Travel Guides

British Isles

Trips out of Town

Feature boxes

Kilkenny Castle. *See p218.*

Getting Started

Get out of town.

Mellifont Abbey. See p204.

It won't take you long to discover that Dublin is a fairly small city. In a few days you'll have seen most of the major sights, imbibed in plenty of its classic pubs and dined in enough of its pricey restaurants. In fact, just about the time you find yourself actually considering checking out the Museum of Banking, perhaps it might be a good idea to rent a car (or hop on a train or bus) and get out of town.

The countryside around Dublin is a lure in itself: to the north, in **Newgrange**, rolling green hills hold mysterious ancient burial sites (*see pp199-204*), while, to the south, the **Wicklow Mountains** surround gorgeous **Glendalough** (*see pp205-212*). Further south still is beautiful **Kilkenny**, with its arts shops, towering castles and rambling ruined abbeys (*see pp213-218*). All are within a couple of hours' journey from the city.

GETTING AROUND

The best way to see the countryside is by car. You can get to the major towns by train or bus, but then you miss out on the lovely scenery and the quaint villages in the surrounding countryside, as most are not accessible by public transport. Some sights are well out of any town and quite isolated, and there's no way to reach them without your own transport. For our list of car rental agencies in Dublin, *see p224*. Otherwise, the train service **Iarnród Éireann** and the bus service **Bus Éireann** (for both, *see pp221-223*) each have wide-ranging coverage to the bigger towns, although connections between rural stations are often lacking. Buses leave from the Central Bus Station (**Busárus**) on Store Street (*see p222*), while trains depart from **Heuston** and **Connolly** stations.

INFORMATION

The **Irish Tourist Board** (Bord Fáilte, *see p235*) has local outposts in most bigger cities, and some small towns have their own tourist offices. In Dublin, your first point of call should be the **Dublin Tourism Centre** (*see p235*), where you'll find reams of literature and maps, as well as advice on hotels, car hire and good routes to take. Those interested in countryside walks may want to check out the helpful website for the wonderfully redundantly named **National Waymarked Ways Advisory Committee**, www.walkireland.ie. The information, though, is bang up to date.

Newgrange & the Boyne Valley

North into Ireland's past.

The rising star of **Drogheda**. See p202.

With its quiet, hilly pastures dotted with fluffy white sheep, the area just north of Dublin may look like your typical Irish countryside, but this is much more than that. This is where Ireland began. This is the home of the **Hill of Tara** – Ireland's Olympus, where kings ruled the country 1,000 years ago, aided, it was said, by fairies.

By then, though, the land was already very old. County Meath's rich soil has attracted settlers for more than 8,000 years, and archaeologists have uncovered burial grounds and ruined settlements that indicate this was a thriving region millennia ago. The best known of the ancient sites is **Newgrange**, with its mysterious carvings and huge stone passage tomb. Nearby, the **Hill of Slane**, a lofty 150-metre (492-foot) mound, overlooks one of the loveliest parts of the Boyne Valley. On this hill, according to tradition, a Welsh priest lit a Christian fire in direct defiance of the pagan

Irish King Laoghaire, thus beginning the first confrontation between religious orders in a country that was to see more than its fair share of them over the centuries.

The chief town of County Meath is **Navan**, but nearby **Kells** is better known because of its famous Book of Kells, the hand-illustrated gospel manuscript on display at Trinity College (*see p59*) in Dublin.

Still, even given the lush, rolling green hills, the charming villages and the bracing sea views, everybody really comes this way for one thing: namely, Newgrange.

Newgrange & Knowth

The ancient site at **Newgrange** is both mythological and real: it's one of the most important Stone Age sites in Europe and also, in Irish lore, the home of the Tuatha de Danainn, cave-dwelling worshippers of the

The ruins of **Mellifont Abbey**. See p204.

goddess Danu. The deep cavern is covered in strange, geometric patterns (of the sort you'll find reproduced on jewellery sold at Glastonbury), and the meanings of the mysterious zigzags, ovals and crazy spirals have never been fully explained.

What is known for certain is that the ancient passage mounds were built 5,000 years ago, when most tools were made of bone, flint and metal, and then not discovered again until 1699. But how and why the members of a small farming community moved rocks weighing 50 tons over massive distances through inhospitable terrain remains a mystery.

For many, the most interesting part of Newgrange is probably this: the tomb's passageway descends 19 metres (62 feet), and the only time light reaches its depths is on the shortest day of the year. The cavern was, therefore, designed to align with the winter solstice so that when the sun rises on 21 December, a ray of light sweeps down the long passageway and strikes the back chamber, where it is believed that the ashes of the dead were once kept.

You can learn more about it all at the helpful **Bru na Boinne Visitor Centre** (see p201), near the town of Donore. The centre also covers (and provides access to) the ancient site of **Knowth**. Like Newgrange, Knowth is a passage mound decorated with spirals, triangles, concentric circles and other stone carvings. Most unusually, though, Knowth has two passage graves, and its central mound has two chambers – one pointing east and the other west; the eastern passage is an impressive 40 metres (130 feet) long. Like Newgrange, Knowth was designed with the sun in mind, but here light shines on the centre chamber during both spring and autumnal equinoxes. While both

Newgrange and Knowth are generally referred to as 'passage tombs', and both undoubtedly functioned as burial places, archaeologists think there may have been much more to them than that; they're just not sure what. They may have been temples or even astronomical observatories.

Access to both Newgrange and Knowth is now handled by the visitor centre. You park at the centre and then are shuttled to the sites from there. In the summertime this system can lead to very long waits, so be prepared. Some swear that if you show up early, you can dodge the masses; we're not so sure, but if you show up late, you might not get to see anything at all. Patience is a virtue… Since you may have to wait for ages, it's a good thing the centre has a museum, informative videos, full-scale models, camp re-creations and decent grub.

If you can't deal with the crowds, you might want to try **Four Knocks** (Na Fuarchnoic), a much smaller, less well-known ancient tomb near the town of Naul. Often deserted in winter, it is quiet even in summer. You can explore it at your leisure and picnic on the grassy roof: it's wonderful to have a 5,000-year-old site to yourself. The key is held by Fintan White and is available (for a refundable deposit) until 6pm daily. Fintan lives about a mile away from the site; for directions and further details, visit www.knowth.com/fourknocks.

Once back at the site (follow the signs from Naul), follow the gorse-lined track. The tomb consists of a heavy iron door and a short passage leading into a wide, pear-shaped chamber. Just inside the main chamber to the left of the entrance is the oldest-known representation of a human face in Europe, as well as many other strange symbols carved in the stone. You'd do well to bring a torch, but if you forget, check the ledge on the left to see if one's still kept there. You never know – this is the countryside, after all.

The passage graves are near the **Boyne Valley**, where the Battle of the Boyne took place in 1690. In 1688 the Catholic King James II was deposed in favour of his Protestant daughter Mary. In a bid to regain his throne, James fought William of Orange's army at Oldbridge, but his troops were routed, and he had to flee to France. This is where you will find **Slane Castle**, whose grounds were landscaped by famed British gardener 'Capability' Brown.

On the **Hill of Slane**, outside the town, Saint Patrick lit an Easter bonfire in 433 as a challenge to the authority of the Kings of Tara; the subsequent spread of Christianity eroded the power of the pagan rulers. A statue of Patrick marks the spot today.

You can see the other side of that story when you're heading back towards Dublin on the N3. On the way, you'll pass the **Hill of Tara**, once the seat of the High Kings of Ireland. Tara is the spiritual capital of ancient Ireland and the fount of much folklore. The site is free, and there's a visitors' centre inside the church at the top of the hill where you can learn more about the ancient rulers. Sadly, a motorway (described by academics and opponents as 'a national and international tragedy') is being built nearby, and it will inevitably affect the ambience.

The *Táin Bó Cúailnge* ('Cattle Raid of Cooley') is set around these parts. First written in the eighth century, it has been described as Ireland's *Iliad*. It tells the story of Queen Maeve of Connaught's efforts to obtain an exceptional Brown Bull from the people of Ulster (100 fighting men could rest in its shade and thrice 50 boys could sport on his broad back), and how she is foiled ultimately by one of Ireland's great folk heroes, Cú Chulainn.

Near the Hill of Tara, the town of **Trim** is well worth a visit. Best among its many sights is **Trim Castle**, an impressive Anglo-Norman castle. Hugh de Lacy began work on its construction in 1172; when completed, the castle's 20-sided tower had walls three metres (11 feet) thick. It was built to be impregnable – three storeys high, protected by a ditch, a curtain wall and a moat – but the English nevertheless managed to get in (twice) during the English civil war. It was abandoned after Cromwell and his cronies departed. If you think the castle looks familiar, that might be because you've seen *Braveheart*, in which it was used as a stand-in for York.

The building across the river from the castle is **Talbot Castle**, a grand manor house that dates back to 1415. Also impressive is **Sheep**

Gate, which is the one remaining segment of the town's original 14th-century walls. No prizes for guessing what it was used for.

If you feel up to a walk from here, you can follow the Dublin road from Trim Castle, crossing the river to the ruins of **St Patrick's Church** (follow the signs). This lovely medieval ruin has well-preserved gravestones, including a 16th-century tomb known locally as the 'jealous couple'; this comes from the fact that the effigies on the tomb lie with a sword carved in between them.

Get maps and local information from the handy local **visitor centre** (*see below*), which also has a small historical display.

About 20 kilometres (12 miles) north of Trim (or 12 miles west of Newgrange), in the north-west of the county on the N52, is the market town of **Kells**. This community was first established as a religious settlement in 550, and is most famed for its *Book of Kells*. The book is now kept in Trinity College, which reduces the town's power of tourist attraction somewhat, although there are some fine Celtic crosses here as well as a Round Tower. There's also the lovely old **Church of St Columba** in the town centre, which is most notable for standing where the monastic settlement that first received the *Book of Kells* once stood.

Bru na Boinne Visitor Centre

Donore (041 988 0300). **Open** *Nov-Feb* 9.30am-5pm daily. *Mar, Apr, Oct* 9.30am-5.30pm daily. *May, Sept* 9am-6.30pm daily. *June-mid Sept* 9am-7pm daily. **Admission** *Centre* €2.90; €1.60 children. *Centre & Newgrange* €5.80; €2.90 children. *Centre, Newgrange & Knowth* €10.30; €4.50 children. *Centre & Knowth* €4.50; €2.90 children. **Credit** MC, V.

Slane Castle

Slane (041 982 4207). **Open** *May-July* noon-5pm Mon-Thur, Sun. **Admission** €7. **Credit** MC, V.

Trim Castle

Trim (046 943 8619). **Open** *Easter-Oct* 10am-6pm daily. *Nov-Easter* 10am-5pm Sat, Sun. **Admission** *Keep (with guided tour)* €3.70; €1.30 children; €8.70 family. *Grounds only* €1.60; €1.10 children; €4.25 family. **No credit cards**.

Where to eat & drink

One of the best things you can do when coming to this area is bring a picnic lunch with you: County Meath is not famed for its cuisine. You can pick up makings of a picnic in Kells at the Tesco on the High Street. If you prefer for somebody else to cook for you, Pebbles (Newmarket Street, Kells; closed Sun, no phone) is a decent greasy-spoon diner popular with the locals. For more stylish fare, try the Vanilla Pod, which uses fresh, local ingredients in its modern

Irish cuisine (John Street, Kells, 046 0084). Lots of pubs have adequate food, particularly in Trim, Slane and Kells. Alternatively, in Trim you could try Kerr's Kitchen (Haggard Street, 046 943 7144, closed Sat & Sun) for sandwiches to go. In Kells, the Ground Floor Restaurant (Bective Square, 046 924 9688, main courses €9.95-€25.50) is an excellent bistro with good food and a great atmosphere.

Where to stay

Near Newgrange try the **Bondique House** in Cullen (Beauparc, 041 982 4823, rates €25-€50 per person), which has affordable rooms, some with en suite. Alternatively, in Trim, the **Wellington Court Hotel** (Summhill Road, 046 943 1108, rates €65 per person) has a grand entrance, 18 rooms and a popular restaurant.

Tourist information

Kells Heritage Centre and Tourist Office

The Courthouse, Headfoot Place, Kells (046 924 7840/www.meathtourism.ie). **Open** *May-Sept* 10am-6pm Mon-Fri; 10am-5.30pm Sat; 2-6pm Sun. *Oct-Apr* 10am-5pm Mon-Sat.

Navan Tourist Office

21 Ludlow Street, Navan, near Newgrange (046 907 3426/www.meathtourism.ie). **Open** *Mar-Dec* 9.30am-5pm Mon-Fri.

Trim Visitor Centre

Castle Street, Trim (046 943 7227/www.meath tourism.ie). **Open** 10am-5pm Mon-Thur; 10am-6pm Fri, Sat; noon-5.30pm Sun.

Getting there

By bus

There are buses to Navan and Slane several times a day from **Busáras** (€10.80 return; 45mins). A number of tour buses run from Navan to Newgrange and Knowth. There are also bus tours from Dublin; check at the tourism centre, which is located on Suffolk Street.

By car

For Bru na Boinne, Newgrange and Knowth, take the N2 out of Dublin to Slane. The N3 leads from Dublin to Navan and the Hill of Tara. For Four Knocks, take the M1 towards Belfast, then turn on the R122 towards Naul. Four Knocks is well signposted from Naul.

Drogheda & Carlingford

Driving due west from Newgrange, you'll get to the town of Drogheda in about 15 minutes. Increasingly vibrant since the onset of Ireland's EU-financed heyday, Drogheda is still a bit tattered around the edges. But then it deserves to be, since it's had the daylights kicked out of it for the last 1,000 years.

The town was founded by the Normans, and was the country's political and ecclesiastical capital in the 14th and 15th centuries, but the Black Death swung its scythe here in 1348, killing hundreds, and the plague arrived again in 1479, bringing more devastation. Then, most infamously of all, Oliver Cromwell's New Model Army came for a visit in 1649, and became the first ever to successfully penetrate the town's encompassing walls. Once they got in, Cromwell's men busily set about butchering thousands of Drogheda's Catholic inhabitants in many creative ways.

Start any tour of the town by picking up maps and other information at the tourist office on Millmount Street (*see p204*). From there, head to the **Drogheda Heritage Centre**, in an old church on Mary Street. As well as information on the town's long, dark history, it also has a piece of the old city walls on its grounds, and local lore holds that the centre stands on the site where Cromwell's hordes finally broke through the wall.

Near the tourist office, the **Millmount Museum** is in an old military barracks with a small but absorbing exhibition exploring the city's past, and some terribly friendly people running the place. They will talk your ear off if you let them.

Walk down the steep hill and across the bridge to reach the centre of the city. Heading up West Street, you really can't miss the Gothic **St Peter's Catholic Church**, the permanent home to the head of the Catholic martyr St Oliver Plunkett, rather gruesomely preserved in a glass altar and holding up surprisingly well, given that it's more than 300 years old. The door to the cell where he was imprisoned before being hanged, drawn and quartered – and, just to make sure, beheaded – in 1681 is neatly mounted nearby. Why did he meet such a grim fate, you ask? Plunkett was a Catholic archbishop believed to have conspired with the French. Something of a fatal combination in those days.

Around the corner and up the hill a bit, on William Street, is another, smaller St Peter's – this one a Church of Ireland version. This is where Catholic residents of Drogheda fled when Cromwell rampaged through the town. Many hid in here, but to no avail: his troops locked the doors and set the church alight. The church is not always open, but the graveyard is quite interesting and, so we are reliably informed, the vicar knows reams about Cromwell, if you happen to catch him in situ.

Grave matters at **Monasterboice**.

Not far from here, traffic flows through the **St Largeness Gate** at the top of Laurence Street – a remnant of the town's old walls, and the finest example of a 13th-century barbican you're likely to come across around here.

Heading north from Drogheda on the N1, signs will direct you to **Monasterboice** (*photos above*), a sixth-century monastery of which little is left except a round tower 27 metres (90 feet) high, and two of the most impressive Celtic crosses in existence. The better preserved of the two is **Muiredach's Cross**, the first one you encounter when you enter the churchyard. Its elegant tenth-century biblical carvings remain quite clear: on the western face are, from the top down: Moses with Hur and Aaron, the Crucifixion, St Peter receiving keys from Christ, doubting Thomas, and finally the arrest of Christ. On the eastern side are, from the top: the wise men, Moses fetching water from the stone, David and Goliath, Cain killing Abel, and the fall of Adam and Eve. Sadly, the other cross, the **West Cross**, is not so well preserved, but there's a sign nearby that offers some explanations concerning its now rather faded carvings.

The ruin adjoining Monasterboice is **Mellifont Abbey** (*photo p200*), founded by a Cistercian monk named St Malachy in 1142, and closed by Henry VIII (with all other monasteries) in 1539. There's not much left of the building now, but the ruins are evocative, and you can make out what was there once upon a time.

Back on the M1, take the exit for the Dundalk bypass (arguably the best thing about Dundalk) and go to the Ballymascanlon Roundabout, where you can take the last exit for Carlingford. About half a mile from here, you'll see the **Ballymascanlon House Hotel** on your left. This hotel is worth visiting, not just because it's pleasant, but also because it has a 5,000-year-old proleek dolmen on its grounds. Dolmens are stone tables unique to Celtic countries, with three portal stones supporting a horizontal roof. In the past, visiting this one involved much clambering over fences and crawling through undergrowth, but the route is now well tended (though there's a mild hazard in the form of flying golf balls from the hotel's course). There's nothing there but the rocks, so this is one for those who care about such things. If you want to know your future, lob a stone (gently) towards the top; local lore has it that if you throw a stone on the roof of the dolmen and it stays there, you'll be married within a year.

From here, it's only a short distance to the charming seaside town of **Carlingford**. Well, a short distance by car, anyway; dedicated hill walkers might want to look for signs for the **Táin Trail**, a scenic 17-kilometre (10.5-mile) walk from Ravensdale to Carlingford (or vice versa). If you choose to do the whole thing, it usually takes two days; on the other hand, if you drive, you can be there in a few minutes.

The name Carlingford derives from the Norse *Carlinn Fjord,* and, sitting as it does between the bay and a lough, this is indeed a fjord town. Its pretty boats, magnificent panoramic views, narrow winding streets, ancient buildings and cosy olde-worlde pubs make it an extremely pleasant place in which to while away a day or two, far from Dublin's bustle. There are a few sights to take in, although just soaking up the atmosphere is what you really come here for. Near the town centre, the **Mint** (on Tholsel Street) is a 15th-century tower house with mullioned windows decorated with pre-Norman Celtic motifs. Also of note is **King John's Castle**, by the lough; the eponymous king stayed here soon after it was built in 1210.

Mellifont Abbey & Monasterboice

Tullyallen (041 982 6459). **Open** *May-Oct* 10am-6pm daily. *Nov-Apr* 10am-6pm daily (but visitors' centre closed). **Admission** €2; €1 children; €5.50 family. **No credit cards**.

Where to eat & drink

In Drogheda, try **Weavers**, **Jalapenos** and the **Westcourt Hotel**, all on West Street. You'll find the backpackers hanging out at the **Salt House** restaurant at the Green Door Hostel (*see below*). Down by the riverside on Shop Street, **Monks Expresso Bar** and the **Keyside** serve meals in a slightly trendier environment. If you fancy a drink, **Peter Matthews** pub (universally known as McPhails) is the liveliest place in town, while **Carbery's**, on North Strand, is good for traditional music sessions, especially on Sunday afternoons.

Along with some fabulous pubs, Carlingford also has a couple of excellent restaurants including the superb **Ghan House** (042 937 3682, main course €29.50), the reliably good **Roscoff's Brasserie** (Newery Street, 042 937 3223, main courses €14-€22, closed Mon & Tue Oct-May) and the **Oystercatcher Bistro** (Market Square, 042 937 3989, main courses €18-€25, closed Mon-Wed Oct-May), where the fresh brown bread and oysters are a local speciality, and the magic ingredient in the Oystercatcher Porridge is a shot of whiskey.

Where to stay

The cheapest rooms are to be found in the town of Drogheda, which has a number of hostels, including the endlessly popular **Green Door Hostel** (47 John Street, near the bus station, 041 983 4422, www.greendoor.hostel.com). It's the backpackers' favourite, with all the hostel extras (lockers, linens, TV lounge) and the laid-back Salt House restaurant for cheap, hot meals. If you want to spend a bit more, try **Westcourt Hotel** in the town centre (Wall

Street, 041 983 0965, www.westcourt.com, rates €65-€135); its history is long, and its location is excellent. Down by the water there's the **Neptune Beach Hotel** (Bettystown, 041 982 7107, www.neptune beach.ie, rates €120-€160), which also has a good restaurant. Near Bettystown, the **Boyne Haven House** (on the Dublin Road, 041 983 6700, www.boyne haven.com, rates €37.50-€45 per person) is an excellent B&B famed for its breakfasts.

You can stay out in the countryside at the **Ballymascanlon House Hotel** (Dundalk, 042 935 8200, rates €170). The hotel is excellent, and the restaurant does good traditional Irish food. There is also an 18-hole golf course and a leisure centre. If you prefer your rural life quieter, try **Glebe House** (Dowth, 041 983 6101, rates €95 double), an ivy-covered country house about 15 minutes' drive from Drogheda, with big, beautiful rooms and fireplaces.

In Carlingford, the **Oystercatcher** not only does good food (*see above*), but also has bright, wood-floored rooms (rates €45-€60 per person). **Beaufort House** (Ghan Road, 042 937 3879, www.beauforthouse.net, rates €35-€43 per person) is a pleasant guesthouse near the water, while the **Carlingford Adventure Centre & Holiday Hostel** (Tholsel Street, 042 937 3100, www.carlingfordadventure.com, rates €17-€30 per person) is an IHH hostel with good food, lots to do, dorm beds and a few private rooms. Finally, there are good **campsites** at Giles' Quay and Ravensdale if you fancy roughing it.

Tourist information

Cooley Peninsula Tourist Office

Carlingford (042 937 3033/www.carlingford.ie). **Open** 10am-5pm Mon-Fri; 11am-5pm Sat.

Drogheda Tourist Office

1 Millmount Street, Drogheda (041 984 5684). **Open** 9am-1pm, 2-5pm Mon-Fri.

Getting there

By car

From Dublin take the M1 to Drogheda (about 45mins). For Carlingford take the M1 to Dundalk and follow signs to Carlingford on the R173 (1hr 30mins). A €1.50 toll will be charged on the M1.

By bus

Bus Éireann runs a regular service from Dublin-Drogheda (041 983 5023, in Dublin 836 6111; 1hr 15mins). For Carlingford, change at Dundalk.

By train

There is a regular daily train service to Drogheda from Dublin on the Dublin-to-Belfast line. The station is located just to the east of the town centre (041 983 8749).

The Wicklow Mountains

Summit special.

Walk the **Wicklow Way**.

Sipping a cappuccino at a seaside café in trendy Bray, at the outer edge of Dublin's suburbs, you can see the mountains of County Wicklow off in the distance. And what an inspiring sight it is. The green and hilly countryside of Wicklow starts just a dozen or so miles south of central Dublin, making it one of the easiest and quickest day trips from the city. There's plenty to do there, whether you prefer to picnic by the river in the **Vale of Avoca** (*see p210*) or hike through the isolation around **Glendalough** (*see p208*): this is country living. Take some good walking shoes (and some waterproofs).

A raised granite ridge runs through the county, peaking at two of the highest mountain passes in Ireland – the **Sally Gap** and the **Wicklow Gap** – and the scenery is dramatic. Ramblers, hikers and rock climbers will be in their element here, as you can strike out on foot on the well-marked **Wicklow Way** (*see p209*), which wanders past mountain tarns and secluded glens. You can pick up a map at any tourism office, and then choose a stretch of the path to explore. If you've got a car, head down to the picturesque villages of **Roundwood**, **Laragh**, and **Aughrim**, or splash about on the **Blessington Lakes** (*see below*).

Blessington & around

The roads south of Dublin rapidly leave the dreary south-western suburbs behind; and a green, mountainous landscape opens up swiftly. Between the road and the hills lie the lovely **Blessington Lakes** (*photos p206*). These deep expanses of water cover thousands of acres and have attracted Dubliners for generations. Well, a few generations, anyway: they're not natural lakes, but man-made reservoirs created when the Poulaphouca Dam was built in the 1940s to supply Dublin's water. Several deep valleys were drowned in the process; the smooth lake waters actually hide whole villages long-since covered over in the name of progress. Although you'd never know it, gazing out over their untroubled waters.

Dubliners spend summer weekends boating and fishing here; the banks tend to get quite crowded, though the area is tranquil enough out of season. If you want to hit the water yourself, the **Blessington Adventure Centre** (04 586 5800) provides equipment and instruction for canoeing, kayaking, windsurfing and sailing, as well as archery and abseiling. The village of

Trips Out of Town

Blessington Lakes. *See p205.*

Blessington is a pleasant spot, loved for its wide main street, quaint market square and grand Georgian buildings.

Russborough House and its demesne lie just a few miles south of Blessington on the N81. This vast Palladian mansion, built in 1741, its lush grounds still intact, commands a wide sweep of the surrounding countryside, but its views are not the attraction. Nor is the draw the building itself, which was designed by Richard Castle, who also created nearby Powerscourt (*see p209*). No, the draw is definitely what's inside – a fine, diverse, vast art collection including works by Vernet, Vermeer, Guardi, Goya, Gainsborough and Rubens. Amassing artworks was the hobby of mining magnate Sir Alfred Beit, a member of the de Beers diamond family, who bought the house in 1952 almost exlusively because he thought his paintings would like nice there.

Of course, planting hundreds of priceless paintings in a country that has long been torn by sectarian violence might look like a bad idea in hindsight… and so it was. Over the last few decades, Russborough has been the victim of several brazen and highly successful robberies. In 1974 the IRA made off with 16 of the paintings, and more were stolen in 1986.

Then, astonishingly, there was a third robbery in 2001, carried out in broad daylight. The 16 paintings originally stolen were all subsequently retrieved, but after the third-time unlucky heist, the authorities at Russborough decided to call time before the house was stripped bare, and the more precious parts of the collection are now safely (we hope) on display at the National Gallery in Dublin (*see p76*). Still, much gorgeous art remains at Russborough, but you get the distinct impression that staff who lead the guided tours do not welcome jokes about burglaries. Something in their thin, tense smiles tends to give it away.

Once you've soaked up the art, a wander in the demesne is recommended: walks across the grounds offer any number of sweeping views down into the valley and across to the mountains. The estate and house are privately run and so by no means prettified in the National Trust style: the gift shop is relatively basic and the tearoom positively spartan. The general tone, in fact, is refreshingly non-commercial, and you probably won't leave the place clutching jars of chutney that you don't really want – unless, of course, you actually seek them out.

South of Blessington and the lakes, the road continues towards Baltinglass. There are a number of fine detours at this point, and the best of the bunch is the much-signposted **O'Dwyer Cottage**. Michael O'Dwyer (1771-1826) was a leader of the 1798 Rising (*see below*) and took refuge in the Wicklow uplands after the rebellion failed. He was hunted by the British for years, finally run to ground in 1803 and transported to Australia. The cottage is the scene of one of O'Dwyer's most daring escapes: in 1799 he was hiding here when British troops got word of his location as they approached, he fled, leaving his companions to defend the house to their death.

The main reason for taking this brief detour, though, is not the cottage itself, but the gorgeous landscape surrounding it: this is the **Glen of Imaal**, a narrow and atmospheric space that winds into the hills and offers splendid views across the fields to Lugnaquilla.

Baltinglass, a pretty town on the banks of the River Slaney, is agreeable rather than thrilling. Its heritage centre offers insights into local history, and has reconstructed and satisfyingly unpleasant 18th-century prison cells. The main sight here is the 12th-century Cistercian **Baltinglass Abbey** north of town

(follow the signs). The abbey began to decay in the 16th century, but even so, its remains are powerfully evocative.

O'Dwyer Cottage
Derrymuck, Knockancarrigan, Co Wicklow (045 404 781/www.wicklow.ie). **Open** *Late June-late Sept* 2-6pm daily. **Admission** free.

Russborough House
Blessington, Co Wicklow (045 865 239). **Open** Guided tours *May-Sept* 10am-5pm daily. *Apr, Oct* 10am-5pm Sun. **Admission** €6; €3-€4.50 concessions. **Credit** MC, V.

Where to eat & drink

You may want to stop in Blessington, even if it's out of your way, if only to sample an excellent breakfast or lunch at the **Grangecon Café**, on the town's main street (045 857 892, closed Sun, main courses €7-€14). It's worth seeking out for its delicious and sophisticated food at café prices. Otherwise, there are pubs in and around Blessington that have good food, including **O'Connor's**, on the main street. If you really want to splash out on a dinner, though, head to **Rathsallagh House** in Dulavin (*see p208*) for traditional Irish food.

Trips Out of Town

Avondale House. *See p210.*

Where to stay

If you fancy a treat, **Rathsallagh House** is a grand country hotel and golf club at Donard, just off the main road midway between Baltinglass and Blessington (045 403 112, www.rathsallagh househotel.com, rates €125-€175). Here you'll have no choice but to relax. If you're staying for a week, you can rent one of the rustic, self-catering stone cottages from the good people at **Fortgranite** (on the R747 near Baltinglass, 059 648 1396, rates €300-€600 per week), a working farm in the Wicklow foothills near Baltinglass. Perfect for hiking and exploring.

Tourist information

Blessington Tourist Office
The Square, Blessington (045 865 850).
Open 10am-5pm Mon-Fri.

Getting there

By bus
Dublin Bus (872 0000) runs from Eden Quay in Dublin to Blessington on its suburban 65 route. Bus Éireann (836 6111) offers service to Blessington on the routes to Waterford and Rosslare Harbour.

By car
The N81 from Dublin runs through west Wicklow, between the western edge of the mountains and the horse-racing flatlands of Kildare. The drive to Blessington takes about 45mins.

Glendalough & around

The lovely area known as Glendalough (which translates from the Irish as 'the valley of two lakes') was the refuge of the sixth-century saint and hermit Kevin, who founded a monastery in the valley. By medieval times, Glendalough's fame as a seat of learning had spread across Europe, and countless monks toiled in the monastery's scriptoria, churning out precious books and works of scholarship. Unfortunately, its success, as with so many early Irish religious sites, was also its downfall, and Glendalough came to the attention of the Vikings, who pillaged it repeatedly between 775 and 1071. But it was always rebuilt, stronger than ever, until 1398, when the English finished what the Vikings could not do and virtually wiped the settlement off the map. Attempts were made to resuscitate it, and it limped on in some form until the 17th century as barely a shadow of its former greatness; then it was abandoned altogether.

Approaching Glendalough from Dublin, the road passes through the saddle known as the

Sally Gap, to the high moors and into farmland and forests that give way to woodland and meadows as the land drops into the narrow glacial valley. The place is powerfully atmospheric under any sky and at any time of the year: its Round Tower rises from the trees – its door three metres (ten feet) above the ground – and the scant, evocative remains of other buildings are dotted here and there across the valley floor, encircled by hills and wreathed in isolation and silence. Late on a summer evening, or under frosty winter skies, the beauty of Glendalough is truly captivating. Not that the valley today is truly isolated or silent: this is a very popular tourist attractions, so tour buses are legion in summer. It's worth arriving very early or rather late in order to have some quiet in which to think. Still, Glendalough usually manages to absorb the crowds without too much difficulty. Its size – covering the valley floor and surrounding hills – is sensitively landscaped and well managed, and so it seldom feels overwhelmed.

Most people come to Glendalough to walk. The Wicklow Way passes through the valley on its way south, and other trails meander through the woods around two lakes: the **Lower Lake** tends to be more crowded in high summer (most of the sights are clustered around it), so take the short walk up to the **Upper Lake** if you're looking for tranquillity.

On the Lower Lake you'll find the Round Tower and the **cathedral**, which date to the ninth century. There's a 12th-century **Priest's House** and the excellent **St Kevin's Church**, which dates to the sixth century. The **Visitors Centre** (*see p210*) is quite comprehensive and succeeds admirably in communicating the essence and unique history of the valley. On the other side of the centre from St Kevin's Church the lovely 12th-century **St Saviour's** is well worth a visit.

Up by the Upper Lake is the Romanesque **Reefert Church**, from which you can follow stone steps to the **Pollanass Waterfall** and a cave known as **St Kevin's Bed**. Even further along are a few ancient remains of **Teampull na Scellig**, 'the church of the rock', believed to be the oldest structure in the area.

The nearest town of any size is **Laragh**. It's no metropolis, but it services the monastic site pleasantly enough, and if you want to stay the night, it's here that you'll find the best accommodation options.

The scenic roads (R755 and R760) heading back north towards Dublin from Glendalough skirt the pretty village of **Roundwood**, whose altitude of 230 metres (754 feet) lets it claim to be the highest village in Ireland. It's a favourite refuge of weary walkers and ramblers. A few

miles north of Roundwood, and only ten miles from Dublin itself, is **Enniskerry**, a tidy, thriving town built around a sloping market square and thronged with weekenders in the summer. Enniskerry was formerly the satellite settlement for the great estate of **Powerscourt** (*p210*), which borders the village to the south. The stately pile at Powerscourt is splendid, with beautifully managed grounds sprawling for miles of lush gardens, smooth lawns and shady woodland walks – all ideal for picnicking. Once you're here, there's probably enough to keep you busy for the better part of a day. For all the glories of the estate and surrounding countryside, the company behind Powerscourt have ensured that all manner of shopping opportunities are available here. At present the estate is marketed with a certain degree of taste, although we wonder how long this will last: a plan to build dozens of new apartments in the demesne, for example, was recently blocked – which leads one to wonder what the owners ultimately have in mind.

The house itself is a sad story. You can tell from looking at its exterior that it was once magnificent – it was designed in the 18th century by Richard Castle, the architect of Russborough House (*see p207*) and Dublin's Parliament building. The same family lived in the building for 350 years, until the 1950s. After they moved out, Powerscourt was finally to be opened to the public. Its renovations took more than 20 years (clearly, nobody was in a hurry). Then, in 1974, on the day before it was finally scheduled to open, it caught fire and the interior was completely destroyed. It's been closed ever since, as those doing the restoration clearly decided to beat their previous record. In essence, the renovation here has already taken half a century. And counting. Parts of the house are now open to the public, but not much. Still, they give you an idea of what the place must once have been like.

There's a garden center where you can learn all there is to learn about the plants that thrive here, and pick up a few seeds to take home. There are also plenty of good gift shops, should you feel like spending a bit more money. The café at Powerscourt is run by the brilliant Avoca chain, and serves up rich cakes, hot soups and healthy salads at reasonable prices with a breathtaking view. If you feel energetic, follow the well-marked path for seven kilometres (just over four miles) to the **Powerscourt Waterfall**. It's the highest in Ireland, at 121 metres (397 feet). If you're not feeling energetic, you can drive, following signs from the estate. But note: nothing comes cheap here – you even have to pay to watch the water fall.

Trips Out of Town

Powerscourt House & Gardens

Enniskerry, Co Wicklow (01 204 6000/www.powers court.ie). **Open** *Mar-Oct* 9.30am-5.30pm daily. *Nov-Feb* 9.30am-4.30pm daily. **Admission** €9; €5-€7.50 concessions. **Credit** MC, V.

Powerscourt Waterfall

Enniskerry, Co Wicklow (01 204 6000/www.powers court.ie). **Open** 10.30am-dusk daily. **Admission** €4.50; €3-€4 concessions. **Credit** MC, V.

Where to eat & drink

Like many tourist attractions, Glendalough is not awash with good restaurants, so your best bet is to look to the hotels. Both **Lynhams** (main courses €8-€15) and the **Glendalough Hotel** (main courses €8 lunch, €25 set dinner; for details for both, *see below*) have good restaurants and bars, and both offer reasonable food that stretches beyond hamburgers; the former has a fire crackling on chilly days.

If you pop into the charming village of Roundwood, the **Roundwood Inn** (on the R755, 01 281 8107) is a well-restored 18th-century coaching inn, with good pub food.

Where to stay

Around Glendalough, you can try **Lynham's of Laragh** (040 445 345, www.lynhamsof laragh.com, rates €65-€95 per person), which has 18 pleasant bedrooms at relatively reasonable prices. Nearer to Glendalough itself is the lovely **Glendalough Hotel** (040 445 135, www.glend aloughhotel.com, rates €75-€105 per person), which is well worth a look.

There are no hotels at Powerscourt, but there are plenty in Enniskerry. Try the small, pretty **Powerscourt Arms Hotel** in the centre of the village (01 282 8903, rates €45 per person).

Near the tiny town of Dunlavin, the **Tynte House** is a well-preserved 19th-century family farm with a varied mix of rooms, apartments and self-catering cottages to rent at good prices (045 401 561, rates €70 per-night double B& B, €365-€520 per week self-catering).

Tourism office

Glendalough Visitors Centre

Glendalough, Co Wicklow (040 445 352/www. heritageireland.ie). **Open** *Mid Mar-mid Oct* 9.30am-5.15pm daily. *Mid Oct-mid Mar* 9.30am-4.15pm daily. **Admission** €2.90, €1.30-€2.10 concessions; €7.40 family. **No credit cards**.
There is a tourism office inside this centre, but access to Glendalough itself is free, so you need not visit the centre (which is not free) if you don't want to. There is another visitors' centre at the Upper Lake (040 445 425) in the high season.

Getting there

By bus

St Kevin's Bus Service (281 8119) runs from Dublin's Royal College of Surgeons on St Stephen's Green to Glendalough, departing 11.30am and 6pm daily (€12.65 return). Dublin Bus 44 (872 0000) makes the hop from Hawkins Street to Enniskerry. Bus Éireann (836 1111) offers tours of Glendalough and Wicklow (Apr-Oct, €22.86); buses leave from Busáras. Alpine Coaches (286 2547) runs a summer service from Bray DART station to Powerscourt and Glencree.

By car

The Military Road (R115) – so called because it was built with the intention of hunting down the rebels who sought refuge in the mountains after the 1798 Rebellion – leaves the southern suburbs of Dublin at Rathfarnham and passes over the high moors before descending into the valley of Glendalough.The drive takes about an hour. This is wild country indeed: in winter, the Sally Gap is always the first in the region to be closed by snow. Returning by R755 or R760 will take you through Enniskerry.

Avoca & Wicklow Town

Eastern Wicklow is, for the most part, mild pastoral landscape, softened by the influence of the nearby sea. This is where you'll find **Avondale House & Forest Park**, the country seat of Charles Stewart Parnell, a 19th-century leader of the nationalist movement, near the small town of **Rathdrum**. The house was built in 1777 and decorated in a plain but elegant Georgian style, although the Wedgwood Room and rich plasterwork are startling exceptions to its understated rule. The guided tours, though not exhaustive, are quite good and help to contextualise the house. For many people, though, the beautifully landscaped country park surrounding the house is the highlight. It stretches for miles and is an ideal spot for a walk; several routes are laid out on nature trails in the forest park. As the place is relatively far from Dublin, its footpaths and trails are never crowded. Facilities include a restaurant, gift shop, children's play area and deer pen.

From Avondale it's just a short drive to the small village of **Avoca**, which has managed to capitalise amazingly well on its limited charms to become a major tourist attraction in this part of Ireland. The village was the location of the BBC soap opera *Ballykissangel*, and always pulled in hordes of tourists at the height of the programme's success. Avoca is pretty enough, although there's comparatively little to do there. It is near the overrated **Meeting of the Waters** (where the rivers Avonmore and Avonbeg join to form the Avoca River), the beauty of which inspired the famous poem by Thomas Moore. The main draw for most visitors, however, are the **Avoca Handweavers Woollen Mills**. These are, of course, tourist-oriented but still worth a visit for the excellent crafts, the colourful clothes and for the ubiquitous, but good, Avoca Café food, if nothing else.

From here, the coastal road back towards Dublin makes for a lovely drive. There's nothing especially rugged or spectacular on this stretch of the Irish coast; what you get instead are beautiful beaches and small coves that attract Dubliners through the summer – the glorious three-kilometre (two-mile) stretch of **Brittas Bay** is probably the best example. Heading on, **Wicklow Town** is agreeably bustling, with narrow, steep streets climbing up from a pebble beach and fine harbour. The district is home to interesting sights, including the **Wicklow Gaol** and the lovely **Mount Usher Gardens**.

The gaol was built in 1702 and all manner of inmates passed through its portals. As you would expect, it hosted many participants in

the 1798 Rising; later, prisoners were held here before being transported to Australia. The gaol is an impressive and literate attraction, so you'll emerge knowing more than you would probably care to about the gruesome conditions of prison life in the 18th and 19th centuries; it also draws in the background of the 1798 Rising and the famine admirably. The gaol even features a reconstructed prison ship (just in case you wanted more appalling information) and is altogether impressive.

Mount Usher comes as something of a relief after all that grimness: it's another world entirely. The gardens were laid out in 1860 in a lovely informal style, and now unroll over a large area along the banks of the River Vartry. The waters are used to great effect in any number of cascades and rivulets, and there's even a mini suspension bridge. Happily, there's the usual clutter of craft shops and tearooms.

If you want to get in some exercise, you can take a walk up the splendid three-kilometre (two-mile) coastal trail that runs from Wicklow Town's seafront and beach past the gaol to Wicklow Head, where it takes in the granite

Proceed with caution

Cross-country walking is not the popular activity in Ireland that it is in some other countries: property owners have the right to deny walkers access to their land, and many do so enthusiastically. While 'rambling' is a great British tradition, here you could face a shotgun with an angry farmer behind it, demanding to know why you're scaring his sheep. There's no right of access to the countryside, and fences generally mean 'keep out'. The basic rules are: don't assume you can wander wherever you wish; stay on marked paths and be nice to any farmers you meet.

The good news, though, is that rambling is slowly becoming more organised across the country – and in Wicklow, in particular, it has taken off in the last few years. The fully signposted **Wicklow Way** footpath – which begins at Marlay Park in the south Dublin suburbs and runs 130 kilometres (80 miles) or so south over the mountains – is the longest trail in the country and passes through some spectacular landscapes. The Way is, at all times, a manageable, if occasionally stiff, climb: it rises to 630 metres (2,066 feet) before gradually falling from the mountain passes to the gentler countryside in the southern part of County

Wicklow. It can be walked in its entirety in five or six days, and its various vantage points offer unsurpassed views: of Dublin spread out to the north; of the Irish Sea and Snowdonia to the east; and of the uplands and peaks of the National Park. There are ample refuelling stops and **An Oige** (Irish Youth Hostel Association, www.anoige.ie) hostels at regular intervals along the route. The main footpath is joined by shorter trails, such as **St Kevin's Way** (formerly a pilgrimage route), which runs from Holywood down to Glendalough. The main tourist office in Dublin offers trail maps and information, and the excellent Walk Ireland website (www.walkireland.ie) is full of advice and information.

Remember that if you're visiting the uplands, and especially if you're planning a walk, it's a good idea to go prepared: while the mountains are not exactly the Andes, they nonetheless feature wild and empty terrain, and snow falls up there when it's only raining in the city below. Every winter has its share of 'incidents', with hikers lost, hurt or even killed. So you should always follow the basic rules if you're planning to hike: let someone know your route and when you plan to return – and always carry the correct gear with you.

lighthouse at the end. And, incidentally, you can also spend the night at the solid old lighthouse, which is one of the properties in the Irish Landmark Trust portfolio.

If you want to continue further from here, turn towards **Aughrim** and follow the narrow roads north through the beautiful and isolated Glen of Imaal, before rejoining the main N81 road to Dublin. If you're looking for yet more spectacular scenery, this is the way to go, and Aughrim has hotels, food and drink.

Possible detours include the seaside town of **Greystones** (which is also on the DART line from Dublin) and the less attractive but more trendy seaside town of **Bray**; the two towns are linked by a six-kilometre (3.7-mile) cliff walk.

Avoca Handweavers
Avoca, Co Wicklow (040 235 105/www.avoca.ie). **Open** 9am-6pm daily. **Credit** AmEx, MC, V.

Avondale House & Forest Park
Rathdrum, Co Wicklow (040 446 111). **Open** *mid March-Oct* 11am-6pm Tue-Sun. **Admission** *Grounds* €5 per car. *House* €5; €2.50-€4.50 concessions; €15 family. **Credit** MC, V.

Mount Usher Gardens
Ashford, Co Wicklow (040 440 116). **Open** *Mar-Oct* 9.30am-6pm daily. **Admission** €6; €5 concessions; free under-5s. **No credit cards.**

Wicklow Gaol
Wicklow Town, Co Wicklow (040 461 599/ www.wicklowshistoricgaol.com). **Open** *Mar-Oct* 10am-6pm daily. **Admission** €6.50; €3.75-€4.50 concessions; €17.50 families. **Credit** MC, V.

Where to eat & drink

Yes, we keep banging on about it, but the **Avoca Café** is pretty darn good, and therefore worth visiting for lunch if you're sick of fish and chips (040 235 105, open 9.30am-5.30pm daily, main courses €6-€13). In nearby Arklow, the bar in the **Woodenbridge Hotel** (040 235 146) is an excellent option for traditional pub food in wonderfully historic surroundings (main courses €9.95), or you can pull out the stops and try its excellent restaurant (set menu €35). Both Michael Collins and Eamon de Valera dined here in their day.

In Wicklow Town it's a short walk from the tourist office (*see below*) to the **Bakery Café & Restaurant** on Church Street (main courses €12-€28), which does excellent bistro food. The **Old Court Inn** (040 467 680,mains €11-€19, closed Mon) in the Market Square is known for its excellent seafood. Or you could try **Tinakilly House** (Rathnew, 040 469 274, set meal €45), which specialises in truly fine, country-house cooking. **Philip Healy's** is the

liveliest pub in Wicklow Town (Fitzwilliam Square, 040 467 380). It's packed to the rafters nightly with locals and tourists, who are drawn here by the good vibe (dare we say, *craic*?) and the decent food.

In Aughrim, the Brooklodge Hotel (*see below*) and its **Strawberry Tree** restaurant are the best, and most expensive, game in town, but undoubtedly worth it.

Closer to Dublin, if you stop off in Greystones you'll want to eat at the **Hungry Monk** (Church Road, 01 287 5759), which is known for its outstanding seafood.

Where to stay

In Aughrim, you can stay at the **Brooklodge Hotel** (040 236 444, www.brooklodge.com, rates €105-€120 per person). It isn't cheap, but the food and standards are excellent if you can afford it.

Near Wicklow Town, the **Woodenbridge Hotel** (040 235 146, www.woodenbridge hotel.com) has pleasant rooms with questionable decoration schemes in historic environs. In Rathnew there's the **Tinakilly House**, which is posh but lovely, with a fine foodie reputation (040 469 274, www.tinakilly .ie, rates €128 per person).

The **Wicklow Head Lighthouse** is a fabulous place to stay: it offers comfortable self-catering accommodation for up to six people, and amazing views across the Irish Sea, though you should book ahead (Irish Landmark Trust, 25 Eustace Street, Temple Bar, Dublin, 01 670 4733, www.irishlandmark.com, rates €440 per week low season, €1,175 per week high season).

Tourist information

Wicklow Town Tourist Office
Rialto House, Fitzwilliam Square, Wicklow Town (040 469 117). **Open** *June-Sept* 10.30am-1pm, 2-6pm Mon-Fri; 9.30am-1pm Sun. *Oct-May* 10.30am-1pm, 2-5pm Mon-Fri.

Getting there

By bus
Bus Éireann's 133 service (836 6111) travels between Dublin and Avoca, including Wicklow Town and the Meetings. Buses are rarest on Sundays.

By car
Take the N11 south in the direction of Wexford and Rosslare, and then follow the signs.

By train
Trains from Dublin to Rosslare Harbour stop at Wicklow Town (040 467 329). Call ahead for timetable information.

Kilkenny & Around

Find art in the countryside.

Kilkenny Castle. *See p218.*

Just beyond the Wicklow Mountains, a couple of hours' drive from Dublin, you're in the real Irish countryside. Roads ascend dark green foothills and tumble down into lush valleys where rushing rivers are bothered by nothing more troublesome than thirsty horses and old fishermen. This is a peaceful region, but not immune from tourists, all drawn to Kilkenny Town's many art and pottery shops, and Wexford's small villages and adorable shops.

Here you can relax in the rural tranquility and take your time exploring the grandeur of **Kilkenny Castle** and **Rothe House**, and the lost wonder of **Jerpoint Abbey** (for all three, *see p218*). Still, for those coming from Dublin, the main attraction is what isn't here: traffic jams, crowds and pollution.

County Wexford

Enniscorthy

There's little to make you linger in the small stone-built river town of Enniscorthy at the northern edge of County Wexford, save for the

National 1798 Visitor Centre. This interesting, interactive museum explains the events that took place in the spring of 1798, when a group of republican rebels seized the town and declared their independence. What followed was a phenomenon in which 20,000 men and women flocked to the village from throughout the country and joined the group's unsuccessful raids on the nearby towns of New Ross and Arklow. With the British sending in thousands of well-armed reinforcements to put down the revolt, the poorly armed rebels took positions on Vinegar Hill, where they made an ill-fated last stand on 21 July. Five hundred rebels were killed or injured that morning; the rest fled into the countryside. Thousands of men and women were slaughtered by the English troops in the subsequent days. Within days it was all over, and the British had reassumed control. With interactive exhibits – some more impressive than others – the centre does a good job of explaining what led to the rebellion (one section makes you listen to a debate between Edmund Burke and Thomas Paine). But it's all generally targeted at school

Trips Out of Town

Kells. *See p217.*

groups. If you wish to explore it all further, you can reach **Vinegar Hill** itself by crossing the bridge in town and taking the first right after Treacy's Hotel, then following the signs. Or you could join a guided walking tour from the Castle Hill Crafts Shop (054 9236800) on Castle Hill. Tours, which are thorough and interesting, last an hour (€5; €2.50 concessions).

Wexford Town

County Wexford is loved by sun worshippers and boaters for its stretches of often empty beach, while charming **Wexford Town** (*photos p216*) makes an excellent base for exploring the countryside. The town's array of statues are your first indication that this place has a heroic reputation for resisting authority; in the mid 17th century the locals stood up to Oliver Cromwell's soldiers when the English troops arrived to occupy the town. They lost, of course, and Cromwell handled the victory with his usual flair: he gathered 1,500 of the town's 2,000 residents and slaughtered them. This massacre – which took the lives of every one of the county's Franciscan friars – made Wexford a beacon of Irish resistance for centuries. It was here that the 1798 Uprising took hold, before spreading out into the countryside.

Start your exploration by getting maps at the **tourist office** (*see p216*) on Crescent Quay, where you can also inquire about free guided walks organised by the Wexford Historical Society. The statue near the office is the likeness of Admiral John Barry, who at 14 emigrated from Wexford to the US, where he is credited with founding the US Navy and firing the last shot in the American War of Independence.

In the centre of the town (at the intersection of Common and Main streets) the square known as the **Bull Ring** has a memorial stone that commemorates the rebels of the 1798 Uprising. Not far from the square, on North Main Street, the impressive Venetian Gothic building is the grand **St Iberius Church**.

A few parts of the medieval town walls remain intact, and you can visit the **West Gate** (on Westgate Street), one of the six original tollhouses. Not far from there, on Slaney Street, are the ruins of **Selskar Abbey**. Henry II is believed to have spent Lent 1172 at the abbey doing penance for the murder of Thomas à Becket, but its historican significance did not interest Cromwell, who had it destroyed in 1649.

Outside Wexford Town

About eight kilometres (five miles) north of Wexford Town at Ferrycarrig, the **Irish National Heritage Park** is a pseudo-historical theme park whose tours take you from Neolithic to Norman times in 90 minutes or fewer; there's even a replica Viking longboat at anchor on the River Slaney just outside. Grown-ups might prefer to head north to the more rustic pleasures of **Curracloe Beach**, a long, beautiful stretch of sand and dunes just made for lounging with a good book on a sunny day.

On the road to Rosslare, the 19th-century **Johnstown Castle** combines a research centre and the Irish Agricultural Museum with some delightfully lush, Italianate gardens. Deep in the woods around it is a ruined medieval tower house that makes for spectacular photographs.

If you continue on south towards the Hook peninsula, the next points of interest are the evocative ruins of **Dunbrody Abbey**, a 12th-century Cistercian monastery founded, it is said, by the uncle of the Norman conquerer Strongbow. Its excellent visitors' centre connects with more ruins – those of the once-lovely **Dunbrody Castle**. The building may be long gone, but its reasonably easy full-size hedge maze remains.

It's not far from here to the 15th-century **Ballyhack Castle**, less castle than tower house with a hazy history that may or may not have something to do with the Knights Templar, depending on who's talking. Just to the east of Ballyhack, the well-preserved ruins of the 12th-century **Tintern Abbey** (*photo right*, named after the bigger and more famous abbey in Wales) stand mournfully; it's often overlooked but well worth a vist.

Ballyhack Castle

Ballyhack (051 389 468). **Open** *8 June-15 Sept* 9.30am-6pm daily. Closed Oct-May. **Admission** free.

Dunbrody Abbey, Castle & Visitors' Centre

Dunbrody Park, Arthurstown (051 388 603/ www.dunbrodyabbey.com). **Open** *June-Aug* 11am-5.30pm daily. Closed Oct-May. **Admission** *Abbey* €2; €1 concessions; €5 family. *Visitors' centre* €4; €2 concessions; €10 family. **No credit cards**.

Irish National Heritage Park

Ferrycarrig (053 9120733/www.inhp.com). **Open** *April-Sep* 9.30am-6.30pm daily. *Oct-Mar* 9.30am-5.30pm daily (last admission 3.30pm). **Admission** €7.50; €6 concessions; €19 family. **Credit** AmEx, DC, MC, V.

Johnstown Castle & Gardens

4 miles (6.5km) south-west of Wexford Town (053 42888/www.johnstowncastle.com). **Open** *Garden* 9am-5pm daily. *Museum Apr, May, Sept, Oct* 9am-12.30pm, 1.30-5pm Mon-Fri; 2-5pm Sat, Sun. *June-Aug* 9am-12.30pm, 1.30-5pm Mon-Fri; 11am-5pm Sat, Sun. *Nov-Mar* 9am-12.30pm, 1.30-5pm Mon-Fri. **Admission** *Garden* €5 per vehicle. *Museum* €5; €3 concessions; €15 family. **No credit cards**.

National 1798 Visitor Centre

Mill Park Road, Enniscorthy (053 9237596/www. iol.ie/~98com/english.htm). **Open** *Mar-Sept* 9.30am-5pm Mon-Fri; noon-5pm Sat, Sun. *Oct-Feb* 9.30am-4pm Mon-Fri. **Admission** €6; €3.50 concessions; €16 family. **Credit** MC, V.

Tintern Abbey

Near the village of Saltmills, off the R734 road (051 562 650/www.wexfordweb.com/tintern.htm). **Open** *Mid May-late Oct* 9.30am-6.30pm daily. **Admission** €2.10; €1.10-€1.30 concessions; €5.80 family. **No credit cards**. **Photo** *below*.

Where to stay

In Wexford Town, pick between **St George Guesthouse** (George Street, 053 43474, www.stgeorgeguesthouse.com, closed 23 Dec-Jan, rates €35-€50 per person) or the 200-year-old surroundings of **Westgate House** (Westgate, 053 22167, rates €35 per person), where you can sleep in a four poster bed. A good budget option is **Kirwan House Tourist Hostel** (3 Mary Street, 053 21208, www.hostels-ireland.com, closed Dec-Feb, rates per person €18 dorm, €24 double). Elsewhere, you can try **Ballinkeele House** (off the N11 north of Wexford at Oylgate, 053 38105, €160-€180 double, closed Dec-Jan), a grand, 19th-century manor converted into a luxurious guesthouse and surrounded by sprawling gardens.

Tintern Abbey

Trips Out of Town

Where to eat

Forde's Bistro (The Crescent, Wexford Town, 053 9123832, main courses €19.95-€38) is arguably the town's most popular restaurant, with an emphasis on French cooking techniques and seafood. Try some of the finest food in the county in the town of Rosslare at **La Marine Bistro** in Kelly's Resort Hotel (053 32114, www.kellys.ie, closed Dec-Feb, main courses €25-€45), where Eugene Callaghan turns out brilliant dishes at decent prices. Kelly's Hotel is a four-star establishment with extensive leisure facilities, and yet its prices are not particularly high (rates €80-€105 per person).

Tourist information

Tourist Office

Crescent Quay, Wexford Town (053 9123111). **Open** *July-Aug* 9.30am-8pm Mon-Fri; 10am-6pm Sat; 11am-5pm Sun. *Sept-June* 9am-5.30pm Mon-Sat. There are also offices in New Ross (051 421 857) and Enniscorthy (054 34699).

Getting there

By bus

There are up to 11 Bus Éireann trips daily between Dublin and Wexford Town (3hrs), and 12 between Wexford and Rosslare Harbour (30mins). Ardcavan Coach (053 9124900) also runs a daily Dublin-Wexford Town service (2hrs 30mins). Wexford bus station (053 9123939) is next to the railway station.

By train

The Dublin-Rosslare Harbour service stops at Wexford Town's O'Hanrahan Station (053 91225 220, 3hrs). A reasonably regular local train service connects Rosslare Harbour and Wexford Town. Note that all trains for Rosslare Harbour depart from Dublin's Connolly Station.

By boat

Irish Ferries (0870 517 1717 from the UK) runs a ferry service from Pembroke in Wales to Rosslare; Stena Sealink (0870 5707 070 from the UK) handles the Fishguard-Rosslare route. There are also ferries to Le Havre and Cherbourg in France; contact Transport et Voyages (042 669 090).

Kilkenny & around

Compact and picturesque, with cobbled streets and a singular medieval atmosphere, Kilkenny is a busy, pleasant town, filled with good pubs and restaurants. It's also a major crafts centre and the locus for summer festivals, most notably the Kilkenny Country Roots festival in May, and the Arts Festival in August.

The main reason the town packs 'em in year after year is obvious as soon as you arrive, as the imposing granite edifice of **Kilkenny Castle** (*photo p213*) overlooks the River Nore with a kind of determined nobility. Historians believe a castle or fort stood on the site long before Strongbow's son-in-law built a castle here in 1192, but one has certainly been around ever since. The existing outer walls date from Strongbow's time, but the rest of the building has been rebuilt, restored and renovated often

Wexford Town. *See p214.*

since then. The most recent work was completed in 2001 and made the building more impressive than ever. The castle grounds are a pretty, well-manicured park leading to a castle yard filled with artists', potters' and jewellers' studios. None of this has escaped the notice of the operators of tour buses, but don't be scared away by the crowds: it's worth a visit and, if you stay long enough to get hungry, the restaurant is excellent.

Like the castle, the large, medieval **St Canice's Cathedral** has also undergone many changes over the centuries, but the chancel, transept and nave date from the 13th century. Enough has been retained for it to rate as a fine example of early Gothic architecture. For those ambitious enough to climb it, the adjoining tower offers tremendous views.

Elsewhere in Kilkenny, the charming **Tholsel** ('toll stall') on Main Street is an 18th-century council chamber still used as an office. On Parliament Street, the sturdy Elizabethan **Rothe House** has been tastefully restored and is now a museum displaying period costumes and a few assorted artefacts; it's not terribly interesting, but the old building is gorgeous and merits a visit on its own: it has unusual octagonal chimneys and plenty of original detail.

So much of Kilkenny is as it has always been that parts of the town seem lifted from history books. Even the **tourist office** building on Rose Inn Street is of note: it's one of the few Tudor almshouses in Ireland.

Attractive though Kilkenny Town is, tear yourself away – the rest of the county is all pretty villages and meandering rivers and should not be missed. With an old watermill and stone bridge, the riverside town of **Kells** (*photo p214*; not to be confused with its more famous namesake north of Dublin) is a lovely place. It's near the ruins of **Kells Priory**, a remarkably complete monastic settlement where most of the ruins date from the 14th and 15th centuries, and only a few minutes' drive from the extraordinary **Jerpoint Abbey** (follow the signs from the town centre). This Cistercian complex was founded in 1160 and thrived until it was suppressed by Henry VIII. It may be in ruins, but the carvings on the walls and tombs are exquisite: as you walk around its ancient columns, you can make out long-faced saints, sombre bishops, playful kittens and doe-eyed ladies. In some places the early pigment remains, giving a glimpse of how colourful and lavish the place must have been in its day. Staff in the small museum are friendly and well informed about the history of the abbey and the surrounding area, so it's a good place at which to seek recommendations for other sites nearby.

If ancient abbeys are your thing, there are further Cistercian settlements at **Holy Cross Abbey** in Kilcooley and **Duiske Abbey** at Graiguenamanagh, a delightful village near the Waterford border whose name means 'the granary of the monks'. Duiske was extensively restored in the 1970s and it's now used as the parish church, but its door dates from the 13th

Trips Out of Town

Near Tintern Abbey. See p215.

century, as does the rather striking effigy of a knight kept behind glass.

If you have time you might want to make a side trip to the small valley town of **Inistioge**, even though it's slightly out of the way from here. It's an exquisite village by the River Nore with a wonderful aura of peace, especially down by the river and on its wide and ancient ten-arch stone bridge.

Jerpoint Abbey
Thomastown (056 772 4623/www.heritageireland.ie). **Open** *Mar-May* 10am-5pm daily. *June-Sept* 10am-6pm daily. *Sept-Oct* 10am-5pm daily. *Nov* 10am-4pm daily. *Dec-Feb* by appointment only. **Admission** €2.90; €1.10-€1.30 concessions; €7.40 family. **No credit cards**.

Kilkenny Castle
The Parade, Kilkenny (056 772 1450/www.kilkenny.ie/hist/castle.html). **Open** *Apr-May* 10.30am-5.30pm daily. *June-Aug* 9.30am-7pm daily. *Sept* 10am-6pm daily. *Oct-Mar* 10.30am-1pm 2-5 pm daily. **Admission** €5.30; €2.10-€3.70 concessions; €11.50 family. **Credit** AmEx, MC, V.

Rothe House
Parliament Street, Kilkenny (056 772 2893/www.kilkennyarchaeologicalsociety.ie). **Open** (last admission 4.15pm) *Mar-Oct* 10.30am-4.30pm Mon-Sat; 3-5pm Sun. *Nov-Feb* 10.30-4.30pm Mon-Sat. **Admission** €3; €1-€2 concessions. **No credit cards**.

St Canice's Cathedral
Irishtown, Kilkenny (056 776 4971/www.southeastireland.com). **Open** *Easter-Oct* 10am-1pm, 2-5pm Mon-Sat; 2-5pm Sun. *Oct-Easter* 10am-1pm, 2-4pm Mon-Sat; 2-4pm Sun. **Admission** €5; €3 concessions. **No credit cards**.

Where to eat

In Kilkenny, **Café Sol** on William Street (056 776 4987) offers splendid lunches and beautiful afternoon teas in a delightfully feminine room. In a centuries-old building on narrow Butterslip Lane, **Pordylos** is a cosy, relaxed restaurant, serving imaginative modern food (off High Street, 056 777 0660, main courses €16-€40). **Lacken House** (Dublin Road, 056 776 1085, prix fixe five-course dinner €59) is where you go for elegant dining in a stately Victorian building. For the hippest locale in town, though, you'll have to head for **Zuni** (26 Patrick Street, 056 772 3999, www.zuni.ie). Have a cocktail in the bar before enjoying some slick food in the main restaurant (main courses €19.95-€26.95).

Where to stay

In Kilkenny there are plenty of B&Bs on Parliament Street, Patrick Street and the roads leading out of town. Again, **Zuni** (*see above*) has sleek modern rooms done out in soothing colours (rates €120-€170 double). If you can't get in there, try the **Butler House** on Patrick Street, a fanciful 18th-century house with sweeping staircases and marble fireplaces (056 776 5707, www.butler.ie, rates €140-€200 double). A cheaper option is the **Metropole Hotel** (High Street, 056 776 3778, rates per person €35-€60), which offers B&B in 12 rooms; or you could try **Lawcus Farm Guesthouse** (off the N10 on the Kells Road just outside Kells, 056 772 8949, www.lawcusfarmguesthouse.com, rates €100 double), a rustic, 200-year-old stone cottage at the edge of the King's River, nicely renovated into a quiet country paradise.

Tourist information

Kilkenny Tourist Office
Shee Alms House, Rose Inn Street (056 775 1500). **Open** *May-Oct* 9am-6pm Mon-Sat; 9am-6pm Mon-Sat; 11am-5pm Sun (July, Aug only). *Oct-Apr* 9.15am-5pm Mon-Sat.

Getting there

By car
Take the N7 out of Dublin as far as Naas in County Kildare; follow the N9 through Carlow to the junction at Paulstown; then take the N10 into Kilkenny Town.

By bus
Regular Bus Éireann services (051 879 000) connect Dublin with Kilkenny (2hrs).

By train
Trains run several times daily from Dublin's Connolly Station to Kilkenny (2hrs).

Directory

Directory

Getting Around

By air

Dublin Airport is about 13 construction-plagued kilometres (eight slow miles) north of the city, and is managed by **Aer Rianta** (814 1111, www.dublin-airport.com). It's small, but packed with shops begging for every last bit of your euro cash before you board the plane for home. There's a little Guinness shop selling those charming Guinness posters, and a half-dozen Irish-themed shops selling food, sweaters and every imaginable Irish everything. The airport also has currency exchange facilities and car rental desks, plus a tourist information office (open from 8am to 10pm daily) that can provide maps and information as well as accommodation booking. For getting to and from the airport, *see p221*. For left luggage (storage), *see p228*. For lost property facilities, *see p229*.

The following airlines run regular flights to Dublin:

Major airlines

Aer Lingus *0818 365 000, UK tel 0870 876 5000 www.aerlingus.ie*
Air Canada *679 3958, www.aircanada.com*
Air France *605 0383, www.airfrance.com*
Alitalia *677 5171, www.alitalia.it*
bmi (British Midland) *283 0700, www.flybmi.com*
British Airways *1-890 626 747, www.ba.com*
City Jet *870 0300, www.cityjet.com*
Continental Airlines *1-890 925 252, www.continental.com*
Delta Airlines *1-800 768 080, www.delta.com*
Lufthansa *844 5544, www.lufthansa.com*
Ryanair *0818 303030/UK tel 0871 246 0000 www.ryanair.com*

US Airways *1-890 925 065, w.usairways.com*

By coach

Travelling by coach in Ireland is a good deal cheaper than travelling by rail, though the Irish road network is still not as good as it might be. The largest nationwide coach service is **Bus Éireann** (836 6111, www.buseireann.ie), which operates out of Dublin's Central Bus Station (Busáras). Private bus companies include **Rapid Express** (679 1549, www.jjkavanagh.ie).

Central Bus Station (Busáras)

Store Street, Northside (information 836 6111 6am-11pm daily/www.bus eireann.ie). **Open** *Information desk 9.30am-6pm daily.* **Map** p251 G2.
The information desk here can provide details of local and national bus and coach services, as well as tours, including all services to Northern Ireland.

By train

The national railway network is run by **Iarnród Éireann** (836 6222, www.irishrail.ie). Trains to and from Dublin use **Connolly Station** or **Heuston Station**, both on the city's north side. As a rule of thumb, Connolly serves Belfast, Rosslare and Sligo; Heuston serves Galway, Westport, Tralee, Killarney, Kildare, Cork, Limerick, Ennis and Waterford. The Enterprise service to Belfast is clean, fast and comfortable, but it's not representative; some other InterCity services can be slow, grotty and uncomfortable.

Bikes can be carried on most mainline routes; ask where to store them, as regulations vary with the type of train.

By ferry

Ferries are still likely to remind you of backpacking trips, but even in these days of cheap trans-channel flights, some people prefer them – if only for the views and the lure of spending time out on the water. While those on driving tours may find that it makes economic sense to take the car along (especially if travelling in a group), it's no longer cheap to cross by boat: two people with a car can expect to pay around £200 to sail from Liverpool to Dublin. Note that some lines give a 20 per cent discount to members of youth hostel organisations.

Ferries from Dublin sail to Holyhead (North Wales), the Isle of Man and Liverpool. There are two ferry ports in and around Dublin: **Dublin Port**, about three kilometres (two miles) from the centre (on Alexandra Road, 872 2777, www.dublinport.ie, bus 53A, 53 to/from the centre), and **Dún Laoghaire** for the Stena Line (*see p221*).

Irish Ferries

2-4 Merrion Row, around St Stephen's Green (reservations & enquiries 1-890 313 131/recorded information 661 0715/www.irish ferries.com). **Open** *9am-8pm Mon-Sat.* **Credit** AmEx, DC, MC, V. **Map** p251 G4.
This company operates the world's largest car ferry, the *Ulysses*, which can carry more than 1,300 cars and has 12 decks to explore on the run between Dublin Port and Holyhead in North Wales.

P&O Irish Sea

From the UK 0870 24 24 777/ within Ireland 01 407 3434/www. poirishsea.com). **Open** 8am-8pm daily. **Credit** AmEx, DC, MC, V. Operates between Dublin Port and Liverpool.

Stena Line

Ferry Terminal, Dún Laoghaire Harbour, Dublin Bay (reservations & enquiries 204 7777/www.stenaline. com). **Open** 8.30am-10.30pm daily. **Credit** AmEx, DC, MC, V.
Stena's massive ferry carries up to 1,500 passengers on its regular runs between Dún Laoghaire and Holyhead.

To & from the airport

By bus

As there's no rail service to Dublin Airport, the only public transport option is Dublin Bus (*see below*), which runs the very useful **Airlink** coach service (873 4222/ www.dublinbus.ie) to and from the airport. There are two routes: the **747** (5.45am-11.30pm Mon-Sat; 7.15am-11.30pm Sun) runs from the airport to O'Connell Street (in the centre) and Central Bus Station, while the **748** (6.50am-9.30pm Mon-Sat; 7am-10.05pm Sun) runs from the airport to Central Bus Station, Tara Street (DART Station), Aston Quay (in the centre), Wood Quay (by Christchurch) and Heuston Rail Station. On the 747

route, the buses run every ten minutes on Monday to Saturday, and every 20 minutes on Sunday. On the 748 route, buses run every 30 minutes daily. If you need to be going to the airport, **747** buses run 5.15am-10.50pm on Monday to Saturday and 7.35am-11.15pm on Sunday; the **748** runs 7.15am-10.10pm on Monday to Saturday and 7.50am-10.50pm on Sunday. Both journeys take around 25 minutes to the centre of town and 40 minutes to Heuston Rail Station; tickets, which can be bought from the driver, are €5 (€2 for children). A family ticket for two adults and four under-16s costs €8.50.

Two non-express buses, the **16A** and **41**, also serve the airport (€1.80 single); timetables are displayed at the bus stops outside the airport's Arrivals terminal. Take note: no large items of baggage are allowed on these buses.

By car

To get into town from the airport, follow signs to the M1, then take it south toward Dublin. When you get to the M50 ring road, either loop

around to enter Dublin from whichever side is closest to the part of town you need, or stay on the M1, which becomes the N1 when it enters the city limits. The journey into town takes about 20 minutes, although the frequent construction on the M1 may slow you down, particularly during rush hour.

By shuttle

The big, blue private **Aircoach** service (844 7118/ www.aircoach.ie, 9am-5.30pm Mon-Sat) runs from the terminal to Ballsbridge in the southern suburbs via the city centre (O'Connell Street). A second route runs from the airport to Leopardstown taking in the city, Donnybrook and Stillorgan: its buses run hourly between midnight and 4.30am; every 20 minutes 4.30-6.30am and 8pm-12am; and every ten minutes 6.30am-8pm. The trip usually takes 40 minutes, but can take up to an hour at rush hour.

It's marginally more expensive (€5-€7 single, €8-€12 return, under-12s free), but makes up for that by being impressively prompt, pleasant and reliable. You can buy tickets just outside the arrivals lounge. Aircoach also sells **The Dublin Pass** which provides a guide book and entry to over 30 attractions for €29.

By taxi

Taxis are plentiful at the airport, and a journey into the city centre will usually cost around €25-€30.

Public transport

Iarnród Éireann runs the **DART** electric rail and suburban rail services, while **Dublin Bus** (Bus Atha Cliath) is responsible for the city buses. Several combined bus

Bus & rail tickets

Combined pre-paid tickets can be the cheapest way to get around, especially if you're going to be doing a lot of travelling in Dublin. These can be purchased from the offices of Dublin Bus and DART (*see p221*), from central newsagents and at the Dublin Tourism Centre (*see p236*).
• **One-day Short Hop:** unlimited bus, suburban rail and DART travel – €8.50; €13 family.
• **Three-day Short Hop:** Three days unlimited bus, Suburban Rail & DART travel – €16.70.
• **Student Seven-day Travelwide** – unlimited bus travel for seven days – €16.70.
• **Weekly rail pass:** €23.
• **Weekly Short Hop:** unlimited bus, suburban rail and DART travel – €29.20.
• **Weekly Rambler:** unlimited bus travel for one week – €20; €6 children.

Dublin by bus

Nearly all buses in Dublin display the mysterious legend 'Via An Lar'. This odd mingling of Latin and Irish is arguably deliberately misleading and off-putting to the uninitiated. But in fact, it simply means 'via city centre' (*an lar* means city centre in Irish) and it holds the key to understanding Dublin's ostensibly intricate bus system.

There are dozens of bus routes through the city and dozens of route numbers, with As, Bs and Xs added for good measure. But the system is not half as wilfully and hellishly confusing as it might appear. The main rules of thumb are these: nearly all buses cross the city from north to south; and nearly all are channelled through, or depart from, O'Connell Street and its immediate riverside environs – Eden Quay, Beresford Place, Aston Quay, D'Olier Street, Westmoreland Street and Dame Street. If you bear in mind Dublin's relatively small city centre, this means that you are never very far from the bus stop you need.

Of course, you may not need to take a bus at all – especially if you're here for just a few days. If you enjoy walking, many of the places in the Sightseeing section of this guide can be reached on foot. You can stroll from, say, Trinity College to Smithfield in 20 minutes, and from St Stephen's Green up to Parnell Square in 15 minutes.

Still, if you're planning to go to some of the outlying attractions such as the Phoenix Park and Kilmainham, then a bus might come in handy. And when the weather's bad, sometimes walking just isn't a lot of fun, so we've included some of the most useful bus routes below.

City Centre to National Botanic Gardens and on to Helix Concert Hall

Buses 13 and 13A (catch them at Merrion Square North and O'Connell Street).

City Centre to Guinness Brewery and on to Kilmainham

Bus 78A (departs from Aston Quay and Essex Quay).

City Centre to Heuston Station

Bus 25X (departs from Westmoreland Street).

City Centre to Dún Laoghaire, via University College

Bus 46A (departs from O'Connell Street and D'Olier Street).

City Centre to Howth Village and Howth Summit

Buses 31 and 31B (both depart from Eden Quay).

City Centre to Smithfield, Four Courts and Parkgate Street

Buses 25 and 26 (depart from Wood Quay).

City Centre to Phoenix Park Visitors' Centre at Ashdown Castle

Buses 37 and 39 (depart from Dame Street).

and rail tickets are available, so work out where and how much you want to travel and see which type suits best.

Bus

Bus stops look like tall green or blue lollipops. They usually (though not always) display a timetable but rarely have a shelter. 'Set down only' means the bus only lets passengers off there, so don't hang around waiting; look for a bus sign that doesn't bear those three words. Note a Dublin curiosity: you board buses at the front and get off at the front, too: the middle doors seldom open.

More than 150 bus routes crisscross the city centre, so you'll usually find a bus stop close by. Timetables at bus stops are often defaced, so your best bet is to get up-to-date versions from Dublin Bus's offices on O'Connell Street (*see p223*). Buses are generally reliable and frequent, but most only keep loosely to their schedules, so allow plenty of time – especially in rush hour and during the whole of Friday afternoon.

Fares are set by city zone, or 'stage'. There are more than 23 stages in and around Dublin, and you can check timetables to see what stage your destination is in. Fares are 90c for a journey within stages one to three, €1.35 for stages four to seven, €1.65 for stages eight to 13, and €4.05 to take a bus from the centre to a far-flung suburban stage. For some useful bus tips, *see left* **Dublin by bus**.

You can buy tickets or bus passes from tourist offices and newsagents, or you can pay the driver the appropriate fare on boarding the bus. If you choose to do the latter, exact change is a good idea: drivers can't give change, though they will issue you a ticket for the amount of the overpayment, and you can then have this money returned at Dublin Bus offices. Banknotes are not accepted. If you need to buy a ticket, board on the left-hand side of the front entrance; the right-hand side is reserved for passengers who have pre-paid bus passes, which are easier and cheaper. If you plan to do a lot of travel by bus, it's a good idea to buy one of these passes. Options include a one-day pass (€5), three-day pass (€10.50), five-day pass €16.50), seven-day pass (€20) and one-day family pass (€8.50). All offer unlimited use of all Dublin Bus services for their specified period. There's also a range of student offers, for which you need ID and a Travelsave stamp from the Dublin Bus offices.

For other passes, *see p221* **Bus & rail tickets**.

Nitelink

Normal bus services end at around 11.30pm, but Nitelink buses run every night except Sunday along many routes from the city centre to the suburbs. Services leave from D'Olier Street, Westmoreland Street and College Street, starting at around 12.30am, then departing every half hour or so until around 3am. The fare is €4. Check with tourist offices or Dublin Bus for timetables and routes.

Dublin Bus

Head Office, 59 Upper O'Connell Street, Northside (information & customer services 873 4222/www. dublinbus.ie). Open 8.30am-5.30pm Mon; 9am-5.30pm Tue-Fri; 9am-2pm Sat. Map p251 F1.

Rail services

The **DART** (Dublin Area Rapid Transit, www.irishrail.ie) and **Suburban Rail** lines provide a faster and arguably more pleasant alternative to buses for journeys beyond the city centre. Central DART stations include **Connolly**, **Tara Street**, **Pearse** and **Grand Canal Dock**. Most of the DART runs outside the city

centre, serving the north and south suburbs from Greystones and Bray in the south to Howth and Malahide in the north. The DART is supplemented by Suburban Rail routes that range as far as Dundalk in County Louth, Arklow in County Wicklow, Mullingar in County Westmeath and County Kildare. See the map on p255 for more stations.

Rail tickets are available from all DART and Suburban Rail stations, as well as from the **Rail Travel Centre** (*see below*). On buying a single or return rail ticket, specify the final destination so the ticket can be validated for a connecting bus service if necessary.

A new transport option is the LUAS tram system (1 800 300 604/www.luas.ie). This state-of-the-art light rail system connects you to the city centre, many of Dublin's top tourist attractions and the best shopping areas. Luas (the word is Irish for 'speed') has two routes. The red line runs from Connolly Rail Station to Tallaght in south-west Dublin. The green line runs from St Stephen's Green in the centre to Sandyford in the southern suburbs.

Luas operates 5.30am-12.30am Mon-Fri, 6.30am-12.30am Sat and 7am-11.30pm Sun. Single fares start at €1.40; an adult pass for one day costs €4. Combined Luas and Dublin Bus tickets cost €6.20. Buy tickets before boarding; there are ticket machines on the platform at every stop.

DART (Iarnród Éireann)

Connolly Station, Northside (836 3333/passenger information 836 6222/www.irishrail.ie). Open 8.30am-6pm Mon-Fri; 9am-6pm Sat; 9.30am-6pm Sun. Map p251 H1.

LUAS

Red Cow Roundabout, Clondalkin, Dublin 22 (1-800 300 604/www. luas.ie). Open 9am-5pm Mon-Fri. Credit (over €5) MC, V.

Rail Travel Centre

35 Lower Abbey Street, Around O'Connell Street (836 6222/www. irishrail.ie). Open 8.30am-6pm Mon-Fri; 9am-6pm Sat; 9.30am-6pm Sun. Credit AmEx, DC, MC, V. Map p251 F2.

Taxis

A multitude of taxi companies operate in Dublin, and taxis tend to be plentiful (though finding one on Saturday nights can be tricky). Expect to pay high prices round the clock. There are 24-hour ranks at Abbey Street and Upper O'Connell Street on the northside, and at Aston Quay, College Green and St Stephen's Green (north). Taxis can often be found outside major hotels.

If you have any complaints, contact the **Irish Taxi Drivers' Federation** (836 4166). *See also p24* **Taxi!**

Fares

Some private companies offer fixed rates for certain journeys and don't charge a pick-up fee; licensed cabs run on a meter. The minimum charge is €3.40 for the first half-mile or four minutes; each additional sixth of a kilometre or 28 seconds is charged at 15c (8am-10pm) or 20c (10pm-8am), 20c all day on Sundays and public holidays. Extra charges of 50c are levied for extra passengers, animals (other than guide dogs) and for every item of luggage that needs to be stowed in the boot of the cab. (Two children are charged as one passenger. Children travel for free). You'll be charged an extra €1.50 if you hire a taxi by phone, or if you pick up a cab from the airport rank.

Phone cabs

Castle Cabs 802 2222
City Cabs 668 3333/
872 2222/475 0800
Co-Op Taxis 676 6666
NYC Taxis 677 2222
Pony Cabs 661 2233

Directory

Chauffeur services
Charlemont Chauffeur Service
087 270 0506/www.charlemont
chauffeurservice.com
Emerald Limos 087 223 1350/
www.emerald-limo.ie
The Limousine Company 843
9055/www.thelimousinecompany.ie.

Driving

Dublin's roads are truly
hellish: traffic jams at rush
hour (morning and night)
make the daily commute a
grind for locals, and driving
an ordeal for visitors. Worse
still, the street signs in Gaelic
and English are too dark and
the writing too small for the
names of the streets to be
easily read in either language
– which means it's all too
easy to get very lost, very
quickly. The system of one-
way streets in the centre –
often not shown on maps –
can get drivers unfamiliar
with the city into a flat spin.
Then there's construction
disruption. Also, public
transport is quite good in
Dublin, so there's even less
reason to drive; buses are
reliable and frequent, and
have a special lane for faster
trips; the DART rail system
will whisk you out to the coast
in a few short minutes. Most
people who spend all of their
time in the city don't even
bother renting a car. If you
do bring your own car, or
rent one on the spot, do drive
carefully. And be sure to
get out of town. Country
roads may not always be
of the highest standard, but
they're rarely choked with
traffic and construction.

EU, US and international
driving licences are valid in
Ireland. Speed limits are
50kph in urban areas, 80kph
in suburban areas, 100kph on
main roads (excluding urban
areas and motorways) and
120kph on dual carriageways
and motorways.

Seatbelts must be worn by
drivers and all passengers

of cars and light vans. The
alcohol limit, as in the UK
and most US states, is 80
milligrams per 100 millilitres
of blood.

Americans and Australians
take note: as in Britain, cars
drive on the left.

Breakdown services

There are many garages in
Dublin that will help if you
have a breakdown. The
following places all offer
24-hour support.
Automobile Association
23 Suffolk Street (677 9481/www.
aaireland.com)
Glenalbyn Motors 460 4050
RAC 1-800 535 005/www.rac.ie
Tom Kane Motors 833 8143

Parking

Parking spaces in the centre
are expensive and can be
difficult to find. Expect to
pay at least €2 per hour.
Computerised billboards
throughout the city list
availability in the major car
parks. All on-street parking in
the city centre is pay-to-park:
there should be an automatic
ticket machine on each street.
Be warned: clamping is widely
used, even in residental areas.

Vehicle hire

Unless you're a committed
(and patient) car driver, there's
no point hiring a car for your
stay in Dublin. However, if
you plan to travel outside it,
a vehicle is essential, since
public transport is far less
reliable away from the city.
You must have a valid
driving licence and a credit
card in order to hire a car.
All the car hire companies
listed here also have outlets
at Dublin Airport. All advise
that you pre-book.

Avis
*1 Hanover Street East, around
Trinity College (1 890 405 060/
www.avis.com).* **Open** 8.30am-
6.30pm daily. **Credit** AmEx, DC,
MC, V.

Budget
*151 Drumcondra Road Lower,
Northern suburbs (837 9611/
9802/airport 844 5150/www.
budget.ie).* **Open** 9am-5pm Mon-Sat;
10am-4pm Sun. **Credit** AmEx, DC,
MC, V. The airport branch is open
5.30am-midnight daily.

Hertz
*151 South Circular Road, Southern
suburbs (709 3060/airport 844
5466).* **Open** 9am-5.30pm Mon-Fri;
9am-3pm Sat, Sun. **Credit** AmEx,
DC, MC, V. The airport branch is
open 6am-midnight daily.

National Car Rental
*Cranford Centre, Stillorgan,
Southern suburbs (260 3771/
airport 844 4162/www.carhire.ie).*
Open 9am-5pm Mon-Sat; 9am-
noon Sun. **Credit** AmEx, DC, MC, V.
The airport branch is open 6am-
midnight daily.

Cycling

The biggest problem with
cycling in Dublin is not the
air pollution, nor avoiding
the mad drivers, but rather
finding a safe place to keep
your bike: Dublin railings
are filled with single wheels
dangling from locks. If you
have to park outdoors, try to
use two locks – a strong one
for the frame and back wheel
and another for the front
wheel – and take your lights,
saddle and any other
detachables with you.

Bicycle hire

For cycle hire you can
expect to pay something
in the region of €20 per day
(based on 24 hour period),
although there are usually
weekly rates (€80) and group
discounts that will reduce the
price somewhat. A refundable
deposit of €200 is required;
you'll get it back when you
return the bike.

Cycle Ways
Bike Rental
*185-186 Parnell Street, Around
O'Connell Street (873 4748/www.
cycleways.com).* **Open** 9.30am-
6pm Mon-Wed, Fri, Sat; 9.30am-
8pm Thur. 10am-4pm Sun. **Credit**
AmEx, MC, V. **Map** p251 E1.

Resources A-Z

Addresses

There is no system of postal or zip codes in the Republic of Ireland, and this can make addresses look dangerously vague – this is especially true in rural areas where an address can consist simply of the nearest town or village. Don't worry, though. This is a small country and the system works just fine.

Dublin is slightly different from the rest of the country in that it has a system of postal districts, numbered from 1 to 24. The system is simple: even numbers cover the area south of the River Liffey; odd numbers are north of the river. As a quick guide, locations in the city centre will either have a Dublin 1 (northside) or a Dublin 2 (southside) post code. The area immediately west of Christ Church is Dublin 8; Ballsbridge, Ringsend and Donnybrook, south-east of the centre, are Dublin 4, and the area around the Four Courts and Smithfield is Dublin 7.

Age restrictions

● Entry to pubs: officially 18, although children are tolerated before 9pm (at bar owner's discretion, so this can be earlier; hotels are best)
● Entry to nightclubs: usually 18, although some may have an over-21 or over-23 policy
● Buying alcohol: 18
● Buying and consuming cigarettes: 16
● Driving: 17
● Marriage: 18
● Sex: 17

Business

Conferences

Dublin Castle Conference Centre *Dublin Castle, Dublin 2 (679 3713 www.dublincastle.ie). All cross-city buses.* **Map** p251 E3.
Westbury Hotel *Grafton Street, around Trinity College (679 1122/ www.jurysdoyle.com). Cross-city buses.*

Couriers & shippers

Call **DHL Worldwide Express** (1 890 725 725, www.dhl.com) or **Federal Express** (1-800 535 800, www.fedex.com).

Office hire

Regus
(402 9401/www.regus.ie). **Open** 9am-5pm.

Travel advice

For current information on travel to a specific country – including the latest news on health issues, safety and security, local laws and customs – contact your home country's government department of foreign affairs. Most have websites with useful advice for would-be travellers.

Australia
www.smartraveller.gov.au

Canada
www.voyage.gc.ca

New Zealand
www.safetravel.govt.nz

Republic of Ireland
http://foreignaffairs.gov.ie

UK
www.fco.gov.uk/travel

USA
http://travel.state.gov

Secretarial services

Firstaff Personnel Consultants

85-86 Grafton Street, around Trinity College (679 7766/www.firstaff.ie). All cross-city buses. **Map** p251 F3.

Useful organisations

Business Information Centre

Ilac Centre, Henry Street, around O'Connell Street (873 3996/www. dublincitypubliclibraries.ie). All cross-city buses. **Open** 10am-8pm Mon-Thur; 10am-5pm Fri, Sat. **Map** p251 F2. A business reference service/library.

Chamber of Commerce

17 Merrion Square, around St Stephen's Green (661 2888/www. chambers.ie). All cross-city buses. **Open** 9am-5.30pm Mon-Fri. **Map** p251 G4.

Dublin Chamber of Commerce

7 Clare Street, around Trinity College (644 7200/www.dub chamber.ie). All cross-city buses. **Open** 8.30am-5.30pm Mon-Fri. *Documentation* 9.30am-12.30pm, 2.30-4.30pm Mon-Fri. **Map** p251 G4.

Consumer

For consumer complaints, contact the **Office of the Director of Consumer Affairs** (4-5 Harcourt Road, Dublin 2, 402 5500, www. odca.ie), which has the power to prosecute traders; or contact the **European Consumer Centre** (809 0600, www.ecc dublin.ie) for free legal advice. Another option is to check out the handy Oasis website, **www.oasis.gov.ie**.

Customs

If you're entering Ireland from outside the EU, you're entitled to the following duty-free allowances:
● 200 cigarettes or 100 cigarillos or 50 cigars or 250 grams tobacco

- 2 litres port, sherries or fortified wines or 1 litre spirits or strong liqueurs (over 22 per cent alcohol)
- 2 litres of table wine
- 60 millilitres perfume
- 250 millilitres toilet water
- €184 worth of goods, including gifts and souvenirs.

If you're entering Ireland from inside the EU (excluding new member states), you're entitled to the following duty-free allowances:

- 800 cigarettes or 400 cigarillos or 200 cigars or 1kg tobacco
- 10 litres port, sherries or fortified wines or 10 litre spirits or strong liqueurs (over 22 per cent alcohol)
- 90 litres of table wine
- No limits perfume
- No limit toilet water
- €175 worth of goods, including gifts and souvenirs.

Customs & Excise

Main office *Ship Street Gate, Dublin Castle, around Temple Bar (647 5000/877 6222/877 6223/www. revenue.ie). All cross-city buses.* **Open** 9am-5pm Mon-Fri. **Map** p251 E3.

Disabled travellers

More and more places provide facilities for the disabled – the easiest way to find out is to call ahead and see if a venue can cater for your needs.

Dublin Bus has a lot of wheelchair-accessible buses, and more are added all the time; contact Dublin Bus for details (*see p223*). Few railway or DART stations were built with wheelchair users in mind, but Iarnród Éireann (*see p223*) makes an effort to accommodate those who contact them in advance: staff will meet you at the station, accompany you to the train, arrange a car parking space and set up ramps. All Luas trams have designated spaces for wheelchairs. Wheelchair users should enter through the double doors in the middle of

the tram, where information on where and how to position the wheelchair is shown.

For details of access to stations nationwide, call any DART station or train station and ask for the 'InterCity Guide for Mobility Impaired Passengers'. For further information, contact the **Department of Transport** (44 Kildare Street, Southside, 670 7444, www.transport.ie).

Useful organisations

Enable (Cerebral Palsy) Ireland 269 5355, www.enableireland.ie.
Central Remedial Clinic *01 8336 633/www.crc.ie.*
Cystic Fibrosis Association of Ireland *496 2433, www.cfireland.ie.*
Irish Deaf Society *860 1878, www.irishdeafsociety.ie.*
Irish Wheelchair Association *818 6400, www.iwa.ie.*
National Council for the Blind of Ireland *1 850 334 353/from outside Ireland +353 1 8307033/www.ncbi.ie.*

Drugs

The official attitude to drug abuse in Ireland remains draconian. Although police attitudes are often relaxed, there are no signs that soft drugs are about to be decriminalised here. Drug problems in some sections of the city remain appalling.

If you get caught with illegal drugs, the result can be an official caution, a night in a cell or much worse.

Drug Treatment Centre

30-31 Pearse Street, around Trinity College (677 1122/www.addiction ireland.ie). All cross-city buses. **Open** 9am-5pm Mon-Fri; 10am-noon Sat, Sun. **Map** p251 G3.

Electricity

Like the rest of Europe, Ireland uses a 220-240V, 50-cycle AC voltage, with three-pin plugs (as in the UK). Adaptors are widely available at airport shops. Note too that Irish and UKVCRs and televisions use a different frequency from those in the USA.

Embassies & consulates

For embassies and consulates not listed below, consult the Golden Pages. Note that many countries (such as New Zealand) do not maintain a full embassy in Dublin. In those cases the embassy in London usually acts as the country's chief representative.

American Embassy *42 Elgin Road, Ballsbridge, Southern suburbs (668 8777/dublin.usembassy.gov). Bus 4, 5, 7, 7A, 8, 45, 63, 84/ DART Lansdowne Road.* **Open** 8.30am-5pm Mon-Fri.
Australian Embassy *Fitzwilton House, Wilton Terrace, around St Stephen's Green (664 5300/www. australianembassy.ie). Bus 10, 11, 13.* **Open** 8.30am-4.30pm Mon-Fri.
British Embassy *29 Merrion Road, Ballsbridge, Southern suburbs (205 3700/www.britishembassy.ie). Bus 8.* **Open** 9.30am-5pm Mon-Fri. Passport enquiries 9.30am-12pm; passport and other enquiries 2-3.30pm; visa enquiries (by appointment only) 9.30am-11am.
Canadian Embassy *65 St Stephen's Green, around St Stephen's Green (417 4100/www. canada.ie). All cross-city buses.* **Open** 8.30am5pm Mon-Fri. **Map** p251 F4.
New Zealand Consulate General *46 Upper Mount Street, around St Stephen's Green (all enquiries to New Zealand Embassy in London: 0044 207 9308 422/ voice message service in Ireland 660 4233/www.nzembassy.com). Bus 7.* **Map** p251 H5.
South African Embassy *Alexander House, Earlsfort Centre, Earlsfort Terrace, around St Stephen's Green (661 5553). All cross-city buses.* **Open** 8.30am-noon Mon-Fri. **Map** p251 H5.

Emergencies

Dial **999** or **112** for Fire, Garda (police) and ambulances.

Gay & lesbian

See also pp170-173.

Help & information

Gay Switchboard Dublin

872 1055/www.gayswitchboard.ie. **Open** 7.30-9.30pm Mon-Fri; 3.30-6pm Sat. Help and information for the gay community in Dublin.

Lesbian Line
872 9911. **Open** 7-9pm Thur.
Advice and information.

Other groups

Drugs/HIV Helpline
freephone 1-800 459 459. **Open**
9.30am-5pm Mon-Fri. For basic
health information and advice by
phone.

Gay Men's Health Project
*19 Haddingdon Road, Ballsbridge,
Southern suburbs (669 9553/669
9500/www.gaymenshealthproject.ie).
Bus 10.* **Open** 6-8pm Tue; 5.30-
7.30pm Wed. Free, confidential drop-
in clinic for gay and bisexual men.

Outhouse
*105 Capel Street, North Quays (873
4932/www.outhouse.ie). All cross-city
buses.* **Open** 12.30-5pm Mon; 12.30-
9pm Tue-Fri; Sat 1-5pm. **Map** p251
E2. An accessible meeting place for
the lesbian and gay community.

Health

The national health service in
Ireland is rightly maligned;
state investment has risen in
recent years, but this follows
years of cutbacks. A number
of city centre hospitals have
moved to the suburbs even as
the population in the centre
has grown. For details of
health insurance, *see p228.*

Complementary medicine

Holistic Healing Centre
*38 Dame Street, around Trinity
College (671 0813/www.hhc.ie). All
cross-city buses.* **Open** 10am-7.30pm
Mon-Thur; 10am-6pm Fri; 10am-6pm
Sat. **Map** p251 E3.

The Inspired Centre
*67 Camden Street Lower, around
St Stephen's Green (478 5022). All
cross-city buses.* **Open** 10am-10pm
Mon-Fri; by appointment only Sat.
Map p251 E5.

Nelson's Homeopathic Pharmacy
*15 Duke Street, around Trinity
College (679 0451/www.nelsons.
co.uk). All cross-city buses.* **Open**
9.30am-5.45pm Mon-Sat (except
Thur); 9.30am-7.30pm Thur.
Map p251 F3/4.

Contraception & abortion

Abortion is illegal in Ireland,
and a highly inflammatory
subject. Its prohibition became
part of Ireland's constitution in
1983. Irish women generally
travel to Britain for a
pregnancy termination.

For women's health matters,
visit a **Well Woman Centre**.
These offer services including
breast exams, pregnancy
counselling, smear tests and
the morning-after pill. You
don't need an appointment,
and staff are friendly.

Condoms are available in
pharmacies and in some
newsagents, as well as from
vending machines in many
pubs and from **Condom
Power** (57 Dame Street,
Around Temple Bar, 677
8963, www.condompower.ie).

Well Woman Centres
*35 Liffey Street Lower, around
O'Connell Street (872 8051/www.
wellwomancentre.ie).* **Open** 9.30am-
7.30pm Mon, Thur, Fri; 8am-7.30pm
Tue, Wed; 10am-4pm Sat; 1-4pm Sun.
Map p251 E2.
Other locations: 67 Pembroke
Road, Ballsbridge, Southern suburbs
(660 9860); Northside Shopping
Centre, Coolock, Northern suburbs
(848 4511).

Dentists

Gallagher's Dental Surgery
*38 Fenian Street, Dublin 2 (670
3725). All cross-city buses.* **Open**
8am-8pm Mon-Wed; 9am-5pm
Thur, Fri.

Irish Dental Association
(295 0072, www.dentist.ie) A quick
and easy online search to find a
registered dentist in your area.

Doctors

You must pay for doctor visits.
This can be quite as expensive,
as doctors' charges usually
range from around €30 to €50,
but can go much higher. It's
always a good idea to check
a doctor's fees in advance.

Grafton Medical Practice
*34 Grafton Street, around Trinity
College (671 2122/www.grafton
medical.ie). All cross-city buses.*
Open 8.30am-6.30pm Mon-Thur;
8.30am-6pm Fri. **Map** p251 F4.

Mercer Medical Centre
*Stephen Street Lower, around St
Stephen's Green (402 2300/www.
rcsi.ie). All cross-city buses.* **Open**
9am-6pm Mon-Thur; 9am-5pm Fri.
Map p251 E4.

Hospitals

In an emergency, call 999/112.
The following area hospitals
all have 24-hour accident and
emergency departments. Note
that all casualty patients must
pay a flat fee of €60 in order to
be treated. EU citizens should
see also p228.

Beaumont Hospital
*Beaumont Road, Northern suburbs
(809 3000/www.beaumont.ie). Bus
27B.*

Mater Hospital
*Eccles Street, Dublin 7 (803 2000/
www.mater.ie). Bus 13, 13A, 16, 16A.*

St James's Hospital
*James Street, Dublin 8 (410 3000/
www.stjames.ie). Bus 19, 78A, 123,
Luas.*

Pharmacies

See p152.

STDs, HIV & AIDS

Drugs/HIV Helpline *freephone 1-
800 459 459.* **Open** 9.30am-5pm
Mon-Fri; Advice and counselling on
HIV- and AIDS-related issues.
Dublin AIDS Alliance *53 Parnell
Square West, 873 3799/www.dublin
aidsalliance.com.* **Open** 10am-5pm
Mon; noon-5pm Fri. A care and
education service for drug users and
people with HIV and AIDS.

Helplines

In addition to the helplines
listed below, there are others.
For women's support and
services *see above*; for gay and
lesbian helplines *see p226*;
for helplines related to AIDS
and HIV *see above.*

Directory

Alcoholics Anonymous 453 8998 in office hours/1 890 412 412/www. alcoholicsanonymous.ie.
Asthma Line *freephone 1-850 445 464/www.asthmasociety.ie.* **Open** 9am-5pm Mon-Fri. Nurse available for advice 10am-1pm Tue-Thur.
Focus Ireland *881 5900/www. focusireland.ie.* **Open** 24hrs daily. 9.30am-5.30pm Mon-Fri. Emergency accommodation.
Narcotics Anonymous Information Line *672 8000/www. na.ireland.org.* **Open** 24hrs daily. Samaritans *freephone 1-850 609 090/www.samaritans.org.* **Open** 24hrs daily.

Insurance

If you're an EU citizen, an E111 form will cover you for most medical (though not dental) emergencies. In the UK, get an application form from the post office. It is always advisable to take out medical insurance, too: it'll save you the effort of trying to wade through the red tape and ensures more comprehensive coverage.

Non EU citizens are advised to have travel insurance that covers health, as they will be responsible for any healthcare costs. Organise your travel insurance before you leave your country of origin; it's impossible to sort out once you get to Ireland. Alway read the small print before agreeing to an insurance contract. There's usually an excess or deductible.

Internet

Many hotels now offer some kind of internet access: luxury hotels should have broadband internet and wireless connection points in each room and hostels tend to have a clutch of terminals. Look out for the many cafés, bars and restaurants that provide wireless as an added extra to customers. If you want to set up an internet account for your stay, good local ISPs include **Eircom Broadband** (701 0022/www.eircom.ie) and **BT Broadband** (1 800 924 924/ www.btireland.ie).

Internet access

If you can't get online in your hotel, you can guarantee that internet access won't be far away; Dublin is positively crawling with cybercafés, most offering a decent number of terminals and other services such as printing, faxing and photocopying.

Central Café Internet
6 Grafton Street (677 8298/www. centralcafe.ie) **Open** 9am-10pm Mon-Fri; 10am-9pm Sat, Sun. **Rates** *varies.* **No credit cards.**

Global Café Internet
8 Lower O'Connell Street (878 0295/www.globalcafe.ie) **Open** 8am-11om Mon-Fri; 10am-11pm Sat; 10am-11pm Sun. **Rates** *varies.* **No credit cards**

Language

In the rush towards cultural homogenisation, much has been lost – but the English language as spoken in Dublin is still a breed apart. The real Dublin accent is rapid and clipped with a dropped 't'. It can be heard to best advantage at the markets on Moore Street and Henry Street.

Entirely different is the 'posh' southside, 'D4' or 'DART' accent (so called because most exponents live near the coastal DART railway line in places like Dalkey and Howth). This accent is nasal and, critics would tell you, rather uptight; most real Dubs don't consider it part of the local vernacular at all.

Left luggage

Busáras
Bus Éireann 703 2434. **Open** 9am-5pm Mon-Fri. *Lockers* 7am-11pm daily. **Rates** €5-€10 locker. **No credit cards. Map** p251 G2.

Connolly Station
Platform 2 (Iarnód Éireann 703 2358). **Open** 6.30am-midnight Mon-Sat; 8am-10pm Sun. **Rates** *for 24hrs* €4 small, €6 large. Will hold for up to 7 days. **No credit cards. Map** p251 H1.

Dublin Airport
Greencaps Left Luggage & Porterage (814 4633). **Open** 6am-11pm daily. **Rates** *for 24hrs* €4.50 small; €6.50 medium; €9 large. **No credit cards.**

Heuston Station
Next to the ticket office (703 2132). **Open** *7am-9pm Mon-Sat.* **Rates** €1.50 small; €3 medium; €5 large. **No credit cards.**

Legal help

AIM Family Services
6 D'Olier Street, around Trinity College (670 8363/www.aimfamily services.ie). All cross-city buses. **Open** 10am-1pm Mon-Fri. **Map** p251 F2/3. Legal counselling and mediation.

The Equality Authority
2 Clonmel Street, off Harcourt Street, around St Stephen's Green (417 3336/www.equality.ie). All cross-city buses. **Open** 9.15am-5.30pm Mon-Thur; 9.15am-5.15pm Fri.

Legal Aid Board Centres
Head Office, Montague Court, Montague Street, around St Stephen's Green (477 6250/www.legalaid board.ie). All cross-city buses. **Open** 9.30am-5.30pm Mon-Thur; 9.30am-5.15pm Fri. **Map** p251 E5. **Other locations:** 45 Gardiner Street Lower, (874 5440); Law Centre, 9 Ormond Quay Lower, North Quays (872 4133); 47 Upper Mount Street, Around St Stephen's Green (662 3655).

Libraries

There are a number of local city- and state-run libraries in Dublin with ample services including, sometimes, internet access. In addition to those listed below, note that most local universities will allow foreign students a temporary reader's pass for their libraries. For this, you'll need a student ID, and, in some cases, a letter of introduction from your college. For a list of local universities, *see p233.*

Those listed here are Dublin corporation libraries.

Central Library
Ilac Centre, Henry Street, around O'Connell Street (873 4333/www. dublincity.ie/living_in_the_city/ libraries). **Open** 10am-8pm Mon-Thur; 10am-5pm Fri, Sat. *All cross-city buses.* **Map** p251 F2.

Pearse Street Library

138 Pearse Street, around Trinity College (674 4888/www.iol.ie/dublin citylibrary/www.dublincitypublic libraries.ie). **Open** *10am-8pm Mon-Thur; 10am-5pm Fri, Sat. Bus 3.* **Map** p251 G3.

Lost property

Make sure you always notify the police if you lose anything of value, as you will probably need a reference number from them to validate any subsequent insurance claims. To track down your lost property, call the following numbers:
Bus Éireann 703 2489.
Connolly Station 703 2359
Dublin Airport 814 5555
Dublin Bus 703 1321.
Heuston Station 703 2302
Luas 1 800 300 604.

Media

Newspapers

Dublin is the centre of Ireland's publishing world and all but one of the Republic's national newspapers are based here.

National broadsheets

The *Irish Times* acts as Ireland's serious intellectual broadsheet. Offering objective and insightful reporting of city, national and international affairs, it has truly transformed itself over its long life from an organ of the Anglo-Irish ruling class into the main voice of a relatively liberal and progressive Ireland.

The *Times'* main rival, the *Irish Independent*, is tabloid in spirit, although it masquerades as a broadsheet. It's a more actively national paper, and is generally more approachable than the *Times*, as it features less of that paper's metropolitan bias. This said, it is often sensationalist and sometimes could be accused of lacking in objectivity. The third national broadsheet, the Cork-based *Irish Examiner*, is decent reading.

National tabloids

The *Evening Herald*, peddled on the streets and newsstands from lunchtime on, is a tabloid, but is a little loftier in tone than some of the morning rags. In some circles, it's required reading: if you need a flat to rent, then look no further. The *Star* is

Ireland's very popular response to Britain's *Sun*, though with a little more conscience and a lot less cleavage. The *Irish Sun*, meanwhile, is the British *Sun* with a few pages of Irish news inserted to keep the locals happy. When the mother paper has one of its frequent fits of Irish-bashing, its Dublin equivalent quietly pulls the relevant pages.

Sunday papers

Of the many papers you will find lined up in a Dublin newsagent on Sunday morning, few will be Irish. The British press has saturated the Irish market in recent years, offering cheaper cover prices and more pages as a means of boosting circulation figures at home. Most of the papers follow the practice of The *Sun* (*see above*) in modifying their editorial stance, where appropriate, for the Irish market: the *Sunday Times* is a particularly brazen offender. Of the indigenous newspapers, the *Sunday Tribune* and the *Sunday Business Post* both offer good news coverage, comment and columnists. The *Post*, like the *Financial Times*, is good for more than just money talk, and is, at times, the most outspoken of all the papers. The *Sunday Independent* is much like its daily stablemate. Sunday tabloids include the popular *Sunday World. Ireland On Sunday* is a new Sunday paper that offers easy reading and current affairs.

Magazines

Listings magazines

Hot Press, which appears fortnightly, offers a slightly more intellectual take on life in general and on music in particular. It remains the best guide to the Dublin music scene, with comprehensive listings and reviews, and its debate pages are pretty lively. Alternatives to *Hot Press* include the amiable and very comprehensive *Event Guide,* which is a handy freesheet available in central cafés and bars. There are also a few websites with listings; *see p238*.

Other magazines

Dublin's shelves are as packed with glossy mags as any city's. All the international mainstays are there, some in special Irish editions. Titles unique to the Irish market include *U, Irish Tatler, Social & Personal* and *Image.* Good for a horrified laugh is *VIP*, which is modelled on *Hello!* and shares that publication's high-minded ideals.

The *RTÉ Guide* offers the usual celebrity gossip plus full TV and radio listings. For buying and selling stuff, check out the aptly named *Buy and Sell*, or for satire

try the *Phoenix. Village Magazine*, a new addition to the shelves, is a straight-talking look at Irish politics, current and international affairs. For comprehensive, in-depth coverage of Irish literature and cinema, try *Books Ireland* or *Film Ireland.*

The quarterly *Dublin Review* offers excellent, well thought-out essays on literature and the arts. The monthly *Dubliner* is an upmarket glossy carrying comprehensive reviews and news articles. It often has excellent writing, and occasional bouts of solid investigative reporting. *Totally Dublin* is a monthly entertainment and lifestyle mag.

Some free magazines can be had at bars, cafés and shops around the city. *Mongrel* has lots of comedy, editorial, fashion, music and more. *Backpacker* is a must for new backpackers arriving in Ireland.

Television

Dublin is one of Europe's more heavily cabled cities, and the full range of UK channels should be available wherever you stay. The national station, RTÉ (Radio Telefís Éireann) runs three national channels: RTÉ1, RTÉ2 and TG4. The station, in spite of a recent licence fee hike, is usually hard up for money, and its perceived lack of adventurous programming and unflattering comparisons with the BBC make it a prime target for public criticism. Still, it does generally excellent current affairs, creative children's programming and highly regarded sports reporting.

RTÉ1

RTÉ1 seldom offers anything challenging or controversial. The daytime diet in Ireland largely consists of soap operas, bland chat shows and DIY programmes. Prime-time programming is better. The most significant programme on Irish TV remains Friday night's *Late Late Show,* formerly hosted by national institution Gay Byrne and now in the hands of Pat Kenny. The *Late Late Show* is the longest-running chat show in the world and countless important events and interviews have taken place on the programme over the years. Today, however, it is a tired shadow of itself, and pressure is building on RTÉ to put it and its unctuous host out of their misery.

Alarmingly for RTÉ, the station lost the rights to the British soap opera *Coronation Street* (for decades the ratings-topper) to new upstart channel TV3, and this has blasted great holes in the station's tried and tested schedule. If you need a soap fix (or a good laugh) there's always the Dublin-based *Fair City*.

RTÉ2

RTÉ's second channel reinvented itself a few years ago, and it did so with largely successful results. RTÉ2 is now a smoother and more stylish operation than its sister channel. At night, music and chat shows aimed at a younger, hip audience come to the fore, and the channel has also commissioned several new series, such as the well-received comedy drama *Bachelors Walk*. Saturday nights are in the hands of Ryan Tubridy, who hosts *Tubridy Tonight*, the new chat show with little appeal. The most popular American imports, such as *Lost* and *Desperate Housewives*, generally appear on RTÉ screens well before they show up on the UK's main channels.

Telefis na Gaeilge (TG4)

A predominantly Irish-language station based in Galway, TG4 does imaginative home-grown drama and a few pretty good documentaries, punctuated by smartly selected art-house movies dubbed for those who have not yet fully mastered the native tongue. It's stylish and slick and well worth a look.

TV3

Ireland's newest (and its first independent) station was born in 1998, and has used populist scheduling to carve a successful niche for itself. No nonsense about public service broadcasting here, as its schedule is filled with low-budget American TV movies, excitable news broadcasts and low-budget sitcoms. It has also poached many of RTÉ's sporting contracts, and a link with Granada has meant that *Coronation Street* and a raft of other popular British shows are shown here.

Radio

RTÉ

RTÉ operates four national stations: **RTÉ Radio 1** (88.2-95.2 FM; 567, 729 AM) offers a fairly safe mixture of news, sports programming and phone-in talk shows during the day, and an excellent range of interesting music slots and offbeat docs at night. **RTÉ 2FM** (90.4-97 FM; 612, 1278 AM) is aimed more at the kids, and so, as you might expect, it has the usual pop and rock shows during the

day and the ever-reliable *Hotline* request show at 7pm daily. **RTÉ Lyric FM** (96-99 FM), based in the town of Limerick, is the classical music station. It offers a mixture of arts programming as well as a wide variety of music and live concert coverage from various Irish and internationsl soloists, ensembles and orchestras. Another option is **RTÉ Raidio Na Gaeltachta** (92.6-94.4 FM), which is the national Irish-language station. Based in Co. Galway, it offers news, current affairs, arts, music and talk shows.

Other stations

A number of new licensed stations have challenged the hegemony of RTÉ in the last ten years. After a rocky start, **Today FM** (100-102 FM) has now quite successfully established itself, offering a broad combination of music shows, news and chat. **Anna Livia FM** (103.2 FM) is Dublin's community station, putting out a good selection of programmes made by people who love radio; while chart enthusiasts prefer the same-old, same-old diet of **98FM** (er, 98 FM), **FM104** (oh, find it yourself) and **Lite FM** (95.8 FM). **NewsTalk 106** (106 FM), which has been climbing up the ratings ladder over the past few years, offers rolling news, debate and occasional documentaries and is well worth a listen.

Pirate radio

The diet of blandness offered by the mainstream music stations, however, has meant that the city's handful of pirate stations have come to fulfil certain music needs in the city. Among the best are **Power FM** (97.2 FM) – a lot of techno and other dance music; **Phantom FM** (91.6 FM) – generally loud indie rock; and **XFM** (107.9 FM) – more loud indie rock. If you want originality, you're most likely to find it here.

Multimedia

Generally speaking, Ireland has spent the last decade enthusiastically embracing new technology, and nowhere more so than in Dublin. The country's economic boom was largely fuelled by the growth in information and media technology jobs and companies such as Iona (which began as a student initiative in Trinity College) continue to perform impressively on the world stage. However, Ireland has

not been immune to the cold wind blowing through the virtual world, and lately there has certainly been a good deal of retrenching to be seen around town. Modest success stories abound, though, and include www.ireland.com, linked to the *Irish Times*, as well as a number of other websites; *see p238*.

Money

In February 2002 the euro became Ireland's sole currency. Ireland was one of the first countries to sign up to the single European currency, along with Austria, Belgium, Germany, Finland, France, Italy, Luxembourg, the Netherlands, Portugal and Spain. Greece joined later, taking the number of countries participating up to 12.

The currency was officially launched on 1 January 1999, and cash in the form of euros (€) and cents (c) came into circulation on 1 January 2002. The Irish pound was then withdrawn on 9 February 2002, with the euro becoming the sole legal tender. Since then there have been cries of what has become known as 'euro inflation' – meaning that when the currency changed over prices went up across the board. This could go a long way towards explaining how expensive things often seem in Dublin, which was formerly known as one of the world's less expensive tourist towns. Still, the Irish government has not endorsed this theory, and denies there has been any euro inflation at all, and some economists deny that it even exists, although others insist that it is a real situation, or a valid problem in any euro member state.

Note that the United Kingdom did not join the euro and retains the pound as its sole currency.

The euro comes in seven notes – €5 (grey), €10 (red), €20 (blue), €50 (orange), €100 (green), €200 (yellow) and €500 (purple) – and eight coins. One face of each coin features a communal map and flag illustration and the other a country-specific design(all can be used in any EU nation). Irish coins all display the emblem of the harp.

ATMs

Automatic cash machines can be found outside most banks and some building societies and in many shops around the city. Most are linked up to international networks (such as Cirrus), so you should not anticipate any problems withdrawing money directly from your account with your standard cash card, although you should expect a nominal charge for each transaction.

Banks

In general, banking hours in Dublin are 10am to 4pm Monday to Wednesday and Friday, and 10am to 5pm on Thursday (closed on Saturday and Sunday). The main Dublin branches of the major Irish banks are listed below.

AIB (Allied Irish Bank) *AIBBank Centre, Ballsbridge, Southern suburbs (660 0311/www.aib.ie). Bus 7.* **Open** 10am-4pm Mon-Wed, Fri; 10am-5pm Thur.

Bank of Ireland *Baggot Street Lower, around St Stephen's Green (604 3000/www.boi.ie). Bus 10.* **Open** 10am-4pm Mon-Wed, Fri; 10am-5pm Thur. **Map** p251 G5.

Ulster Bank *33 College Green, around Trinity College (702 8600/ www.ulsterbank.com). All cross-city buses.* **Open** 10am-4pm Mon-Wed, Fri; 10am-5pm Thur. **Map** p251 F3.

Bureaux de change

Nearly all banks, building societies and post offices have foreign exchange facilities, so you shouldn't have any trouble finding places to change your currency into euros.

There are desks at the airport and at the main bus station, **Busáras** (*see p220*), so you can stock up on euros as soon as you arrive.

Another option if you need to change once you're in the city itself is the bureau de change inside Clery's department store (*see p138*).

Other useful bureaux de change include:

First Rate Bureau de Change

3 Westmoreland Street, around Trinity College (671 3233/www. boi.ie). **Open** 9am-6pm daily (summer late opening until 8pm Thur-Sat). **Map** p251 F3.

Foreign Exchange Company of Ireland

Tourist Information Building, Suffolk Street, (661 1800/www.fexco. com). All cross-city buses. **Open** 9am-5pm Mon-Sat. **Map** p251 F3.

Joe Walsh Tours (JWT)

69 O'Connell Street Upper (872 5536). All cross-city buses. **Open** 8am-8pm Mon-Sat; 10am-6pm Sun and bank hols. **Map** p251 F1.

Thomas Cook Foreign Exchange

118 Grafton Street, around Trinity College (677 1307). **Open** 9am-5.30pm Mon, Tue, Thur-Sat; 10am-5.30pm Wed. **Map** p251 F4. **Other locations:** *51 Grafton Street, (677 7422).* **Open** 9.30am-5.15pm Mon, Tue, Thur-Sat; 10.30am-5.15pm Wed.

Credit cards

Ireland is still a cash culture, but most places will accept MasterCard and Visa, although only a few accept American Express or Diners' Club cards.

If your credit cards are lost or stolen

As you would at home, it's best if you first inform the police and then contact the 24-hour numbers listed below.
American Express Customer Services *1-800 282 728.*
American Express Travellers' Cheques *1-800 626 000.*
Diners' Club *0818 300 026 authorisation service 1 800 709 944.*
MasterCard *1-800 557 378.*
Visa *1-800 558 002.*

Tax

Sales tax (VAT) in the Republic is set at 20 per cent. Visitors from outside the EU can get a refund by filling in a tax-free shopping cheque (available from participating stores) and handing it in to the Refund Desk at Dublin Airport.

Opening hours

General business hours are 9am to 5.30pm Monday to Friday. Banks are open 10am to 4pm Monday to Wednesday and Friday, and from 10am to 5pm on Thursday. Shops in the city centre generally open between 9.30am and 6pm on Monday, Tuesday, Wednesday, Friday and Saturday, and from 2pm to 6pm on Sunday, with late-night opening until 8pm on Thursday and Friday. Hours during which alcohol can be sold have been tightened once more after an experiment in slackness resulted in excessive drinking and late-night violence; pubs are now usually open from 11.30am to 11.30pm Monday to Thursday, and 11.30am to 12.30am Friday and Saturday (though many pubs in Dublin have permission to open until 1.30pm and later) and noon to 11pm on Sunday.

Smoking is banned in all Irish pubs and restaurants. This has brought a new outdoor flavour to Irish bars, as most pubs have a designated outdoor smoking area. Under new law, children are allowed in pubs, with adults, until 9pm. This is however at the discretion of the pub owner and you may see signs stating earlier times.

Police stations

The emergency telephone number for police (called Garda), fire and ambulance is 999 or 112. City centre Garda stations are located at the following addresses; all are open 24 hours daily. Non-emergency confidential calls to the Garda can also be made on 1-800 666 111.

Garda stations

Pearse Street, around Trinity College (666 9000); Store Street, North Quays (666 8000); Fitzgibbon Street, Northside (666 8400); Metropolitan HQ, Harcourt Square, Southside (666 6666).

Post

Post boxes are green and many have two slots: one for 'Dublin Only' and one for 'All Other Places'. It costs 48c to post a letter, postcard or unsealed card (weighing up to 20g) inside Ireland, 60c to the UK, 65c to anywhere in the EU and also 65c to elsewhere in Europe as well as other international destinations. All airmail letters – including those to the UK – should have a blue priority airmail *(aerphost)* label affixed: you can get these free at all post offices. Post is generally delivered in fairly quick order within Ireland itself, and you should expect letters sent from Dublin to reach their destination within a day. International mail varies: it takes several days for letters or parcels to reach Europe and about a week to reach the US, or slightly more than that to reach Australia, South Africa or New Zealand.

Post offices

Generally speaking post offices are open from 9am to 5pm Monday to Friday. Larger branches are also open from 9am to 1pm on Saturday. This rule is not inviolable, as offices have varying opening hours. Note that many smaller post offices still close for lunch from 12.45pm to 2pm.

General Post Office

*O'Connell Street, around O'Connell Street (705 7000/www.anpost.ie). All cross-city buses. **Open** 8am-8pm Mon-Fri; 8am-1pm Sat. **Map** p251 F2.*

Poste restante

If you need to have mail kept in a post office for collection, ask the sender to put your name clearly on the envelope and send it to Post Restante, General Post Office, O'Connell Street, Dublin 1 (*see above*). Bring photo ID when you collect it.

Religion

There are many churches in and around Dublin. Check the *Golden Pages* for more listings.

Church of Ireland

Christ Church Cathedral

*Christchurch Place, around Temple Bar (677 8099/www.cccdub.ie). Bus 50, 77, 123. **Services** Morning prayer 10am; peace prayers 12pm. Eucharist 12.45pm Mon-Fri (Lady Chapel). Choral evensong 6pm Wed, Thur; 5pm Sat (except July, Aug); Sung Eucharist & sermon 11am Sun; Eucharist 3pm Sun. **Map** p250 D3.*

St Patrick's Cathedral

*Patrick's Close, off Patrick's Street (453 9472/www.stpatrickscathedral. ie). Bus 50, 54A, 56A. **Services** Mon-Fri Choral Matins (during school term only) 9.40-10am; Holy Eucharist (in Lady Chapel) 11.05-11.25am; Choral Evensong 5.45-6.25pm Sun Holy Eucharist (in Lady Chapel); 8.30-9am; Choral Eucharist and Matins 11.15am-12.30pm; Choral Evensong 3.15-4.30pm. **Office** opens 9am-5pm and deals with the Self-Guided Tours of the Cathedral (€5 per person. Group bookings available.) **Map** p250 D4.*

Roman Catholic

Church of St Francis Xavier

*Upper Gardiner Street, around O'Connell Street (836 3411). All cross-city buses. **Services** Mass 8.30am, 11am, 1pm, 7.30pm Mon-Sat; 8.30am, 10am, 11am, noon, 7pm (gospel choir mass, except July & Aug) Sun.*

St Mary's Pro-Cathedral

*Marlborough Street, Dublin 1 (874 5441/www.procathedral.ie). All cross-city buses. **Services** Mass 8.30am, 10am, 11am, 12.45pm, 5.45pm Mon-Sat; 10am, 11am (Latin mass), 12.45pm, 6.30pm Sun. **Map** p251 F1.*

Other Christian

Abbey Presbyterian Church

*Parnell Square, top of O'Connell Street (837 8600). All cross-city buses. **Services** 11am Sun. **Map** p251 F1.*

Grace Baptist Church

*28A Pearse Street, around Trinity College (677 3170/www.grace.ie). All cross-city buses. **Services** 11am Sun. **Map** p251 G3.*

Methodist Church

*Abbey Stree, City Centre (874 4668/ www.irishmethodist.org). All cross-city buses. **Services** 11am, 7pm Sun.*

Islam

Islamic Centre Dublin

*163 South Circular Road, Southern suburbs (453 3242/www.islamin ireland.com). Bus 19, 22. **Services** 5 prayers daily, plus Friday prayers. Check website for prayer times.*

Judaism

Dublin Jewish Progressive Congregation

*7 Leicester Avenue, Rathgar, Southern suburbs (285 6241/www. jewishireland.com). Bus 15A, 15B, 15C. **Services** phone for details.*

Safety & security

Levels of street crime in Dublin have risen dramatically in the last decade. Pickpockets and bag-snatchers have always been fairly prevalent in the city, but in recent years some assailants have been known to use syringes as weapons – threatening their victims with the possibility that whatever is in them is tainted with HIV. They have even, if rarely, robbed people on city buses, walking the victim off at needle-point to get to a cash machine.

The majority of safety hints amount to little more than simple common sense. If you're worried about travelling on buses, then sit downstairs and in sight of the driver. When wandering around town, avoid wearing ostentatious jewellery that says 'rob me'. Always strap your bag across your chest with the opening facing towards your body. When withdrawing money from cash machines, don't stand around counting your money; put it away quickly, and, if there's a machine inside the bank, use that instead. Never leave your wallet in your back pocket. In bars, don't leave your wallet on a table, and keep your bag with you at all times.

Most of all, safety is about being aware and looking confident. This is especially important at night: if you're on your own, stay in well-lit, populated areas and try to avoid consulting a huge map every couple of streets. Arrange to meet people inside a pub or restaurant rather then waiting outside on your own.

Smoking

In March 2004 a wide-ranging law banning all smoking in the workplace came into effect in Ireland. It is viewed as the most far-reaching anti-smoking legislation in the world and has proved to be a big success. It prohibits smoking in any bar, restaurant or public space in the country. The effect has been dramatic: all Dublin pubs, for example, became no-smoking areas overnight. Most bars have an outdoor, heated and seated area for smokers. However, some pubs don't; get used to seeing small groups of people standing at bar doors having a puff. Don't even think of lighting up in any enclosed space in the country, including shops, bars, restaurants, airports, trains or buses. *See also p131* **Ave paria**.

Students

Considering the sheer number of language schools, business colleges and universities in Dublin, it's not surprising that the city's student population is considerable. It's also diverse: over summer, thousands of people come to Dublin to study English, and for the rest of the year colleges are filled with academic students from Ireland and abroad.

Citizens of roughly 60 countries (including all EU-member states) do not require visas to study here. However, the law requires long-term visitors to register with the Immigration Department at the Garda National Immigration Bureau, Harcourt Square, Southside (666 9100). For more information consult the website (foreignaffairs.gov.ie) or get in touch with the Irish Department of Foreign Affairs, Visa Section, Hainault House, 69-71 St Stephen's Green, Southside (478 0822).

If you do end up going to school here, you'll find that rents in Dublin have risen sharply in the last decade: expect to pay upwards of €100 a week for a reasonable place. The rental market has become much less cut-throat in the last few years, but is still fairly frantic around September when all the students return to Dublin to sort out lodgings. Summer, therefore, is the best time to look for bargains.

The *Evening Herald* is probably the best paper to check for ads, though you might get lucky at USIT (*see p234*). You could also go through your college's accommodation service if it has one, or a letting agency. Best of all, though, is the DAFT website (www.daft.ie) which is excellently designed and easy to use.

Language schools

French
Alliance Française *1 Kildare Street, around St Stephen's Green (676 1732/www.alliance-francaise.ie). All cross-city buses.* **Map** p251 G4.

German
Goethe-Institut *62 Fitzwilliam Square, St Stephen's Green (661 8506/www.goethe.de/dublin). Bus 10, 11, 13.* **Map** p251 G5.

Irish
Gael-linn *35 Dame Street, around Temple Bar (675 1200/www.gael-linn.ie). All cross-city buses.* **Map** p251 E3.

Spanish
Instituto Cervantes *58 Northumberland Road, Ballsbridge, Southern suburbs (668 2024/www.dublin.cervantes.es). Bus 7, 45/DART Lansdowne Road.*

Universities & colleges

The three biggest colleges in the Dublin metropolitan area are as follows:

Dublin City University
Glasnevin, Northern suburbs (student services 700 5165/www.dcu.ie). Bus 11A, 11B, 13A, 19A.

Trinity College Dublin
College Green (students' union 677 6545/www.tcd.ie). All cross-city buses. **Map** p251 F3.

University College Dublin
Belfield, Southern suburbs (269 3244/www.ucd.ie/international). Bus 3, 10, 11B, 17.

Other schools & colleges

American College Dublin
2 Merrion Square, around St Stephen's Green (676 8939/www.amcd.ie). All cross-city buses. **Map** p251 G4.

Dublin Business School
Aungier Street, around St Stephen's Green (475 1024/www.dbs.edu). Bus 16, 16A, 19, 19A, 83. **Map** p251 E4.

Dublin Institute of Technology
Cathal Brugha Street, around O'Connell Street (402 3000/www.dit.ie). All cross-city buses. **Map** p251 F1.
There are six DITs in and around the city, offering a wide range of courses, including in popular areas such as architecture, music, engineering and tourism.

Directory

Griffith College Dublin

South Circular Road, Southern suburbs (454 5640/www.gcd.ie). Bus 16, 19, 122.

Useful organisations

Union of Students in Ireland Travel (USIT)

19-21 Aston Quay, around Trinity College (602 1600/www.usit.ie). All cross-city buses. **Open** 9.30am-6.30pm Tue, Wed, Fri; 9.30am-7pm Mon, Thur; 10am-5pm Sat. **Map** p251 F2.

USIT handles all student travel arrangements, so wherever you're going, it can tell you the cheapest way to get there. It's also very much a meeting of the ways: its noticeboards are filled with details of flatshares, language tuition, jobs and cheap flights. You'll probably have plenty of time to browse through the small ads while you're waiting to be served: you should expect at least 30 minutes' queuing.

Telephones

Dialling & codes

The dialling code for Dublin is 01, although you don't need to use the prefix if you're calling within the Dublin region itself. Local phone numbers in Dublin all consist of seven digits, though you'll notice that elsewhere in Ireland phone numbers may be either shorter or longer. As in the US, numbers with the prefix 1 800 are free.

All Dublin numbers listed in this book have been listed without the city code of 01. If you need to dial any of these numbers within Dublin, simply use the numbers as they appear in the listings. If you are dialling from outside Dublin but within Ireland, add 01 to the front of the numbers listed. If you are dialling from outside Ireland, you need to dial the international dialling code + 353, then the Dublin city code 1 (omitting the initial 0), then the number as it appears in the guide.

To make an international call from within Ireland, dial 00, then dial the appropriate international code for the country you're calling (*see below*), and then dial the number itself, omitting the first 0 from the area code where appropriate.

- Australia: 00 61
- United Kingdom: 00 44
- USA &Canada: 00 1
- South Africa: 00 27
- New Zealand: 00 64

Making a call

If you have access to a private telephone, the charges for your calls will be significantly lower than they would be from your hotel or your mobile: for example, a three-minute local call will cost around 24c during the day, and the same amount of money will net you double minutes' chat during off-peak hours at night or on weekends.

Reduced rates are available for calls made between 6pm and 8am from Monday to Friday, and all day Saturday, Sunday and Bank Holidays. If you need to make international calls, try to wait until these off-peak hours, as it is considerably cheaper.

If you can't use a private phone, the next easiest way to make long-distance calls is to buy a phone card, available from most newsagents and post offices, which you can use on public pay phones. These days, the majority of pay phones only accept these cards, not cash. The cards are especially useful outside Dublin, where payphones of all kinds are scarce, and it's best to be prepared.

With hotel phones, check rates in advance. It is unlikely that there will be any off-peak reductions, and prices can be dizzyingly high.

Public phones

Cash- and card-operated pay phones are found in phone boxes across the city. They are not cheap, however, as a local telephone call from a pay phone generally costs 40c for around three minutes during the day.

Operator services

Call 10 to reach the operator for Ireland and the UK, and 114 for international assistance.

Reverse-charge ('collect') calls are available but will cost about 77c extra.

For directory enquiries, dial 11811 or 11850 for Ireland and Northern Ireland, and 11818 for international numbers, including UK numbers.

UK visitors planning their trip should note that when calling directory enquiries from the UK, Irish numbers are now listed on the myriad UK directory enquiries numbers, not under international directory enquiries.

Telephone directories

The *Golden Pages* is Dublin's equivalent of the *Yellow Pages*. You can search online at www.goldenpages.ie to find addresses in a given area. The 'Independent Directory', distributed annually, is a smaller version, with the added bonus of fairly good restaurant listings.

Mobile phones

There are several mobile networks in Ireland. Vodafone Ireland, O2, Meteor and Three each have about 98 per cent coverage across the country. Ireland's network uses the 900 and 1800 GSM bands, and a UK handset will therefore work in Ireland as long as you have a roaming agreement with your service provider. Holders of US phones (usually 1900 GSM) should contact their service provider to check compatibility.

If you find that you need to buy a mobile phone (for instance, if you will be in the country for an extended period of time), or if you need to buy a new handset for your existing service, or if you want to sign up to an Irish mobile phone network, there are plenty of options. If you're here for just a short period of time, contact one of the following companies and get a pay-as-you-go phone that lets you buy talk time in advance.

If you intend to rent a mobile phone to use during a short stay in the country, contact the Dublin Tourist Information office for vendors (*see below*).

Carphone Warehouse *30 Grafton Street, around Trinity College (670 5265/www.carphonewarehouse.ie). All cross-city buses.* **Map** p251 F4.
Vodafone *48 Grafton Street, around Trinity College (679 9938/ www.vodafone.ie). All cross-city buses.* **Map** p251 F4.

Time

Ireland is in the same time zone as Britain, so it runs to Greenwich Mean Time. In spring, on a Saturday towards the end of March (exactly as happens in the UK and the US) the clocks go forward one hour for Summer Time. Clocks return to normal towards the end of October – on the same dates as the UK.

If you're not sure what time it is, call the 24-hour speaking clock by dialling 1191.

Tipping

You should tip between 12 and 15 per cent in restaurants. However, if – as is often the case – a service charge is included on your bill, ask waitstaff if they actually receive that money: you have every right to refuse to pay it if they don't. Always pay the tip in cash where you can, to make sure the people it's intended for.

Tip hairdressers and beauticians if you feel like it, and don't feel obliged to tip taxi drivers. A lot of city bars and clubs now have attendants in their lavatories, but don't feel that you have to tip them.

Toilets

Clean and safe public toilets are thin on the ground in central Dublin. It's perfectly acceptable to use the toilets in bars and shopping centres. The toilets at Bewley's on Grafton Street (*see p117*), in the Jervis Centre on Henry Street (*see p139*), and at Marks and Spencer on Grafton Street (*see p138*) are all generally clean and pleasant.

Tourist information

Located in a lovely converted church, this almost absurdly helpful centre will do just about everything but your laundry. It has a bureau de change, a car rental agency, a booking service for tickets for tours and travel excursions, a ticket booking desk for concerts, theatre performances and other events, a friendly café and a surprisingly good souvenir shop with fair prices.

You might check out the Dublin Pass, a newly launched 'smart card' which, for a fee, gets you in 'free' to sights across the city. How affordable it is depends on how much you were planning to see – prices start at €29 for a one-day card to €89 for a six-day pass.

You can book hotel rooms here, too, though you will have to pay a booking fee for each reservation. To make a booking before you arrive, call ResIreland (1-800 668 668; 0800 783 5740 from the UK; 00800 6686 6866 from the rest of Europe; 1-800 398 4376 from the US and Canada; or 00 353 669 792 082 from all other countries, or try online at www.goireland.com).

Dublin Tourism Centre
St Andrew's Church, Suffolk Street, around Trinity College (605 7700/ www.visitdublin.com). All cross-city buses. **Open** *Jan-May, Oct-Dec* 9am-5.30pm Mon-Sat; 10.30am-3pm Sun. *June-Aug* 9am-8pm Mon-Sat; 10.30am-3pm Sun. **Map** p251 F3.

Irish Tourist Board
Information 1 850 230 330 from within Ireland; UK office 0800 039 7000/www.Ireland.ie. **Call centre:** Mon-Fri 9am-8pm; Sat 9am-6pm.

Other tourism centres
14 Upper O'Connell Street. **Open** 9am-5pm Mon-Sat. **Map** p251 F1. *Baggot Street Bridge, around St Stephen's Green. Bus 10.* **Open** 9.30am-noon, 12.30-5pm Mon-Fri. **Map** p314 K7. *Dublin Airport. Bus 747, 748.* **Open** 8am-10pm daily. *Dún Laoghaire Ferry Terminal, Dublin Bay. DART Dún Laoghaire.* **Open** 10am-1pm, 2-6pm Mon-Sat.

Visas & immigration

Citizens of the USA, New Zealand, Australia, South Africa and Canada do not require special visas to enter Ireland and are permitted to stay in the country for a maximum of three months. British citizens and members of all EU states have unlimited residency and employment rights in Ireland.

Passport control at Dublin's airport is surprisingly strict and suspicious, even of American visitors. So be prepared for the third-degree.

As with any trip, countries can change their immigration regulations at any time, check visa requirements well before you plan to travel, either at the Irish embassy in your country or on www.irlgov.ie/iveagh/services/visas.

If you require a visa, you can apply to the Irish embassy or consulate in your country. It is best to do so months in advance. If there is no Irish representative in your country, you can apply to the Foreign Affairs Department in Dublin (*see below*).

Directory

Consular Section, Department of Foreign Affairs

13-14 Burgh Quay, beside Tower Street DART (616 7700/foreign affairs.gov.ie). All cross-city buses. **Open** *Office* 10am-12.30pm Mon-Fri. *Phone enquiries* 2.30-4pm Mon-Fri. **Map** p251 F2.

Weights & measures

The Republic of Ireland is now (very nearly) fully metric, although the good old imperial measurements are still readily used and understood – most importantly, pints are still pints at the bar.

When to go

The high tourist season runs from July to August; these are the months when the majority of major festivals and events take place across the country. It will come as no surprise to learn that accommodation is at its most scarce and expensive during this period of time, special offers are few and far between, and Dublin and other popular districts are at their most crowded. Prices are lower and the weather is generally better in May, June and September, so these months might be the best time to visit.

In winter, prices are lowest of all, but the weather is rather dismally wet and cold. Note that during the St Patrick's weekend (around 17 March), Dublin is packed to the gills, so you'll need to plan months ahead if you want to come to town for that festival.

Climate

It will come as no surprise to get an Irish weather report that emphasises rain and chill. Winters tend to be very chilly with lots of rain, and a heavy coat will be necessary from about November through February. Throughout the rest of the year the weather is so variable that, even after winter is long gone you would be wise to expect the worst and pack a warm sweater and a raincoat. Do it even in the summer, just in case. If the weather takes a turn for the worse you'll be glad you did.

For an up-to-date weather forecast for Dublin, telephone 1-550 123 854 (calls cost about 75c per minute).

Public holidays

The following public (bank) holidays occur annually:
1 January New Year's Day
17 March St Patrick's Day
Good Friday
Easter Monday
First Mondays in May, June and August
The Monday closest to
Hallowe'en (31 October)
25 December Christmas Day
26 December
St Stephen's Day
29 December

Women

Although Ireland has made impressive economic progress, over the recent years, changes in the still fundamentally patriarchal social structure have been much more gradual, and many women's issues remain, on the whole, largely neglected.

One item of good news is that the number of women in Irish politics is gradually increasing, thanks in part, no doubt, to Mary Robinson's groundbreaking presidency. Along with that, there has also been an enormous increase in awareness of women's rights over the last 15-20 years. That said, public funding for women's aid is tragically scarce. Divorce is now legal in Ireland, although it is a much longer process than it is in countries like England or the US, and abortion is illegal.

These organisations offer support and/or information:

Albany Women's Clinic
Clifton Court, Fitzwilliam Street Lower, around St Stephen's Green (661 2222). **Open** 8am-6pm Mon-Fri. **Map** p251 H5.

Rape Crisis Centre
70 Leeson Street Lower, around St Stephen's Green 1-800 778 888/661 4911/www.drcc.ie). **Open** *Telephone lines* 24hrs daily. **Map** p251 G5.

Women's Aid
1-800 341 900/www.womensaid.ie. **Open** 10am-10pm daily. Offers advice and support.

Women's Refuge & Helpline
496 1002. **Open** 24hrs daily. Offers support and advice.

Average temperatures

Month	Maximum	Minimum
January	8°C/46°F	1°C/34°F
February	8°C/46°F	2°C/35°F
March	10°C/51°F	3°C/37°F
April	13°C/55°F	4°C/39°F
May	15°C/60°F	6°C/43°F
June	18°C/65°F	9°C/48°F
July	20°C/68°F	11°C/52°F
August	19°C/67°F	11°C/52°F
September	17°C/63°F	9°C/48°F
October	14°C/57°F	6°C/43°F
November	10°C/51°F	4°C/39°F
December	8°C/46°F	3°C/37°F

Directory

Further Reference

Drama & poetry

Samuel Beckett *Waiting for Godot* Two blokes hang around for a couple of hours.
Brendan Behan *The Quare Fellow* A shocking drama from the notorious Dublin drinker.
Eavan Boland *In a Time of Violence* Collected poems.
Nuala Ni Dhomhnaill *The Astrakhan Cloak* Well-rated works by the best-known poet writing in Irish today.
Seamus Heaney *Opened Ground: Poems 1966-1996* Good introduction to the Nobel Laureate.
Patrick Kavanagh *The Great Hunger* The Famine as metaphor.
Tom Murphy *The Gigli Concert* Art, addiction and music: a masterful play by Dublin's greatest living dramatist.
Sean O'Casey *Collected Plays* Politics and morality in 1920s Ireland, including *The Plough & the Stars*.
George Bernard Shaw *Selected Plays* 'My Fair Lady' wasn't really his fault. Honest.
JM Synge *The Playboy of the Western World* Championed by Yeats, this play caused riots in the streets, although we fail to see why.
Oscar Wilde *Plays, Prose, Writings and Poems* In which the 19th century's finest wit declares his genius.
WB Yeats *Collected Poems* Dublin's mighty bard.

Fiction

John Banville *Ghosts* A haunting narrative with Beckett-like overtones.
Samuel Beckett *Murphy* A darkly humourous Irish portrayal of London life. *Molloy/Malone Dies/The Unnamable* Compelling, and compellingly odd, fiction.
Brendan Behan *Borstal Boy* Extraordinary autobiographical novel of a Dublin childhood with the IRA.
Dermot Bolger *The Journey Home* A hard-hitting account of life lived on the edge.
Elizabeth Bowen *The Last September* Quintessential Anglo-Irish 'big house' novel.
Emma Donoghue *Stir-fry* A wry lesbian love story, and a fine debut.
JP Donleavy *The Ginger Man* The high japes of a drunken Trinity student; banned by the Catholic Church.
Roddy Doyle *The Commitments* Most Dubliners agree that the book was much better than the film.
Jeffrey Gantz (trans) *Early Irish Myths and Sagas* For those who want to learn more about the country mystical heritage.
Henry Glassie (ed) *Penguin Book of Irish Folktales* Fairies, leprechauns and big potatoes.
Seamus Heaney *Sweeney Astray/Buile Suibhne* The crazy King Sweeney updated.
Jennifer Johnston *How Many Miles to Babylon?* Protestant gentry and Catholic peasant bond.
James Joyce *A Portrait of the Artist as a Young Man* Cuts through superstition like a knife. *Dubliners* Compelling short stories from the master at his most understandable. *Finnegans Wake* defines the phrase 'unreadable genius'. *Ulysses* The most important 24 hours in literary history.
Pat McCabe *The Butcher Boy* A hilariously grotesque tale of an Irish childhood.
Edna O'Brien *The Country Girls* Bawdy girlish fun that roused clerical ire.
Flann O'Brien *At-Swim-Two-Birds* Hilarious novel about a struggling writer.
Joseph O'Connor *Star of the Sea* Fascinating emigration drama on the high seas.
Liam O'Flaherty *The Informer* Terse social comment from a civil war veteran.
Jamie O'Neill *At Swim Two Boys* A homosexual *bildungsroman* set against the backdrop of the Easter Rising.
Sean O'Reilly *The Swing of Things* Dark comic thriller set in contemporary Dublin.
Stephen Price *Monkey Man* Savage parody of Dublin's media darlings during the boom years of the late 1990s by an ex-producer at Radio Ireland who saw it all.
Bram Stoker *Dracula* The original horror novel.
Jonathan Swift *Gulliver's Travels* The political satire to beat all political satire.
Colm Tóibín *The Heather Blazing* An elderly city judge is forced to confront history.
William Trevor *The Ballroom of Romance* Short stories by the Northern Irish master, set in rural Ireland.

Non-fiction

John Ardagh *Ireland and the Irish* An acute look at present-day Ireland.
Douglas Bennett *Encyclopaedia of Dublin* Just packed with vital information.
RF Foster *Paddy and Mr Punch* A media-savvy study of modern 'Irishness'.
FS Lyons *Ireland Since the Famine* A definitive text.
Frank MacDonald *The Construction of Dublin* Exploration of the city's architectural development during its Celtic Tiger days.
Robert Kee *The Green Flag* A chunky nationalist history. *The Laurel and the Ivy* Parnell, Gladstone and Home Rule.
Máire & Conor Cruise O'Brien *A Concise History of Ireland* A thorough overview.

Jacqueline O'Brien & Desmond Guinness *Dublin – A Grand Tour* A useful guide to the Irish capital.
Nuala O'Faolain *Are You Somebody?* Dublin memories from a respected columnist.
Seán O'Faolain *The Great O'Neill* Queen Elizabeth I, Hugh O'Neill and the battle of Kinsale.
Paul Williams *Gangland, The General* Two fine dissections of Dublin's organised crime.
Cecil Woodham-Smith *The Great Hunger* The definitive study of the 19th-century Great Famine.

Film

About Adam (dir Gerard Stembridge, 2000) Sharp, witty drama about *menage à cinq* of young Dubliners.
Bloom (dir Sean Walsh, 2004) The brave new adaptation of *Ulysses,* starring Stephen Rea.
Breakfast on Pluto (dir Neil Jordan, 2005) The story of Patrick 'Kitten' Braden (Cillian Murphy), who leaves behind small-town Ireland and becomes a transvestite cabaret singer in '70s London.
The Butcher Boy (dir Neil Jordan, 1998) Entertaining version of Pat McCabe's surreal novel.
The Commitments (dir Alan Parker, 1991) Love it or hate it, we can all hum the tunes.
The General (dir John Boorman, 1998) Gritty urban drama about Dublin's most notorious gangster.
Intermission (dir John Crowley, 2003) Colin Farrel goes back to his roots in this lively urban romance.
In The Name of The Father (dir Jim Sheridan, 1993) A man fights for justice to clear his father's name.
Michael Collins (dir Neil Jordan, 1996) A fine bio-pic using lots of Dublin locations.
Nora (dir Pat Murphy, 2000) Superior bio of James Joyce

and his highly tempestuous paramour.
Reefer and the Model (dir Joe Comerford, 1987) Quirky psychological thriller that continues to split the critics.
Veronica Guerin (dir Joel Schumacher, 2003) A dark, fact-based film with Cate Blanchett playing the doomed investigative reporter.
When Brendan Met Trudy (dir Kieron J Walsh, 2000) Boy loves girl. Girl nicks stuff. Etc.

Music

Paddy Casey *Living (2004)* Brilliant Dublin singer and writer who recently supported U2 at their home concerts.
Adrian Crowley *When you are here, you are family* (2001) The second album from this eclectic and popular singer/songwriter.
Damien Dempsey *Seize The Day* (2003), *Shots* (2005) Dublin singer/songwriter who made his name at home, and is now taking the UK by storm.
Dinah Brand *Pale Monkey Blues* (2003) Melodic country rock in the vein of Big Star from respected Dublin songwriter, Dylan Philips.
The Frames *Set List* (2004), *For the Birds* (2001) This critically accclaimed Dublin band may make it big at last.
Gemma Hayes *The Road Don't Love You* (2006) Second album from Tipperary gal and Mercury Prize nominee.
Barry McCormack *We Drank Our Tears* (2003) Critically-acclaimed acoustic folk music from a fine Dublin songwriter.
Christy Moore *Live at the Point* (1994) An institution in Irish music.
Declan O'Rourke *Since Kyabram* (2005) Sensational debut album.
Planxty *Planxty* (1972) Seminal trad band (newly reformed) that inspired many of today's biggest Irish music stars.

Redneck Manifesto *Cut Your Head Off From Your Head* (2002) Second album from instrumental punk band.
Damien Rice *O* (2003) The Kildare man, currently doing great things in the US, still plays regular gigs in Dublin.

Websites

www.abbeytheatre.ie Ireland's national theatre.
www.andrewslane.com Andrew's Lane Theatre – a Dublin favourite.
www.cluas.com Excellent independent Irish music site.
www.dublinks.com Detailed listings of the best events in town.
www.dublinbus.ie The official city bus website has a useful bus route search facility.
www.dublinevents.com Online entertainment listings for the city.
www.dublinpubscene.com Invaluable guide to the city's many watering holes.
www.dublintourist.com Tourist guide to the capital.
www.dublinuncovered.net Everything from taxis companies to shopping tips.
www.entertainment.ie Comprehensive event listings.
www.eventguide.ie Dublin's best fortnightly guide.
www.eventsoftheweek.com All major sporting events, festivals and more.
www.gate-theatre.ie Offical website of the Gate Theatre.
www.ireland.com Online version of the *Irish Times*.
www.ireland.ie The Irish tourist board.
www.local.ie If it's in Ireland, you'll find it here.
www.nch.ie National Concert Hall: classical music aplenty.
www.ticketmaster.ie Online ticket sales for all major Dublin gigs and concerts.
www.visitdublin.com Culture, events, getting around and special offers.
www.whelanslive.com A must for live music lovers.

Directory

Index

Index

Index

Advertisers' Index

Please refer to the relevant pages for contact details

Place of interest and/or entertainment	
Railway station	
Hotel	
Park	
Hospital	
Neighbourhood	RANELAGH
Pedestrian street	
Main road	
Church	✚
Airport	✈
Luas	Ⓛ
Hotels	➊
Restaurants	➊
Bars	➊

Maps

Ireland

NORTHERN IRELAND

Giant's Causeway
Rathlin Is.
Dunfenaghy
Glenveagh National Park
Aran Is.
Coleraine
Letterkenny
Londonderry
Londonderry
ANTRIM
DONEGAL
LONDONDERRY
Larne
Glencolumbcille
Killybegs
Donegal
Ballymena
Omagh
Belfast Internt.
Ballyshannon
L. Lough Erne
Belfast
Donaghadee
Donegal Bay
LEITRIM
Enniskillen
Lough Neagh
DOWN
FERMANAGH
Harbour Airport
Sligo
U. Lough Erne
Armagh
Portadown
Achill Is.
Ballina
Monaghan
N2
ARMAGH
Lough Conn
SLIGO
Lough Allen
MONAGHAN
Newry
MAYO
Cavan
Dundalk
Clare Is.
Castlebar
Knock
Carrick-on-Shannon
LOUTH
Dundalk Bay
Clew Bay
Westport
Knock
CAVAN
Drogheda
ROSCOMMON
N3
CONNAUGHT
Longford
Roscommon
Clifden
N17
LONGFORD
N3
Connemara
Tuam
Lough Ree
N4
Kells (Ceanannas Mór)
MEATH
Oughterard
Lough Mask
Athlone
WESTMEATH
N3
GALWAY
Lough Corrib
Ballinasloe
Mullingar
N4
Galway
Galway
LEINSTER
Dublin
DUBLIN
See pp247
Aran Islands
N6
OFFALY
Tullamore
KILDARE
Dún Laoghaire
Bray
Galway Bay
IRELAND
Doolin
Birr
Kildare
Wicklow Mtns
The Burren
Port Laoise
Cliffs of Moher
N18
Lough Derg
N7
Roscrea
LAOIS
Athy
Wicklow
CLARE
Ennis
Carlow
WICKLOW
N7
Shannon
N8
CARLOW
Arklow
Limerick
Thurles
Kilkenny
N24
KILKENNY
N11
LIMERICK
TIPPERARY
IRISH SEA
N20
Tipperary
KERRY
WEXFORD
MUNSTER
N25
Wexford
Tralee
Rosslare
Great Blasket Is.
Dingle
Killorglin
Kerry County
Waterford
Dingle Bay
Killarney
Mallow
WATERFORD
Waterford
Lough Leane
CORK
Dungarvan
Valentia Is.
Cahirciveen
Kenmare
Macroom
N25
Sneem
N22
Cork
Youghal
Cork
Glengarriff
Cork
Dursey Is.
Bantry
Kinsale
Bear Is.
Clonakilty
Bantry Bay
Skibbereen
Clear Is.

ST GEORGE'S Channel

0   100 km
0   60 miles

© Copyright Time Out Group 2007

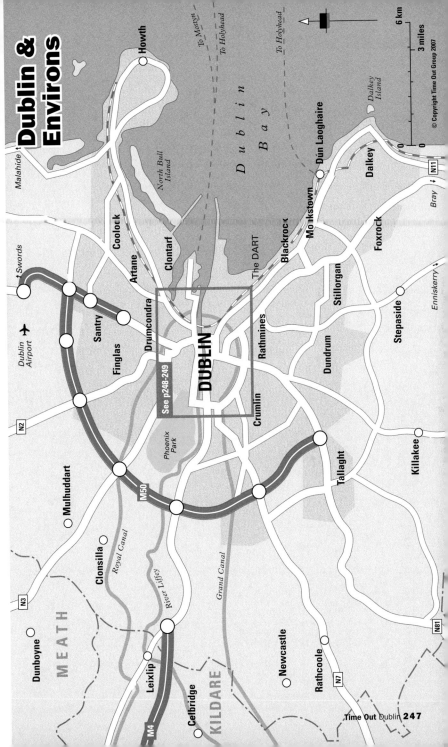

Dublin & Environs

Malahide

Howth

To Mostyn

To Holyhead

To Holyhead

To Holyhead

Dublin Bay

North Bull Island

Dalkey Island

Dún Laoghaire

Dalkey

N11

Bray

Enniskerry

The DART

Blackrock

Monkstown

Foxrock

Coolock

Artane

Clontarf

Swords

Dublin Airport

Santry

Finglas

Drumcondra

Rathmines

Stillorgan

Dundrum

Stepaside

DUBLIN

See p248-249

Crumlin

N2

M50

Phoenix Park

Killakee

Tallaght

Mulhuddart

Clonsilla

Royal Canal

River Liffey

Grand Canal

Newcastle

Rathcoole

N81

N7

N3

MEATH

Dunboyne

Leixlip

Celbridge

M4

KILDARE

6 km

3 miles

© Copyright Time Out Group 2007

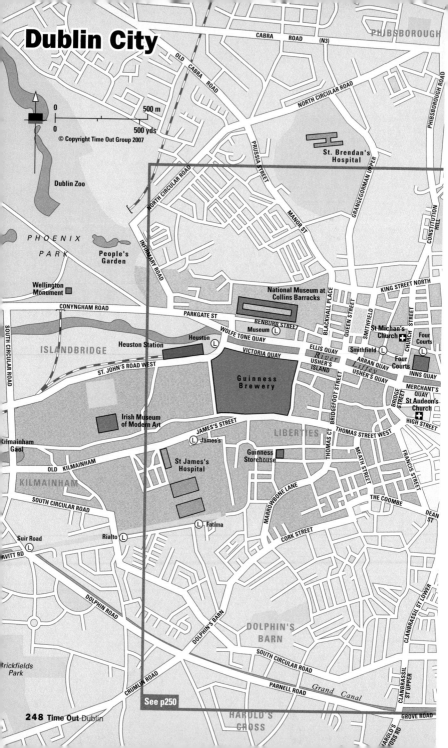

Dublin City

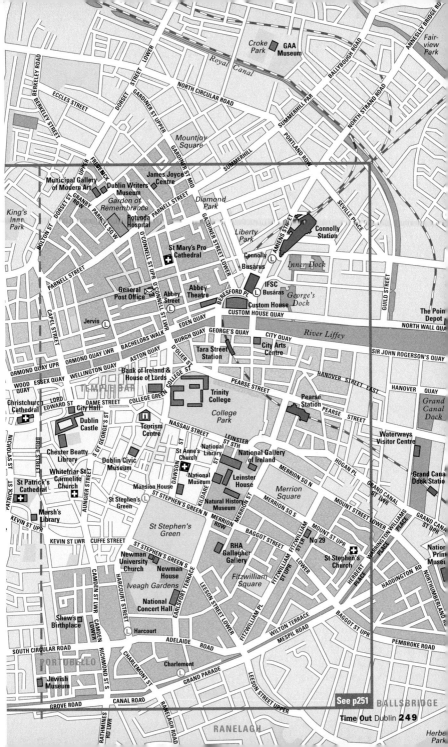

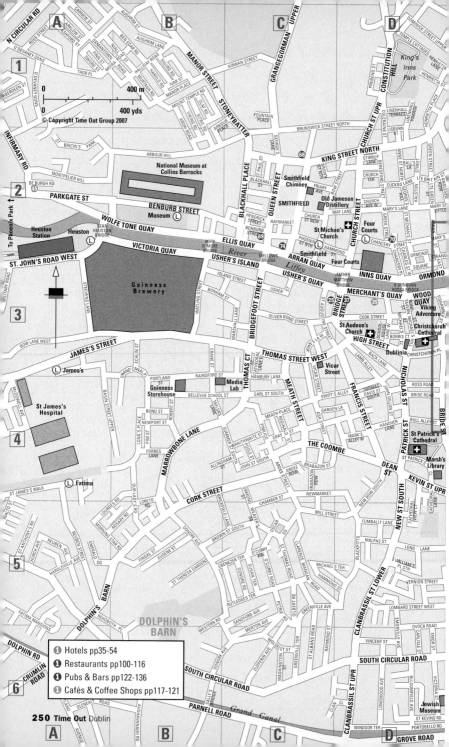

Map legend / keys

- **Hotels** pp35-54
- **Restaurants** pp100-116
- **Pubs & Bars** pp122-136
- **Cafés & Coffee Shops** pp117-121

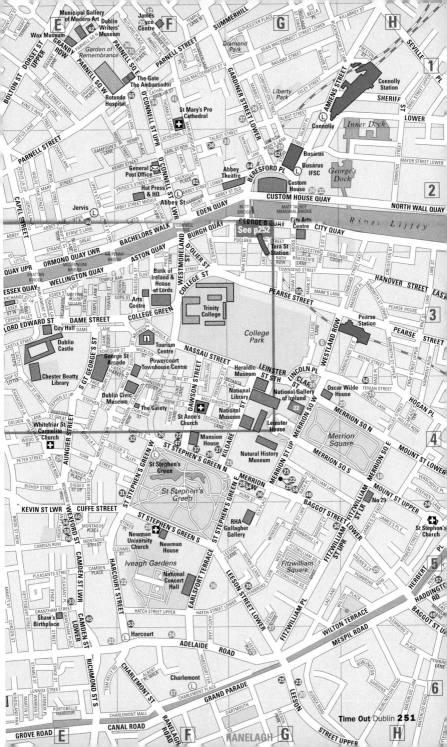

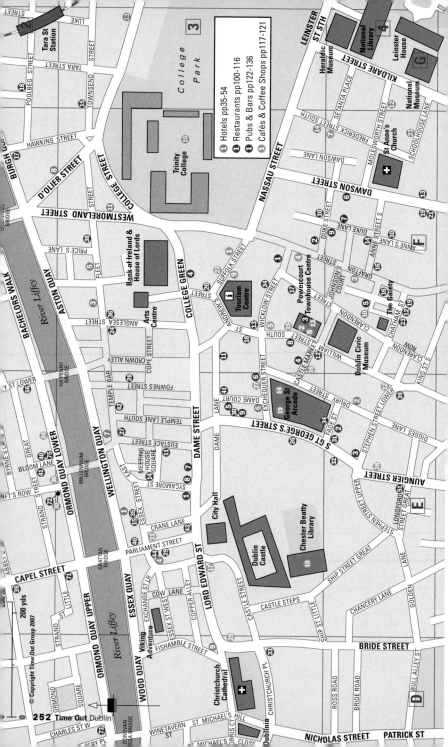

STREET

LUKE

Tara St
Station

TARA STREET

STREET

POOLBEG STREET

TOWNSEND

STREET

HAWKINS STREET

BURGH QUAY

D'OLIER STREET

COLLEGE STREET

WESTMORELAND STREET

3

College
Park

Trinity
College

15

Hotels pp35–54
Restaurants pp100–116
Pubs & Bars pp122–136
Cafés & Coffee Shops pp117–121

LEINSTER
ST STH

Heraldic
Museum

National
Library

Leinster
House

KILDARE STREET

4

G

National
Museum

SCHOOLHOUSE LANE

MOLESWORTH STREET

SETANTA PLACE

FREDERICK STREET SOUTH

DAWSON LANE

St Anne's
Church

NASSAU STREET

DAWSON STREET

DUKE STREET

DUKE LANE

ANNE STREET S

ANNE'S LANE

F

GRAFTON STREET

JOHNSON'S COURT

The Gaiety

CHATHAM ST

CHATHAM ROW

CLARENDON ROW

KING ST S

Bank of Ireland &
House of Lords

Arts
Centre

COLLEGE GREEN

ANGLESEA STREET

CROWN ALLEY

TEMPLE BAR

FLEET

PRICE'S LANE

River Liffey

BACHELORS WALK

ASTON QUAY

HAPENNY BRIDGE

Y ST LOWER

GREAT

BLOOM LANE

ORMOND QUAY LOWER

MILLENNIUM BRIDGE

WELLINGTON QUAY

FOWNES STREET

TEMPLE LANE SOUTH

MEETING HOUSE SQUARE

EUSTACE STREET

SYCAMORE ST

ESSEX STREET EAST

SUFFOLK STREET

ANDREW'S ST

Tourism
Centre

WICKLOW STREET

Powerscourt
Townhouse
Centre

WILLIAM STREET SOUTH

Dublin Civic
Museum

CASTLE MARKET

DAME STREET

DAME LANE

DAME COURT

EXCHEQUER STREET

George St
Arcade

FADE ST

DRURY STREET

S GT GEORGE'S STREET

STEPHEN STREET LOWER

DIGGES LANE

AUNGIER STREET

STEPHEN STREET UPPER

LONGFORD STREET GREAT

E

City Hall

Dublin
Castle

Chester Beatty
Library

LORD EDWARD ST

CASTLE STREET

CASTLE STEPS

SHIP STREET LITTLE

SHIP STREET GREAT

CHANCERY LANE

GOLDEN LANE

BRIDE STREET

BRIDE ROAD

ROSS ROAD

BULL ALLEY ST

D

CAPEL STREET

ESSEX QUAY

River Liffey

ORMOND QUAY UPPER

EXCHANGE ST LR

COW LANE

WOOD QUAY

Viking
Adventure

FISHAMBLE STREET

ESSEX ST WEST

COPPER ALLEY

Christchurch
Cathedral

CHRISTCHURCH PL

WINETAVERN ST

ST MICHAEL'S HILL

MICHAEL'S CLOSE

Dublinia

NICHOLAS STREET

PATRICK ST

PARLIAMENT STREET

CRANE LANE

GRATTAN BRIDGE

STRAND

ABBEY

CHARLES ST W

O ORMOND
SQUARE

© Copyright Time Out Group 2007

200 yds

200 m

0

252 Time Out Dublin

Street Index

254 Time Out Dublin

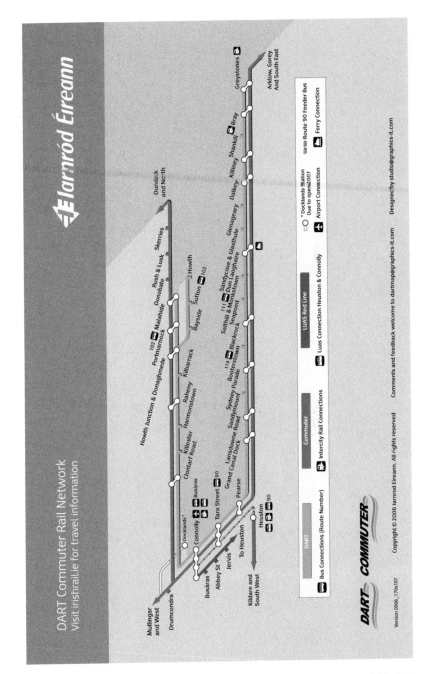

DART Commuter Rail Network
Visit irishrail.ie for travel information

Iarnród Éireann

Mullingar and West
Drumcondra
Docklands*
Connolly
Tara Street 90
Pearse
Busáras
Abbey St
Jervis
To Heuston
Heuston 90
Kildare and South West

Howth Junction & Donaghmede
Clontarf Road
Killester
Harmonstown
Raheny
Kilbarrack
Grand Canal Dock
Lansdowne
Sandymount
Sydney Parade
Booterstown
Blackrock
Seapoint
Salthill & Monkstown
Dun Laoghaire
Sandycove & Glasthule
Glenageary
Dalkey
Killiney
Shankill
Bray
Greystones

102 Malahide
Portmarnock
Donabate
Rush & Lusk
Skerries
Dundalk and North
Bayside
Sutton 102
Howth

111
114

Arklow, Gorey And South East

DART
Bus Connections (Route Number)

Commuter
Intercity Rail Connections

LUAS Red Line
Luas Connection Heuston & Connolly

*Docklands Station Due to open 2007
Airport Connection

Route 90 Feeder Bus
Ferry Connection

DART COMMUTER

Version 0906_170x107

Comments and feedback welcome to dartmap@graphics-it.com   Design by studio@graphics-it.com

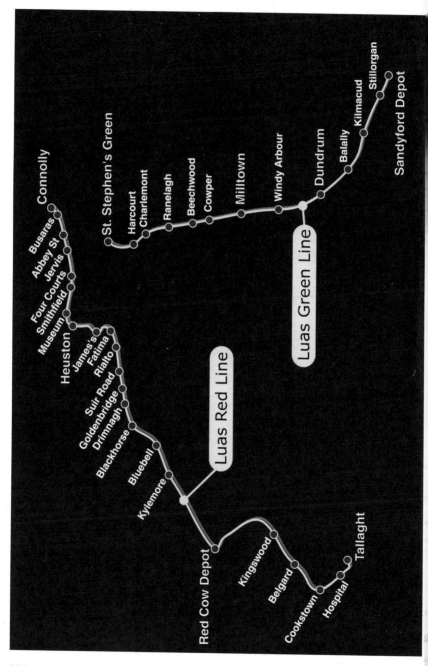

Connolly
Busaras
Abbey St
Jervis
Four Courts
Smithfield
Museum
Heuston
James's
Fatima
Rialto
Suir Road
Goldenbridge
Drimnagh
Blackhorse
Bluebell
Kylemore
Red Cow Depot
Kingswood
Belgard
Cookstown
Hospital
Tallaght

St. Stephen's Green
Harcourt
Charlemont
Ranelagh
Beechwood
Cowper
Milltown
Windy Arbour
Dundrum
Balally
Kilmacud
Stillorgan
Sandyford Depot

Luas Red Line

Luas Green Line